KING CON

KING CON

THE BIZARRE ADVENTURES OF
THE JAZZ AGE'S GREATEST IMPOSTOR

PAUL WILLETTS

CROWN
NEW YORK

All rights reserved.
Published in the United States by Crown,
an imprint of the Crown Publishing Group,
a division of Penguin Random House LLC, New York.
crownpublishing.com

CROWN and the Crown colophon are
registered trademarks of Penguin Random House LLC.

All quotations from the Lucullus V. McWhorter Papers, Manuscripts, Archives and Special
Collections by kind permission of Washington State University Libraries.

Library of Congress Cataloging-in-Publication Data is available upon request.

ISBN 978-0-451-49581-5
Ebook ISBN 978-0-451-49583-9

PRINTED IN THE UNITED STATES OF AMERICA

Book design by Andrea Lau
Jacket design by Elena Giavaldi
Jacket photograph by The National Archives Image Library, UK

10 9 8 7 6 5 4 3 2 1

First Edition

In memory of Robert Hastings (1966–2017) and Chris Stephenson (1939–2017), two charming, witty, and much-missed friends.

Through others we become ourselves.

L. S. Vygotsky

CONTENTS

A NOTE ON SOURCES

King Con is entirely a work of nonfiction, made possible by the surprisingly extensive paper trail that its main character left behind. It draws upon a vast array of historic newspapers, letters, and other archival material, cited in the notes. All quoted speech comes from these sources, which provide glimpses into people's thoughts and feelings. The notes also include occasional background information about the story.

KING CON

PART I

The Fake's Progress

The waiting was almost over. Within the next few minutes, Tom Longboat, an Onondagan marathon runner who had just stopped off in San José, California, would be entering the pulpit of the First Baptist Church. Now twenty-eight years old, Tom was way past the age when newspapers carried stories about him winning race after race and twice competing on Canada's Olympic team, but he remained famous enough for his presence in town to spark excited chatter. That evening—Sunday, March 4, 1917—several hundred people filled the pews. Speaking to them from the pulpit of this balconied modern church was its resident preacher, the Reverend James W. Kramer, who had a reputation for staging services "better than a movie show."

Broad-shouldered and as fidgety as a marionette midperformance, Kramer had a large, bulging-browed face, its youthful smoothness extending to his prematurely bald crown. In deep, sonorous tones, he said, "I'm sorry the world has still got to be watched. There is something the matter with the world. It wants a religion that not only says, 'This is the way,' but *walks* in that way." He was nearing the end of that evening's sermon. "You need religion," he assured the congregation. "And don't forget that genuine religion works!" He went on to announce the imminent unveiling and illumination of a newly commissioned ecclesiastical painting, which he described as a masterpiece. "During the illumination, our friend Tom Longboat will sing ..." Kramer meant to say that Tom would be performing the well-known hymn "Just as I Am, Without One Plea," but he muddled his words and said, "Just as I Am, Without One *Flea*."

Laughter from his audience compounded Kramer's embarrassment. Distraction was, luckily for him, on hand. The lights were shut off, ready for the painting to be unveiled and then spotlit.

Here was the cue for the boyishly handsome Tom to take center stage. The much-talked-about wound he'd incurred while serving with the Canadian medical corps in France—heart of the war America had not thus far joined—didn't prevent him from carrying himself with nonchalant grace, his physique still lean and muscular. Just shy of six feet, "the big Indian," as Kramer referred to him, was tall by the standards of the period. Tom had high cheekbones, olive skin, and full lips that often flexed into a captivating smile, his intelligence and gentle authority projected by soulful brown eyes. He wore his thick, jet-black hair in a neatly parted, collar-length style. On the lapel of his dark suit, he liked to display a Red Cross pin.

When Tom launched into the opening hymn, the Baptist Harmonic Orchestra provided the ponderous musical accompaniment. "Just as I am, without one plea / But that Thy blood was shed for me," Tom sang in a mellow yet powerful voice, its crisp phrasing accentuating the vocal similarity between him and the hugely popular tenor Chauncey Olcott.

Afterward Tom addressed the congregation, which included numerous latecomers, standing at the sides because all the seats were taken. He was a natural in front of an audience. "This is the first time that I have ever stepped into a first-class Baptist church with a first-class Baptist spirit," he said, his speech no less rich and melodic than his singing. Relaxed, engaging, and genially self-assured, he spoke of breaking the record for the marathon and receiving trophies from the kings of England and Greece. It was clear why Kramer had awarded him such a fulsome endorsement on the ads promoting that evening's service. "I never heard a greater man singer than this Indian," the preacher had declared. "Hear his story of the war and hear him sing. Yes, he is a Christian man. He will move and thrill you."

Tom proudly informed the congregation that he was a graduate of Carlisle. Just that one word was sufficient to identify Carlisle Indian Industrial School, the celebrated Pennsylvania boarding school where Native American youngsters—many of them unwillingly uprooted from their families and culture—received a classical as well as vocational education. Tom served as a living advertisement for that institution and dozens of other such eastern boarding schools to which generations of Native Americans had been sent. As a mark of his assimilation, Tom said he'd completed a three-year medical course in Chicago. He also revealed that he'd traveled around the world, learning several languages in the process. And he delivered a brief but engrossing account of his work with the medical corps on the muddy battlefields of France.

His description carried the distinctive imprint of firsthand experience. There were none of the allusions to glory and patriotism deployed by people who had never set foot in the trenches. For him, the horrors of the current war "could not be exaggerated."

"The thing to do," he suggested, "is to take the sovereigns of the different countries, place them in a pit, charge admission, and let the sovereigns fight."

Energetic applause greeted this suggestion.

An incredulous young girl, who was impressed by Tom's performance, dragged her mother up to the pulpit for a closer look at him. Tom suspected racial prejudice lay behind the girl's disbelief. "Why, he looks just like a man," her mother said. Tom would later joke about how the girl's mother must have wondered where his war paint and feathered headdress had gone.

Sharing the bewilderment of both mother and daughter was another member of the congregation—a local real estate agent named Charles Millar. Like so many people there, he'd been drawn to the service by the gravitational pull of Tom's fame. Millar was doubly curious because he'd raced against Tom in Montreal close on a decade earlier. But Millar didn't recognize the man in the pulpit, who looked nothing like the marathon runner he'd trailed behind. The Tom Longboat *he* knew had even darker skin. *And* he was a tad shorter. Millar couldn't figure out why the man in the pulpit wanted to go around pretending to be Longboat. Whatever the reason, Millar made up his mind to expose him as an impostor at the end of the service.

The man calling himself Tom Longboat continued to soak up the applause. It was soon replaced by the sound of the church orchestra playing several more hymns. These were followed by a singing duet, a series of baptism ceremonies, and the closing hymn. Dr. Kramer made a few announcements before the large congregation began to disperse.

Millar could now unmask the impostor in front of everyone. But, almost as if the man was being protected by an Onondagan guardian spirit, Millar suffered a last-minute loss of nerve. Instead of facing a torrent of angry questions, Edgar Laplante—the impostor exploiting Tom Longboat's name and celebrity—was free to collect a large appearance fee.

WHILE PUTTERING AROUND SAN JOSÉ, where the two- and three-story downtown buildings were framed by mountains and where horse-drawn buggies and electric streetcars shared broad avenues with open-topped automobiles appropriate to the mild, cloudless weather next day, Edgar would have to be careful. If he was going to sustain his image as a paragon of wholesome American manhood, he couldn't afford to be caught doing many of the things he normally did—smoking cigarettes and seducing young women, to name but two. Kramer detested these practices. Still more abhorrent to Kramer's way of thinking was Edgar's penchant for seducing young men. By gratifying *that* particular appetite, Edgar wouldn't just be endangering his relationship with the preacher. He'd also be risking trouble with the police, as sex between men was punishable in California by up to fifteen years of jail time.

His taste for hard liquor—scotch, if he could lay his lips on it—was something else Edgar had to conceal from Kramer. Among the leading temperance campaigners, Kramer had already helped to instigate legislation against the manufacture, sale, and delivery of alcohol in both Idaho and Washington State. He would have been horrified by Edgar's recent behavior. Not two months prior, Edgar had gotten so drunk he'd been slung out of a Sunday morning service in the town of Bisbee, Arizona. Were Kramer to detect as much as the faint tang of alcohol on Edgar's breath, the invitation to perform a solo concert at the First Baptist Church was sure to be withdrawn. Even the glowing testimonials from Edgar's regimental commander and several well-known Baptist ministers wouldn't save the concert, scheduled for that evening.

To publicize his show, Edgar gave an interview to a reporter from the *San José Evening News*. He said he was in town to recover from the year and a half he'd spent on the front line in France. What really caught the reporter's interest was Edgar's condemnation of the English war effort. Any military successes chalked up by the Allies had been achieved by soldiers from Canada and other English dominions, he contended. "England has done nothing save send over some officers—but I won't say what *sort* of officers. Oh, yes, I *will* say that England has put up a lot of money. She has been a good meal ticket, but a poor fighter."

"When do you figure the war will be over?" the reporter asked.

"Don't know. And I wouldn't venture a guess. I know one thing: The Germans are far from being whipped. The Germans are sending boys into the trenches now but—let me tell you—these boys can fight better than their daddies. They call this a boys' war. It may be that, but it's an awful war just the same. People over here have no idea of the horrors that are being enacted." He spoke about how young children were being targeted. "When little, defenseless children are used for gun fodder it is going some . . ."

Edgar then unbuttoned his shirtfront and, in a graphic illustration of the brutality of war, showed the reporter a prominent scar on his chest. It was the size of a dollar coin. "A German woman gave me that," he explained. "Yes, I was on German soil when she ran her saber through my breast. She thought I was there to destroy her home, and she came out to defend it. We were about fifty yards on German territory when we came upon this house, and that was as far as we got. When the poor woman discovered the red cross on my arm and found out that I was in the medical corps, she felt so dreadful about it that she broke out in tears. She gave me a sound thrust all right. The doctors had to remove two of my ribs in order to fix me up."

AT HIS SOLO SHOW LATER THAT DAY, Edgar continued to reminisce about his battlefield ordeal. He also fielded questions from the big crowd, talked about his athletic career, and performed a selection of popular songs, which led one member of the audience to declare his singing had "seldom been equaled in this city."

So many people wanted to speak with him and shake his hand after the show that he needed to take refuge in a side room to avoid being crushed. He only ventured back into the main body of the church once the brouhaha let up.

For the better part of an hour he mingled with his fans. He was partial to speaking about himself, but he was happy to listen to other people, to let them feel their opinions mattered, to satisfy their desire to warm themselves in the fireside glow of celebrity.

His success in convincing the residents of San José that he was Tom Longboat tempted him to feed them another barefaced lie. Now he started talking about how he'd played football alongside the great Jim Thorpe on Carlisle's equally celebrated team. He took pride in his ability to make people buy cockamamie stories like that. Outside his fecund imagination, the closest he'd been to gridiron stardom appears to have come through his stepmother's job as an inspector of footballs at a sporting goods plant. Merely to be an ex-teammate of Jim Thorpe was not sufficient for him, though. As if he wanted to map the limits of people's credulity, he embellished his story by claiming to have been on the team that had defeated Harvard.

To sports fans of that era, Carlisle's win over Harvard rated as one of football's greatest upsets. Professing involvement in such a game was a rash move. Some football fanatic might be in a position to check the Carlisle team's lineup and find no mention of Tom Longboat. Or someone familiar with the story might recall that Carlisle had triumphed only through exploiting a loophole in the rules of football. By associating himself with such underhand tactics, Edgar might encourage people to question his integrity, to scrutinize all the other things he'd told them, all the lies about competing as an athlete and training as a doctor. People might even wonder about his racial identity: In truth, he was no more Onondagan than he was an Olympic athlete or an army veteran.

2

Any minute there might be a knock on the door of Edgar's hotel room. He might then find himself being quizzed by an officer from the San José Police Department. Once the police got ahold of him, Edgar's life could veer in several directions, none of them good. Even allowing for the absence of a countrywide criminal database, there was always the fear that the authorities might discover he was a career con man with outstanding warrants against him in the states of Arizona and New York.

Before any of these scenarios could play out, Edgar quit town and headed south. He had with him only a single valise.

The Southern Pacific railroad's Coast Line furnished the most convenient means for him to make the 416-mile journey to San Diego. Bordering the track were orchards, vineyards, and prosperous rural towns that would have made attractive subjects for his paintings and drawings. Just past Santa Barbara the bucolic scene gave way to a herd of seesawing oil derricks that strayed some distance into the ocean.

For travelers such as Edgar, whose mouth was seldom without a cigarette, the passing views were seen through the misty filter of the smoking car. The landscape had little in common with Central Falls, the close-packed blue-collar Rhode Island city where he'd been reared amid cotton mills, well-maintained tenements, and brick-paved streets, alive with the clip-clop of horse-drawn wagons, the rattle of trains on the elevated railway, and the clucking of the chickens kept in the barn to the rear of where he lived. He and his three younger siblings had grown up on Lincoln Avenue with their parents, both from Quebec. The Laplantes were surrounded by a sizable colony of other French-Canadian émigrés, many of them carpenters like Edgar's father. Despite retaining their own Roman Catholic festivals and holidays, their own church and school, their own correct if homespun brand of French, their own cuisine, and even their own newspapers, their community's potent sense of cultural identity had somehow never defined Edgar, whose failure to acknowledge his French origins must have been one of the many sources of conflict with his now-estranged Francophile father.

Persistent in his rejection of the life into which he'd been born, Edgar was still pretending to be the Onondagan athlete Tom Longboat when he reached San Diego on Thursday, March 8, 1917—three days after his solo show at the First Baptist Church. He found his way to the downtown stretch of Sixth Street, where he walked into the mahogany-swathed interior of the Hotel St. James and rented a room. Snazzy hotels like this were important to Edgar and his fellow grifters, who needed to mix with influential and well-heeled types. Eleven stories tall, the St. James rated among the city's loftiest and most up-to-date structures. It even boasted a roof garden from which Edgar could survey the grid of chiefly low-rise blocks covering the shallow grade that angled toward San Diego Bay, numerous large steamships necklacing the waterfront.

His first night at the St. James was spent befriending F. C. Dean, the hotel's manager. Within seconds Edgar could beguile men and women alike with his smooth-talking charm, bantering humor, and counterfeit stardom. As was so often the case, this must have blinded Dean to the obvious flaw in Edgar's Tom Longboat shtick. Though he presented himself as a famous Onondagan athlete, Edgar did not possess the facial characteristics of *any* indigenous North American people. His daring act of racial imposture was surely assisted by general ignorance of what those people looked like. Dean and many other white Americans probably had no memory of encountering them, no memory of seeing photos of them; just the memory, perhaps, of white actors playing them on-screen—white actors who lacked Edgar's uncanny plausibility. For Dean and other white Americans, their prejudices nurtured by then-fashionable racial theories, much of that plausibility would have been due to the manifest illogic of a white American willfully trading places with a member of what was considered an inferior race. Edgar's maybe unconscious masterstroke was to legitimize himself by displaying an authentic Onondagan's eagerness to discredit those widespread misconceptions.

Such were Edgar's acting skills that he gave his new acquaintance the impression that his wartime experiences had left him craving "the milk of human kindness." Later that evening, Dean obliged by taking him to an event at the nearby Maryland Hotel, where the light, sparsely appointed, pale mosaic–floored public rooms possessed a modernity absent from the St. James. Edgar and Dean hobnobbed there with the all-male membership of the local chapter of the Hotel Greeters of America, a group whose aim was to boost the hotel industry. Dean and the other members treated Edgar as a hero, the atmosphere of bonhomie likely abetted by alcohol. Further ingratiating himself with his host, Edgar presented Dean with a cane that was, he said, made from a spear used by a colonial soldier fighting in the British army.

Probably at the Maryland that evening, Edgar ran into a journalist from the *San Diego Union.* By talking to the press, he'd render the locals more receptive to his scam, yet publicity increased the chances of his being caught. Risk and reward were one and the same for Edgar, though, because he was addicted to the attention that came from speaking with reporters, to the frisson of risk that accompanied it—risk that courted arrest and imprisonment.

He told the journalist he was planning to settle in San Diego, where he'd arranged to meet his mother, who was heading west at that very moment. But he neglected to mention that any such reunion would require supernatural intervention, his mother having passed away more than a decade earlier. He said he was recuperating from a bayonet wound he'd sustained while serving in France. The wound had, he explained, put him "permanently out of the running game." He also talked about fighting alongside the Canadian forces. And he spoke about wanting to rectify the common misapprehension that he was "a Canadian Indian." He added that he'd been "born in New York State." Weak though he claimed to be, he said, "If America goes to war with any nation, I am ready to donate my services to my own country."

For all his storytelling skills, which enabled him to pass off fiction as reality, he couldn't hide the truth from himself. Behind his jaunty double-dealing lay a sorrowful recognition that no matter how hard he tried to be someone else, someone worthy of acclaim, he'd always be that no-good boy from Central Falls.

INEVITABLY ASSISTED BY HIS CONVIVIAL evening with the Hotel Greeters, Edgar became a cherished fixture in the lounges, bars, and dining rooms of San Diego's tonier hotels over the next few days. Swank establishments such as the Grant Hotel—where his debonair looks led swooning young women to declare that "he surely knew how to wear a dress suit"—gave him access to the affluent San Diegans who socialized there. He then lined up those hapless marks for the con artist's quintessential sleight of mind, for the sad story of how he was "temporarily embarrassed by lack of funds," a story that applied just the right amount of psychological pressure to ensure they *insisted* upon lending him money. Flimflam merchants like him accepted these loans only after a show of prideful reluctance.

In search of extra leverage, he began saying he'd served in the trenches with Princess Patricia's Canadian Light Infantry, known as "the Princess Pat Regiment." Almost wiped out at the Second Battle of Ypres, where it had fought a dogged but futile defense of its position, the unit was synonymous with military martyrdom. Edgar's latest embellishment may have been inspired by a recent syndicated newspaper story about Lieutenant Sylvester Long Lance, a Carlisle graduate who happened to be one of the regiment's few survivors. By attaching himself to that tragic tale, Edgar could exploit people's desire for glory through association.

Soon he was being pampered by a number of prominent citizens, including Judge George J. Leovy, the gray-mustached, pince-nez-wearing commodore of San Diego's ritzy and very popular Yacht Club. Edgar also plied his trade at the city's similarly exclusive Rowing Club, where he suckered two of the young bucks into wining and dining him. They even elected him as an honorary member. In return, he pledged to donate three Indian-style canoes to their club. The minute they started asking after the canoes, he would know his time in San Diego was drawing to a close and he'd have to skip town.

"Hopscotching" from place to place—as grifters like Edgar termed this—was fundamental to his line of work. Whenever exposure loomed, he'd move elsewhere. It was a tactic rendered effective by the absence of national newspapers, by the lack of a countrywide radio or highway network, by the disconnectedness of the budding coast-to-coast law enforcement system, and by the inconvenience of long-distance phone calls, which could take upward of seven minutes to put through. Edgar also benefited from the mileage between the cities out west, mileage that conspired with poor communications to make those cities feel like remote islands. Each time the situation necessitated it, he could just go to a new place and begin afresh, debts and friendships casually shrugged off at a moment's notice.

COLONEL JOSEPH P. O'NEIL invited Edgar—or, rather, he thought he was inviting Tom Longboat—to be guest of honor at San Diego's Panama-California Exposition. The role carried such kudos that Edgar's predecessor was the world-famous opera singer Nellie Melba, who had visited the exposition a few days before.

Deep into its final month, the event, held to celebrate the opening of the Panama Canal, represented the latest in a series of ostentatious displays of progress that had been staged in America and Europe over the previous sixty-five years. The exposition was spread across the abundant, rugged acreage of Balboa Park, not far from Edgar's hotel. At the core of the event were a host of gargantuan, specially constructed Spanish-style buildings, which looked deceptively old. Their elegant towers and domes might have put Edgar in mind of Greater Dreamland, the oceanfront amusement park on Coney Island, where he'd worked seven summers earlier. But, unlike

Coney Island that summer, Balboa Park had an off-season feel. Most of its buildings and their themed exhibitions had already closed. Tourists were nonetheless encouraged to wander around the surrounding courtyards, tropical gardens, and citrus groves.

Edgar's diminutive host commanded the Second Battalion of the Twenty-First Infantry Regiment, which had been staging parades and mock battles as part of the exposition. Colonel O'Neil and his officers were based in what people called the Indian Village—an imitation of a New Mexico or Arizona pueblo. Three terraced rows of houses appeared to have been cut into the rock face, homemade ladders connecting each level. Yet Edgar just needed to tap those rocks with his foot to understand that he was a sham Indian in a sham Indian Village. The rock face had been fabricated by laying cement over chicken wire. Until just a few months earlier, two hundred genuine, traditionally clothed Native Americans had been paid to live there.

O'Neil acknowledged Edgar's supposed record as a war veteran by giving him a U.S. Army uniform to wear at the exposition, where Edgar schmoozed with O'Neil and other officers. Like Nellie Melba before him, Edgar was asked to present the Stars and Stripes at the Twenty-First Infantry Regiment's twice-weekly dress parade.

Behind a marching band, O'Neil's men conducted their complex drill on the huge expanse of asphalt that comprised the Plaza de Panama. All around Edgar and the parading soldiers were ornate architectural confections, each of which could have been plucked from some Spanish city. The parade culminated in Edgar presenting the flag, his latest escapade offering no more than temporary sustenance to the overpowering compulsions that drove him, compulsions destined to push him into ever more extreme scenarios.

FROM O'NEIL, EDGAR FINAGLED a letter of recommendation. It was addressed to Lieutenant Robert Gross, the officer in charge of the USS *Paul Jones,* a destroyer berthed in San Diego Bay. Lieutenant Gross was fixing to recruit junior officers for the city's newly formed naval reserve, established to patrol the harbor and neighboring shoreline. His recruitment campaign had attracted the interest of several people from the Yacht Club, where Edgar was a frequent guest of Judge Leovy.

Always on the lookout for new ways of gratifying his unquenchable thirst for attention and status, Edgar applied to become a naval reservist. Judge Leovy's son was among the other applicants. Before they could be enrolled, ready to commence training later that year, Edgar and the others had to go through a medical exam. Not that it presented any obstacle to him, because he was so fit. (While pretending to be Tom Longboat during a recent visit to an army training camp near the Mexican border, he'd validated all the stories about his athletic prowess by winning a one-mile race against a bunch of soldiers.) Predictably, he sailed through the reservists' medical and joined ten other recruits for a ceremony aboard the USS *Paul Jones*. There, Edgar was assigned the rank of ensign, lowest position in the hierarchy of U.S. Navy officers.

His fake identity as a famous athlete led to his recruitment triggering stories in newspapers on both coasts. A self-confessed "souvenir fiend," who collected press clippings about himself, Edgar would surely have wanted a copy of the *San Diego Union*'s article about his enlistment. Edgar would have been able to obtain this from one of the local "newsies," the typically homeless, grubby-faced boys aged between ten and fourteen who prowled the sidewalks hawking newspapers. "Although still suffering from a severe bayonet wound in the chest," purred the article, "Longboat's superb physique enabled him easily to pass the physical examinations."

Reading multiple newspapers each day was a ritual common to bunco artists like Edgar. It enabled them to stay abreast of topics that might facilitate conversations with potential marks. And sometimes it alerted them to lucrative opportunities, or kept them one jump ahead of the law.

THAT WEDNESDAY—HIS SIXTH DAY in San Diego—Edgar paid another visit to Balboa Park. Not to the Plaza de Panama, but to the area abutting both the Indian Village and the encampment where the Twenty-First Infantry's enlisted men lived. An audience of seven hundred soldiers had already gathered at the Tractor Demonstration Field, where an afternoon of entertainments was laid on to reward the regiment for its work.

Edgar had cause to feel pleased with himself. In recognition of both his singing and the fame he'd pilfered from Tom Longboat, he would be appearing on the same bill as Carrie Jacobs-Bond, one of America's preeminent singers. She'd even performed at the White House, though there was nothing starry about this homely, rheumatic fifty-four-year-old Midwesterner. By a happy coincidence, her hit song, "The End of a Perfect Day," was part of Edgar's repertoire, yet that day already threatened to end far from perfectly for him, thanks to concurrent developments in Toronto, hometown of the real Tom Longboat. News of an impostor pretending to be Tom and receiving a hero's welcome in San José had reached the *Toronto Telegram*.

Edgar would surely have known nothing about the potential trouble brewing north of the border while that afternoon's entertainments got under way. These commenced with a series of boxing bouts, featuring what was presented as a comic brand of pugilism called a "battle royal." Dating back to the days of slavery, these brutally dehumanizing contests entailed groups of anywhere between four and thirty blindfolded African American men swinging at one another until all but one of them had been bludgeoned into unconsciousness, the winner often collecting a meager purse. Battle royals were recurrent attractions at Jim Crow–era carnivals, fairs, and boxing shows. They were certainly familiar to Edgar. Over in Bisbee, Arizona, just a shade under seven weeks earlier, he'd shared the bill with a battle royal.

Into the ring at the Tractor Demonstration Field stepped a good-looking African American boxer nicknamed Speedball. He'd lately been bragging about how he could lick any two men in town. Confronting him in the ring were not two but *five* other African Americans. By the end of the bout they were lying concussed at Speedball's feet.

Edgar had the unenviable task of going onstage immediately afterward and striving to capture the audience's attention. Fortunately, he'd had plenty of practice at that sort of thing, not least when he'd worked as a "ballyhoo man" on Coney Island. Perched every afternoon and evening on a small stage outside Bostock's Animal Arena, he'd been required to attract a crowd by any means. No sooner had he distracted people from the competing sights, sounds, and smells than he'd make way for the "barker"

who began a shouted spiel designed to coax those people into the show.
Edgar was consequently well-prepared almost seven years later for going
onstage in front of the huge crowd of excited soldiers, fresh from yelling
at Speedball and the other fighters. The soldiers were rapidly enthralled
by Edgar's rendition of a traditional Irish song.

How a star athlete could perform with the virtuosity of a professional
singer may have puzzled one or two of them. The answer was simple.
He *was* a professional singer, who had worked in vaudeville, one of the
country's most popular forms of mass entertainment. Vaudeville performers like Edgar honed their ability to interact with audiences, banter
with them, and swat hecklers with smart put-downs—skills that would
surely have been tested by the crowd currently facing him. Singing loudly
enough to be heard in the back rows of cavernous theaters was another
of those skills.

When Edgar finished belting out his closing number, its last line dispersing through the spring air, he received sufficient applause to justify
an encore. He wound up providing further encores before finally handing over to Carrie Jacobs-Bond. She accompanied herself on the piano as
she performed numbers from her lachrymose back catalog, their repeated
emphasis on home and ultimate reunion apposite to her military audience.
Once she'd finished the last of her songs, her place was taken by the exposition's director, who praised the soldiers and thanked them for playing
a part in its success. Much to their surprise, a commemorative medal was
issued to each of them. With these pinned to their uniforms, they were
treated to a performance by a Hispanic song-and-dance troupe. Meanwhile, a well-known Los Angeles chef barbecued generous quantities of
beef. Soon the soldiers were waiting in line to have their cups filled with
coffee and their plates heaped with meat, beans, tamales, and olives, as
well as bread and butter.

To this subsequently sated audience, Edgar made a speech urging the
men to be careful at all times to uphold the dignity of their uniforms. His
speech displayed an eloquence that flouted his paucity of schooling: "My
people have buried the tomahawk and the hatchet and war paint, but they
are ready to go to war with you boys and protect our Star-Spangled banner, if necessary."

Within hours of Edgar speaking those words in Balboa Park, a Morse code message from a journalist in Toronto was stuttering down the network of telegraph wires linking Canada with San José. Delivered to the offices of the *San José Evening News,* the message read:

MAN POSING IN YOUR CITY IS FAKER. THE REAL TOM LONGBOAT IS NOW IN ENGLAND WITH A TORONTO BATTALION WHICH LEFT HERE ONLY FIVE MONTHS AGO. HE HAS NEVER BEEN TO FRANCE.

3

Edgar returned to Balboa Park at 1 p.m. the next day. Secretive about his true self yet garrulous and extroverted in the role he'd chosen, he socialized with his officer friends at the Indian Village. He couldn't stay there long, however, because he had just ninety minutes to spare until he was scheduled to take the stage once again.

To reach that afternoon's concert venue, he had to saunter past a big open-air theater and some formal gardens. Beyond the huge façade of the Christobel Café, which advertised "cabaret and dancing," were the grand entrances to a half-dozen other substantial buildings, all of them closed. Edgar then needed to cross the Plaza de Panama and head down a wide avenue leading to a smaller square, where big crowds assembled to listen to daily concerts. Before him was an almost semicircular Roman-style arcade. It bordered a wide stage that protruded from the base of Spreckels Organ Pavilion, which resembled the gatehouse to some colossal Spanish palace. Embedded within the pavilion's central arch lay the world's largest outdoor pipe-organ.

From the pavilion, Edgar provided vocal interludes to an hour-long selection of opera and classical music played by a middle-aged English organist. In addition to singing the saccharine Victorian hit "Goodbye," Edgar performed "Mother Machree," his soundalike Chauncey Olcott faux-Irish number.

After the concert, Edgar was buttonholed by the owner of one of San Diego's downtown stores. In recent days the two men had grown friendly. The store owner was due to buy Edgar dinner at a fancy hotel that evening, but their arrangement wasn't what Edgar's friend wanted to discuss. Instead, his friend mentioned the story on the front page of that day's *San José Evening News*. It began, "The man who early this month attracted much attention in this city, explaining that he was Tom Longboat, the famous Indian runner, and that he had just returned from service with the Red Cross Corps in France, is a faker."

Edgar's friend asked whether there was any truth in the accusation. The phrasing of the question left no scope for evasion.

Poise, mental agility, and a poker face were Edgar's key assets in situations like this. Sure enough, he achieved the seemingly impossible by ad-libbing a swift response that dodged his friend's question. When they parted, the other man remained under the impression they'd still be dining together later on.

Around 5 p.m. Edgar phoned the Hotel St. James. Ostensibly leaving a helpful message for anyone who wished to speak with him, Edgar told the manager he wouldn't be back until ten o'clock that night. If the police or the press came hunting for him at his hotel, this would buy him additional time. He also appears to have fed people a line about being on his way to Tijuana.

Even though he still had some clothes and a suitcase of possessions at the St. James, he didn't risk attempting to collect them. Without settling the hefty bill that the hotel's manager had permitted him to run up, he made his exit from San Diego. He had just enough time to get over to the Santa Fe Railway's station and catch the 6:10 p.m. train, not south to Tijuana but north to Los Angeles, which was a little under four hours away, much of that spent tracing the shoreline, its passage marked by seaside towns, beaches, a concrete pier, and a rocky promontory. Seeing America spooling past like this was just a normal part of Edgar's far-from-normal life. Over the past ten weeks alone, he'd ricocheted around Arkansas, Texas, Arizona, New Mexico, and California.

His nomadic existence had started not long after his widowed father had remarried and transplanted their family from Rhode Island to the leafy boomtown of Springfield, Massachusetts, where his father had secured a job at the Highland Brewery. Quickly tiring of life as a day laborer in Springfield, Edgar cut loose from his family, then drifted to Coney Island via New York City.

And now he was in fast-expanding Los Angeles, where the broad downtown roads were made hazardous by so-called motormaniacs. Flanking many of those thoroughfares were continuous lines of billboards, large enough to hide all but the crowns of the palm trees beyond. The billboards—a relatively new phenomenon, symptomatic of the rapid growth in people's spending power and the attendant emergence of mass-market consumerism—emphasized the surfeit of choice open to Edgar. Different products. Different forms of entertainment. Different lives. Of course Edgar had already succumbed to a number of the advertised temptations, among them cigarettes, available in upward of eight brands, ranging from Chesterfields to Egyptian Deities ("The Utmost in Cigarettes").

Logic overridden by his compulsive flirtation with trouble, Edgar kept up his Tom Longboat scam. He'd netted a gig as the celebrity speaker at a Red Cross fundraiser. Slated for the Wednesday after his departure from San Diego, his role in the event was already advertised. It must've set people talking, because the Red Cross soon discovered that the real Tom Longboat was in Europe. So they contacted the downtown address Edgar had provided. Maybe because he'd been spooked by his close shave in San Diego, he'd taken the precaution of giving them a phony address.

If Edgar had any illusions about prospering in L.A., these would have been banished by the sight of a piece in that Friday's *Los Angeles Herald*. It covered his dealings with the Red Cross and alerted people to the arrival in town of the "bogus Tom Longboat," currently generating more column inches than the famous athlete whose identity he'd stolen. His prospects took another turn for the worse when the Sunday edition of the *Los Angeles*

Times disclosed that the Bureau of Investigation had launched a hunt for the man pretending to be Tom Longboat.

The bureau, which represented America's sole form of nationwide law enforcement, was an understaffed, nine-year-old precursor of the FBI, operating under the control of the Department of Justice. Edgar's choice of crime placed him within the scope of the bureau's severely restricted investigative boundaries. Amid escalating tensions with Germany, these had widened to include aspects of national security. The suspicion that the fake Tom Longboat's involvement with both the Twenty-First Infantry Regiment and the U.S. Navy Reserve might be linked to espionage lent added impetus to the bureau's hunt for him.

EDGAR PROMPTLY PUT HUNDREDS of miles between himself and the City of Angels. His less-than-angelic instincts guided him east through Montana, where snowy mountains presided over livestock-sprinkled pastures and lonesome huddles of frame houses, lit by candles or kerosene. These vast open spaces offered a reminder of just how easily he could evade the short arm of the law.

As an extra precaution, Edgar began calling himself Chief Harry Johnson, a stage name he'd adopted the previous year when he was doing vaudeville down in Key West. To go with his new persona, Edgar—who understood the value of appearance in projecting an identity—disguised himself in a long black wig, a pale headband, moccasins, and buckskin pants decorated with beads. Around his shoulders he wore a dark, striped Native American blanket.

Dressing in a similar hodgepodge of Native American attire was nothing unusual for him in particular or white Americans in general. He'd first done it at least six years earlier, and white Americans had been doing it since at least the eighteenth century, latterly at the annual parades of quasi-Masonic societies, for which it was used as a token of patriotic pride. Due to the expansion of one such society, calling itself the Improved Order of Red Men, the practice of white people wearing what purported to be Native American costume had grown more extensive in recent years. By the time Edgar left L.A. and recast himself as Chief Harry Johnson, whites-only chapters of the Red Men and its women's auxiliary, the Daughters of Pocahontas, were active in most states. Among the organization's half million or so members was former president Theodore Roosevelt.

In Central Falls, where Edgar was raised, the Red Men had a strong presence. He'd likely been part of the crowds that cheered and lit red flares during the group's parades past his family home. Those parades featured marching bands and floats depicting white America's interpretation of Native American life. As many as one thousand members of the local chapter and its affiliates joined in, their faces daubed with war paint, heads adorned with feathered bonnets and long black wigs of the type Edgar had on now.

He seems to have first worn that style of getup during the summer he worked on Coney Island, where his employer kitted him out in a costume that followed the tradition of exotically accoutered white ballyhoo men. Talent-spotted that summer, Edgar had soon landed another job requiring him to impersonate a Native American. It was with Dr. W. H. Long's Big Indian and Medicine Concert Company, which belonged to the flourishing breed of itinerant medicine shows. These sold quack remedies to customers lured by the prospect of as much as two hours of free—or at least very cheap—entertainment. A self-titled "Great Disease Detective," the eponymous Dr. Long—who had died just before Edgar joined his outfit—claimed to be able to diagnose every disease just by gazing into someone's eyes. Dr. Long's Philadelphia-based troupe, which toured the eastern states, exploited the vogue for Native American–themed medicine shows, tapping into white Americans' widespread belief that *Native* Americans enjoyed superior health.

Roughly two-thirds of such shows were given over to vaudeville—anything from eight to ten routines, from banjo solos to conjuring acts, from ventriloquism to quickfire exchanges of jokes between a blackface comedian and a straight man. Supplementing these were contributions by what were billed as "genuine Indians," often pale-skinned African Americans. Two or three times a night, Edgar's boss had him reprise his moccasined and feathered Coney Island role. He was, of course, well-equipped to take part in the vaudeville show. Between its constituent routines, the pretend Native Americans danced, chanted, drummed, and gabbled nonsense that the audience was meant to mistake for an authentic language. The resulting hubbub underscored a couple of lectures by a flamboyant "doctor," whose bellowing, whooping monologues interspersed sales of soap and candy as well as patent medicines that promised to vanquish any disease. Appropriately for someone who was the personification of a misleadingly labeled product, Edgar helped pitch supposedly traditional concoctions like "The Great Indian Hair Grower"—concoctions no more Native American than him. Though he'd been hustling people since he was at least fourteen, his time with the medicine show appears to have provided his formal apprenticeship in the techniques of the professional con man.

"Ladies and gentlemen, some good folks devote their lives to saving souls, others to accumulating wealth," ran the sales pitch for this sort of cure-all. "I am here this evening not only to entertain you but to relieve suffering humanity of its aches and pains. I call your attention to this bottle I hold in my hand, containing one of the greatest gifts to man. This famous Indian herb medicine is made from a formula handed down from generation to generation by my forefathers, who were chiefs of the Osage Indians. Did you ever hear of an Osage Indian having rheumatism? No, ladies and gentlemen, a thousand times no! It is written in the white man's bible that three score and ten is a long life, but it is a common occurrence for an Osage Indian to live to be a hundred years old and never suffer a pain or an ache. How does he accomplish this wonderful feat? He does it with the aid of this wonderful medicine I now hold before me."

Salesmen clutching only a couple of bottles of the stuff would then offer it to people in the crowd. "All sold out, doctor!" they'd chorus as soon as they needed to replenish their inadequate supply, thus conveying an impression that the medicines were even more popular than they were.

The specialty of Edgar's show was a patent tapeworm killer. Hunger, insomnia, fatigue, and other ordinary complaints were presented as signs that someone harbored a giant tapeworm. The standard sales ploy involved a member of the troupe gesturing toward a long jar containing an enormous pickled tapeworm, purchased from a slaughterhouse but portrayed as living inside him until he'd taken Dr. Long's patent worm killer. Available in the form of large pills, the cure was sold at the show or from an improvised surgery. Each pill contained a fake tapeworm or sometimes just a length of string that could be mistaken for a tapeworm, which would pass through the customer's digestive tract, offering spurious proof of the pill's effectiveness.

Medicine show doctors tended to promote that sort of product by recounting how its secret formula had come into their possession. The doctor would tell melodramatic stories in which he was, for instance, saved from certain death by a Native American who found him in the wilderness and took him back to a village where the tribal medicine man cured him with a homemade remedy. By smuggling some of this mysterious substance back to a chemist and having it analyzed, the doctor claimed to have created the miraculous patent medicine now on sale. Yarns like that probably taught Edgar just how far he could in the future push tales he told. He wouldn't have to content himself with pretending to be a Native American. He could be a war hero and a famous athlete, too.

After leaving Dr. Long's show, Edgar set up as a vendor of patent medicines, which he'd either have bought wholesale or mixed in hotel bathtubs. Still sporting a feathered headdress and tasseled buckskins, he pitched his merchandise everywhere from Boston to St. Louis. Unlicensed pitchmen like him, who learned to show their heels whenever a beat cop appeared, were nicknamed "T. and K. men" because they peddled their wares out of a "tripes and keister"—a tripod with a suitcase mounted on it. For them, no distinction existed between pitching and grifting, their sales patter enabling them to capitalize upon people's simplicity and ignorance.

Along with patent medicines, Edgar sold what masqueraded as snake oil, later to become a synonym for fraudulence. The traditional Chinese version of snake oil, obtained from Oriental water snakes, had first reached America during the nineteenth century. Edgar said his oil—which he marketed as a form of sun cream—was made from snakes he'd caught himself, yet the bottles contained nothing but olive oil.

His career as a pitchman took him to Woonsocket, just eighteen miles to the northwest of his hometown, yet he didn't bother getting in touch with his father, who had moved back to Rhode Island. A friend of Edgar's had by then shown his father a photo of him in Native American costume—a photo that, his father said, "almost left me speechless." Hearing that Edgar was performing a publicity stunt in the window of a drugstore, his father hurried over to Woonsocket, only to discover that Edgar had already moved on. And he'd kept moving ever since.

UNDER THE REGULATIONS RECENTLY ENACTED after the United States had declared war on Germany and her allies, Edgar—whose days as a patent medicine salesman were far behind him—should have been registering for military service on the evening of Tuesday, June 5, 1917. But instead he was riding a train through the rural Midwest.

Soon he'd be arriving in Eau Claire, Wisconsin, where he had speaking engagements. He was due to meet Thomas Goodale there. Formerly a big-name reporter on the *Detroit Times,* Goodale had become Edgar's publicist. Borrowing from vaudeville, whose performers often hired their own press agents, Edgar had employed Goodale to represent his current alter ego: not Chief Harry Johnson but Chief Tewanna, who hailed from the Oklahoma branch of the Cherokee, his surname carrying more than a faint echo of the surname of the Carlisle-educated Olympic athlete and gridiron star Louis Tewanima.

Goodale had publicized Chief Tewanna's arrival by circulating posters and placing an article in that morning's *Eau Claire Leader.* The chief would, according to the article, be spending a few days in Eau Claire as part of a tour of the northern and eastern states, campaigning for "the right of the Indian to vote as well as fight for this country." Edgar used the article to highlight other ways in which Native Americans suffered discrimination. And he claimed to be the designated spokesman for the Oklahoma Cherokee and Osage, supposedly on his way to Washington, DC, where he was due to meet President Woodrow Wilson, "the great white chief." Relinquishing his previous pose as a peace campaigner, he now proclaimed that his mission was to volunteer the military services of an additional thirty thousand Cherokee and Osage who wanted "to show their white brothers that the red men are as loyal as any man or group of men." All rather ironic in view of Edgar's status as a draft dodger.

When Edgar rolled up in Eau Claire at 9 p.m., the city's military registration office had—conveniently for him—just closed. Everyone at the railroad depot ogled him as he stepped off the train, wearing a feathered headdress over his braided wig. The headdress elicited numerous admiring remarks. Always cognizant of the way detail lent verisimilitude to fiction, he said it had been given to him by President Wilson. He made out that the gift was a token of the president's appreciation of "his service in bettering the condition of the Indian."

EDGAR'S LATEST PERSONA POSITIONED HIM to exploit white America's long-standing fascination with Native Americans and the Wild West. This was, of course, a relationship freighted with tragic irony, given that it co-existed with systematic discrimination *against* Native Americans, whose culture the government sought to eliminate through a policy of assimilation.

Nourishment for white America's interest in Native Americans came not just from medicine shows but also from a broad span of mass-market entertainment. Much of it cast them as villainous adversaries to cowboys and white settlers, an approach epitomized by short, pocket-sized paperback "dime novels," so named because they'd cost ten cents when they first appeared nearly sixty years earlier.

Yet a significant branch of popular entertainment provided seductive portrayals of Native Americans. Most famous of these was the by-then-defunct Buffalo Bill's Wild West touring show, which depicted Native Americans as heroic representatives of a vanishing culture. Other alluring depictions of them featured in the novels of James Fenimore Cooper, Helen Hunt Jackson, and some of their contemporaries. There were even movies—typified by D. W. Griffith's *Ramona*—that also portrayed them as heroes, as idealized embodiments of the natural world, set against the urban sleaziness of their white adversaries.

Some of that stereotypical nobility was annexed by Edgar, who had an appointment at Eau Claire High School the morning after his arrival. There, he gave a stirring address to the student body, arguing for Indians to be granted the vote. His mixture of oratorical flair and heartfelt passion earned an enthusiastic response (though his apparent sincerity was just another theatrical prop).

As he may have pointed out, denial of voting rights and full citizenship for Native Americans had its roots in the formation of the United States. Despite being the country's original inhabitants, Native Americans were treated like members of foreign nations. Not until 1887 were they offered so much as limited citizenship—and even *that* was granted only on the condition they accepted ownership of just a portion of their land, renounced tribal allegiances, and took up what was presented as "civilized life."

To lend weight to what he'd been telling the students, Edgar posed a riddle. He offered a handsome blanket as the prize for the first correct answer. The blanket was, he said, woven by "an Indian princess" on the Cherokee reservation. Many of the students tried their luck before he awarded the blanket to one of them.

He then milked the adoring students for yet more adulation by soliciting trinkets that he could take back to the children at the Chieasher Indian Mission School in Oklahoma. The recipients of these donations would, he promised, "write to their paleface friends and thank them." Gifts for the imaginary children attending this fictitious school in this fictitious town swamped him the following day.

By Friday of that week, he had embedded himself in Eau Claire's communal imagination no less as a philanthropist than as the owner of fourteen oil wells "running day and night." Like a drug addict who requires higher and higher doses to achieve the same effect, he had an urge to keep magnifying the scale of his boasts. He took to professing fluency in nine languages, and to presenting himself as a noted runner and footballer; a collector who had amassed historic relics from the world over; and someone accustomed to conversing with "men and women high in the affairs of their nations." He even posed as a close friend of King Edward VII, whom he said he'd met while touring England.

So persuasive were Edgar's self-aggrandizing tales that the *Eau Claire Leader* ran an article proclaiming, "It is doubtful if any Indian living is so widely known as Chief Tewanna." One of the reporters on that paper was nonetheless skeptical enough about Edgar to start investigating him.

The reporter fixed up a Friday afternoon interview with D. L. Hunt, a local man with financial ties to the oil business in Oklahoma, Edgar's supposed home state. Hunt had also spent a decade living there, running the Southwestern Business College, which left him "extensively acquainted with conditions there." He could hardly have been better placed to contradict Edgar's portrait of himself as a well-known Oklahoma businessman and sports personality.

At the interview, Hunt talked knowledgeably about the "great strides" made by the Cherokee "in the matter of education." He told the reporter that they had "taken up in nearly all cases the white man's ways." He praised them for how well they ran the district's schools, banks, stores, and other businesses. He referred to their ownership of "vast oilfields valued at millions of dollars." And he lamented the paucity of wider recognition for their achievements. Unwilling to admit he'd never heard of Chief Tewanna—which represented a freakish stroke of luck for Edgar—Hunt declared that in Oklahoma "the name of Tewanna was a prominent one."

It was becoming so in Wisconsin, too. Edgar's local celebrity could, as his time in California had taught him, be parlayed into friendships with Eau Claire's most influential and moneyed citizens. Since his arrival in the city on Tuesday evening, several such people had given him presents and hosted meals for him. Each of them was informed that he'd be sending them a large box of Indian blankets, currently stored in Chicago, where he claimed to be scheduled to appear at the Great Northern Hippodrome. Admittedly, he *was* aiming to leave Eau Claire that Saturday, but he had no such booking in Chicago.

ONLY A DAY BEFORE HE was due to depart, Edgar presented himself at Eau Claire's Grand Opera House, a gabled Victorian redbrick building distinctly lacking grandeur. It didn't host opera, either. Like most similarly titled small-town venues, its name served not to describe its function but to distract customers from the louche associations acquired by ordinary theaters.

Edgar had been hired to perform there immediately after that evening's screening of a new silent movie. Interspersing short movies with vaudeville acts had long been common. Acts such as Edgar's, which referenced ethnic and racial stereotypes, were a staple of vaudeville. Though the dominant variation entailed white performers wearing blackface makeup and lampooning African Americans, other acts caricatured German Americans, Chinese Americans, Jewish Americans, and Native Americans.

In this case, Edgar or his press agent had duped the management into believing that he'd appeared in the main movie about to be screened. Titled *Her Own People,* it was about a doomed love affair between a white man and a half–Native American girl, played by a white actress. Edgar must have known that some of the Native American actors would—thanks to a mixture of smudgy cinematography, feathered headdresses, and the haze of tobacco smoke in the theater—be hard to identify, enabling him to get away with the audacious claim that he was one of the Native Americans on-screen.

Music at the show was provided not by a lone pianist but by an orchestra, playing to an audience of about five hundred. Edgar had worked as a pianist at similar venues back east. He couldn't read music, so the improvisatory aspect of the job was a godsend. It had also helped him to become still more attuned to the art of showmanship, to the ways he could steer the reactions of his audience. Vaudeville audiences—especially those at venues such as the Grand Opera House—tended to be quick to hoot, boo, clap, or heckle performers. But experienced performers like Edgar referred to themselves as "mechanics of emotion," coaxing the desired response at the desired moment. In that sense, vaudeville artistes had more in common with con artists than they may have cared to admit.

When the movie finished, Edgar took to the stage and presented a prize to one of the city's Boy Scout troops. He described the prize as "a beautiful solid silver trumpet, valued at about $75," though it was actually made from tin and worth closer to $3. After the presentation, he gave a lecture and performed some songs and piano solos. Practiced vaudevillians like him positioned themselves in the footlights' glare, close to the rim of the stage, from where they were best able to read the audience, establish a rapport with it, and then create an illusion of spontaneity and intimacy. Edgar had a flawless singing technique, probably drummed into him by the music instructor at the surprisingly enlightened reformatory to which he'd been consigned as a fourteen-year-old.

His act went down so well that people begged him to stay in Eau Claire and play some extra dates. He graciously consented to extend his booking at the Grand Opera House for another couple of days, but dispatched his press agent, Thomas Goodale, to Detroit, where Goodale could solicit publicity that might generate speaking engagements in Michigan.

Twice daily that weekend, Edgar worked as a support act for movies at the Grand Opera House, yet even that didn't satisfy the demand. It didn't satisfy Edgar, either, because he lacked the single-minded patience required to parlay his talent into the big-league vaudeville stardom it deserved. In any case, he needed more than just the applause from a sizable audience and the fat paychecks that came with that. No matter how large the paychecks were, it would never be enough for a spendthrift like him.

Promising to return to Eau Claire on the final Thursday of that month, he borrowed a suitcase from one person and eighteen dollars from another before heading to Detroit, his press agent's home turf. Edgar nonetheless had a total of only thirty dollars in his billfold.

Just prior to his arrival, Goodale bagged a story for him in the *Detroit Free Press*. Headlined BIG CHIEF OFFERS BRAVES FOR WAR, it plugged his services "lecturing to the palefaces" and applied daring enhancements to the fiction he'd dreamed up. Now his portrait could be seen on the ceiling of the lobby in Detroit's new Statler Hotel. Now he was "a personal friend" of President Wilson. Now he'd be returning from their meeting in Washington, DC, with a party of forty Indians who, at each stopping place, would perform an opera, written especially for them, all proceeds being donated to the school system.

Detroit was a flourishing city of grand civic buildings and spacious, remarkably clean avenues, on which the sounds of street piano players and shouts from Italian fruit sellers were common. The city's early embrace of Prohibition had spawned illicit businesses catering to Edgar's affinity for the warm, anesthetic embrace of liquor. Down by the river he had a choice between not only secret rooms housing speakeasies, but also what were known as "blind pigs" or "blind tigers." These circumvented the law by charging customers to see a blind pig or some other form of sideshow attraction, and then serving a complimentary glass of moonshine—something with which Edgar was well-acquainted in both senses of the word.

He did not, however, have any significant successes to toast during his short time in Detroit. For all Goodale's efforts, Edgar failed to secure the bookings he needed to generate the cash he lacked. Still worse, his arrival overlapped with the widely publicized introduction of a government campaign to arrest men who had failed to register for military service. If Edgar was caught, he faced a year in prison—and a lot longer than that if the authorities figured out who he really was.

4

Sticking around in Detroit was not a prudent option, yet Edgar took until late June to find a means of escape. It necessitated stooping to the level of the pickpockets who were viewed with such disdain by con artists like him. Preoccupied as he was by status, that wouldn't have sat easily with Edgar. Whatever misgivings he felt, he stole his press agent's suitcase, together with some clothes and money. Then he headed more than one hundred miles southwest to Fort Wayne, Indiana, still calling himself Chief Tewanna, his lineage morphing from Cherokee to Sioux.

He warded off awkward questions about the military draft by claiming he'd already enlisted in the Oklahoma Field Hospital Corps. And he circulated the story that, until he shipped out, he'd be working as an army recruiter "under the direction of Uncle Sam." Over a period of just three days, he visited a couple of industrial plants and made recruiting speeches to their workforce, his efforts aided by a squad of artillerymen. He also headlined in four "Enlistment Day" vaudeville shows, hosted by the Lyric Theater, which was, name aside, grander than the equivalent venue in Eau Claire.

Vaudeville programs typically comprised as many as nine acts, each lasting between ten and thirty minutes, the full show spanning upward of three hours, through which the house orchestra provided an accompaniment. Some of Edgar's colleagues at the Lyric Theater had probably been touring the same act for years, because only a few thousand people at most could see any show in a single day. Changing a successful act was said to bring bad luck, but Edgar's lack of superstition gave him scope for incessant tinkering.

The manager of the Lyric would have been responsible for slotting Edgar and the other acts into a well-tested framework, always beginning with a visual routine, since any vocals would be rendered inaudible by chattering latecomers taking their seats. For the show headlined by Edgar—"Chief Tewanna" to the audience—a dance or juggling act would have functioned as the opener. It was followed by singers, a pianist, a comedian, and one of the short films that often featured on vaudeville bills. There was an elaborate theatrical sketch as well. Edgar must have been conversant with the term for this: "a flash act." Such acts were prone to *flashy* production values—flashy enough to come with their own scenery on occasion. Flash acts generally preceded the moment when the curtain came down for the intermission.

As that evening's headliner, Edgar would have been left to hang around until the penultimate spot in the show—a coveted position that came with the best dressing room and highest salary. While waiting backstage, he'd likely have heard language reflective of vaudeville's role as family entertainment. Even mild profanities such as "goddamn" were seldom uttered, despite the constant pressure under which he and his fellow performers labored.

Whenever they went onstage, their careers were at stake. Only a single lucky break away from stardom, they had to hope their acts provoked applause, or "drew blood" in vaudeville slang. The duration and intensity of that applause would be noted on "Act Report" cards written by the theater manager, who also commented on the quality of each act and how suitable it was for families. His report would then be submitted to the central booking office run by that chain of theaters. Were Edgar or any of the other artistes to receive an unfavorable write-up, they could forget about securing any more bookings from other theaters in the same chain. Just the *threat* of a bad report served to keep performers in line. It was a system sure to exacerbate the often-strained relationship between theater managers and the likes of Edgar.

Theater managers usually resented the fact that their paychecks were far smaller than those of the performers. And the performers had cause to resent the fact that managers policed the length of every act. For the managers, timing was crucial. If a matinee overran, it reduced the time available before the next show and thus reduced income from the theater's food and beverage concessions. The repercussions were even more serious when an evening show fell behind schedule. Under those circumstances, the theater risked incurring high-rate overtime payments to the orchestra, the stagehands, and the front-of-house staff. In the event that the artistes going onstage before Edgar were running late, the manager would have visited Edgar's dressing room and instructed him to shave a few minutes off his act.

Onstage at last, Edgar sang a patriotic song and performed a couple of his standard Chauncey Olcott numbers, which were, he told his audience, Olcott's favorites. He added that Olcott himself had suggested he sing them. Also he bragged about his experiences of army life and encouraged members of the audience to enlist in the military.

Charismatic and talented though he was, show business could at present give him nothing more than a fleeting respite from his money problems. These were compounded by the authorities getting wise to his activities. He became worried enough to drop his Chief Tewanna charade.

NECESSITY LED HIM TO IGNORE any qualms he had about returning to New York City, where he'd once served jail time for impersonating a government official. By the start of August he was back in the Big Apple, back amid its smoke-wreathed skyscrapers, yellow taxicabs, congested tenements, fashionable women, and jostling rush-hours, the brash modernity and nocturnal sparkle of its streets emblematic of the myriad ways in which the world around him had altered since he was a kid. Not that he had trouble adjusting to new things. One thing that had changed during the time he'd been away was the ubiquitous presence of gaggles of soldiers and sailors on the sidewalks, pestering women who strayed into their orbit.

Edgar's return to the city coincided with a protracted heat wave of record-breaking severity. Numerous stores and factories were forced to shut down, their sweat-soaked employees decanted into the parks. Fire escapes and rooftops became improvised bedrooms. Cart horses crumpled in the street. People succumbed to heat exhaustion, too. And wisecracks about the temperature circulated more readily than the clotted air. "It is impossible to get soft-cooked eggs," one of these went. "The hens are laying 'em hard-boiled."

Both the heat and the humidity reached their zenith that Thursday when Edgar crossed lower Manhattan's financial district, where the streets were shaded by office blocks of up to forty-one stories. Servicing those were men-only lunch counters that attracted the kind of people his father had wanted him to become. Regular people with regular jobs. On Broad Street—a gorge-like thoroughfare culminating in the stock exchange— Edgar would have had to slalom down the sidewalk, which was, despite the heat reflected off all those hard surfaces, crowded with brokers. They formed the chaotic "curb market," trading securities not listed on the stock exchange.

Midway down the street, Edgar disappeared into a building where the U.S. Army Transport Service was based. He must have heard they were recruiting civilian crewmen, so he'd gone to sign up, his need to raise some cash and escape from the authorities blending perhaps with a desire for adventure.

When he showed up at the busy but understaffed Labor Employment Section, he was recognized by one of the officers there. In all probability, the officer—who knew him as Tom Longboat—belonged to the Twenty-Second Infantry Regiment, which had transferred to New York City from Fort Douglas, Arizona, where Edgar had seven months earlier spent time. Possibly swayed by Edgar's past experience as a nightwatchman on a merchant ship, his acquaintance at the Labor Employment Section offered him a job as an ordinary seaman aboard the SS *Antilles,* due to transport American troops to France. The job paid ninety dollars a month. Very low, even with the inclusion of a forty-five-dollar-a-month bonus. To make matters worse, the offer was contingent upon Edgar providing either a passport or a Certificate of Identification confirming his identity. Since he wasn't the man he said he was, that left him in a bit of a fix.

SQUADRONS OF DARK CLOUDS HAD by lunchtime assembled west of the city, muffled thunder mimicking the ominous, far-off drumroll of artillery fire. Edgar just needed to shut his eyes and he'd be able to imagine himself a hero in the trenches. Within about half an hour, rain started sheeting down. Children shrieked delightedly in the flooded streets. Adults, meanwhile, leaned from windows to savor the refreshing downpour. It didn't last long, but it left behind much cooler air.

Before that afternoon was over, Edgar set out for the U.S. Army Transport Service's headquarters. He could get there via the nearby Hudson Terminal, marked by twin office blocks that resembled a giant tuning fork. From the underground platforms, where nicotine addicts like him were not allowed to light cigarettes or pipes, electric trains slithered beneath the river on their brief journey to Hoboken, the so-called port of embarkation for American military personnel shipping out to fight the Germans. Ironically, it was synonymous with German immigrants, who made up a quarter of its population. Along Hoboken's waterfront were scores of German saloons and hotels, advertising bock beer—the type of German ale brewed at the plant where Edgar's father had worked.

Young soldiers from the Twenty-Second Infantry Regiment—several of whom remembered Edgar as Tom Longboat—guarded the big iron gates through which he entered the docks. It felt like a military encampment. Army-issue pup tents covered much of the yard space. Beyond lay a series of giant piers extending into the Hudson River. Six of those, formerly owned by German shipping lines, had been commandeered by the U.S. government, which had replaced most of the German-born dockworkers, lest they remain loyal to the kaiser. The piers were already stacked with bags, crates, and vast quantities of barbwire, all pending shipment.

Pier 4—a weather-beaten, single-deck wooden structure—housed the well-staffed port utilities offices, where Captain D. F. Chamberlain worked. Like the other offices, his would have been sparsely furnished: just a map on the wall, a chair, and a paper-strewn desk with a candlestick-style phone on it. Edgar—who had little choice but to play along with the notion that he was Tom Longboat—asked the nearsighted, gray-haired Captain Chamberlain for a Certificate of Identification under that name.

The two of them seem to have got along, meaning Edgar had a good chance of obtaining what he wanted. On the application Edgar claimed to have been born in Syracuse, New York, nearly six years before his real date of birth. There was nothing out of the ordinary about a Native American not possessing a birth certificate, so he showed Chamberlain a forged Certificate of Naturalization, a type of document issued in Oklahoma, where Edgar's purported tribe had its reservation. The forgery helped Edgar to fool Chamberlain into issuing him a Certificate of Identification, bearing the captain's signature, a government seal, and a photograph of himself in a seaman's uniform. If anyone challenged his identity, he could now prove that he was, according to the U.S. government, Tom Longboat.

HE HAD FIVE DAYS BEFORE setting off for Europe: five days during which the temperature and humidity soared to levels almost as energy sapping as they had been prior to the rainstorm. In that time he could mingle with his fellow crewmen, reacquaint himself with shipboard life, and familiarize himself with his uncomfortable new floating home. He could enjoy his celebrity (or, more accurately, *Tom's* celebrity) among the soldiers from the Twenty-Second Infantry Regiment. He could quench his thirst in Hoboken's waterfront saloons. He could pick up women—or even men, if he wanted to risk trouble with the police. And he could sample the revolutionary new "slam-bang, knock-'em-down-and-drag-'em-out confusion of noises," which people were referring to as "jazz"—music that made his own repertoire sound so much more conventional than he was in other regards.

During this five-day hiatus, he must've talked to someone who maybe talked to someone else who alerted the Underwood & Underwood photographic agency to the presence in Hoboken of Tom Longboat. A man from the agency came looking for him. When the photographer eventually tracked him down, Edgar appears to have lied about enlisting in the U.S. Army Transport Service, for which he was merely working as a civilian crewman. He may even have used his newly acquired Certificate of Identification to dispel any doubts.

Arrayed in a white sailor's top, worn over a matching T-shirt, he posed for a photograph, eyes staring into the lens, cheekbones underscored by the light, his expression suitably serious, cowlicks of black hair flopping on either side of his forehead. He could have passed for a movie star—a newish breed. The photographer was left in no doubt that the handsome features visible through the camera's lens belonged to one of North America's most famous athletes, now on the crew of the SS *Antilles*.

The *Antilles* was a steamship that used to ply the New York City–New Orleans route, carrying cargoes of bananas and other fruit, along with a modest number of passengers. Before being redeployed as a troopship, she had been fitted with extra accommodation, toilets, and cooking facilities. She'd also acquired lookout stations, a speaking-tube communication system, a generous supply of life rafts, and several artillery platforms on the deck. The sight of these was likely to make Edgar and his crewmates worry about the German submarines lying in wait for them.

KIT BAGS SLUNG OVER THEIR SHOULDERS, a long column of khaki-clad troops in wide-brimmed hats marched down the quayside on the morning of Tuesday, August 7, 1917. Despite the heat, they were wearing heavy winter coats. Military personnel shepherded them onto the pier where Edgar's ship was moored. They then filed along the gangplanks linking the pier to the *Antilles*. In advance of the moment when they'd set sail for France, the troops were ordered belowdecks, which gave rise to a lot of grousing. By keeping them out of sight, the authorities maintained the forlorn hope that nobody, especially the local German population, would recognize that the *Antilles* was transporting troops.

She cast off at half past one that afternoon. From her deck, Manhattan's clustered towers continually realigned as she chugged down the Hudson River. A little later, the gigantic Statue of Liberty drifted into view, thrusting skyward as if it had just burst from its mid-channel island.

None of the *Antilles*'s military passengers were visible at that stage, yet the crews aboard other vessels must have figured she was a troopship because they gave supportive whistle blasts. And the band on a nearby tour boat, which had been playing a jerkily urgent ragtime number, lurched into a rendition of "Goodbye, Good Luck, God Bless You."

Only after the *Antilles* had skirted Brooklyn's huge wharves and entered Gravesend Bay were the troops at last permitted on deck. They reappeared in time to witness their ship's rendezvous with the rest of what was only the second American military convoy to Europe since the president's declaration of war. Four other troopships, a battleship, and two smaller escort vessels made up the remainder of the convoy, which soon dropped anchor within sight of the Coney Island lighthouse, tantalizingly close to Edgar's old haunts.

He'd have been surrounded over the next few hours by the clatter of boots and blur of passing faces as the *Antilles*'s human cargo was ushered from one part of the ship to the other. By nightfall the soldiers had all been allocated cramped quarters. Unlike Edgar, few of them would've had the nautical experience to recognize the metallic clanking of the anchor being hauled up, at which point the *Antilles* followed the other ships on an easterly course into the uninterrupted darkness and out of the throttling grip of the New York City summer. When dawn broke, Edgar's military shipmates were astonished to discover their home country's shoreline had vanished as unexpectedly as a silk handkerchief during a conjuring routine.

The *Antilles* was second in a line of lumbering troopships, escorted by destroyers on both flanks. But the battleship was out of view somewhere ahead. Though the convoy had not yet left U.S. waters, Edgar knew that he could suddenly be pitched into the type of military scenario within which he'd so often depicted himself. A U-boat attack was possible even at that early stage in the convoy's transatlantic voyage. Off Nantucket nearly six months before America entered the war, an enemy submarine had demonstrated that by sinking five vessels—one Dutch, one Norwegian, and three British.

Any temptation for Edgar to relax was quashed by constant reminders of this threat. Day and night, teams of sixteen soldiers were assigned to lookout duty. Each of them devoted a maximum of thirty minutes to using binoculars to scan a preassigned fifteen-degree sliver of ocean. Lookouts were drilled until they grew accustomed to making prompt and accurate reports on everything sighted.

Daily "Abandon Ship" drills heightened the sense of danger. Edgar also had to comply with a series of orders that decreed that all the watertight doors belowdecks should be kept closed in order to restrict the flooding caused by a torpedo strike, that nothing should be thrown overboard lest it alert submarines, and that no light should be visible from the ship after dusk. Even the smoking of cigarettes and the carrying of matches was prohibited at night, because the glow from a cigarette or the flaring of a match would be discernible up to half a mile away—well within the range of an enemy torpedo. The captain of the *Antilles* and his officers were nonetheless reassuring about the ship's ability to withstand an attack. In the event she *was* torpedoed, her construction would, they said, enable her to stay afloat.

PUT EDGAR IN A NEW PLACE and he'd soon charm people. Already he had made friends with personnel from the First Telegraph Battalion, most of whom hailed from Pennsylvania. With them they had a little black-and-white-spotted terrier named Smoke, who functioned as their mascot. They passed much of the voyage lounging around the deck, rows of soldiers standing along the rails or sitting on the life rafts. Frequent references to how they'd be in "heaven, hell, or Hoboken" by Christmas were commonly heard among outward-bound troops.

To relieve the monotony, Edgar's pals from the First Telegraph Battalion started putting on evening entertainments in their stuffy quarters. Behind portholes draped with blankets, they arranged for a performance by a comedian and, on another occasion, a musical quartet, all recruited from their unit. Taking advantage of the presence of what seemed to be a bona fide star, they invited the famous Tom Longboat to appear at one of their shows. He obliged with a selection of anecdotes about his experiences with the Canadian army at Ypres.

On the men's eighth evening at sea, bad weather began to brew. Everyone lining the deck kept anxious track of the rest of the convoy as dusk approached, complete darkness gradually enveloping them. Around midnight Edgar and his crewmates finally felt the full force of the storm, which had the ship bucking like a roller coaster. The officers dismissed it as a mere squall, but Edgar's friends from the First Telegraph Battalion rated it "a very real storm."

Between then and the afternoon when the *Antilles* had commenced her voyage, the *Brooklyn Daily Eagle* had, through a tip-off that probably emanated from the Hoboken waterfront, run a story about Tom Longboat's enlistment in the U.S. Army Transport Service. Next to the story was a photo of the *real* Tom Longboat, though the article focused upon Edgar's fictionalized version of the athlete's past. "Soon after the European war broke out, Longboat enlisted in the Queen Victoria Grenadiers and fought in the first drive on the Somme front," the article stated. "He was struck by a piece of shrapnel and was laid up in a hospital for eight months. After his convalescence he returned to the United States and spent some time on the Mexican border, teaching the boys training there at the time the finer points of the running game."

Numerous other newspapers, everywhere from New York City to Vancouver, from Kansas City to Indianapolis, picked up the story, which came to be paired with the photo of Edgar taken by Underwood & Underwood. Staff at the *Brooklyn Daily Eagle* then discovered that there were *two* Tom Longboats, one of them now in the mid-Atlantic, the other reportedly serving in France with the 180th Sportsmen's Battalion. The newspaper launched an investigation to determine which of those men was the noted marathon runner. It came down on Edgar's side. *He* was tagged as the genuine Tom Longboat, and the genuine Tom Longboat was branded an impostor. Referring to the photo of Edgar, the article declared, "If it is not Tom Longboat, it is his twin brother."

While Edgar endured another day and night of strong winds and heavy rain, his photo in the *Daily Eagle* prompted a spate of letters and phone calls to the newspaper from track-and-field devotees. Most of them insisted the man in the photo was *not* Tom Longboat. Someone suggested he was the same person who had been in California masquerading as Longboat. And someone else wrote, "This picture is not one of Tom Longboat, but an Indian who was employed on a vessel with me some three years ago. Know that face . . . Kept me company during the long, dreary night watches for four months, with a voice like Caruso. Bull like a frog."

If Edgar succeeded in bypassing heaven and hell and made it back to Hoboken instead, the chances of him winding up in another jail cell were growing.

DURING THE EARLY HOURS of Friday, August 17, 1917, the storm abated, by which time the convoy had dispersed. None of the other vessels could be seen from the deck of Edgar's ship. A single distant light soon appeared in front of her, marking the battleship at the head of the convoy. Now the *Antilles* and the other ships had a point around which to reassemble. Yet passing U-boats were bound to be attracted by such a bright light. Exacerbating the tension for Edgar and his crewmates was the pace at which the scattered ships maneuvered into their allotted positions, a pace that replicated the dawdling gracelessness of a party of geriatrics trying to find their seats in a darkened theater.

Not until the end of the morning was the convoy safely back together. The escort ships then sailed off, and were replaced by a fresh group of destroyers. As the convoy steamed east, the destroyers circled it, later chasing away an unidentified vessel that materialized on the horizon.

When dusk fell, Edgar and his shipmates were warned that they were about to enter the most dangerous part of the Atlantic. Their lives depended upon them remaining vigilant. Sighting the frothing wake left by a torpedo could win the *Antilles* vital seconds in which to evade it, or at least lessen its impact. In case Edgar and the others were forced to abandon ship, the officers had them sleep in their clothes. And they were told to have their life preservers always within reach.

Somewhere to the west of the *Antilles,* the flashing of Morse code from a British ship punctured the darkness. The message read MY CONVOY WAS ATTACKED BY A SUBMARINE TEN MILES FROM THE PRESENT POSITION.

SHORTLY BEFORE NOON THAT SUNDAY, a sudden spurt of water broke the sea's sculpted surface, pinpointing where a U-boat had ducked beneath it. The alarm rapidly sounded aboard Edgar's ship, those half-dozen blasts on a steam whistle heralding the precise moment when his military fantasies became real. With a violent sideways movement that must have yanked at Edgar's body, the *Antilles* commenced the standard zigzagging anti-submarine course, which was replicated by the other troopships. Military personnel and crewmen alike sprinted down the swaying corridors and gangways, their boots hammering on the decks, their shouts no doubt bouncing off the ship's metal walls. While crewmen manned the gun platforms, soldiers in life preservers crowded the deck, where the unfolding drama could be watched with lip-biting anxiety.

Like sheepdogs nipping at the heels of their flock, the escorting destroyers kept veering close to the *Antilles* and the rest of the convoy. In the meantime, a torpedo's fizzing trail was spotted. It etched a line across the water, extending toward one of the destroyers. A simple geometry assignment would now help to determine whether Edgar and his shipmates lived or died. If that moving line intersected with the destroyer, Edgar's ship was a lot more likely to end up being sunk or disabled. From the masts above him, the lookouts would have seen the tip of the line getting closer and closer. Forty yards. Thirty yards. Twenty yards until it bisected the ocean in front of the destroyer, and then exploded harmlessly.

The destroyer and its fellow escort vessels converged on the area where they suspected the U-boat was lurking. What looked like garbage cans were rolled from the rear of these ships. Each can was a fifty-pound depth charge, attached by a length of rope to a marker buoy. For a few anticlimactic moments, the buoys would crest the waves in a silent preamble to a stifled *boom* and a frothing ring of water. Yet no debris surfaced, nothing to imply that the submarine had been hit.

Everyone aboard Edgar's ship awaited the next attack. Two more alerts that afternoon propelled the gunners to their positions. Once again the U-boat scored no torpedo strikes.

COMING INTO VIEW AT DAYBREAK was a fleet of small fishing boats with weather-stained red, yellow, and sometimes blue sails. Their presence implied that the convoy didn't have far to go until it reached Saint-Nazaire. Edgar could look forward to practicing his fluent French when he disembarked. Before the *Antilles* made landfall, though, she had to negotiate a stretch of water where several shipping lanes bunched into a single narrow channel that doubled as a shooting gallery for waiting U-boats.

At 8:32 a.m., a faint bristle on the horizon resolved itself into a lighthouse, set on an island just off the coast. Within a few hours Edgar's perilous journey would be over. A mood of elation prevailed among his shipmates. The sonorous explosion of a depth charge, dropped by a destroyer to the left of the *Antilles,* cut short the euphoria. Instantly, the gunners aboard Edgar's ship dashed to their posts. They fired three inconclusive shots at a U-boat that was briefly visible above the surface.

More gunfire was audible at intervals over the next half hour. Toward the rear of the convoy, someone sighted a submarine's periscope. Half a dozen shots were fired before the periscope vanished.

A couple of French airplanes flew over the zigzagging fleet and bombed the submarine. One of their bombs exploded dangerously near a troopship.

Before the convoy reached the mouth of the river Loire, some twelve further shots were aimed at what now appeared to be multiple U-boats. A torpedo sped toward the troopship just ahead of the *Antilles.* By swerving like a quarterback sidestepping an opponent, the troopship dodged the projectile, which passed only twenty feet from its hull.

At last the attack was over. It had gone on for more than an hour, relieved conversations about it only now breaking out around Edgar. A debate raged as to how many U-boats had been sunk. While the ship's officers plumped for a single hit, others insisted that ten had been destroyed.

The truth was more prosaic. Not even a single enemy submarine had been sunk.

Edgar's shipmates were still arguing as the convoy steamed slowly into Saint-Nazaire, gliding past beaches that sloped up to green, sunlit

hills with cottages scattered across them. After thirteen days at sea, everyone on board relished the prospect of escaping from the discomfort and
claustrophobia of seagoing life. But the low tide prevented the *Antilles*
and her sister ships from entering the congested little harbor until about
five o'clock that evening.

On either side of the *Antilles,* much smaller boats bobbed about. The
crews of these waved their hats and shouted, *"Vive les Américaines!"* A
cheering throng of Frenchmen and black-clad women was already on the
quayside as the ship docked. Edgar's friends from the First Telegraph Battalion were soon streaming down the gangplank. As they marched across
the cobbled quayside, children scampered alongside them, tossing flowers
in their direction and reaching out to touch their hands—just the sort of
schmaltzy scene within which Edgar so often portrayed himself.

When the *Antilles* completed the return journey to Hoboken about a month later, Edgar was immediately taken away for questioning. Captain H. C. Craig, an army officer who worked out of an address on River Street, just across from the docks, undertook the interrogation. Presumably as an upshot of the articles published by the *Brooklyn Daily Eagle* while Edgar was en route for France, Craig accused him of being an impostor.

Edgar began by denying this accusation. Under the pressure of cross-examination, though, he was forced to admit he wasn't Tom Longboat. But he said his real name was also an Indian name. It was, he claimed, Thomas Tewanna. His story may well have elicited pity because Craig didn't take the matter any further. Instead of feeling the chill grasp of handcuffs around his wrists, Edgar was allowed to collect his meager wages from his time aboard the *Antilles,* and then leave Hoboken.

No longer trading on Tom Longboat's fame, he had, by the second week of October, found his way to cold, blustery upstate New York, where he called himself Chief White Elk, the name he'd been given when he worked for Dr. W. H. Long's Big Indian and Medicine Concert Company. Edgar assigned Chief White Elk a rich backstory. Predisposed to cast himself as a macho yet cerebral man, he borrowed aspects of his jazzed-up version of Tom Longboat's past, sparing him the inconvenience of learning a new role. Chief White Elk thus became a survivor of the Princess Pat Regiment and a onetime member of Carlisle's crack football team.

He also led people to think he was on furlough from his duties as a wireless operator aboard a U.S. Army Transport Service vessel, where he'd been serving since being invalided out of the trenches—not that he'd even visited the trenches during his brief sojourn in France, much of which appears to have been spent unloading his ship's cargo of military equipment. With vivid specificity, he detailed the wounds he'd incurred at the Battle of Verdun. A silver and steel plate was, he said, implanted in his chest, where several ribs had been blown away. Shrapnel had blinded him in one eye—an illusion that required a piratical eye patch. Rubber bandages swathed his legs, which had been burned by a flamethrower and "practically shot to pieces." Worse still, he'd lost his hearing in one ear.

Experience was teaching him that the bigger the lies he told, the more avidly people seemed to embrace them. He'd surely have realized that those people probably wanted to feel a connection—however loose—to world events, to have something out of the ordinary to tell their friends, something that made them feel special.

Stopping in Poughkeepsie, its brick and timber buildings lining the east bank of the Hudson River, Edgar picked up an engagement to lecture about the war. Three days after the lecture, news broke that the real Tom Longboat had been killed on active service. Coverage of his demise was sometimes illustrated by photos of Edgar pretending to be him.

While news of the celebrated athlete's death spread across the Eastern Seaboard, Edgar headed north. As Chief White Elk, he visited Schenectady, another small, prosperous riverside city. There, he spun a yarn about being on his way to visit his birthplace—the Onondaga Reservation, near Syracuse.

That Wednesday he hobbled along the section of State Street traversing the city's business district, his imaginary war wounds signposted by the cane he used. Austere three- and four-story edifices, intermingled by fussily decorated storefronts and theaters, served as an honor guard for this ample, brick-paved thoroughfare, along which streetcars trundled. Edgar limped into the building that housed Schenectady's *Daily Gazette.* He captivated one of its reporters with his broad grin, his colorful tales of football stardom and military service, his account of how the French respected and appreciated the American troops, his stoic acceptance of his war wounds, and his confidence in the successful outcome of the war. When the reporter inquired whether he thought the Allies would win the conflict by next spring, Edgar heaped his response with feigned bemusement: "The *Allies*?" A sardonic smile preceded the moment he added, "Not the Allies—you mean *America* will finish it *for* the Allies."

Seemingly overcome by quivering rage, he spoke about what America was fighting against. He described entering Belgian villages and seeing infants who had been skewered with bayonets. These sort of atrocity stories had been making the rounds since the early days of the war, so Edgar upstaged them by saying he'd witnessed some Scottish soldiers—"kilties," he called them—being crucified by the Germans.

"Maybe you haven't heard just how it was done," he continued with the gleeful aplomb of a born raconteur. "The horrible thing took place right before our eyes and we were unable to help them. The four men were placed against a structure and their arms were pulled out with ropes so that the cords or tendons stuck out and could be seen. Then several German soldiers—'barbarians' is a better term—took knives and cut off the men's ears and noses and other parts of their bodies. After the Germans had cut holes through their shoulders, they literally pulled the skin from their bodies.

"Barbarism in the primitive stage is far superior to German warfare. They stop at nothing and won't ever stop until they are beaten—and beaten badly. That will be the part which America will play before summer."

In the next day's *Gazette,* a lengthy piece about Chief White Elk appeared. The piece softened up the citizens of Schenectady for his usual shakedown.

By that weekend he had reason to feel as if fate had intervened on his behalf. Word was circulating that the SS *Antilles* had been torpedoed off the French coast. Up to seventy personnel were missing, presumed drowned. Of those, the majority belonged to the civilian crew. Edgar could so easily have been among them. But he'd lived to flimflam another day.

ACCOMPANYING HIM ON THE last Thursday of that month was a man who went by the name of H. H. Klein. They'd met somewhere between Schenectady and the industrial city of Wheeling, West Virginia, slightly less than four hundred miles away. In Wheeling, the pair entered the McLure Hotel. The largest and fanciest hotel in the vicinity, it was just the class of establishment where Edgar and his fellow con artists sought their prey. It offered a sharp contrast to the boardinghouses and hotels at which he and his coworkers in Dr. W. H. Long's medicine show would have stayed. Rooms open to folk like them tended to be dark, dirty, and vermin infested, their thin walls giving rise to a popular quip about how "you could hear the fellow in the next room making up his mind."

Klein signed the visitors' book at the McLure with a few indecipherable squiggles. Though he showed up at the same moment as Edgar, Klein told the desk clerk that he'd known Chief White Elk just a matter of hours. The scene of their meeting, he stated, was Zanesville, Ohio— seventy-four miles east. He said he'd taken pity on the chief and brought him to Wheeling.

In the argot of con men, Edgar's companion was "a shill": a person who helped to perform short cons. On the day of their arrival at the McLure, Klein orchestrated a conversation with a Jewish visitor from Pittsburgh. Klein ended by inviting him to a talk set to take place at the hotel that evening. The talk was being given by a soldier lately returned from France.

Along with the man from Pittsburgh, a substantial crowd showed up to hear Edgar speak. He told the audience that Germany was whipped and that the war was pretty much over. Flattering them with the impression they were privy to inside information, he spoke about how the government had covered up the sinking of an American troopship. Two thousand soldiers had, he said, lost their lives. He described his time in the trenches as well, his reminiscences spiced with the sort of "weird tales" so characteristic of his habitual straining toward the extraordinary, the unexpected. And he referred to the metal plate inserted after he'd suffered a serious chest wound—a cue to tap on his rib cage. Something must have been concealed under his clothes, because the tapping produced a metallic noise. It also aroused his audience's sympathy. With Klein's help, he collected donations from many of the people there.

Edgar and Klein checked out of the McLure next morning. A short time afterward they went their separate ways.

Newspapers across the eastern states meanwhile carried stories that Tom Longboat hadn't, contrary to previous reports, been killed in France. These stories about his resurrection could easily have been triggered by the confusion Edgar had sowed, which had led people to mistake him for the famous athlete. But on closer inspection it turned out that the real Longboat *was* indeed alive.

Most of the press stories quoted the same extract from a letter he'd written to his former manager:

> *I was over the front lines last night and I was sweating like an old horse. I was covered with mud from head to feet and I don't know how many times I fell in the shell holes over the wires. They cut me all up. Everything was flying around, high explosives, shrapnel, whizz-bangs, coal boxes, rum jars, oil-drums. That made me real sore on this fellow having [a] good time all over the country on my reputation, so I am going to put an action against that man. I am going to have three charges against this man, one for making false statements, second for impersonation, third [for] intent to defraud the public at large.*

If Longboat was ever going to follow through with his threats, he'd have to identify Edgar and track him down first, neither of which was remotely probable so long as the two men were on different continents. Besides, Longboat had plenty of other things to worry about—little things like trying not to get shot or blown up.

· · ·

LESS THAN TWO WEEKS AFTER leaving the McLure, Edgar was in the one-horse Kentucky town of Dry Ridge. He needed only to glance around to see how small-time his life was in comparison to his big-time dreams. As he schmoozed his way through that evening's audience, which had just heard him deliver a speech in the persona of Chief White Elk, he harvested money from them. Half the proceeds would, he said, go toward his living expenses, and the other half would be donated to the local branch of the Red Cross.

Resisting the temptation to let greed derail a good scam, he did in fact pass on some of his takings to the Red Cross. Yet he still aroused the suspicions of the town's postmaster, who appears to have been a member of the American Protective League. This business-supported volunteer organization, which functioned as a semiofficial adjunct to the Department of Justice, had already enrolled more than one hundred thousand members, each pursuing the financial bounty awarded for the identification and capture of German spies. Over that weekend, the meddlesome postmaster went to the trouble of placing a long-distance phone call to the Cincinnati office of the Bureau of Investigation. He apprised the bureau of his vague misgivings with regard to Chief White Elk.

But providence favored Edgar, because the bureau had no reason to link the chief to its earlier hunt for the fake Tom Longboat. The bureau's Cincinnati office did, nonetheless, have access to a report about the chief, previously deemed important enough for it to have caught the attention of the organization's director, Bruce Bielaski. The report concerned the chief's layover at the McLure Hotel, during which he'd publicly accused the government of conducting a cover-up. His accusation placed him within the expanded remit of the bureau. Since America had entered the war, this had shifted toward not only apprehending spies but also implementing recently passed legislation that criminalized anything liable to hamper the war effort. On the evidence of what the chief had said at the McLure, the bureau suspected he might be peddling pro-German propaganda. Accordingly, Dry Ridge's postmaster was directed to converse with the chief and look for signs of anti-American bias.

Four evenings later, the postmaster waylaid Edgar at another of his Red Cross fundraisers. He met the postmaster's questions with what appeared to be honest, his apparent frankness likely helping to quell the man's suspicions. He said he'd be heading down to Lexington, Kentucky, that evening for a speaking engagement, after which he meant to travel to Corinth and then Knoxville, Tennessee. His entire itinerary was hogwash, though. By the following day he wasn't even in Kentucky. He was the better part of seven hundred miles away in warm, humid New Orleans—a city of crumbling houses garlanded by cypress vines, of alleyways strung with washing, of doors opening into dark courtyards, of precarious-looking iron balconies decorated with pots of geraniums, of passersby speaking in the slow-tempo lilt of Creole French, of banner headlines about the revolution in Russia, where Moscow had just fallen to Communist forces.

For his next move, Edgar employed Tom Longboat's name to write to Captain Chamberlain, the Hoboken-based army officer who had helped get him the job on the SS *Antilles*. The letter depended upon Chamberlain having missed all the newspaper stories about the real Tom Longboat's anger at the man impersonating him. Edgar announced that he envisaged giving talks about his time aboard the *Antilles*. He requested a statement confirming he'd been part of her crew when she sank. No such statement was forthcoming, which suggests that Chamberlain had read about the real Tom Longboat or else studied the pertinent crew roster and failed to find the athlete's name on it.

Undeterred by Chamberlain's silence, Edgar resorted to forging a type-written letter of endorsement from the U.S. Army Transport Service. He also amended his old Certificate of Identification, referring to his time on the *Antilles*. Where Tom Longboat's name had featured, he skillfully added a new one. In what amounted to a cheeky in-joke, he used Chief White Elk's initials and the covering letter to reinvent himself as a onetime vaudeville singer named C. W. Ellis. He could now profit from the marketable topicality of being a survivor of the *Antilles,* but he had a powerful disincentive to remain in New Orleans, because the local police had lately declared a crackdown on the common practice of impostors masquerading as current or past members of the military.

. . .

EDGAR UTILIZED HIS SHIPBOARD EXPERIENCE to secure a berth on a vessel carrying refrigerated fruit to California. Probably docking in the Port of Los Angeles, he then traveled inland. By the second week of December, he was in Laramie, where eastbound Union Pacific trains halted every few hours, often pausing while large numbers of sheep and cattle were loaded onto freight cars.

Despite being Wyoming's oldest city, its rectilinear street plan punctuated by huge Colonial-style properties, Laramie was no older than many of its residents. Mingling with them, Edgar introduced himself as C. W. Ellis, veteran of the Princess Pat Regiment and survivor of the sinking of the *Antilles*. Ostensibly striving to raise funds to return to his home in Portland, Oregon, he spoke with the management of the Empress, a palatial movie theater where he hoped to secure a booking.

To verify his claim about having been aboard the *Antilles*, he showed them his forged paperwork. He could also back up his story by displaying what passed for war wounds. These may have been self-inflicted or even the result of an assault several weeks earlier. One thing was for certain: He kept applying some form of cream that prevented them from healing.

Satisfied that he was "no faker or impostor," the Empress's management hired him to provide a live component to the 8 p.m. movie show on Monday, December 10, 1917. Edgar agreed to perform a few French songs, talk about the battlefront horrors he'd witnessed, and award what purported to be "a French watch direct from France" to the cutest woman in the audience—an old medicine show gimmick. His seventy-five-minute performance was slated to follow a couple of short, silent comedies and a newsreel—a brand of current affairs bulletin. For his efforts, he'd receive 50 percent of the box office takings.

AFTER THE SHOW, EDGAR COLLECTED his half of the ticket sales—which may have earned him a sizable sum, as the theater seated more than 1,500 people. He then took off without settling the bill at his lodgings. Grifters like him commonly bilked landladies and hoteliers by resorting to what was dubbed "a boardinghouse deceiver"—a cheap and often empty cardboard suitcase, left behind in the grifter's room to imply he'd be returning later that day.

From Laramie, Edgar rode the train almost 180 miles across the prairie to Rock Springs, Wyoming. He could have used some rest, but napping on these long rides was never easy due to the noisy "train boy" who paraded up and down the aisle, selling books, candy, and assorted merchandise. In the remote yet ethnically varied city of Rock Springs, its crooked streets dominated by black smokestacks and the gray shaft houses of coal mines from which emanated the metallic heartbeat of machinery, Edgar jettisoned his most recent alias. He went back to styling himself as Chief White Elk, one of just seven survivors from the Princess Pat Regiment. But he had the misfortune to be in town at the same time as another so-called war pretender, whose arrival appears to have put the police on high alert.

During the third weekend of December, Edgar and the other man were rousted on suspicion of being impostors. Edgar landed in the city jail, which probably bore the scars of an incident that had occurred less than forty-eight hours earlier. This involved a gang of vigilantes breaking into the jail, seizing an African American prisoner, and then lynching him on a nearby railroad bridge.

When questioned by the Rock Springs police, Edgar conceded that Chief White Elk wasn't his given name, yet he remained insistent about being an Oklahoma-born Cherokee. At various times he said his real name was W. C. Ellis, C. W. Ellis, and W. E. Ellis.

The subsequent investigation by the county prosecuting attorney and the city's mayor revealed that Edgar had been carrying forged U.S. government documents—a revelation that prefaced one of his rare bursts of truthfulness. He confessed that, contrary to what he'd told the audience at the Empress Theater, he hadn't served with the Princess Pat Regiment. And he finally came clean about the fact that his self-professed war wounds hadn't been incurred aboard the *Antilles*.

He was in enough of a hole without the investigators digging up anything else from his criminal past, but they swiftly unearthed two of the outstanding warrants against him, the most recent of which stemmed from his failure to settle his rooming house bill in Laramie. The other warrant, dating back to the previous December, had been issued against Chief

White Elk. It referred to an alleged fraud committed in Albany County, New York State.

A few days after Edgar's arrest, the Albany County Sheriff's Department was notified that the warrant from Laramie took precedence.

SHERIFF CARL JACKSON ESCORTED EDGAR from Rock Springs to the Laramie County Jail. There, he joined nineteen other inmates, among them a young cowboy charged with stealing money from a fellow ranch hand. Edgar would have had no trouble fitting in or acclimatizing to the familiar jailhouse regimen.

Both Sheriff Jackson and Laramie's chief of police interviewed him. Responding to questions about his true identity, Edgar gave the same names he'd supplied the Rock Springs police.

Soon he had to face a fresh allegation. The manager of the Empress Theater accused him of obtaining money under false pretenses. In his defense, Edgar maintained that he'd been paid for his singing, *not* for talking about the war. Lack of evidence prevented the authorities from taking the matter any further, so the county attorney charged him with "false representation" instead. For some reason the charge of defrauding the owner of the boardinghouse had, in the interim, been dropped.

On Friday, December 21, 1917, Edgar was taken from the county jail to the city's large, brick-built courthouse for his arraignment. As he waited to appear in front of the judge, his mind may have drifted back to his courtroom debut when he was just fourteen. He'd been playing hooky from the Roman Catholic school on his street, and mixing with other truants his age—boys whom his sardonic father had labeled "bums." Those boys had, as his father put it, helped Edgar to get "into a lot of little jams," which culminated in him hustling several of the downtown storekeepers in Central Falls. Seeking nothing more than excitement, he'd go into one store and spin a tale about being sent to fetch change for a nearby store. Even at that age he was plausible enough to persuade people to give him money. He'd then pocket the cash and hand it to his father under the pretense that it was his weekly wage from a part-time job. But he came unstuck one afternoon when he took a shot at scamming a saloon owner, who detained him and summoned the police. The next morning Edgar found himself charged with larceny, which provided his ticket to a quasi-military Rhode Island reform school, where he became Cadet Laplante.

Ushered into the courthouse in Laramie just over a decade and a half later, he stood before a placid, bespectacled judge. Edgar pled guilty to the charges against him under the name of C. W. Ellis, yet even then he got lucky. The judge wouldn't accept his plea on the grounds that it had no basis in evidence.

Sheriff Jackson requested more time to build a case against the defendant, so Edgar was remanded into his custody, pending another court appearance.

While Edgar languished in his cell, Jackson contacted police departments outside Wyoming. He also wrote to the Hoboken offices of the U.S. Army Transport Service, which furnished him with Edgar's plump file. It revealed that Edgar had been pretending to be the athlete Tom Longboat.

Despite the sheriff's efforts, there remained insufficient evidence to prosecute Edgar on charges of either fraud or false representation. The county attorney released him, but only after he was made to promise that he'd "quit posing as a hero." Edgar said he had learned his lesson and "would never again be caught in a similar mess."

Late on the afternoon of Wednesday, January 16, 1918, he walked out of the Laramie county jail. He'd been allowed to keep the amended Certificate of Identification and the forged letter from Captain Chamberlain. For all the contrition Edgar had displayed in front of the county attorney, his continued possession of these documents indicated that he hadn't learned his lesson. Unlike most people, he couldn't simply assess his options and choose to behave differently. Choice never entered the equation. He didn't *have* a choice. He just couldn't stop himself.

Edgar traveled south across the state line into Colorado and over mile upon arid mile of the high plains, which receded toward the far distant Rocky Mountains. When he got to Denver, where an electric lightbulb–encrusted "Welcome Arch" greeted visitors emerging from the rail depot, he would have had no difficulty buying liquor, even though Prohibition—almost two years away from being imposed throughout the country—was already on the Colorado statute book. He only had to approach the boys hawking copies of the *Denver Times* on the downtown streets, along which there was a dense crop of twelve-story office blocks. The boys would have been happy to sell him a quart of "Sugar Moon"—a type of local moonshine, concocted using sugar beet.

Just a day after his arrival in Denver, Edgar moved on to Pueblo, Colorado. Under a cold blue sky, the city's outlying districts were rimmed by a much more fertile landscape, irrigation canals slicing through lush, farmstead-dotted fields. Yet there was nothing rural about Colorado's second city. Behind its drably functional buildings and grand mansions were the smokestacks of steel mills and smelting plants, which had people likening it to Pittsburgh. Edgar didn't have happy associations with smelting plants. Several years back, he and a Rhode Island buddy had worked in just such a plant over in Bartlesville, Oklahoma, but they'd soon walked out because they couldn't handle the backbreaking work.

In Pueblo, where enforcement of Prohibition was no more effective than in Denver, Edgar registered at a hotel owned by an independent woman with a passion for off-road auto racing. Her four-story establishment hosted not only regular meetings of the Catholic Women's League but also a share dealership for a new car company.

Fresh acquaintances of Edgar, now calling himself Clyde White Elk, were encouraged to believe he was a full-blooded Cherokee chief from Oklahoma, who had been educated at Carlisle. He couldn't be content with this familiar deceit, though. He also had to tell people that he spoke six languages and fourteen Native American dialects. Yet even *that* wasn't enough. So he claimed to have studied at the prestigious Rush Medical Institute in Chicago. Again, that fell short of the level of distinction he lusted after. Ornamenting his persona still further, he characterized himself as a nomadic adventurer, who was nonetheless a man of means—part owner of 480 acres and eight big oil wells.

Like a novelist reconfiguring and embroidering his own experience in order to make a better story, he talked about being aboard the SS *Antilles* as a seaman and interpreter when the decisive torpedo struck. He substantiated his story by brandishing the documents he'd brought with him from Laramie. To illustrate what—with calculated jingoism—he painted as the everyday heroism of American servicemen, he recounted an incident that occurred, he said, the day before the sinking of the *Antilles*.

She and another homeward-bound troopship were, his fabricated tale began, sailing almost side by side out of a French port. In the five-hundred-yard gap between the two vessels, a periscope suddenly broke the surface. Both troopships were set to fire at the submarine, yet neither did so. The risk of hitting the ship opposite was simply too great.

Before the submarine could attack them, a large airplane flew low overhead. Somewhat implausibly, Edgar claimed to have heard the pilot shout, "I've got him!" The airplane then swooped down over the periscope and dropped a depth charge. He described the airplane going into a steep climb, its pilot unfurling an American flag. Everyone aboard the *Antilles* cheered. At that point there was an explosion. The force of it supposedly blasted the wrecked submarine high into the air. It sank stern-first as soon as it struck the sea.

ONLY ABOUT TWELVE HOURS AFTER his arrival in Pueblo, Edgar was in his hotel room when he received unexpected visitors. They were from the Pueblo Police Department. With them was Special Agent R. Lee Craft, local representative of the Bureau of Investigation. The bureau had become accountable for enforcing the seven-month-old requirement that men between the ages of twenty-one and thirty should register for military service. On suspicion of failing to comply with that law and thus being what was known as "a slacker," Edgar was again arrested. This time he gave his name as Clyde White Elk.

Special Agent Craft and the police officers took him across town to city hall, adjacent to a big construction site where work was well-advanced on a much larger replacement. Inside the current building were the police headquarters, where the staff treated Edgar with surprising politeness. He expressed confidence in his ability to satisfy the authorities as to his status. Until that could happen, though, he'd have been held in the cramped, frowzy, and windowless bullpen, the occupants of which inhabited a perpetual dusk.

WHEN SPECIAL AGENT CRAFT INTERVIEWED him later that day, Edgar trotted out bogus stories about his background. He said the title of "chief" was just a nickname, given to him by his friends. Proudly labeling himself "an original American"—a synonym for Native Americans in widespread use then—he referred to his Cherokee parents who lived in Chickasha, Oklahoma. Though he admitted knowing it was a legal requirement for him to register for the military draft, he confessed he hadn't done so. He mentioned that numerous men from his reservation had gone to Washington, DC, to offer their services to the military. The sole reason for him not going with them, he stressed, was that such a journey would have been pointless, because he wasn't fit for military service. He explained that he had injuries to his side and chest, along with a detached retina in his right eye. Even so, he assured the special agent that he'd be happy to register. As evidence of his willingness to do his bit for his country, he said he'd left home last July and traveled to New York City, where he had signed on as an ordinary seaman with the U.S. Army Transport Service.

He described making two trips to France on the *Antilles*. Then he told what proved "a most thrilling" account of the sinking of that vessel. He and the other survivors had, he said, been taken back to France prior to being repatriated. They'd landed in San Francisco, from where he had traveled to Laramie, planning to spend a few days there before returning to Chickasha.

But he claimed that the authorities in Laramie had been instructed to arrest all strangers, leading to him being detained there for a month while the police made inquiries about him. With what must have been intended to mimic disarming openness, he remarked that he *deserved* to be punished if he'd violated the law.

A disagreeable surprise awaited him. Special Agent Craft outlined the full reasons why he was being held. Edgar was suspected of being a German spy as well as a draft dodger.

Infuriated by what he'd just heard, Edgar replied that his failure to register for the draft was his only crime. He said he'd find out who had accused him of spying for the Germans. Far from losing his nerve, he countered with a reference to having "a brother in Washington who would take up the matter for him"—something of a veiled threat against Special Agent Craft. Edgar also tried to apply psychological leverage by saying he needed to resume his journey in order to get home before the anticipated death of his aged mother, who was awaiting a reunion with him.

After the interview, a reporter from the local newspaper approached a city hall official and asked how the bureau's Pueblo branch was progressing with its investigation. The official kidded that Clyde White Elk appeared to be able to speak nine languages "and lie like a pirate in nine of them."

Oblivious to the extent of those lies, Craft arranged for a telegram to be sent to the military draft board in Chickasha, notifying them of Clyde

White Elk's arrest. The draft board was sure to expose Edgar as an impostor and force him to register for military service.

"WE HAVE NO KNOWLEDGE OF THE CASE," came the swift response from Chickasha. Edgar was fortunate that the draft board wasn't inspired to launch a futile hunt for Clyde White Elk in their roster of Cherokee residents. Instead, Special Agent Craft merely received instructions that the prisoner should be made to register at the nearest draft board.

For the time being, however, Edgar was left in the bullpen at city hall, where his companions included a bootlegger, the proprietor of a speakeasy, and a vagrant awaiting medical treatment. Over the next five days, snow meanwhile powdering the streets outside, Edgar had time to contemplate the tight spot into which he'd gotten himself.

If Craft linked him to the man posing as Tom Longboat—the man sought by the bureau in California—Edgar would be in big trouble. Even if he avoided such a scenario by catching another lucky break, officers from the local police department made it clear that he needed to explain a lot of things. He'd otherwise face "severe penalties."

ASSISTED BY SHERIFF CARL JACKSON, who passed on the fruits of the Laramie investigation, Special Agent Craft became aware of many of Edgar's aliases, Tom Longboat among them. Craft was now just one step away from tying him to the cons he'd pulled in San Diego and elsewhere.

Maybe realizing that he had to keep the bureau from digging any deeper into his past, Edgar devoted some of Thursday, January 31, 1918, to writing a confession. It contained admissions that he hadn't been aboard the *Antilles* when it was torpedoed, and that he hadn't put his name down for the draft.

"I am sincerely sorry," he wrote, "and am willing to do what my government wants me to do." In a bid to fend off the allegation that he was working for the Germans, he stated, "I am American and proud of it." He added that he'd been traveling the country, singing and lecturing. "I even helped to recruit for our army by encouraging our boys by telling them I had been in France." He concluded by insisting that his songs had been patriotic and his lectures had tackled the question of how the country could best fight autocracy and respond to the demands of President Wilson. At the end of his confession, he declared, "The above is true so help me God." Then he signed it, "Chief White Elk."

Later he submitted a request to speak to Craft again. The request was granted.

Edgar used Craft's visit to affect a display of counterfeit candor. He said he'd been "confused" on the day of their previous discussion. Using astute flattery, he explained that he'd been thrown off balance by the authorities' speed and accuracy in excavating his past. He mentioned that the police had shown him "so many courtesies" that he'd felt ashamed to acknowledge he had done anything wrong. Apparently keen to set the record straight, he presented Craft with his confession.

SIX MORE DAYS PASSED, during which Edgar was joined in the cells by a Greek vagrant and another suspected draft dodger. But just when it seemed as if Edgar might be spending a lot longer in Pueblo's jail cells, he was led out of the murky bullpen at police headquarters.

Another hour went by before he was taken to an office in a different part of city hall. The office housed one of the local draft boards. Edgar's tactic of writing a confession had worked.

District Attorney Harry B. Tedrow, a dimple-chinned Midwesterner thirteen years his senior, manned the office. Under Tedrow's supervision, Edgar filled out a draft registration form. He gave his name as Touaxonanna, his title as Chief White Elk, his birthplace as Syracuse, his place of residence as Chickasha, and his occupation as "vaudeville performer."

The registration process completed, he was advised to remain in Pueblo until he received a military serial number. He was then permitted to walk out of city hall, where he'd spent almost thirteen days.

· · ·

GUNSHOTS ECHOED AROUND THE THEATER. They were fired by the Cheyenne Brothers, a sharpshooting vaudeville duo featured in a benefit show the following Monday. Held at a theater in Pike's Peak, a blue-collar neighborhood of Pueblo, where line upon line of close-set frame houses knelt in supplication to the smoky presence of a massive steelworks, the show was in aid of the Our Boys in France Tobacco Fund—"The boys want tobacco and it's our duty to help them get it."

Edgar was on the same bill as the Cheyenne Brothers, necessity presumably drawing him back into the world of lower-echelon vaudeville, a world of Spartan dressing rooms, negligible backstage assistance, shabby lodgings, and nearly inedible food, a world from which he'd long been straining to break free. Every time he finished a song, the capacity crowd at the Pike's Peak Theater demanded an encore. His Chief White Elk act, which also featured him playing the piano, went down so well that the management had him stay on for a couple more shows that week. These were headlined by the Speedway Girls—a dozen-strong troupe of petite and glamorous girls whose peppy song-and-dance numbers pulled in big audiences. Touring with the girls was a veteran comedian named Ben Lambert. On Tuesday evening someone handed Lambert a telegram just as he stepped offstage partway through his act. The message reduced him to a state of such debilitating grief that he was unable to complete his routine. So the theater's manager strode in front of the audience, explained the reason for the comedian's absence, and read out the telegram he'd received:

VANCOUVER BARRACKS, WASHINGTON. 2.12.18. BEN LAMBERT, PUEBLO, COLORADO. YOUR BROTHER, ALVIN LAMBERT, WAS KILLED HERE AT 5:50 O'CLOCK TODAY. SIGNED COMMANDANT.

If Edgar needed any reminder of the danger awaiting him in the military, then here it was. Disinclined either to stick around until he was drafted or to persist with vaudeville, he skipped town and went back to Denver. He tried to safeguard himself against problems with the Pueblo draft board by sending them a postcard affirming his readiness to serve his country. "Will you please notify me when called, addressing me 'General Delivery, Denver,'" he wrote. "I hope I am called soon, as I have made one trip to France and what I saw there makes me feel like fighting." Yet he quickly placed a considerable distance between himself and the Denver post office where he'd asked the draft board to send his call-up papers.

7

Thick snow lay on either side of the track. Short of cash but sleek and recognizably theatrical in his blue serge suit, Edgar was aboard a train rattling through Utah. After leaving Denver, he'd tried his luck in a mining town where he masqueraded as an employee of a West Coast debt collection agency, but this latest grift had proved to be a dead end.

On Wednesday, March 6, 1918, he disembarked in Salt Lake City at what looked more like a French château than a railroad depot. Its grand, echoing concourse, overlooked by stained glass windows and a mural of covered wagons, led into a huge parking lot. Beyond was a road so wide that it could accommodate parallel streetcar lines. Jabbing through the adjoining roofline were the neo-Gothic spires of the vast Mormon temple.

At the theatrical costumier's several blocks from the station, Edgar announced that he wanted to rent a traditional chief's rig. He said he was "awaiting the arrival from the east of his Indian clothes." Gaudy next to the muted colors prevalent in the men's fashions of the day, his new getup featured a deerskin, moccasins, a beaded belt, and a feathered headdress, plus a brightly colored blanket draped around his shoulders.

Influence was a scent Edgar could sniff out at fifty paces, so he lost no time in zeroing in on Frank R. Newman, among Salt Lake's most noteworthy citizens. Within walking distance of the costumier's, Newman's 44 East Broadway office stood opposite a downtown store somewhat optimistically advertising NEW SPRING HATS. A sign for Pantages Theater marked the entrance to the office. From this drab, three-story block, Newman—a snappily dressed, middle-aged huckster with slicked-back hair, puffy features, and a slightly gauche smile—managed the western sector of the vaudeville circuit named for its Greek owner, Alexander Pantages.

Reasonably safe in assuming that word of Chief White Elk's fraudulence as a war hero hadn't bridged the 425-mile gap between Pueblo and Salt Lake, Edgar must have told Newman about being aboard the *Antilles* on its final voyage. And Newman must have auditioned Edgar as a singer, because Newman booked him as a last-minute addition to Thursday's lineup at Pantages's Salt Lake venue.

Edgar, meanwhile, moved into the Hotel Utah, the monumental milky-white façade of which contrasted with the gray stone of the Salt Lake Temple, just across the street. Neatly uniformed women piloted the elevators connecting his hotel's stupendous chandeliered marble and gilt lobby to its elegantly accoutered rooms, Turkish bath, roof garden, and multiple dining areas. Impressive though its amenities were, it lacked a bar, Utah being another of the so-called dry states that had enacted Prohibition. But Edgar didn't need to go far to quench his thirst.

Despite the efforts of the local police department's purity squad, which staged periodic raids, neighboring shoeshine stores trafficked in such large quantities of rotgut whiskey that their proprietors could afford to buy monogrammed silk shirts. The shoe shiners sold liquor made from raisins, molasses, and fresh fruit, its amber hue imparted by tobacco juice or sometimes iodine. His sleep probably deepened by a bellyful of this bootleg hooch, Edgar awakened to find the city had gotten much less congenial all of a sudden.

AN IMPENDING STATEWIDE CLAMPDOWN on what were dubbed "Indian slackers"—Native American draft dodgers—was announced in that morning's edition of the *Salt Lake Telegram*. Motivated by a desire to continue his own draft dodging, Edgar headed through the freezing streets to the Keith Emporium, a department store only a ten-minute walk from his hotel. Within the store was the U.S. Navy Recruiting Office. He must have read the previous day's newspaper story announcing that the recruiters had already filled their latest quota, because he made a token attempt to volunteer for the navy's aviation service. To ensure he didn't wind up on a list for future recruitment, he referred to a fictitious eye injury (maybe the detached retina he'd mentioned in Pueblo), which would be sufficient to exclude him.

Gossip about Edgar's presence in the city spread rapidly, and his visit to the recruiting office attracted a reporter from the *Salt Lake Herald*. Edgar led the reporter to believe that his "love for the fighting profession" hadn't been diminished by being thrown from the crow's nest of the *Antilles* when she was torpedoed, or by having to survive adrift at sea until he was rescued. This alternate version of reality had also seen him return to the U.S. Army Transport Service and make "numerous trips across the danger zone of the submarine-infested Atlantic without mishap." As the owner of oil wells that pumped cash into his bank account, he said he intended "to pay for treatment of his eyes with a view to making them serve his country." He even jested about wanting to scalp Kaiser Wilhelm II.

In what was shaping up to be a busy morning, set to conclude with the usual rehearsals for the vaudeville show at Pantages Theater, Edgar ran into a petite thirty-one-year-old Native American woman. Her moccasins, buckskins, and headband surely gave him the chance to engage her in conversation and then catch her in the powerful spotlight of his charisma. She had a clear and educated-sounding voice, her manner demure yet charming and witty, her turn of phrase self-evidently smart and sporadically poetic. Her allure was physical, too. People often commented upon how pretty she was. The daughter of a Native American mother and a white father, she had a tawny complexion; button nose; dark, lustrous eyes; plump cheeks dabbed with rouge; and black hair that she fixed into braids that hung over her ears.

She was most commonly known as Burtha Thompson, but she also had a name drawn from the language of her mother's tribe, the Klamath, one of a cluster of small tribes living in northwest California. Her Native American moniker was Ah-Tra-Ah-Saun, which meant "Valley of the Mountain."

Despite being ostracized by the Klamath community for being what they labeled "a half-breed," she took pride in her heritage. She'd been raised with a strong sense of her tribal identity. Just a few years earlier, she'd helped prepare a book about the traditions of the Klamath. On the grounds of her white ancestry, those customs barred her from inheriting her mother's title as a "Talth," a member of the Klamath high priesthood, comparable to the chiefs of other tribes and to European royalty. Staunchly ethical though she was in other regards, Burtha nevertheless insisted on styling herself *Princess* Ah-Tra-Ah-Saun.

Her royal title and passion for Native American culture must have heightened her appeal to Edgar. Conversely, Burtha's response to him must have been shaped by his apparent status as a Cherokee chief, his good looks, casual magnetism, and talent for dispensing well-timed quips. He likely projected an aura of stardom by getting her a ticket to the vaudeville show in which he was performing that evening. Other young, middle-class women would have needed to obtain their parents' blessing before accepting a theater invitation from a stranger, but Burtha faced no such constraints. She was a trained nurse who lived an independent, unmarried life away from her northwest Californian hometown. As such, she embodied the growing feminist phenomenon of the "New Woman," for whom living away from home and smoking cigarettes—"liberty torches"—represented defiance against gender conventions.

That day there were three performances of Edgar's show, each combined with a screening of a short film. Music from the theater's seven-piece band must have filled the building as the cast shuttled between their shared dressing rooms and the modestly proportioned stage. Edgar probably exercised his charm on the other performers: a trio of acrobats, a comedian, a song-and-dance duo, and the headline act, a lion tamer and his half-dozen lions, advertised as THE GREATEST ANIMAL ACT IN VAUDEVILLE. The rich odor of lions would likely have brought back memories of the badly treated creatures at the Coney Island amusement park where he used to work.

Also backstage at Pantages was the cast of what those in the business called "a girl show"—an eleven-strong chorus line, fronted by the daintily glamorous Marjorie Lake, a longtime vaudeville favorite who had a surprisingly deep singing voice. She and the chorus girls performed a one-act musical comedy set on a college campus. The girls whizzed through several costume changes before its flag-waving finale, so Edgar would've seen them skittering past in everything from evening dresses to scholastic caps and gowns.

Solo singers like him tended not to perform until just before the headline act. Through the usual blaze of spotlights that greeted him as he took his place onstage, Edgar would have seen an elegant three-tiered auditorium seating almost two thousand. He spoke about being "on the masthead of the United States ship *Antilles* when it was torpedoed," an incident when he was "severely wounded." And he sang a medley of numbers that included the maudlin Great War–themed "You're a Long Way from Broadway (When You're Somewhere in France)." It would have appealed to the gushingly patriotic Burtha, who was fixing to go to France and tend to the wounded. So impressed was she by Edgar's singing that she regarded him as "a man with wonderful talents."

On rather less evidence she swallowed his enticingly tragic rise-and-fall yarn, in which he'd been rated as "one of the world's greatest singers" and "one of the world's greatest athletes," formerly "a great chieftain" with millions of dollars to his name. He also convinced Burtha that he was a qualified physician. No easy task, given that his quick-witted new acquaintance had spent years nursing alongside genuine doctors. What made him so plausible was his capacity to absorb a superficial knowledge of subjects that might prove useful.

Inside twenty-four hours of meeting Burtha, he'd installed her as his girlfriend. Shrewd and calculating as he was, he'd have been aware of how much her presence would aid his act. With a Klamath "princess" in tow, he'd appear more convincing as a Cherokee chieftain. And he'd become a still more romantic figure. He may even have realized that his fake identity could be both endorsed and enriched by Burtha's patriotism and seemingly incompatible outrage at the ways in which "their people" were being treated.

Whites' condescension toward what Burtha called "the race of red men" was one of many things she resented. Another was the discriminatory system inflicted upon Native Americans. Having been herded onto reservations set up by the government and left under the almost unsupervised control of agents from the Bureau of Indian Affairs, a quarter of a million or so Native Americans lived in poverty. Disease, malnutrition, and even starvation added to their suffering.

Parcels of reservation land were allotted to individual Native American families, the objective being to transform them into farmers, and to break tribal loyalties, thus assimilating them into white society. But numerous corrupt county court judges had declared them incapable of managing their allotted land, some of which featured rich pasture, with oil and gas deposits beneath it. Guardians had then been appointed to act on behalf of its owners, who sometimes wound up paying 50 percent of their income in management fees. The lucrative nature of this racket saw attorneys vying for control of dozens of guardianships. Forgery, embezzlement, blackmail, kidnapping, and sometimes murder became the tools employed by those wanting to steal from Native Americans.

So Edgar's new girlfriend had good reason to be highly critical of the Bureau of Indian Affairs and the conditions that prevailed on reservations—conditions that made her feel lucky not to have been raised in such circumstances. "I was everything but a reservation Injun," she believed, "and never had been, thank God for that."

THE SALT LAKE HEADQUARTERS of the U.S. Army recruitment service was at Main and Second South Streets. Under the businesslike command of a retired lieutenant, fifteen soldiers—all of them declared medically unfit for deployment overseas—staffed its hectic offices. Edgar and Burtha walked into these on the morning after his performance at Pantages. Their relationship buttressed by their shared patriotism—or the *appearance* of patriotism, in Edgar's case—they volunteered to assist the city's recruitment drive. Seeing as the recruiters were looking to enroll speakers to go into movie and vaudeville theaters, Edgar and Burtha's offer was accepted. The couple would now be contributing to the campaign to fill numerous vacancies in the 145th Field Artillery Regiment, caused by men avoiding enlistment on medical grounds. Until the regiment reached its full numerical strength, it couldn't be sent to France.

Edgar seems to have begun by setting up two recruiting talks for that evening: Friday, March 8, 1918. One of these bookings came courtesy of Frank R. Newman, his contact at Pantages. The other probably came through Otis Skinner, an aging and very famous American stage actor who had only the previous morning checked in to the same hotel as Edgar.

Donning war paint to go with his chief's apparel, Edgar went to the Salt Lake City Theater for the first of that evening's recruiting talks. From the stage, he spoke before the opening performance of the hit play Otis Skinner was taking around the country. Afterward Edgar and Burtha reported to Pantages, where they'd been shoehorned into the show. Both of them would be giving talks this time. Shy though she appeared, Burtha had experience in public speaking, albeit about Native American culture rather than recruiting. Large crowds appeared to hold no terror for her, either. Three years earlier she'd marched past thousands of people as leader of the "Native Daughters of California" section of the inaugural parade at the Panama-Pacific International Exposition, a giant jamboree held in San Francisco.

When Burtha and Edgar appeared backstage at Pantages, they'd have met Marjorie Lake, the singer topping the bill. Edgar had already worked with her, enabling him to introduce Marjorie to his girlfriend. Marjorie and her husband, a former actor named Harry C. Lewis who helped to run their touring theater company, struck up a friendship with the young couple.

Ripples of excitement passed through the full house as Chief White Elk and Princess Ah-Tra-Ah-Saun took to the stage. In his recruiting speeches, Edgar liked to refer to his own military service and to denounce "slackers"—hypocritically, of course, as he himself was a draft dodger. He urged "the palefaces not to let the Red Man outdo them in patriotic response to the country's call."

Though much of what Edgar said was bunk, his references to the willingness of American Indians to report for military service were entirely accurate. Disproportionate and inexplicable numbers of them were already in the uniform of the country that denied citizenship to more than two-thirds of their people.

Once the talks by Edgar and Burtha were over, Frank Newman joined the two of them onstage. Newman endeavored to bolster his own political aspirations by having Chief White Elk and Princess Ah-Tra-Ah-Saun present him with an American flag as a symbol of their appreciation of his patriotism and willingness to allow them to appear at his theater.

Presumably through Newman, Edgar met a couple of prominent local politicians—namely, Simon Bamberger, governor of Utah, and W. Montague Ferry, mayor of Salt Lake. Newman was also most likely responsible for introducing Edgar to the local lodge of the Benevolent and Protective Order of Elks. An exclusive social club to which Newman belonged, the Elks granted honorary membership to Chief White Elk, whose name suggested kinship with the organization. It maintained a midtown clubhouse only a short stroll from the Hotel Utah, where Edgar was staying.

Edgar reveled in the attention. By Saturday afternoon he'd taken a decision that promised to make him the focus of even more of it. Just two days after his chance meeting with Burtha, she'd agreed to become "Mrs. White Elk."

Newman responded to this by suggesting they hold the ceremony at the recently completed state capitol, which housed Utah's legislature as well as the offices of his friend Governor Bamberger, who went along with the idea. What made the wedding seem worthy of such pomp was that it would unite the chief and princess of two tribes, which represented "the incarnation of genuine Americanism."

FAST BECOMING A DOUBLE ACT, recurrent admiring references to them in the local newspapers garnering them citywide celebrity, Edgar and his wife-to-be positioned themselves on the corner of Main and Second South Streets that Saturday afternoon. Burtha wore a traditional Klamath outfit. She and Edgar were poised to speak on behalf of the nearby army recruiting office.

A big crowd gathered to hear them. Burtha talked about the work of the Red Cross and the patriotic duty of Utah's young men. Edgar, on the other hand, reminisced about his experiences in France and on the *Antilles*. He goaded the men in his audience to volunteer for the army: "If America's good enough to live in, it's certainly good enough to fight for." The crowd cheered as eleven young men answered his call to arms.

While standing on the street corner, he reached over to Burtha and removed the necklace she had on—a necklace supposedly "of much value as a historical relic." Demonstrating his skills as a sidewalk salesman, Edgar explained to the eager crowd that he'd be auctioning the necklace and that all bids had to be accompanied by cash. Proceeds from the auction would, he said, be going toward the Red Cross. Everyone who could get near enough rained dollars and other coins into the collecting hat. Bidding terminated at $25—a respectable figure, sufficient to buy a cooker if they'd needed one. Were it not for the high-minded influence of Burtha, from whom he went to enormous trouble to conceal his criminal propensities, Edgar would surely have purloined the cash.

Their afternoon's recruiting at an end, he and Burtha decamped to the local Red Cross headquarters, together with one of the soldiers from the recruiting office. When Edgar handed over the contents of the collecting hat, the Red Cross treasurer issued him a receipt.

His atypical honesty was rewarded by the arrival that day of a telegram at the U.S. Post Office, just a block from Pantages. The telegram had been sent to Special Agent Leon Bone of the Bureau of Investigation's Salt Lake branch. It was from the deputy marshal of Rock Springs. WE HAD CHIEF WHITE ELK IN JAIL HERE AS AN IMPOSTOR, he wrote. I THINK THAT HE IS THE SAME MAN THAT IS IN YOUR CITY.

With the telegram from Rock Springs came a recommendation. It suggested that Special Agent Bone should wire the police in Laramie for further information about Chief White Elk.

Very likely oblivious to the danger he was in, Edgar gave a couple more recruiting talks on Sunday and Monday. For the second of these, he and Burtha returned to Pantages and addressed the vaudeville audience.

Under the expert guidance of Pantages's West Coast supremo, plans for their well-publicized marriage were meanwhile advancing. The couple would be tying the knot on Wednesday afternoon. At the request of county, state, and city officials, they were making the ceremony public—scarcely an imposition for an exhibitionist of Edgar's magnitude. Such was the prestige attached to the wedding that the city's preeminent jewelry store donated its most expensive ring—an eighteen-carat wedding band, made by America's foremost jeweler, Tiffany & Co. What's more, the commander of the Twentieth Infantry Regiment, based a little way outside Salt Lake's city limits, acknowledged Edgar's war service by granting the ceremony full military honors. Music would even be provided by the regimental band.

Obtaining wedding attire suitable for someone of his imagined rank was, however, more problematic for Edgar, who told people that his "best Cherokee dress suit" was back in Oklahoma, thousands of miles distant. As one of the Salt Lake newspapers commented, he wouldn't easily be able to acquire a replacement, because "the ordinary department stores have no buckskin ready-to-wear departments." So he scoured the city's curio stores, where he put together what could pass as a Native American outfit. He was wearing it late on Tuesday morning when he and Burtha, accompanied by Frank Newman and Marjorie Lake, made for an address set in a park four blocks south of the Hotel Utah. Several misguided onlookers who saw his beaded buckskin suit estimated its value as "probably enormous."

Edgar and his companions entered the Salt Lake City and County Building, an immense gray, ecclesiastical-looking Victorian Gothic pile, which dominated that part of town. Beneath vaulted, busily decorated plaster ceilings, they hiked down its long, broad hallways, considerable expanses of oak wainscoting and tiled flooring sliding past. They eventually found their way to the office of the marriage license deputy. Watched by an excited throng of officials, not to mention members of the judiciary and at least one journalist, Edgar and Burtha completed and then signed a marriage license application. The license fee was paid by the local Elks lodge. On their behalf Newman and the county clerk presented the marriage certificate to the soon-to-be-wed couple.

A reporter from the *East Oregonian* appears to have been on hand to speak with Edgar about the wedding. Seldom able to resist embroidering the fantasies he fed people, Edgar seems to have flaunted his patriotism and imaginary oil wealth by saying he'd bought more than $200,000 of the Liberty Bonds used by the U.S. government to finance the war. Newspapers in locations as far away as North Dakota then propagated the story of his generous purchase.

Right after collecting their marriage license, Edgar and Burtha hotfooted it over to the swank Newhouse Hotel, where they attended a lunch hosted by the Utah branch of the National League for Women's Service, a civilian organization dedicated to stateside war work. As guests of honor, they were seated on the sweet-pea-and-carnation-decked high table beside a local blueblood and onetime member of the House of Representatives.

For Edgar, this offered a bracing contrast to his past, when hotel and boardinghouse dining rooms were typically partitioned by drapes to separate respectable guests from riffraff like him and his coworkers on the vaudeville and medicine show circuits.

Exiting the Newhouse Hotel, Edgar and Burtha caught the tail end of an afternoon unusual even by the capricious standards of Salt Lake's weather. Bright sunshine alternated with rain, hail, and snow, conditions likely to make Edgar's feathered headdress look a tad bedraggled. He and Burtha proceeded to a downtown venue where they gave a couple of speeches and auctioned some War Savings Stamps, another new government scheme intended to help pay for the conflict with Germany and her allies. But the self-styled Chief White Elk and Princess Ah-Tra-Au-Saun couldn't stay for the whole event, because they had to hurry across town to the magnificent, Italianate-looking Orpheum Theatre for a big patriotic rally featuring Mayor Ferry. They'd been assigned their own box overlooking the huge auditorium. In his final engagement of the day, Edgar had the privilege of delivering the closing address, which extolled the contribution of American Indians to the war—a genuine contribution that contrasted with the inauthenticity of Edgar himself.

THERE WAS STILL MORE REASON for Edgar to feel triumphant when he surfaced the next day. A story about his wedding had found its way into the *Salt Lake Telegram*. "This is the first time that Salt Lake has married a real princess to a real chief at her State Capitol," the newspaper crowed.

Whether Edgar was about to get married or arrested remained uncertain, though. For his big day, marked by warmer and sunnier weather, he wore his buckskins and feathered headdress. He told people that the buckskins had been given to him by President Wilson's daughter and that they were worth $1,000, close to the annual income for the average American family at that time. Augmenting his everyday outfit were still more feathers, plus birds' claws, ermine skins, bells, and a necklace of bison bones. He also had on robin's-egg-blue moccasins, emblazoned with the Stars and Stripes in beadwork. To round off this display of sartorial understatement, he carried the discordant combination of a tomahawk and a peace pipe.

Not long after lunch he teamed up with his pal Frank Newman and a small entourage for a visit to the Studebaker dealership on South State Street. Included in the group was Marjorie Lake's husband, Harry C. Lewis, who had been named as Edgar's best man. Also in the entourage was his nominated ring bearer, J. Fred Daynes, the wealthy, high-society jeweler who had donated a Tiffany wedding band.

At the downtown Studebaker dealership, Edgar was permitted to borrow a car for his wedding. Under the vigilant gaze of a local journalist, he picked a snouty, five-seater Light Six with wooden spokes, long running boards, and a windshield that folded lengthwise. He passed approving comment upon the vehicle's low, rakish lines. It retailed at $1,295. The journalist was amused by the sight of what he patronizingly regarded as a man perhaps more accustomed to sitting astride a Pinto pony now ensconced in "paleface's most civilized and up-to-date conveyance."

Edgar's chosen vehicle had maroon paintwork, coincidentally described in the sales spiel as "Indian Red." He felt its cushioned leather seats and ran his fingers approvingly across its paintwork and varnished mahogany instrument panel. It represented a significant improvement on the horse-drawn wagon in which he'd traveled when he was with Dr. Long's medicine show. Before he and his cronies drove the Studebaker away, he asked for its soft-top to be lowered. Then they traveled a block and a half to Pantages, where they rendezvoused with the bridal party.

Another dealership had lent Burtha a beautiful National Highway Twelve touring car. Riding in that and other vehicles were the bridesmaids, who comprised three of Burtha's fellow nurses and most of Marjorie's chorus line. Marjorie was, naturally enough, the maid of honor.

Further cars carried khaki-clad officers and enlisted men from the Twentieth Infantry Regiment. Among the enlisted men were five Native Americans, representing the Cheyenne, Choctaw, Cherokee, Chippewa, and Delaware tribes. What they made of Edgar and his fancy dress is anybody's guess, though Private Lincoln Bird of the Cherokee must have known that the self-proclaimed leader of his tribe was a fraud.

Heading the motorcade, assembled outside Pantages, was the thirty-one-piece band of the Twentieth Infantry Regiment. In time to a zestful rendition of Mendelssohn's "Wedding March," it paraded along East

Broadway, past a hotel that had been shut down for serving liquor to its guests, past Auerbach's department store, and past an indoor market (THOUSANDS OF THRIFTY SHOPPERS BUY FROM US). Edgar's Studebaker and the rest of the vehicles followed the regimental band as it turned onto State Street and marched up the shallow incline toward the capitol. Overflowing streetcars and packed automobiles clogged the road. They were crawling in the same direction as thousands of pedestrians, many of them schoolchildren. Incessant ballyhooing by the local newspapers had given them a thirst to witness the closest thing Utah was likely to get to a royal wedding.

Upon passing through the gates at the top of State Street, the procession had to cross the extensive lawns skirting the capitol, its enormous white façade already in view, a domed rotunda projecting above a classical-style colonnade. As Edgar's Studebaker drew closer to it, a pair of giant American flags came into focus. These were draped from windows above the front steps, around which five thousand excited people had congregated. Edgar had, in all likelihood, never previously appeared in front of such a large crowd, the scale of his success growing with the scale of his lies. Officers from the U.S. Navy and Marine Corps, along with the armies of Britain, France, and Serbia, were among his audience. Groucho Marx and other members of the Four Marx Brothers, who so often mined comic diamonds from the ornately garbed pretentions of officialdom, may have been there, too, fresh from rehearsing their show at a local theater.

The dark-suited Mayor Ferry, together with state, county, and city officials, joined Edgar's entourage at the capitol. Escorted not only by his best man and ring bearer but also by Private Lincoln Bird and the other Native American soldiers, Edgar stood at the top of the front steps, which had been decorated with a line of potted palms. Bright sunshine illuminated them.

Now the regimental band once again began to play the "Wedding March." Its stately rhythm complemented the moment when Burtha and her bridesmaids emerged from a mass of photographers and a film crew that had been hired by Frank Newman. Burtha was wearing a pale headband, white moccasins, and a dress emblazoned with carved seashells and strips of beaded and tasseled buckskin.

Out of the sunshine, snowflakes fell like confetti as she and the rest of the bridal party climbed the long, wide flight of steps. The snowfall, which had ornamented Burtha's ascent, stopped just before she reached the top. As a mark of the esteem in which she and Edgar were held, the watery-eyed, septuagenarian Governor Bamberger was there to give away the bride. She and Edgar stood in front of Mayor Ferry, who started declaiming the wedding service. Edgar, meanwhile, had the chance to peer across the sea of faces stretching out before him and to gloat over the spectacular scenario he'd conjured within just seven days of arriving in Salt Lake. Predisposed to treat adult life like a childhood game of "dare," he may have wondered how much further he could take things. Maybe this wasn't the pinnacle of his Chief White Elk scam. Maybe this was just the out-of-town tryout for the big production sometime in the future.

When the service reached its climax and Burtha said, "I will," the crowd gave a massive cheer and the band crashed out the opening bars of "The Star-Spangled Banner." Congratulatory kisses landed on the bride and groom, who were ushered into the governor's sumptuous office, its walls decked with paintings and tapestries. There, the newlyweds signed the marriage register, a ritual witnessed by the mayor and the county clerk. Sundry officials, plus the bridesmaids and Edgar's Native American escort, were then invited into the room, where the officials took the opportunity to glad-hand him.

Anyone who noticed the five little stars tattooed on Edgar's hand as they shook it must have taken them for some form of Cherokee adornment. Yet these supplied him with a constant but fading reminder of the jail time he had served in New York City. Jails were dangerous places for Edgar and fellow grifters, who were sensibly mistrusted by the more violent prisoners from the so-called heavy rackets. Surely using his deception skills by pretending *not* to be a grifter, he had enrolled in the jail's offshoot of the Five Points Gang, New York City's preeminent street gang. Named for the eponymous lower Manhattan slum, this was mainly an Italian American organization.

In what Edgar likely portrayed as a traditional Cherokee gesture of gratitude, he handed Governor Bamberger a bow and a sheaf of arrows as a gift. Afterward Edgar and his bride walked out of the building's west doors, from where they could see the crowd. He climbed onto a stone pier flanking the stairway, then addressed the throng. Showing why he had so speedily established a reputation as one of the finest orators involved in army recruitment, he spoke about how there were five thousand Indians serving on the front—a figure he'd just plucked from his imagination. He closed by issuing a familiar challenge. White men were exhorted to follow his people's patriotic example—a sentiment that provoked more cheering.

DONATIONS FROM SOME OF THE wedding guests replenished Edgar's pocketbook, so he must have been feeling flush when he and Burtha got into the maroon Studebaker. At around five o'clock that evening, they drove back downtown, where they'd arranged to appear onstage at Pantages as part of that evening's show. The audience greeted them warmly, after which Edgar gave yet another of his recruiting speeches. He and Burtha then moved on to the wedding reception arranged by the local Elks Lodge.

Most of the reception was spent fielding wishes of good luck and prosperity. Later that evening, members of the lodge escorted them to the Hotel Utah, where the Elks had reserved the bridal suite as a wedding present. These well-appointed ground-floor rooms faced the mountainous Salt Lake Temple. Hidden from the newlyweds, however, was the nearby U.S. Post Office building, where the Bureau of Investigation had its Utah base.

Since receiving the telegram from the deputy marshal of Rock Springs, Special Agent Leon Bone had been looking into Chief White Elk's activities in Salt Lake. Bone had only now reached a conclusion. He decided that the chief had violated no federal laws and should, for that reason, "be permitted to proceed with his good work." Possibly unaware of the bureau's renewed interest in him, Edgar had yet again eluded a career-threatening tackle.

WHEREVER HE AND BURTHA WENT in Salt Lake over the next few days, they received goggle-eyed attention, their celebrity fortified by coverage of their wedding. Three times daily, a highlights reel of the ceremony was screened at Pantages. Local press coverage was also plentiful enough to give rise to news items in cities as far away as San Francisco and Los Angeles.

Desperate to associate themselves with Chief White Elk and Princess Ah-Tra-Ah-Saun, high-society women threw ritzy parties in their honor. And the couple received invitations to host auctions for the Red Cross and the War Savings Stamp campaign, from which Edgar pocketed some of the takings.

For all the newsprint devoted to these postnuptial activities, Edgar grew resentful at the lack of attention given him by the *Salt Lake Tribune*. On Monday, March 18, 1918, he phoned its editor, vented his disappointment, and arranged to visit the *Tribune*'s offices to "explain his position." His fit of vain peevishness would have significant repercussions.

9

The punch slammed into Heinie Schuman's jaw. He was staggered by the impact, which threatened to bring his challenge for the Inter-Mountain Country's featherweight boxing title to a premature conclusion. But he fought back bravely, landing hard, rapid blows against the champion. These were interrupted only by the bell marking the end of the first round.

Edgar was in the crowd at the Grand Theatre, two dozen blocks south of his hotel. With him that evening—the same evening as his phone call to the *Salt Lake Tribune*—was Frank Newman. They saw not just the ultimately indecisive title bout, but also four undercard contests. Several of these involved soldiers from the Twentieth Infantry Regiment, which had played such a conspicuous role at Edgar's wedding.

His trip to the Grand Theatre turned out to be highly profitable. At the suggestion of a friend—likely Newman—the event's promoter announced to the crowd that Chief White Elk had been carrying out his recruiting work without recompense from the government. "Any contributions would be thankfully received," the promoter added.

In the ensuing collection, seventy dollars was raised—easily enough to cover the bill Edgar had run up at the Hotel Utah before the local Elks began picking up his tab.

ALL AROUND EDGAR AND HIS BRIDE next day were signs of spring: warmer temperatures, a dusting of leaves on the poplars, budding lilacs, and the sight of road crews grading the city's dirt streets. Imminent though the season of renewal was, Edgar's current bonanza was closer to the end than the beginning.

Rumors reached the local sheriff that Chief White Elk was not who he professed to be. Early on the evening of Tuesday, March 19, 1918, Sheriff John S. Corliss started out for the Hotel Utah, where he meant to question Edgar. Newman found out about this, then phoned Edgar and warned him that Corliss was heading over to his hotel. Edgar appears to have hung up before Newman could explain why the sheriff wanted to speak with him.

Despite being due to address the congregation of a local church that evening, Edgar and Burtha quickly vacated the bridal suite. Feeding Burtha a story that played upon her well-merited sense of grievance about the unjust treatment of Native Americans by white society, he settled the bill for his previous room, said they'd be away for a few days, and dragged his wife nine and a half miles north to the small town of Bountiful.

He blamed their hurried departure on a "propaganda campaign" against him, waged by the *Salt Lake Tribune*. Burtha came to believe this stemmed from a time when her husband had stood on the back of a truck outside the army recruiting office and spoken about the *Tribune*'s "refusal to aid enlistments."

FROM BOUNTIFUL, EDGAR PHONED NEWMAN later that evening and asked "what all the excitement was about."

Newman explained that Edgar was suspected of posing as someone he was not. He said Sheriff Corliss had no evidence to corroborate these suspicions.

Edgar insisted that he really *was* Chief White Elk.

"Then, if there is no fake about it, meet me here and show that you are okay," Newman replied.

So Edgar promised to meet Newman in his office at noon the following day.

Averse to relinquishing the stardom and luxury he'd acquired, Edgar did something he didn't often do. He kept his promise. With Burtha in tow, he went back to Salt Lake the next morning.

One glance at the newsstands was enough to tell him that the atmosphere was no longer so favorable. The front page of the *Tribune* bore the headline CHIEF WHITE ELK VANISHES. SHERIFF SEEKS INTERVIEW. Not the type of coverage Edgar had sought when he'd complained to its editor. . . . But the headline seemed adulatory in comparison to the article paired with it. Drawing upon information from the Laramie and Rock Springs police, the paper stated that the chief was an impostor whose real name was C. W. Ellis. It also revealed that he had, in the past, defrauded people and pretended to be the athlete Tom Longboat. Worse still, it declared that he'd never sailed on the *Antilles* and that his wartime exploits were fictional. It even went so far as to suggest that Princess Ah-Tra-Ah-Saun was not an Indian, either. Little wonder that so many people in the damp streets that morning were chattering about Edgar and his wife. Simply turning around and taking a train out of town was an enticing prospect for the couple, but they lacked the necessary cash.

True to his word, Edgar went with Burtha to Pantages for his noonday appointment at Newman's office. When they got there, Edgar mustered the anger he required to play the role of the wronged man endeavoring to clear his name.

He had a brief discussion with Newman, who was plainly fearful about scandal tarnishing his own reputation and damaging his political aspirations. Newman then rang the *Deseret Evening News* and other Salt Lake papers. Their reporters were invited to his office that afternoon to put questions to Chief White Elk. Probably at the behest of Edgar, who had no cause to feel well-disposed toward the *Tribune,* its journalists were omitted from the guest list.

If Edgar could muster plausible answers to the press corps' questions, there was a chance that he might be able to deter them from further probing his activities. That way, he and Burtha would be free to remain in the city and continue their charmed existence.

At the press conference, he faced accusations that he'd fled from the police.

"It's no real crime, so far as I know, to leave Salt Lake City without notifying the sheriff," he countered with customary sangfroid. He also clarified why he and his wife had departed with such apparently suspicious haste. Burtha had, he told the reporters, been afflicted by a "sudden illness." He said he'd taken her to a friend's house in Bountiful, where she could convalesce.

The *Tribune*'s story about him was, he blustered, "outrageous and criminal." He insisted that he was a *real* Indian chief, that he owed money to nobody. Commenting upon the allegation about him profiting from his Red Cross and recruiting talks, he referred to it as "a deliberate lie" and "a damnable outrage" and said he'd be consulting his attorney. He added, "I have given sixty-two talks in the interest of recruiting and the Red Indians, and have *never* received a penny."

In response to the *Tribune*'s accusation that he'd posed as Tom Longboat, he said that one time someone in the crowd at a Wyoming track meet had remarked to him that he looked very similar to Longboat. Edgar went on to say he'd either replied that he was as good an athlete as Tom Longboat, or else he'd joked that maybe he *was* Tom Longboat. And *that* accounted for how some people got the idea about him being the famous runner.

But he still had to contend with questions pertaining to the stories he'd told about making five transatlantic voyages on the *Antilles*. He answered using a clever ploy, demonstrative of honesty. He conceded that his stories had been "somewhat exaggerated," in that he'd completed only a single round-trip. All the same, he maintained that he *was* on board the ship when she sank. Being an Indian, he submitted that the government wouldn't initially allow him to join the ship's crew. He said he'd been forced to register under the assumed name of C. W. Ellis, the name quoted in the *Tribune*. To confirm what he'd just told the reporters, he showed them his amended U.S. Army Transport Service discharge certificate.

Another of the *Tribune*'s central allegations—that he'd pretended to be a veteran of the Princess Pat Regiment—awaited a response. But once more, Edgar came up with a deft reply, cloaked in the illusion of frankness. He owned up to the reporters that he *had* given a lecture at a movie theater and that he *had* spoken about being one of the regiment's seven survivors. Yet he said he'd only done so at the insistence of the Empress Theater's manager, who had prevailed upon him to do it "for patriotic effect."

Even under awkward scrutiny like this, Edgar comported himself with the easygoing courtesy that was taught by the staff at the reformatory where he'd been sent as a fourteen-year-old. "Courtesy is to business and society what oil is to machinery," they'd asserted. In highlighting the career opportunities available to the courteous, Edgar's teachers were unlikely to have anticipated his choice of career, which flouted another of their maxims: "Do not try to pass for what you are not."

AFTER THE PRESS CONFERENCE, Edgar and Burtha (who retained her belief in her husband's tall stories) cabbed across town. They were heading for the First Ward Chapel, where an event in their honor was scheduled. En route, they saw lots of people who expressed support by clapping. At the chapel, Edgar and Burtha found a crowd so large that it flowed into the street.

The audience gave Mr. and Mrs. White Elk a rousing reception when they stepped onto the platform. Edgar started by pledging that he'd remain in Salt Lake until the allegations against him had been rebutted. Firecracker applause met the declaration that he'd continue to assist the Red Cross and various branches of government. He followed this with a long, patriotic speech, then played the piano and sang.

Requests to speak at numerous other local venues came Edgar's way. If he accepted these and remained in the city, he might be pushing his luck, so he turned them down. But he worried that people might figure he was "afraid to face the music." To disprove that, he arranged with Frank Newman to return to Pantages and appear with Burtha at that evening's show, which featured the usual miscellany of vaudeville talent, headlined this time by the jowly, moonfaced comedian and future movie star Harry Langdon.

Newman strode in front of the footlights and vouched for Chief White Elk's authenticity. Then Edgar and Burtha made their entrance to hooting and frenetic clapping. Edgar assured the audience that he had no intention of running away, even though he'd been maligned and had his feelings hurt. Defending himself against rumors that he was wanted in New York State, he explained he was merely wanted as a *witness*, and that he'd left the state before he could be apprised of this.

"They were civil actions, such as any man might have, and not in any sense of a criminal nature," he said. "If a man is wanted as a witness, for instance, that does not make him a criminal. If the New York or any other authorities want me, I am here and will go without the formality of extradition. My record is clear and I am going to stand pat until everything is put right." And he went on to say how bitterly he resented the *Salt Lake Tribune*'s inference that his wife was not an Indian.

THE *TRIBUNE* REMAINED UNCEASING IN its pursuit of the truth about Edgar. Its headline the next morning read IMPOSTOR HAD MANY ALIASES. Juxtaposed with that was a reproduction of a photo taken when Edgar was posing in Montana as Chief Harry Johnson. Beneath the picture were damning items of evidence against him, gleaned through dogged investigative reporting, which had involved the police departments in Rock Springs, Pueblo, and Laramie.

Since the *Tribune* had already contacted the police, Edgar must have figured that the paper would soon disinter the incontrovertible and inglorious truth about his time in Uncle Sam's service. His safest bet appeared to be to come clean about most things and try to buy himself sufficient time to raise the money he and Burtha would need to leave town.

Before paying a visit to the *Tribune*'s offices, he seems to have confided in Burtha about the lies he'd be acknowledging. He probably justified those lies, however, with *more* lies, featuring some convoluted story about how he'd have to confess to things that weren't true. So talented an actor was he that he made even the most far-fetched statements sound irrefutable. And that was *without* taking into account the otherwise bright and skeptical Burtha's paradoxically naïve devotion to him.

Whatever he said to her, it worked. In a show of support, she accompanied him to the *Tribune* that morning.

On arrival, he was asked if he had anything to say for himself.

"Well, what you have printed in the paper is true," he said as he scooped up a convenient copy. "But I can't see *why* it should be printed." He subsequently admitted that he hadn't been among the survivors from the Princess Pat Regiment. "I have since learned that not one of those seven survivors is able to move around at all."

"Were you ever on the battlefront in France?"

"No, I was not. I went across once, but the leave of absence from a boat for a seaman is very short, and I was never on the battlefront or in the trenches."

"How about your story of the *Antilles*—that you were thrown from the crow's nest when she was torpedoed and you lost five ribs?"

"That is a fake," he replied. "I was not on the *Antilles* when she was torpedoed. She was sunk in October. I went across on her in August as a common seaman and left her when we got back to this side. The story about being thrown out of the crow's nest, there's nothing to it. You know, men who are in the show business exaggerate sometimes. . . ."

His protracted confession even involved him conceding he wasn't an Indian chief. He pointed out "almost every Indian is called 'chief.'" The title tended to be nothing more than a derogatory nickname applied to most Native American men. "I just appropriated that title," he explained contritely.

IN WHAT REMAINED OF THE MORNING, Edgar and Burtha went over to the U.S. Army Recruiting Office, where they told the soldiers on duty that they were broke and wanted to quit town. When the couple said they'd like to raise money by selling portrait photos of themselves, one of the soldiers took pity on them. He promptly went out and bought them a five-dollar street vendors' license.

At midday Edgar and Burtha climbed onto the rear of the army truck parked near the recruiting office. Interest in them remained so feverish that a crowd soon clustered around the truck. After addressing the huge audience outside the capitol just eight days ago, this must have felt like going from Carnegie Hall to the back room of a saloon, yet Edgar still went ahead with his recruiting speech. Once he'd finished, a soldier joined him and Burtha on the rear of the truck, brandishing a sheaf of photos of them in their Native American regalia. The soldier peddled these for twenty-five cents apiece. Clutching similar photos, the remaining soldiers threaded their way through the crowd. They shouted, "Who wants to buy a picture of White Elk and his bride?"

But a reporter from the *Tribune* cut in and said, "Are those pictures being sold for the personal benefit of the chief?"

"Yes," answered the nearest of the soldiers. His response did nothing to increase sales of the photos. Soon there were no more customers, leaving Edgar and Burtha to count the paltry takings. The couple now had to rely on the lecture Edgar had lined up that evening to generate the money they needed to escape from Salt Lake.

DURING THE HOURS LEADING UP to the lecture at the Rio Grande Baptist Church, he and Burtha received a summons from Special Agent Bone of the Bureau of Investigation. They had little choice but to report to the U.S. Post Office, a titanic, five-story granite structure glowering through a neoclassical colonnade. The building filled the entire block next to the Newhouse Hotel, where Edgar and Burtha had been fêted by the local bluebloods not so long back. The couple entered via a broad flight of steps leading through massive bronze doors into the cavernous lobby, which sported the kind of marble and tile floors that registered every footstep.

Along with numerous other federal government employees, Bone had an office on the west side. He was a shortsighted forty-three-year-old whose austere taste in office furnishings extended no further than a desk, a typewriter, a rug, and a spittoon.

Uncharacteristically flustered, Edgar told Bone that he was striving to do good work, that he hadn't violated any law, and that he wasn't an impostor. In a show of guileful candor, he did, however, admit to having once been arrested in New York for impersonating a government officer. That matter, he added, had since been cleared up and now he was "trying to lead a proper life."

He and his wife were warned by the agent not to break any laws in pursuit of their patriotic campaigning. So long as they followed that advice, Bone assured them, they would not be troubled.

Though the bureau had no intention of troubling Edgar and Burtha, the same certainly wasn't true of the local press. Around when the couple emerged from their interview with Bone, a reporter working for Salt Lake's *Deseret Evening News* asked Edgar about the time he'd been detained in Wyoming.

"Little misfortunes like that occur to nearly every man," Edgar replied coolly. "And, in view of the work done in this city in the interest of recruiting and of the Red Cross, by myself and my wife, we think it unfair that they should be brought to the attention of the public, especially in so one-sided a manner."

HIS ENCOUNTER WITH THE REPORTER served to remind Edgar of why he and Burtha were so keen to get out of Salt Lake. Bankrolled, it appears, by his performance at the Rio Grande Baptist Church, Edgar and Burtha took the late-night train to San Francisco, their hasty and well-timed departure coinciding with a fresh wave of gleefully unflattering newspaper stories about them. Now derisive rather than investigative, these were epitomized by an item posing the question, "Is Chief White an elk, or is Chief Elk a white?" But the localized nature of newspapers in those days ensured that Edgar could leave behind his problems with the Salt Lake press as easily as he'd left behind that suitcase at the Hotel St. James.

San Francisco, where Burtha had begun her nursing career and where she appears to have still had contacts, was nineteen and three-quarter hours and almost a thousand miles away by railroad. Each westbound mile through pasture, mountains, tunnels, deserts, and small towns hastened both the arrival of spring and the moment when they escaped from Prohibition and entered Nevada. Only now could drinks flow freely aboard the train.

Countless invigoratingly different sights and sounds awaited Edgar and Burtha in San Francisco. Lining its steep streets were rows of foreign stores and restaurants. Into the gaps between those buildings flooded views of faraway ocean liners and tall-masted schooners sliding under the Golden Gate Bridge. Flashing electric advertising signs loomed over sidewalks crowded with the city's varied population, from turbaned Sikhs to Chinese waiters carrying trays on their heads. Nocturnal mists gave the place an eerie intimacy, the mournful sound of foghorns providing a requiem for the luxury and acclaim that Edgar and Burtha had surrendered when they'd fled Salt Lake.

Burtha's past as a trainee nurse at the City and County Hospital probably gave her husband his next opening. Edgar landed an expenses-only fundraising job with the San Francisco County Nurses' Association, which was attempting to purchase an apartment where nurses could recover from the traumatic experience of tending wounded soldiers in Europe.

For no more than a few days around the start of April, Edgar and Burtha flexed their fundraising muscles. But Edgar's activities caught the eye of the police, because he seems to have been skimming cash from the proceeds. He was consequently picked up on a charge of obtaining money under false pretenses. Even then, Burtha—who had completely bought the idea of her husband being a blameless victim of persecution—stuck by him.

Lacking sufficient evidence to prosecute Edgar, the cops ended up turning him loose. From now on, though, the San Francisco Police Department was sure to be watching him, so the couple opted for a fresh start in Oakland, just a ferry ride across the bay. Within days of arriving in this modern-looking port city, where U.S. soldiers and sailors dotted the warm, dry sidewalks, Edgar and Burtha were presented with a fortuitous opening that promised to reverse the decline in their fortunes.

From the wedge-shaped rooftop of the First National Bank Building, Edgar could see Oakland's retail district nine stories below. He and Burtha, who were treating their visit to the city as a honeymoon, were in the middle of a publicity stunt worthy of Edgar's erstwhile friend Frank Newman. The event was held under the banner of Oakland's Liberty Loan Committee. Four days earlier, the committee had launched their campaign for the Third Liberty Loan, the latest in a series of nationwide government bond issues used to underwrite the war against Germany and her allies. Having set a vast target of $6.9 million, the Oakland committee had hired Chief White Elk as a fundraiser, his abilities vouchsafed by a stack of testimonials from the mayors of numerous cities.

Most of those documents were forged, presumably by Edgar, who'd shown a prior readiness to fake official paperwork. In the testimonials, he and Burtha received the highest praise for raising enormous sums of money on behalf of the Liberty Loan, War Savings Stamp, and other fundraising drives. Edgar's new employers were left with the impression that they were lucky to obtain his services for such a modest fee.

He'd already delivered an eloquent speech to the members of a women's club in East Oakland, but the event at the bank represented his first big test. Edgar and Burtha were joined on the rooftop by a sizable flock of movie people and local dignitaries, among them a former chief justice of the Oklahoma Supreme Court. For events of this nature, Burtha wore her beaded Native American attire, plus a headband with a feather protruding from it.

Newsreel cameramen with hand-cranked movie cameras were there to record her and Edgar presiding over the event. Its centerpiece involved Edgar auctioning Liberty Bonds. Whoever made the highest single bid would be awarded the bonus of being permitted to kiss Princess Ah-Tra-Au-Saun. At the opposite end of the prize range were lapel buttons issued to anyone who bought a Liberty Bond. Pressure was thus exerted on holdouts, who faced further shaming through the practice of newspapers listing all local purchasers.

Edgar ended up selling $22,000 in bonds—a sum of such magnitude that it would cover the cost of training and equipping almost one thousand infantrymen. The largest individual bid came from S. H. Kitto, one of the senior staff at the First National Bank. Kitto coughed up $3,000.

As Burtha waited for him to claim his prize, Kitto blushed and protested that he was "too far along in years to be up to those tricks." Burtha was left to wonder whether her charms were fading.

"Why don't you kiss her?" the onetime Supreme Court judge said to the embarrassed banker. "If *you* don't kiss her, I will."

"If you *do* kiss her, it won't be . . . official," Kitto answered in a moment of pedantry.

While the newsreel cameramen impatiently cranked their cameras, the judge stared at Kitto, who was still blushing. And Kitto stared back at the judge.

Standing nearby, Edgar grinned at this absurd spectacle.

WELL ON HIS WAY TO becoming the sensation of the Oakland campaign, revered for his ability to chivy bashful dollars out of people's pockets,

Edgar spoke at a lunch hosted the next day by the city's Rotary Club. The diners included a millionaire who reacted by purchasing $50,000 in Liberty Bonds, enough to construct a one-hundred-bed military hospital. Some of that money would surely have snuck into Edgar's billfold without Burtha knowing.

Edgar also gave fundraising speeches at a large public meeting, at the shipyard workers' yearly jamboree, and at an upscale women's club. So effective was he that the Oakland campaign was swiftly awarded an "honor flag," a sought-after trophy created by central government to reward areas exceeding their sales targets. Edgar's newfound renown in Oakland made him a welcome visitor to the city's most affluent homes, where curtsying hostesses acknowledged his eminence.

Seizing the opportunity to translate admiration for him into something tangible, he targeted one of the many automobile dealers along San Francisco's Van Ness Avenue, where their architecturally promiscuous showrooms—part Grecian, part Colonial, part Mission style—featured flouncily lettered advertisements for Buick, Mercury, and other manufacturers painted across their walls. Edgar more than likely viewed the middle-aged founder of the F. J. Linz Motor Company as an easy mark, thanks to his Germanic surname.

In the year since America's entry into the European war, rampant suspicion toward German Americans like Linz had spiraled into outright hostility, which often took absurd forms. Banning German books and music from libraries, for instance. Or renaming sauerkraut "liberty cabbage." Sometimes the same impulse found more oppressive and violent expressions. Yellow paint was daubed on buildings owned by anyone suspected of "pro-Germanism." People were encouraged to spy on German neighbors. And speaking German in public became dangerous, certain jurisdictions even declaring it illegal. Under these circumstances, Linz had a powerful incentive to make a public display of support for America. He was suckered into assisting the Liberty Loan campaign by lending a car to Edgar and Burtha, so they could fundraise more widely. This expensive vehicle was a four-seat Chandler Dispatch. It came with a soft-top, pale bodywork, and stylish whitewall tires.

Edgar and his wife now swelled the number of inexperienced motorists on California's roads. Many of what passed for highways were no more than strips of rutted dirt that turned into mud whenever it rained, and were unlit at night, save for occasional illuminated billboards flaring out of the darkness—tricky conditions for even the most seasoned of drivers.

ON THE MORNING OF THURSDAY, April 18, 1918, Edgar was in Oakland, breakfasting alone. He'd gone to the large and inexpensive Saddle Rock restaurant, which regularly laid on music and "refined dancing"—a term distinguishing it from the more exuberant styles fast becoming popular. Not that Edgar had much time for dancing, refined or otherwise. Another packed day of campaigning beckoned. First, though, he needed to finish his coffee.

He'd positioned himself at a table near Saddle Rock's entrance, where customers couldn't fail to notice him. One such customer was the mailman from the *Oakland Tribune,* based just across Thirteenth Street. The mailman went from table to table, selling both War Savings Stamps and their cheaper alternative—Thrift Stamps. He knew about the money Edgar had already raised on behalf of the Liberty Loan campaign, so he had no intention of trying to sell stamps to him.

Yet Edgar snagged the mailman and said, "Wait a minute." Playing to the gallery, he then insisted upon paying for a dollar's worth of twenty-five-cent Thrift Stamps, the showiness of his gesture outweighing the stinginess of his purchase. He told the mailman to stick them on a Thrift Card—one of the cards used by anyone collecting these stamps. "Give it to the first boy you meet," Edgar instructed.

Dutifully, the mailman affixed the stamps to a Thrift Card. As he walked toward the offices of the *Oakland Tribune,* he crossed paths with a young colleague. The mailman handed the Thrift Card to his coworker and said, "Here's a present to you from the best American in the United States."

SINCE BREAKFAST, EDGAR AND HIS WIFE had traveled across the Bay to San Francisco, where they'd been lunch guests at the opulent Palace

Hotel. Their hosts were a group of industrialists to whom Edgar auctioned more than $4,000 of Liberty Bonds. And in the city of Berkeley, not far north of Oakland, he'd been treated to an early-evening reception at the Shattuck, one of Berkeley's leading hotels, where he gave a short talk and sang for his supper—in both a literal and a metaphorical sense.

For all his exertions, Edgar still possessed lots of energy, which was just as well because he'd gone straight from the Shattuck to his third event of the day. Ahead of him now were three thousand enthusiastic people, gathered around the Gallic-looking white stone façade of city hall. From the top of the steps leading up to its entrance, a waggish local singing star led the crowd in a rendition of a ragtime song popular in the trenches. Backed by the cheerful, brassy rhythm of a seventy-piece school band, they sang, "Good morning, Mr. Zip-Zip-Zip / With your hair cut just as short as mine . . ."

It wouldn't be long before Edgar's big moment arrived. He was the event's principal speaker, described in the ads as a "full-blooded Cherokee millionaire" and "an orator of no mean ability." When the time came for him to address the crowd, he leapt onto the table in front of him, earning a wholehearted ovation. With barely an instant's hesitation, he delivered his opening line. "How many here have Liberty buttons on?"

Numerous hands thrust into the air.

He asked how many people *didn't* have buttons.

Just as many hands were raised.

"I am ashamed of you. Do you have to come here to have an Indian shame you into buying bonds that you ought to be glad to buy?

"I am a real American," he continued. "America belonged to my fore-fathers, and *your* forefathers took it from them. If we were to ask you to pay for what they took from us, it would require a dozen Liberty Loan drives. But we do not ask that. We ask only that you show yourselves as much Americans as we show ourselves to be.

"Of the pitifully few Indians left in the United States today, five thou-sand have given themselves to the service of Uncle Sam." It was an imagi-nary figure he'd used before—a figure that sounded impressively high yet represented well under a quarter of the true number of Native Americans in military and Red Cross units. Referring to the wider Native American population, which had invested generously in the government fundraising campaign, he conjured another figure from his imagination: "Of their money they have given $9 million to the Third Liberty Loan. Can *you* say as much? If you are real Americans, you will subscribe to the loan, and if you are not real Americans, this is no place for you—you should be back with the kaiser where you belong."

Edgar explained that he'd served America in ways other than just selling Liberty Bonds. "I have given myself to my country and my flag," he added. "I plunged fifty feet from the crow's nest of the *Antilles* when she was struck by a torpedo from a German submarine. But it takes more than a U-boat to kill a real American—as they will find out.

"I could tell you dozens of stories of atrocities I saw in France between trips of the transports upon which I served, but I will not. I am here to awaken in you that impulse to buy Liberty Bonds. I want you to buy—and buy tonight. Who is going to be the first to subscribe here?"

Then he invited people to come forward to his makeshift rostrum and open their wallets. So many people bunched around him that a half-dozen members of the Berkeley Liberty Loan Committee were needed to administer their purchases.

After the city's mayor offered to hand over an extra $500 if anyone invested that much, a young woman obliged. She earned a kiss from Edgar.

In total, his assistants obtained pledges to invest many thousands of dollars and collected $19,000 of down payments, comparable to the cost of at least six of the new tanks used on the battlefields of France. People were still waiting to purchase bonds when Edgar began his final duty of the evening more than an hour later.

Two hundred members of the local branch of the Camp Fire Girls—an outdoorsy youth organization whose prize-giving ceremony he'd attended the previous day—converged on city hall. In front of it was a massive bonfire, the glow from which must have been visible for miles. Doing their best to duplicate Edgar's every intricate movement, the Camp Fire Girls performed what he called "the Cherokee Snake Dance," its provenance in all likelihood as bogus as Chief White Elk himself.

AROUND THAT PART OF CALIFORNIA, the scuttlebutt had it that neither Chief White Elk nor Princess Ah-Tra-Ah-Saun were real Indians. Soon those rumors percolated into newspapers as far away as Kansas and Oklahoma.

Only a few days after the end of the Third Liberty Loan campaign, Edgar and Burtha left the Bay Area. Despite all the gossip, they managed to secure employment on a U.S. Navy recruiting tour of some of the state's northern cities. Several marines and almost two dozen musically adept school students from the Oakland Boys' Club Band, which included a brilliant young cornet soloist, were on the tour. Leading it was Frank Spaulding, a roguish twenty-five-year-old with dark, slicked-back hair, a toothy grin, and narrow yet expressive eyes that hinted at his swaggering self-confidence. Edgar had probably first encountered him in Berkeley. He wore the blue uniform of a seaman in the U.S. Navy, his white sailors' cap perched jauntily on the back of his head. The son of a Washington State preacher, Frank held the rank of pharmacist's mate. As someone trained to provide basic medical care for navy personnel, he had access to morphine and cocaine, both legally available on prescription. He may have been responsible for introducing these to Edgar, who developed a taste for how the drugs recalibrated his senses, morphine plunging him into a warm bath of woozy serenity, cocaine giving him a pulse-quickening surge of euphoria and even more boundless self-belief than ever, fostering his more highfalutin fantasies.

The ability to procure prescription narcotics was not the only talent of Frank's that Edgar could appreciate. Frank happened to be a compelling speaker. And he possessed a sweet and tuneful singing voice. It had earned him the tag of "Singing Sailor Spaulding" and made him a popular performer at recruiting rallies, where he sang propagandist and mawkish numbers such as "Somewhere in France Is the Lily."

By Wednesday, June 26, 1918, the tour had, temporarily minus the Oakland Boys' Club Band, arrived in Redding, where orange trees and palms rimmed the small but handsome central plaza. Like many of California's cities, it would, back where Edgar came from, have qualified as nothing more than a town.

Outside St. Caroline's Hospital that day, Edgar and Frank took part in a flag-raising ceremony, but it was marred by the intervention of J. W. Schoonover, a local attorney and rancher. He groused about them raising the Stars and Stripes in front of the hospital. By doing so, they were, he argued, perpetrating an act of spite toward Miss Ehemann, its German superintendent. His remarks got him into an undignified row with Edgar and Frank.

There was a sequel the next day. In the lobby of Redding's leading hotel, the Golden Eagle, which was owned by two brothers of German origin, Schoonover launched another verbal broadside against Edgar and Frank. He said that Frank was guilty of German baiting just by wearing a uniform in the hotel. Then he stated his willingness to defend any otherwise defenseless woman who was proud of her country. Invited to specify *which* woman he had in mind, Schoonover said it was Miss Ehemann.

Yet Edgar delayed exacting his revenge until Friday evening. When he stepped into the spotlight at the Redding Theater, where he was due to sell War Savings Stamps, he couldn't resist accusing a local man of rooting for the Germans, though he coyly omitted the man's name. He must have known that his reticence would whet the crowd's curiosity. There were repeated calls for Edgar to identify the anonymous German sympathizer. With consummate stagecraft, Edgar bowed to these demands by outing J. W. Schoonover. "The words of this man were an insult to me and the uniform I wore—and to Mr. Spaulding," Edgar thundered. "I shall not leave town until he apologizes to me."

An apology was not forthcoming. Instead, Edgar's accusations needled Schoonover into contacting the county police department and asking them to make inquiries about Chief White Elk's war record.

Before Edgar could suffer the consequences of Schoonover's request, he and Frank journeyed south to rejoin the Oakland Boys' Club Band in Marysville, California, where they were set to continue their recruiting campaign despite recent peace overtures by the Germans. About the time Edgar and Frank were traveling through the verdant pastures of the

Sacramento Valley, Burtha left the tour so she could visit her elderly parents in Northern California and, it seems, take a break from her husband's drug taking, which she loathed.

IN THE ATTRACTIVE LITTLE CITY of Chico, only a shade over forty miles north of Marysville, where Edgar and Frank were due next, Frank received some news from France. His teenage brother, Lee, who was a corporal in the Marine Corps, had been awarded a citation for bravery from General John J. Pershing, commander of the American forces. Reference to Pershing would've provided an entrée for Edgar's well-rehearsed stories about meeting the general on the front line and traveling to Europe "with a contingent of Pershing's men." As Edgar must have known, the general was famous for having commanded a company of Apache and Sioux during the earlier war with Mexico.

Frank treated his brother Lee's commendation by the general as mere sibling one-upmanship, ripe for macho banter. BULLY FOR YOU, Frank wired his brother. YOU'VE ANSWERED GERMANY'S PEACE TERMS, AND THERE ARE A HUNDRED MILLION OTHER ANSWERS IN THE MAIL.

BETWEEN CHICO AND MARYSVILLE lay mile after mile of orchards, as well as fields so large they were plowed by lines of up to forty mules. A series of massive levees protected Frank and Edgar's destination, another picturesque yet busy little city, its prosperity evident from the goods in its many stores.

No longer constrained by his wife's scruples, Edgar claimed he was a representative of the federal government. And he must have reverted to his old trick of wearing an eye patch, because he started telling people that he'd lost an eye in combat—"lost for the honor of your flag and my flag," those words spoken in homage to a wartime hit song of that title.

He and Frank, who was happy to play along with Edgar's blarney, passed much of the next ten days fundraising for the Red Cross, each of the duo apparently helping himself to some of the donations. Both men also took to the stage at concerts by the Oakland Boys' Club Band, concerts at which Frank sang and Edgar gave recruiting speeches.

Previous U.S. Navy recruiting drives had never been successful in Marysville, but Edgar and Frank brought about sufficient enlistments to push the city beyond the midpoint of its quota. Yet Superior Judge E. P. McDaniel—who chaired the local county council of defense, one of a nationwide network of committees overseeing aspects of America's militarization—suspected that both Chief White Elk and Frank Spaulding were crooks. He wired a complaint about their activities to Josephus Daniels, President Wilson's secretary of the navy. Though Frank was working with the navy's blessing, Daniels incorrectly assured the judge that neither individual held official status as a recruiter.

WITHOUT GIVING THE JUDGE A chance to take action against them, Edgar and Frank quit Marysville. Conceivably lovers by now, though that would've required extreme discretion, lest they be condemned as "sexual perverts" and reported to the police, they moved the better part of thirty miles east. Their destination was the mining town of Grass Valley, California, where Edgar ingratiated himself with the locals and spoke at a recruiting rally while kitted out in a U.S. Navy uniform.

Charlie Clinch, an enduringly influential former mayor of the city, and Thomas Ingram, a California state senator, meanwhile received notification that Chief White Elk was not an official U.S. Navy recruiter, nor was he an emissary of the U.S. government. These two self-appointed sleuths then summoned Frank Spaulding to a meeting on the morning of Thursday, July 25, 1918. Quizzed about Chief White Elk, Frank insisted that the chief was working on the recruiting campaign for patriotic reasons, even if he *was* "masquerading under false colors" and had been wearing a uniform he had no business wearing.

Ingram and Clinch next went round to see Edgar, who blamed "pro-German sources in Redding" for the allegations against him. Besides stressing that he'd been donating his services to the country for free, he said he'd never claimed to be a government-sanctioned recruiting officer.

He added that he did nevertheless have a certificate from Secretary of the Treasury William Gibbs McAdoo, authorizing him to sell War Savings Stamps. But he was still unable to convince Ingram and Clinch of his legitimacy—a rare failure.

Neither of his two adversaries had the legal right to force him to do anything, yet they ordered him out of Grass Valley right away. Leaving behind Frank and the rest of the recruiting party, Edgar acceded to their demands and took the midday train to San Francisco, his departure sparking front-page coverage in the local press. But he barely had time to reacquaint himself with San Francisco before Frank—who, clearly, didn't want to be separated from him—discovered Edgar still had plenty of support in Grass Valley. This lured Edgar back from the coast.

In front of a big crowd, which had poured into the Strand Theatre, he offered his side of the story. A short time afterward two officers from the regional headquarters of the U.S. Navy's recruiting service pitched up in Grass Valley. Their brief was to investigate Chief White Elk and Pharmacist's Mate Frank Spaulding. Edgar—for whom loyalty remained an alien concept—vanished, and left Frank to field the inevitable fusillade of tricky questions.

COMPELLED TO FIND ANOTHER WAY of supporting himself now that his partnership with Frank was over, Edgar reactivated his dormant vaudeville career by landing dates in Modesto, California, and Reno, Nevada. In mid- to late September, he went back to San Francisco, where he would've had no trouble obtaining his favored narcotics from the illegal sources who were fueling a nationwide rise in drug dependency, which had seen the number of known addicts top one million. When he wanted morphine or cocaine, the latter nicknamed "joy dust," he just had to sashay up to one of the curbside dealers and hand over about a dollar—the cost of several small packs of cigarettes. The dealer would then instruct him to walk down the street. As Edgar did so, a passerby would palm a sachet of his chosen drug into his hand. Known as "a deck" or "a bindle," each of these sachets contained just enough powder for between two and four snorts.

Edgar was fixing to stay in San Francisco awhile, so he moved into the Arrow Apartments, a seven-story property only a block from the mid-section of Market Street. Crossing this busy thoroughfare was seldom easy. Streetcars and automobiles sharked along it, heedless of jaywalkers. Its crowded sidewalks hosted prematurely aged, hoarse-voiced newsies; disabled men selling pencils; and grifters peddling sugar, horoscopes, suspenders, laundry soap, and even bottles of what was sold as the elixir of life. Crowds tended to collect around the grifters as they ran through the type of smooth patter Edgar would have used in his days hawking patent medicines.

Just off Market Street were the offices of I. C. Ackerman and Saul Harris, who ran a notorious West Coast vaudeville circuit. Performers nicknamed it the Death Trail, commercial rather than bodily death awaiting those foolhardy or desperate enough to appear on it. So widely spaced were some of the Ackerman and Harris Hippodrome Circuit's theaters that its artistes would often struggle to break even, because they'd spend so much time and money traveling between engagements.

But Edgar was canny enough to avoid that pitfall by signing up for a short sequence of bookings that didn't require inordinately long journeys. All of his engagements were nonetheless what were known as "split weeks"—badly paid three- or four-day gigs. He'd be part of the fluctuating cast of the Hippodrome Road Show, a nominally "all-star" production, supplemented by a short movie. Poverty or maybe overconfidence even led him to agree to perform in San Diego, where he had, only the previous year, employed his Tom Longboat shtick to defraud many prominent citizens. Mercifully for him, though, he wasn't being sought by the city's police department. Even after the *San Diego Evening News* had produced a front-page exposé of his activities there, none of his victims had been willing to endure the indignity of going to the police and reporting their losses.

With eleven weeks to go until the tour kicked off, he was at his apartment one Monday night when he received an unwelcome visitor—Special Agent H. H. Dolley from the Bureau of Investigation. Dolley had a federal warrant for Edgar's arrest. It dated back to the period before America had entered the war, back to his time at Camp Harry J. Jones in Arizona, where the Twenty-Second Infantry Regiment had been training. Edgar was charged with encouraging American soldiers to fight the Germans by deserting and then joining the Canadian Army.

Press coverage of his arrest soon appeared not only in San Francisco but also in Salt Lake City, Oakland, San Diego, and elsewhere. Nowhere was his comeuppance greeted with more satisfaction than in Salt Lake, where he'd made so many people look dumb.

11

The Bureau of Investigation's San Francisco office received a message from Arizona's attorney general. He revealed that the charges against Edgar had already been dropped for lack of evidence. Just over a day after being arrested—well before the presumed unavailability of alcohol or drugs would have turned the experience into an ordeal for him—Edgar was set free. He then left San Francisco and went north, narrowly escaping the lethal influenza epidemic that wreaked havoc on the city.

In the persona of Chief White Elk, he stopped off in Marin County and performed a couple of shows before continuing through a wilderness landscape that had scarcely changed since the arrival of the first European settlers. The scale of its mountains, rivers, and luxuriant forests of giant redwoods would have forced anyone with a smaller ego than Edgar's to reflect upon his own insignificance.

That fall he rolled up in the port city of Eureka, California, where he was reunited with Burtha, whom he hadn't seen for about three months. She'd probably been staying with her father and stepmother at 1557 Myrtle Avenue, a mile and a half from the waterfront. Accessible via a sharp flight of steps, their home was a pretty, slightly eccentric-looking shingled cottage with a turret in one corner. Burtha had first moved there with her white father and Native American stepmother when she was about fourteen. Previously they'd lived on a ranch much further north. Her father, Jim Thompson, was a sturdy Alabaman in his seventies. He had a gray mustache and a matching beard that flared out from his chin like the cowcatcher on the front of an old-fashioned locomotive. Ever since coming to California, he had been in the lumber business, though he'd still found time to play an instrumental role in educating Burtha.

Whenever Jim ventured down the street with Burtha's stepmother, Che-an-wah Weitch-ah-wah—who also went by the name of Lucy Thompson—the two of them walked hand in hand. Lucy had a spruce European outfit, complete with handbag, fitted coat, and plumed hat. It was an outfit belying her inordinate pride in her Klamath background. Her potent sense of affiliation survived even being shunned by her tribe on account of her marriage to a white man. Approximately a decade younger than her husband, Lucy was a slim-waisted, straight-postured little woman with high-cheekboned, tan features. Her downturned mouth lent her a truculent and crestfallen appearance that didn't chime with her starchy benevolence. Though her sister Nora—Jim's first wife—was Burtha's biological mother, Lucy had raised Burtha as her own.

If Burtha was hoping Edgar had used the time apart from her to wean himself off drugs—a word that, she declared, "haunts me like Satan in hell"—then she was destined for disappointment. She nonetheless restrained herself from confiding in friends or family about any of this. Despite all the anxiety to which her husband had subjected her, she still kept faith in him. She presumably moved in with him when he found accommodation at 1515 Dean Street, just a short distance from her parents' place.

Through Burtha most likely, Edgar met the thirty-nine-year-old photographer Emma B. Freeman, an old friend of Burtha's. Emma was a white Midwesterner with an elfin physique, blue eyes, gray-streaked hair, and a nervous yet playful manner that made people—men especially—relax in her presence. Close friends knew her as "Toots." Willful and ambitious, she had a well-developed sense of fun and an offbeat taste in clothes that sometimes prompted her to wear a man's hat with a rattlesnake-skin band around its crown. She owned a downtown studio, darkroom, gallery, and gift shop called the Freeman Art Company. In the gift shop, she used to sell traditional-style Klamath baskets made by Burtha. As Emma may have mentioned to Edgar, these were so beautifully woven that collectors prized them.

Over the eight months he'd been married to Burtha, Edgar would likely have heard many fond recollections of his wife's friendship with Emma. It stretched back some five years, back to when Burtha had taken a job at a hospital in Eureka after training in San Francisco as a nurse. Nourishing their friendship was a mutual fascination with Native American culture. They were both outsiders, too—a status conferred by Burtha's mixed race and by what was perceived as Emma's scandalous behavior. Around the time Emma's marriage collapsed following an extensively publicized fling with a former governor of Illinois, Burtha had joined Emma's cheery, chattering coterie of young, well-educated, part-white, part–Native American friends. Burtha had meanwhile started modeling for Emma's ongoing series of portraits of Native Americans.

Emma used deep shadows and soft-focus lenses to depict her sitters with appreciative lyricism, communicating her romantic notion of them as what she called "Nature's monarchs of the wild." One of her photos of Burtha ended up being reproduced on the front page of the *San Francisco Chronicle*. Burtha was also represented in a display of Emma's Native American portraits exhibited at the city's Panama-Pacific International Exposition, which the two women visited together.

So consistently enthusiastic was the response to her show that Emma went from being a bohemian outsider to a portraitist much in demand by the West Coast elite. Recently, she'd carried out a series of commissions for the U.S. military. These encouraged her to style herself as an "official government photographer" and to curry favor with the authorities by making public pledges to various wartime fundraising drives.

More than likely Emma's current incarnation as a patriotic minor celebrity helped Edgar and Burtha to become fundraisers for the latest of Eureka's Liberty Loan campaigns. In his familiar role as a famous Cherokee chief and American soldier, Edgar impressed the locals, who were soon able to celebrate Germany's unconditional surrender.

He had cause to celebrate as well. Maybe drawing upon cash he'd skimmed from the fundraising campaign or by simply exploiting the excitement surrounding his Liberty Loan work, he acquired a Studebaker Touring Car, which retailed for as much as $1,695. It was a capacious vehicle that represented an upgrade from even the deluxe vehicle driven at his wedding. Now he and Burtha could motor into the wilderness around Eureka, the onset of seasonal rains and mist granting it an aura of spectral ambiguity.

For Burtha and Lucy, that landscape was dense with mythological associations and family tradition. Not too far beyond the city limits lay the tumbledown property where Burtha's grandmother was born. Tribal legend taught that the house had belonged to the Wa-gas, a beneficent white superrace that had assisted the Klamath and then departed with an unfulfilled promise to return. The property's link to the revered Wa-gas made it a place of spiritual importance for Lucy, whose own mother had vacated it almost twenty years earlier. Until recently, Burtha's grandmother had made trips back to the area with the sole purpose of smashing the stone bowls, trays, and implements purportedly left behind by the Wa-gas. Lucy explained that Burtha's grandmother didn't wish these mementoes of the Wa-gas to be "ruthlessly handled and curiously gazed upon by the present-day white race." Neither Lucy nor her husband, Jim, appear to have realized that Edgar belonged to that race.

Edgar's Studebaker was not only convenient for sentimental journeys to places associated with Burtha's family, but also perfect for trips out to the forests with Burtha and her photographer friend, who wanted to take more pictures of her. Joining the three of them on one such expedition was Bertha Stevens, another of Emma's circle.

An attractive, fashion-conscious twenty-something with Native American blood, Bertha had formerly worked as Emma's cook and photographic retoucher. She'd since married Fred Chamley, a tall, intelligent, strikingly handsome young part-Cherokee, employed in Emma's darkroom. Expert at making an immediate connection with strangers, Edgar would surely have discovered that Bertha Stevens had attended Carlisle, his own supposed alma mater. If the two of them had then swapped recollections of their schooldays, Edgar would've needed to be cautious in talking about Carlisle, reliant as he was upon generalities, secondhand anecdotes, and his facility for ad-libbing.

Emma—whose own spontaneity didn't extend to her working methods—paused to photograph Edgar and their two companions in front of a stand of redwoods. She also posed Edgar and his wife inside the forest, near enough to its periphery for the low, hazy light to penetrate. Until she was satisfied that her subjects were in exactly the position she wanted, Emma would maneuver them, like a child playing with dolls. In a composition expressive of her romantic, somewhat mystical admiration for Native Americans, she had Burtha crouch on the ground at Edgar's feet, almost blending into the scrub. Unsmiling, Edgar towered over his wife, his war-bonneted profile standing out against the dark trunk behind.

Convivial get-togethers with Emma and her circle were probably responsible for Edgar and Burtha's conversations about how they envisioned making their home in Eureka. As tempting as that prospect was, they could not do so until the New Year. Edgar was, after all, committed to touring with the Hippodrome Road Show.

ONCE AGAIN PARTING FROM BURTHA, he went down to San Diego, where his Cherokee chief's disguise would have come in handy if he'd bumped into members of the high-society crowd whom he'd scammed during his previous visit. He began his return to vaudeville with a four-day run at Spreckels Hippodrome. Its nearly two-thousand-seat Baroque-style auditorium, modern facilities, enormous stage, and equally enormous onyx-lined lobby decorated with Tiffany stained glass gave him a tantalizing taste of the big time, though he may not have been too pleased that someone else was headlining the show.

Just a couple of days after taking his final curtain call, directly beneath a ceiling adorned by what would turn out to be a prescient allegorical painting of two angels emptying a horn of plenty, Edgar was in warm, rainy Los Angeles, where he had a Thursday-to-Sunday stint at the local Hippodrome. Despite being even larger than its near-namesake in San Diego, Edgar wouldn't have found it anywhere as comfortably appointed as Spreckels. He and some jugglers, a pair of gymnasts, a whistler, a comedienne, a singer, and an eight-girl song-and-dance troupe billed as "the Beautiful Broadway Song Birds" had to make do with only nine dressing rooms between them.

Christmas and New Year interrupting their tour, Edgar and most of the cast then made the short jump to Santa Ana for a two-day booking. There, they had a grinding itinerary of three shows daily, which required Edgar to perform in a musical comedy starring the all-girl song-and-dance troupe he'd worked with in L.A.

Prior to his final tour dates in nearby Oxnard, where he was advertised as "a whole show in himself," he fulfilled some solo engagements. These included a visit to a women's club in Orange, at which he sang, played the piano, and spoke in favor of the campaign for citizenship to be granted to all American Indians. His appearance at the women's club was probably what got him invited to a dinner party thrown by two society hostesses who claimed to have Cherokee ancestors "three generations back."

Edgar and Burtha arrived in Portland, Oregon, which was enjoying intermittent spring sunshine. They made their way through the prosperous downtown area, where many new buildings had gone up and where statewide Prohibition had swept away the saloons. Clad in full regalia, the couple went into a huge, late-nineteenth-century hotel at Sixth and Morrison. They asked the desk clerk for a suite of rooms, their crisply enunciated English wrong-footing him.

Comparable disbelief was evident when later that day they presented themselves at the home of Emery Olmstead. A young, beaky-nosed, dark-skinned man who would have made a more plausible Cherokee than Edgar, Olmstead served as chairman of the Fifth Liberty Loan, a soon-to-be-launched federal government campaign aimed at raising money to fill the budgetary deficit created by the recently ended war.

Edgar's cheerful demeanor offset the abruptness of his announcement that he was there to help with Portland's contribution to the campaign. Ushered into the comfortable house, he swiftly established such a rapport with Olmstead that Burtha could have mistakenly assumed they were old friends. They were soon deep in conversation about the Liberty Loan campaign, their discussion powered by cigarettes.

Meeting the fundraising target set by the government would be a formidable task, Olmstead's campaign staff had warned, because the public's appetite for anything war related was dwindling. Edgar nonetheless assured Olmstead that the target was attainable so long as the campaign utilized the expertise he'd just offered. He and Burtha brandished their stack of testimonials. Among those, he had a forged letter of commendation from the authorities for working in a Californian hospital where he'd supposedly helped defeat an influenza epidemic, this latest recruit to his army of heroic stories about himself maybe inspired by the epidemic he'd only just avoided in San Francisco.

By the time he and Burtha said goodbye to Olmstead, they'd been engaged as fundraisers.

IN THE PRESENCE OF HIS WIFE, that evening Edgar talked to a reporter employed by the Portland-based *Morning Oregonian*. "From the experience we've had with our own people, from the faithful service they've given—both in lives and money—we have come to feel that all are equal in this America of ours, and that all should be sharers in the liberty that our nation strives for here and overseas," Edgar said. "It is our hope that someday our people may raise their heads and feel that they have a full share in that liberty."

Cigarette in hand, he made emphatic gestures as he spoke, those gestures causing the bone and shell ornaments on his broad chest to jangle and the feathers in his headdress to shiver. He gave every indication that he was conscious of the many admiring glances directed at him.

"We are patriots, we Indians," he continued. "If you question that, look at the records of our race in the war." Backing this up, he said, "One small Indian community in this district gave thirty times its quota to a Liberty Loan. We think that compares well with the records of those who came here and took possession of our land."

Garnished by the usual references to his service on the *Antilles*, his medical qualifications, and his achievements in college football, as well as new stories about Burtha's wartime nursing service in France, and about them raising $1 million for the Red Cross, the resultant newspaper article was published first thing next day—Monday, April 14, 1919.

Later that morning, Emery Olmstead summoned his fellow Liberty Loan Committee members to a meeting at Edgar and Burtha's hotel. Though the federal government wasn't launching its nationwide campaign until the following week, Edgar consented to perform at a fundraising event in Portland the next day. But his plan soon hit its first obstacle.

THE ARTICLE IN THE *MORNING OREGONIAN* caught the attention of staff at the *Salt Lake Tribune*. Before the day was out, they'd wired the director of publicity for Oregon's Liberty Loan campaign. Their telegram, which provided an inventory of Chief White Elk's recent criminal escapades, concluded with the line WE DISPROVED EVERY CLAIM HE MADE AND EX-POSED HIM.

Soon the district attorney for Oregon was involved. At the request of the local Liberty Loan campaign, he started looking into the *Salt Lake Tribune*'s allegations. When the *Morning Oregonian* got wind of those, someone was sent to question Edgar.

Face-to-face with the reporter, he brushed off the telegram from the *Tribune* as "a vicious and baseless attack." To refute the claim that he hadn't served on the SS *Antilles,* he showed the reporter his U.S. Army Transport Service documentation. He also sought to demonstrate his good character by fishing out his stash of testimonials praising his work and Burtha's on successive government fundraising drives.

"If we are the impostors that these charges would make us," he said, his voice replete with indignation, "why is it that the government has permitted us to work on all these drives, and why is it that we have scores of high-official letters of recommendation?" He even added, "We have decided to go to Salt Lake City and take action in court. There has been enough of this slander."

His all-too-credible, point-by-point denial of the allegations didn't pre-clude stories about him from circulating around Portland. Word had it

Studio portrait of Edgar Laplante, ca. 1918.
Washington State University Libraries

Widely reproduced newspaper
photo of the twenty-nine-year-
old Edgar Laplante posing
as Onondagan athlete
Tom Longboat, August 1917.

WHITE ELK KEPT POLICE BUSY

IMPOSTOR HAD MANY ALIASES

CHIEF WHITE ELK, alias Pouaxonanna, alias C. W. Ellis,
posing as Chief Harry Johnson at Lima, Montana. This
picture was taken by a local photographer at Lima last April.

Front-page newspaper story
about Edgar Laplante, aka
Chief White Elk, published in the
Salt Lake Tribune, March 21, 1918.

Onondagan athlete
Tom Longboat
photographed during
an athletic event
at Ebbets Field in
Brooklyn, July 26, 1913.
*Bain News Service/Library
of Congress*

Studio portrait of Edgar Laplante, posing as Chief White Elk, ca. 1918.
Washington State University Libraries

The western apse of the
Varied Industries Building
at the Panama-California
Exposition, ca. 1915.
*Panama-California Exposition
Digital Archive*

Visitors passing the Commerce
and Industries Building at the
Panama-California Exposition, ca. 1915.
*Richard Benton Collection,
Panama-California Exposition Digital Archive*

View from the deck of the SS *Antilles,* August 1917.

Portrait of Burtha Thompson and Edgar Laplante, probably taken in
Washington State by Emma B. Freeman, ca. 1918.

Washington State University Libraries

CHIEF WHITE ELK VANISHES
□   □   □   □.   □   □
SHERIFF SEEKS INTERVIEW

C HIEF WHITE ELK, also known as C. W. Ellis, as he looked on his recent wedding day on the steps of the state capitol.

Antilles "Hero" Quits Hotel
When Friends Question
His Genuineness.

Front-page story from the
Salt Lake Tribune, March 20, 1918.

Edgar Laplante, aka Chief White Elk, and his new bride, Burtha Thompson, photographed just after their marriage ceremony at the Utah State Capitol in Salt Lake City, March 13, 1918.

Dr. White Elk will be at the Odeon tonight in costume. He will sing while you dance.

HALLOWE'EN MASK BALL

$35
In Cash
Prizes
For
Best
Indi-
vidual
Cos-
tumes

DR. WHITE ELK
will lead the Grand March tonight
Irresistible Dance Music by

ODEON
BALL ROOM

——We Don't Insist on You Being Masked——
SPECIAL DECORATIONS
Management Knights of Pleasure Club
No Advance in Prices for This Extraordinary Dance Event

Advertisement for an appearance by Edgar Laplante's alter ego Dr. White Elk in Great Falls, Montana, October 1920.

Portrait of Edgar Laplante's wife Burtha Thompson, probably taken in Washington State by Emma B. Freeman, ca. 1918.

Edgar Laplante's employer-turned-adversary, the Reverend Chief Red Fox Shiuhushi, pictured outside the White House, 1915.
Library of Congress

Bostock's Animal Arena in the Greater Dreamland amusement park on Coney Island, ca. 1905.
Library of Congress

that he wasn't even a real Indian; that he hadn't, as he maintained, been a student at Carlisle; that he was wanted by the police on charges of draft dodging.

Experience alerted him to the fact that the situation would only get worse, so he and Burtha decided to leave Portland. Resolutely protesting their innocence, he said that he and Princess Ah-Tra-Ah-Saun would be traveling to Salt Lake, where they'd be instituting legal proceedings against the *Salt Lake Tribune*. They stayed just long enough for Edgar to sing at the scheduled Liberty Loan event on Tuesday evening. Without explaining themselves to Emery Olmstead or any of the other people they'd come to know, Edgar and his wife went to the station and boarded the midnight train.

BUT EDGAR HAD LIED ABOUT where they were going. They weren't on their way to Salt Lake. They were, instead, going north into Washington State, another supposed bastion of the mandatory teetotalism that nonetheless offered little impediment to the alcohol consumption of hardened drinkers like Edgar.

In and around Seattle, where well-lit streets sloped toward a long waterfront, bordered by mills, factories, and warehouses—the focus of a recent, exceptionally bitter five-day general strike—he picked up bookings as a guest speaker. At one of those, he posed the pertinent question, why are his people deemed good enough to fight for the United States yet *not* good enough to be granted the vote?

Over the fourteen months of his marriage, he'd transmitted the show business virus to Burtha, who contemplated launching herself as a solo performer. She got her big break when she was invited to appear as an "added attraction" at Levy's Orpheum, the most prominent of Seattle's theaters. Alongside the Folly Girls, a troupe of white chorus girls tricked up in faux Native American outfits, she'd be demonstrating "the native dances of her tribe." Despite her commitment to remain in Seattle, Edgar—who wasn't about to let marriage interfere with his own work—accepted an offer to join a summer lecture tour of Canada, organized by the promoter and talent spotter J. W. Erickson.

Tall and burly, dark hair retreating from angular features, Erickson was a kindly, energetic, and high-strung man who worked alongside his wife. They ran one of a number of companies dedicated to staging what were known as "chautauquas," a name derived from Lake Chautauqua in New York State, where the concept had originated at a summer camp almost fifty years earlier. Rooted in democratic idealism and free speech, in the desire to eliminate bigotry and sectarianism, chautauquas had evolved into a thriving movement primarily oriented toward small towns in America's rural provinces. Like vaudeville, chautauquas were based upon itinerant groups of performers, only in this instance performers were chosen for their ability to educate as well as entertain both adults and children. Unlike vaudeville, chautauquas were held in circus tents. And they were limited to the summer months, hence their self-proclaimed status as "the greatest summer school in the world."

Ellison-White Dominion Chautauquas, the outfit run by Erickson and his wife, was in the forefront of expanding the movement into Canada. As Chief White Elk, Edgar became a late addition to the Canadian Six circuit, its title arising from the fact that six days were spent at every stop on the tour. He agreed to lecture on the afternoon of Day Five. His chosen subject was his fictitious experiences at the Versailles Peace Conference between America and the other previously warring nations.

SPORTING A FEATHERED HEADDRESS and flowing robes, Edgar arrived in the handsome port city of Vancouver on the evening of Wednesday, May 21, 1919. His apparent exoticism was tempered by the Chinese immigrants on the sidewalks and by the passengers from Japanese ocean liners. Since leaving Seattle, Chief White Elk had morphed into the dignified figure of Dr. Tewanna, survivor of the sinking of the *Antilles,* Carlisle graduate, college football star, Cherokee chief, and Olympic long-distance runner. Appended to this familiar résumé—which left him well-equipped to chisel cash from the gullible—were tales of how he'd campaigned for the various Liberty Loans and how he'd delivered a speech from the steps of the New York State Capitol.

He checked in to the Hotel Vancouver, easily Canada's most palatial hotel, its amenities including a roof garden and a grillroom specializing in big game. At the hotel, he may have tasted the prevalent Canadian prejudice and discrimination toward non-Anglo-Saxons. While he was staying there, local newspapers ran numerous articles about strikes and threatened strikes in Vancouver and elsewhere in the country. Motivating this unrest were harsh working conditions and the refusal of employers to negotiate with unions. The newspapers carried parallel reports on massive strikes in America, potential strikes in England, and turmoil in Italy, where violent clashes had taken place between communists and supporters of the new fascist movement. Red flags were also reported to be flying in Paris. Even the most cursory flick through the papers would've given Edgar the impression that the revolution, which had already installed a communist government in Russia, would soon sweep the world. That impression was strengthened by the news of a forthcoming general strike in Vancouver.

But Edgar needed time to reach the rendezvous point for the chautauqua, so he'd surely left town before the strike got under way. He had a nine-hundred-mile train ride through a wild landscape for which the observation car was intended, views of mountains, lakes, woods, canyons, and waterfalls ultimately replaced by the seemingly endless wheat fields of Saskatchewan.

When passing isolated farmsteads, vaudevillians like him were in the habit of tossing unwanted magazines and newspapers out the windows—not because they enjoyed littering the landscape, but because they figured that the inhabitants of those farmsteads would relish news from the outside world. Tucked away on the inside pages was a story about Tom Longboat's return to Canada after military service in France. No mention was made of Longboat carrying out his almost two-year-old threat to press charges against the man impersonating him. Evidently, Longboat was more interested in resuming his athletic career, so Edgar had nothing to fear on that score.

Edgar was scheduled to join the chautauqua by Friday, June 6, 1919, its penultimate day in the small town of Stoughton, Saskatchewan. Assuming everything went according to plan, he'd have been preceded in the tent that afternoon by Francis Hendry, a bushy-mustached, middle-aged impressionist whose act involved elaborate makeup and his wife's piano accompaniment. The Hendry Duo was also slated to perform in the lamp-lit tent that evening, its repertoire encompassing dramatic readings and vocal solos, which weren't exactly the most obvious warm-up for the day's final event—a talk on "China's Fight for Democracy."

The talk was due to be given by Dr. Ng Poon Chew. Sometimes billed as "the Chinese Mark Twain," he was a bespectacled and urbane former diplomat who had gone on to become a journalist and set up America's first Chinese-language newspaper. Edgar would've had sufficient time to get acquainted with him and the Hendrys, because chautauqua performers assigned to feature on the same day routinely rode the same trains together and stayed at the same rooming houses and small hotels, where they became a rambunctious presence at the same dining tables.

In theory, Edgar and his three fellow performers had no alcohol to lubricate their acquaintanceship, Prohibition being on the statute books across every Canadian province save Quebec. Yet Edgar had only to visit the local drugstore if he wanted a drink. He could then purchase a bottle of Hostetter's Bitters or one of the other patent medicines that had become a synonym for alcoholic beverages. Many of those were more than five times stronger than beer.

Though the chautauqua continued in Stoughton until Saturday night, Edgar and his companions were free to leave once they'd honored their weekly obligations. From Saskatchewan, they moved into neighboring Manitoba, their small-town destinations marked by grain elevators that spiked the flat landscape, across which an incessant, gritty wind blew, its invisible fingers tugging at the pegs holding up the chautauqua tent. People poured in from outlying districts, filling the makeshift, increasingly stuffy auditorium, numerous children swarming toward the front. These excited youngsters whistled and clapped throughout other people's musical numbers, but they lapsed into an attentive hush during Edgar's spellbinding lectures. And when he'd finished, everyone stood up and gave a hearty rendition of "God Save the King!" One of Edgar's colleagues joked about having helped save the king so many times that he could sing the British national anthem backward.

Inevitably, Edgar would've had plenty of time not only to exercise his talent for painting and drawing, but also to meet the other thirty-five performers on the chautauqua. They were a varied bunch. Among them were a young, headscarfed Syrian woman; an Australian war veteran; a Japanese writer who had to coach people on the pronunciation of his name; a trio of vivacious and attractive female singer-instrumentalists; a husband and wife who lectured on the six years they'd spent in the Malayan jungle; a traditional Serbian tamburica band; and a young man who gave stagy readings from great works of literature.

Late that June, Edgar and the others headed west into Edmonton, Alberta, a burgeoning city reached by way of an absurdly slow, unreliable, and uncomfortable railroad service. The carriages rocked so much that the man who had spent years roughing it in the jungle complained about feeling seasick. Veterans of this route came equipped with a set of straps with which they tied themselves into their sleeping berths. To add insult to any injury sustained falling out of bed, all this discomfort wasn't worthwhile, because there turned out to be little demand for chautauqua in Edmonton.

But Edgar had other things to take his mind off the sparse audiences. He visited a local children's club, where he gave what was regarded as "a very fine address on the aims and aspirations of his people, making a deep impression on those present." He was the star attraction at a big parade, designed to advertise the annual cattle roundup in nearby Neutral Hills—an event akin to a state fair. He appears to have rubbed elbows with everyone from cowboys to members of the Canadian government. Around that time, he also appears to have made a hollow promise to compete in a Toronto marathon due to feature Tom Longboat.

While Edgar was soaking up all this attention, his assumed identity as a Cherokee chief was further validated by a glowing reference in the latest edition of the *American Indian,* a quarterly journal promoting Native American culture and attainments, and the growing movement for Native American rights. In an article about the Liberty Loan, "Chief and Princess White Elk" were proudly but erroneously praised for selling more than $1.8 million worth of Liberty Bonds over a single week.

Through July and early August, Edgar and the rest of the chautauqua moved from one cattle town to another until they reached their final date in Briercrest, Saskatchewan, each day capped by a florid sunset that didn't burn out until midnight. Burtha, meanwhile, had probably been sending

Edgar the sort of long, chatty letters she liked to write. There was a lot for her to tell him about. She had, as planned, been appearing in the show at Levy's Orpheum. Using the stage name Princess White Elk, she'd performed what was marketed as "the Bare-Footed Nature Dance." Theatergoers had flocked to see the show, her act eventually earning top billing.

Her success appears to have led to her being approached by a prominent impresario who had worked with a lot of famous entertainers. She described him as "a wonderful talker, a wonderful man, a wonderful promoter." He wanted to work with her on putting together a lavish dramatization of "the history of the American Indian," starring an all–Native American cast. Burtha rated it "a great plan," one that would advance her people's cause as well as the show business career she now pictured for herself and Edgar.

BACK TOGETHER AFTER THE CHAUTAUQUA FINISHED, Edgar and his wife traveled some 140 miles southeast of Seattle. In the city of Yakima, Washington, they visited Burtha's Native American friend and correspondent Ben Olney, possibly because she wanted to ask him about the proposed stage show. Ben—the name of whose home city derived from his tribe—was a chunky man with a complexion dark enough for him to be taken for a Sicilian immigrant. The owner of a flourishing ranch, he combined effervescence and erudition. He'd long been a vigorous campaigner for a better understanding of Native American culture and for improving the educational opportunities available to the country's indigenous people. Most likely he was the person who introduced Burtha and Edgar to a couple of his locally based friends from the Native American rights movement.

One of those friends was Lucullus V. McWhorter, an unassuming elderly white Virginian rancher and amateur historian whose handlebar-mustached face tended to be crowned by a broad-brimmed cowboy hat. Well over a decade before Edgar and Burtha met him, Lucullus had played a pivotal role in defeating an attempt by Congress to appropriate the majority of what remained of the Yakama tribal land, his work prompting the Yakama to adopt him into their tribe and bestow upon him the prestigious name of Hemene Ka-Wan: "Old Wolf." But his many Native American friends knew him as "Big Foot," a nickname given to him when Yakama children first noticed his footprints in the snow.

Edgar and Burtha took a great liking to Big Foot, whose wife grew close to Burtha, too. In the course of their visit to the city of Yakima, they also met the Reverend Chief Red Fox Shiuhushi, a friend of both Ben Olney and Big Foot. Lately ordained into the Christian Disciples Church (to which Ben belonged), Red Fox was by some distance the country's best-known Native American rights activist.

Aged thirty-five, just three years Edgar's senior, he had dark hair, a slim build, and a face so elongated it might have been squeezed out of a toothpaste tube. He never tired of using his fluent command of English to discourse upon his past. He could talk about traveling around Europe with Buffalo Bill's Wild West, about converting to Christianity, about his days at Carlisle, about meeting the king of England and Kaiser Wilhelm II, about riding his pony from Montana to the White House to speak with the president and submit a petition for every American Indian to be granted full citizenship. Except for the trip to the White House, none of these experiences had occurred—at least, not outside his imagination.

As perceptive as Edgar was about human nature, he failed to see aspects of himself reflected in Red Fox, who was a fellow con man. Like Edgar, Red Fox's only legitimate tribal affiliation was with what real Native Americans would decades afterward wittily brand "the tribe of Wannabe." Yet both Edgar and Burtha took a shine to him and were, in Burtha's words, "impressed by the good ideas he had." Compellingly expressed, those centered upon equal rights and opportunities for Native Americans. Red Fox sought to advance his objectives through the construction of a Christian school not far away on the Yakama Indian Reservation and through the American Tipi Association, a briskly evolving organization over which he presided as "Supreme Most High Chief."

Established by Red Fox and Big Foot, the association began life as the Tipi Order. In that earlier guise, its purpose had been to create a Native American challenger to the Boy Scouts of America. Focused at that stage upon the teaching of the language, customs, and history of the country's original inhabitants, the Tipi Order had since been recast as an adult fraternal society–cum–civil rights campaign group. Only the previous summer, the recently constituted American Tipi Association had obtained far-reaching publicity when Red Fox had granted membership to the leading star of cowboy films, William S. Hart.

The admiration that Edgar and Burtha felt for Red Fox appears to have been mutual. Hardly surprising in view of not only Burtha's attractiveness and eloquent commitment to the cause of Native American rights, but also the current résumé touted by the man calling himself Dr. White Elk. Cocaine surely heightening Edgar's irresistible urge to inflate the fictional accomplishments that concealed his real-life failings, he now claimed to speak twenty-three languages, to hold degrees from two universities, and to have raised $80 million for the various Liberty Loan campaigns.

Red Fox wound up inviting Edgar and Burtha to work for the American Tipi Association. He asked them to give lectures and performances that would "change public opinion toward the American Indian."

On a short-term basis at least, the job was appealing to Edgar and Burtha, because it promised to keep them solvent until their big stage show got off the ground. Accepting Red Fox's offer had the added virtue of advancing a cause of which they were both longtime supporters. It would allow them to work together as well. Since the end of the chautauqua, that was a luxury they'd sampled only briefly when they provided a vaudeville interlude to several movie screenings in Oregon. But they'd been apart pretty much the rest of the time.

While Burtha had continued performing in Seattle, Edgar had swung through Idaho, where he'd held a well-received exhibition of his paintings and picked up a ragbag of engagements. He'd campaigned for all Native Americans to be given the right to vote. He'd bluffed his way into a two-week stint as lecturer-in-residence at the College of Idaho, a Presbyterian university positioned on the western extremity of the state. And he'd performed at movie theaters, his amended routine including "One Hour of Laughs" and a small backing band styled as "the Chief White Elk Orchestra." His routine even featured sharpshooting, which he must have learned from a colleague in vaudeville, where such acts were common. Generally more reliant upon subterfuge than marksmanship, these incorporated flamboyant tricks like the one that opened with a pretty girl standing on a raised platform that faced the audience, her body swathed in a voluminous wrap. Fastening this were large white buttons, at which the sharpshooter aimed from his position at the side of the stage. Those buttons were not what they appeared to be, though. They were, instead, large white balls, painted to resemble buttons when seen from the front. Opposite the sharpshooter was an angled steel sheet, which deflected the special low-velocity bullets into a sand trap. As the last of these smashed its target on its way across the stage, the girl's wrap fell to the floor, supplying the cue for amazed applause.

RATHER THAN SPEND STILL MORE time apart, Edgar and Burtha accepted Red Fox's job offer. At each of the events they organized on behalf of the American Tipi Association, they'd make a collection. Of the cash they raised, they were entitled to set aside 25 percent for their expenses. The balance had to be forwarded to the association.

Before Edgar and Burtha commenced their tour, Red Fox furnished a stack of bona fides. He also made the first payment on a Buick automobile that would allow them to get around more easily. Future repayments would be their responsibility.

During the cold, wet spring of 1920, they drove hundreds of miles across Washington State, calling at Tacoma and Olympia, where they gave performances of what they promoted as a "Unique Indian Concert." Large sums of money were remitted to their employer, yet they were flat broke by the time they hit the thriving city of Spokane.

They couldn't appeal for help from their employer, because Red Fox was traveling and they had no address for him, so Edgar wired Big Foot, the American Tipi Association's cofounder, with whom Burtha had already embarked upon a voluminous correspondence. Edgar's telegram requested a $57 loan from the money they'd already sent back to the association. But he succeeded only in provoking a letter from Red Fox, who turned down his request.

Until they could fix up some events, Edgar and his wife had to get by on starvation rations and whatever assistance they could glean from Sydney Allison, a college junior and talented would-be professional singer whom they came to know. Through Allison's well-connected parents, they obtained a booking at the local Presbyterian church, where Allison sang alongside them.

Edgar's dishonesty held in check by Burtha's honesty and her belief in what appeared to be Red Fox's objectives, they carried on sending him money they could ill afford to relinquish. So malnourished was Burtha that she was taken in and nursed by a local minister when they performed in nearby Cheney. The experience proved a pivotal moment for her. No matter how committed she was to the American Tipi Association's cause, she refused to continue sacrificing her and Edgar's health for it any longer. Whenever they ran low on cash as they drove south across Idaho and into Montana, they felt entitled to borrow from the money they generated. Though they'd already forwarded the sizable sum of $700 to Red Fox, he was infuriated by the discovery that Edgar had dipped into the proceeds for a $10.50 loan.

Red Fox retaliated by sending angry letters to the pair of them—letters that threatened to have Dr. White Elk put behind bars. Those threats coalesced when Edgar and Burtha were stopped by men from the local sheriff's department, who questioned them about the alleged theft of the Buick they were driving. Red Fox turned out to have asked the sheriff's department to seize the car and return it to him, but the deputies figured there were no legal grounds for that.

"Bodily and mentally" sapped by the subsequent flow of threats and accusations gushing from Red Fox, Edgar was taken sick, his condition not helped by the drink and drugs he'd been consuming. On a quest to straighten things out, Burtha made a 450-mile-plus round-trip to Butte, Montana, where she had a showdown with "the Fox," as she referred to their employer-turned-adversary. She told him that he couldn't expect them to give him the car, because *they* were the ones making the payments. Backing down, he signed a document confirming their ownership of the Buick. And he assured her that "everything was good" between them.

The irate letters nonetheless resumed once she got back from seeing Red Fox. He even started writing to people in the towns and cities they were due to visit, causing Burtha to wonder whether he was "going bug-house." His letters resulted in the cancellation of many of their plum bookings. Left with barely enough cash to buy gas, Edgar and Burtha finally gave up working for him.

Among the recipients of Red Fox's letters was the governor of Nebraska. With breathtaking hypocrisy, Red Fox warned him that Edgar and Burtha were "impostors," masquerading as representatives of the American Tipi Association. Red Fox also warned the governor that they were currently in Wyoming and heading his way.

But Red Fox must have been misinformed. The buckskinned duo were not in Wyoming, nor were they en route to Nebraska. In fact, they were still in Montana.

12

On the afternoon of Friday, July 23, 1920, Edgar, Burtha, and close to seven hundred other people boarded a flotilla of motor launches, a steamer, and a spacious barge. These set sail across Flathead Lake, where a vacation ambience was created by music wafting over from the barge. Its passengers were dancing to a band from another part of rural Montana.

Half a mile of choppy water separated the boats from their destination, a small, thickly forested island that broke the waterline like the carcass of some stranded sea monster. Along with the others, Edgar and Burtha—who were in their full Native American finery—had been invited by a Rotary Club–like organization called the Knights Templar of Montana, which was staging its inaugural summer picnic on the island. Edgar had given them the impression that he and Burtha—Dr. and Mrs. White Elk—were fundraisers "working for the benefit of Indian children in order that they may receive good educations."

Safely disembarked on the island, many of the women began sun-bathing on the gravel beach. Other people waded into the lake and tried out surfboards. But the majority of the group spent the next several hours horsing around on the shore, waiting for the big communal picnic. With impressive speed, the meal was served soon after six p.m. The menu choices, not to mention the quality and abundance of the food, drew praise from Edgar's fellow guests.

Once everybody was done eating, the organizers instructed them to find somewhere to sit. Except for Burtha and Edgar, who would be providing that evening's entertainment, the guests perched on the slope rising from the beach.

Taking to the makeshift stage, Edgar began his impersonation of good ol' Chauncey Olcott performing "Mother Machree," the singer's most famous song. When Edgar reached the final line, "Oh, God bless and keep you, Mother Machree," a crackle of applause swept like bushfire across the facing incline.

He followed up with a couple of other cloying numbers—"There's a Long, Long Trail" and "Dear Old Pal of Mine." Both songs received more bursts of exuberant applause. He then entertained his audience with reminiscences of the chautauqua circuit and his friendship with Dr. Ng Poon Chew. Anyone who got the chance, he declared, should hear Dr. Chew speak. Edgar then retold the dramatic story of his close brush with death when he was thrown from the crow's nest of the *Antilles*. The fall had, he revealed, cost him *six* ribs and one lung, though he assured listeners that the "physicians have practically restored all the missing parts."

Eventually, he made way for Burtha, who gave a talk about Native American religion and how her people had worshipped "the Great Spirit" long before the white man had set foot on American soil. She said they'd erected crosses on hilltops as part of their religious ceremonies. And she talked about "the high standard of morality which the Indians held previous to their introduction to the sins of the white races." In what may have been intended as an elegiac conclusion to the show, Burtha declaimed one of the poems she had written about Native American life. She called her composition "Memories." It climaxed with the lines,

Memories! Fond memories of the years that are gone forever
When our race greeted the sun-dawn of their rising nation

But now our dusky maids and swarthy braves are waiting ever
On these sorrowful shores where an alien people rules a broken nation.

That evening's sunset, its glow painting the waters of the lake, had long since dimmed by the time Edgar and the other guests retraced their route to the moonlit boats. For the trip back to the mainland, he joined the throng clambering onto the waiting barge. As it sailed slowly across the lake, the band struck up the first in a series of tunes that included an Irish jig. Lots of the passengers started dancing again. Edgar contributed by singing with the band.

ON THE STRENGTH OF HIS SERVICE as a "practicing surgeon with Uncle Sam's forces," Edgar finagled accommodation at the Montana Soldiers' Home, just a couple of miles outside Columbia Falls. Around a hundred other men and women—who addressed each other as "comrade"—lived in the brick-built, three-story structure. More like a large, comfortably appointed house than an institution, it sat on the bank of the Flathead River. A broad apron of lush pasture, where the veterans grew their own food, surrounded the property. Sharp and clear on some days, soft and blue on others lay the distant Kootenai and Rocky Mountain ranges.

In both its pastoral setting and benign communal regime, the Soldiers' Home was not so different from Sockanosset School for Boys, the reformatory where Edgar had been sent seventeen years earlier. He'd wound up living in one of five large, rustic-looking stone buildings, each of which housed a dormitory for more than fifty boys, some of them as young as eight. For many of Edgar's fellow pupils, who had committed offenses ranging from the theft of a few eggs to manslaughter, Sockanosset had offered a preferable alternative to homelessness or life with their impoverished families. Besides regular meals, it provided a wide range of activities overseen by caring staff. There were school lessons, theatricals, sports, lectures, parties, and occasional outings, plus a music program. Vocational training was also provided—training of such a high caliber that the boys' cabinetmaking exhibit bagged a silver medal at the 1904 World's Fair in St. Louis. Measuring up to Sockanosset's function as a reformatory, significant numbers of its residents were *reformed* by their time there. But Edgar, despite all his father's chivying, didn't land a steady job when he emerged from the school. And nothing in that regard had altered over the intervening years.

He and his wife were now, as Burtha wrote in a letter to Big Foot, gearing themselves up "to start out again as entertainers." Through her correspondence with Big Foot, she'd lately discovered that her friend had, just like she and Edgar, fallen out with Red Fox, affording her the opportunity to compare notes with Big Foot. "Be on your guard for you can't believe a thing he says," she warned her friend. Little suspecting that she shouldn't believe a thing her husband said, either, she added, "He thinks he can break my confidence in my husband and have me turn against him—he can never do that under the high heavens."

NEAR THE END OF AUGUST, Burtha and Edgar left the Soldiers' Home. Probably via Big Foot, who had a sideline as an agent for Native Americans seeking employment as performers at rodeos and state fairs, they secured a booking for all six days of that month's Montana State Fair, due to be held in Helena, two hundred miles to the southeast. Its organizer was delighted by the arrangement, even bragging to the *Helena Daily Independent* about obtaining the services of "the famous Indian Caruso." The booking not only required Edgar to sing but also to supervise "tribal ceremonials and traditional dances" performed by thirty-five Native Americans.

About the time Edgar was negotiating this latest engagement, newspapers elsewhere in the country reproduced the photo of him taken a little before he sailed to France three years earlier. Each of the reproductions carried a caption wrongly identifying the handsome man in the picture as Tom Longboat. Alongside the photo was a story about the real Tom Longboat's decision to retire from athletics and become a farmer on Canada's western prairies.

Well out of reach of the man whose identity he'd stolen, Edgar was soon working with Burtha at the Montana State Fair, which was blessed by warm sunshine and blue skies. Around them were thousands of people, attracted by the exhibitions of livestock and farm produce, the carnival, and the extensive daily program of entertainments. In addition to the rodeo, there were concerts, races on foot and horseback, a beauty pageant, music, auto racing, aerobatic displays, balloon flights, and parachute jumps from the balloons. There were also novelty animal acts such as "Panhandle Pete and His Educated Mule."

Fittingly, Edgar's contribution to the state fair's program was titled "Indian Fantasies." It involved a group of young people from the Bitter-root Salish, Pend d'Oreille, and Kootenai tribes—known to the white population at that time as "Flathead Indians." Under Edgar's supervision, they performed a sequence of trancelike dances every afternoon in front of the grandstand. Now and again he even led the dancing. Supplementing the "Indian Fantasies" show, Edgar and Burtha demonstrated a selection of two-person dances, which proved a great hit with the crowd. His song selections were more successful still, warranting multiple encores.

Visitors returned again and again to see "Indian Fantasies." By Thursday lunchtime—the show's fourth afternoon—the grandstand and both sets of bleachers were sold out. Press photographers stalked the crowd, hunting for evocative pictures.

At the state fair, Edgar and his wife were accosted by a stocky and forthright little woman named Mrs. Georgia Prest. She was a reporter for the *Anaconda Standard,* one of Montana's leading newspapers. In her downtime, she worked as a stunt pilot for movies. She even had her own airplane, which she called *Poison* because, as she remarked, "one drop is fatal." Three days earlier, she'd entertained the crowd with her aerobatics and wing walking.

She was deeply impressed by Edgar and Burtha, by what she saw as their unusual attractiveness, and by their outfits as well. "The chief was garbed in a most bewildering array of feathers, beads, and beaded jacket, which it is impossible for me to attempt to describe," she wrote afterward, "but I will simply say it was one of the handsomest costumes I have ever seen."

Aching to impress still further, Edgar seems to have reeled off his story about scoring the winning touchdown for Carlisle against Harvard in the famous football game.

· · ·

THE FLATHEAD INDIAN RESERVATION WAS a lawless part of western Montana, where bootleggers operated numerous whiskey stills. At the heart of it lay an encampment of tipis and huts, scattered on either side of a railroad track and overlooked by a mountain range. Edgar—and presumably Burtha, too—was one of the guests at a Native American wedding on the reservation, to which they appear to have been invited by a dancer from "Indian Fantasies." During the wedding party, Edgar had a movie camera pointed at him by one of the members of an eccentric group of travelers.

In charge of the group was a dashing yet diminutive Polish sophisticate with a strong accent and a grin that flouted even the rudiments of symmetry. He liked to dress in khaki, pseudo-military attire with leggings and a leather helmet. Titling himself Captain Walter Wanderwell, his name and rank as inauthentic as Edgar's, he was addressed as "Cap" by the fluctuating team of four people who traveled with him and his wife in their beat-up Moon Six car.

No less idiosyncratic than its owner, the vehicle had a human skull and crossbones mounted on its hood. Its bodywork bore the names of many of the Mexican and American places through which it had driven, names abutted by signatures and messages in German, French, Spanish, and English. Within the space of just a few inches were the autographs of the governor of Oregon, the movie star Viola Dana, and the Mexican revolutionary Francisco "Pancho" Villa. These had been acquired during the latest leg of what were designated the "Wanderwell World Tours," through which Captain Wanderwell sought to nurture international understanding and world peace. As a means of financing the journey, he rented seats in the car. He and his team also hawked photos and screened home movies shot along the way. And that was why the man Wanderwell knew as Chief White Elk was currently being filmed.

Edgar and Burtha were probably there with the aging, dark-skinned Chief Little Bear, whom they'd befriended. Little Bear was the leader of the Chippewa-Cree, a tribe based on the Rocky Boy's Indian Reservation in northern Montana. He didn't speak English, but Edgar and Burtha could communicate with him through both Jim Dinney, his son, and Four Souls, his son-in-law. The chief was vocal about the material hardships confronting his people that winter.

Acutely sympathetic to the plight of the Chippewa-Cree, Burtha was likely behind Edgar's decision to commit to a series of charity events for them across Montana. The weather—so mild that people dispensed with their topcoats—made travel a lot easier than it might have been. On the road with her husband, Burtha penned letters and poems, dominated by her desire to improve life for her fellow Native Americans. She also published a children's story in a local newspaper.

Punctuating the charity events for the Chippewa-Cree were a range of other engagements that Burtha obtained for her and Edgar. The two of them were, in her words, "awful busy." There were vaudeville shows, as well as performances in a church, at a Rotary Club dinner, at movie theaters, at a piano shop, and at a fancy-dress party where guests were encouraged to ape the film stars Charlie Chaplin and Mary Pickford. Edgar even substituted for the regular vocalist with a local jazz band, made up of tuxedoed, pomaded young men who proclaimed themselves "Real Jazz Jammers" and marketed their band with the line, "We Play the Blues While You Dance Them Away."

When Edgar and his wife hit the town of Bozeman, she had him sell a ring he'd given her, because she believed it brought her bad luck. He traded the ring for a pearl replacement. "It is a beautiful little ring, and I am glad to get rid of the other one," she wrote to Big Foot, who had become her confidant. Now that she'd divested herself of her old ring, she announced, "I have crushed out most all the bad luck that has come my way for awhile."

APTLY NAMED, THE GRAND HOTEL was a turreted, five-storied establishment. Edgar and his wife found accommodation there in mid-December after they'd breezed into Butte, streetcars and electric lighting attesting to the city's status as Montana's commercial heart.

Courtesy of a Seattle-based film distribution company called Greater Features, Edgar and Burtha were poised to begin work at the giant Broadway Theatre. Burtha had gotten them a contract to perform at screenings of *Before the White Man Came,* the latest example of a breed of appreciably longer movies known as "feature films" because they were intended as the main feature of a movie program. Like the big stage show on which Burtha still hoped to work, the film had an all–Native American cast.

Before the White Man Came was being released as a road show—a type of release associated with prestige productions. For road show movies, only a limited number of prints were produced. These toured from venue to venue, ideally generating a frisson of excitement and exclusivity that would increase the prospect of wider distribution at a future date. Screenings of road show movies were structured around such overtly theatrical devices as musical overtures and intermissions. By splicing Edgar and Burtha into the program, Greater Features would be reinforcing the show's theatricality and thus endowing their movie with a classy, educational aura more often associated with the stage than the screen. Employing them to appear at screenings would also—in theory, at least—promote the movie's much-trumpeted authenticity.

Consistent with its title, *Before the White Man Came*—which told the story of an intertribal romance—was set in the era preceding European colonization. Edgar pretended he was one of the Native American actors who featured in it, some of them on-screen too briefly to identify. He likely told his wife that he'd worked on the movie before she met him. Fortunately for him, the acting credits at the start of the film were visible for only a matter of seconds—not long enough for viewers to read much of the closely spaced list, from which Chief White Elk's name was absent.

But his name could not have been much more conspicuous in the advertisements for the movie, which started appearing in the *Anaconda Standard.* His wife was also given prominent billing: "Princess White Elk Is Considered the Most Attractive Indian Woman Appearing Before the Public."

Leafing through the paper in search of the ad, she or Edgar may have noticed that the strikes and other apparent portents of revolution, which dominated the press just a few months earlier, had fizzled out. Proud of the ads, Burtha mailed a copy to her friend Big Foot.

At least once each day she and Edgar stepped in front of an audience that must have been enlarged by the prospect of leering at her. Edgar prefaced the screenings with some songs and a short lecture. He and Burtha followed this with a rendition of a war dance, during which he could wear one of two feathered bonnets purchased from Little Bear. The war dance and the rest of their act received such acclaim that Burtha gloated about her and Edgar "dynamiting" the city.

For their final three days at the Broadway Theatre, they drafted Little Bear and several of his compatriots into the war dance. It provided a piquant appetizer for the movie's opening images: a long shot of a silhouetted horseman riding down a barren hillside, live music raising the audience's sense of expectation.

BETWEEN SESSIONS AT THE BROADWAY THEATRE, Edgar squeezed in the finale to the charitable campaign in aid of the beleaguered Chippewa-Cree. On the day after Christmas, he and Little Bear, along with Jim Dinney and Four Souls, attended the religious service at the YMCA building, a comparatively new structure occupying almost a full block of West Park Street.

In the run-up to the service, Edgar sang several numbers from his repertoire of popular songs. Then he spoke to the congregation about the difficulties endured by American Indians. He explained that the majority of "full-blooded Indians" were attempting to farm the land they'd been allotted by the government, but they were being stymied by "the adverse climatic conditions of the last four years," which had "put them in a bad way." To deter questions about his own racial credentials and, perhaps, lord it over his mixed-race wife, Edgar fired off a few disparaging remarks about Indians who were not full-blooded. He said he had little sympathy for these so-called "breed Indians" because "most of them lease their lands and live in laziness."

With Jim Dinney and Four Souls functioning as translators, Little Bear wished the congregation a Merry Christmas and Happy New Year. "I am glad to see you," he continued. "The reason I am glad to see you is that God wants us to meet here. Look at me—I cannot read or write. That is the kind of man that tells the truth. I am not going to tell you a lie. You people see me here today in fear. I wish you people here would help me and clear me of my fear." He went on to say, "Many of us are hungry. Some have not enough clothes. I ask you people to write to the government and tell them of our trouble."

A collection for his tribe was taken up afterward. It boosted the campaign's total proceeds to more than $170, just below the average weekly wage for a skilled manual worker. Once the ensuing religious service finished, Edgar handed a peace pipe to the president of that chapter of the YMCA. Edgar joked about hoping the gift would ensure its recipient was "a good Indian all year."

Very much against type, Edgar was endeavoring to prove that he, too, was a good Indian. On top of donating $100 to the fund for the beleaguered inhabitants of the Rocky Boy's Indian Reservation, he and Burtha sent them more than 2,200 pounds of donated clothing, along with large quantities of candy for the children. Yet Little Bear complained because he'd expected a lot more. Burtha had come to resent his frequent grumbling. "Little Bear has grown very selfish and unappreciative of the things that are being done for him," she declared. "The more you do for him, the more he expects, and when you are not in a position to do the things he expects you to do, he complains."

Her husband's efforts were better appreciated at the Broadway Theatre, where he'd proved enough of a box office draw for the management to program an additional matinee—without the movie. Likely deploying knowledge that he'd gleaned during a recent charity event at Butte's Spiritualist Society, Edgar was set to garnish it with a supernatural component.

On the afternoon of what was advertised as "The White Elk Show," the mild weather departed. A combination of a stiff breeze and heavy snow drove the pedestrians from the sidewalks around the theater. Edgar was nonetheless sought out by a sports reporter from the *Anaconda Standard.* The reporter had been tipped off about Edgar by Mrs. Georgia Prest, or perhaps some other colleague of hers who had spoken to him at the Montana State Fair. Happy to hold forth about his imaginary sporting exploits, Edgar provided the reporter with reminiscences of the athletes he'd encountered. But the reporter was most interested in the period when Edgar had been on the famous Carlisle football team coached by the great Glenn "Pop" Warner.

Edgar explained that he'd played under his Indian name, Tewanna, not the English name he adopted for the sake of his theater audiences. Between 1906 and 1910, he said, he'd figured in most of Carlisle's games and been deployed by Warner as a running back. He admitted he wasn't a spectacular player, but he *was* fast, which accounted for why Warner chose him for what the journalist remembered as "one of the most remarkable stunts in the history of the autumn sport."

The journalist listened to Edgar's version of what happened when Carlisle played at the Harvard stadium in late October 1909. Harvard scored first and then kicked off, the ball arcing downfield. Eventually it descended on the Carlisle ten-yard line, where it was caught by one of Edgar's teammates. Instead of embarking on the usual downfield drive, every Carlisle player bunched around the man with the ball. Just as the Harvard team charged toward them, the huddle dispersed. Some of the Carlisle players calmly walked a step or two before standing still. Others ran in different directions. Yet there was no sign of the football.

Momentarily flummoxed, the Harvard players heard a loud hiss. Edgar was the source of this, audible from twenty yards. He was already sprinting for the Harvard end zone, only the ball was still nowhere to be seen. Several of the Harvard players pursued Edgar. They failed to catch him, though, before he crossed the goal line. He then pulled the partially deflated football out from under his shirt, where he'd concealed it while he was in the huddle.

When Carlisle claimed a touchdown, Harvard disputed the legality of their tactic. Edgar insisted the ball had been punctured as he'd charged toward the end zone. After a lengthy argument, the officials declared a touchdown and the game resumed, Harvard going on to win 27 to 12.

People assumed that the hidden ball trick was the reason why the Carlisle versus Harvard fixture did not take place the following year, but that was, Edgar said, down to the failure to find a mutually convenient date. "It was not due to Harvard being stuck up, as is commonly supposed," he added. "They treated us very finely off the field and were not a bit conceited or snobbish in any way. On the field they played hard, rough football and were out to win. I remember Wendell—then playing his first year for Harvard, and twice picked as an all-American half back—as the hardest-hitting, hardest-tackling man I have ever met on the gridiron. The way he put his head down and butted into you, he just couldn't be stopped."

THE NEXT MORNING'S EDITION OF the *Anaconda Standard* carried Edgar's recollections. They were seized upon later that day by a rival Montana newspaper. It described his story about the hidden ball trick as "the best and wrongest yarn concerning football published in Butte in many a year." The article proceeded to explain why that was the case: "Here's the joke: but one such play was ever made between the two colleges. This came in 1903, when Dillon of Carlisle hid the football under his sweater and ran through the full Harvard team for 105 yards for the only touchdown of the game. . . . Further, rule books show that in 1904, five years before the alleged feat of Dr. White Elk, the hidden ball trick was ruled out of the game and has never returned."

As a result of the article, a representative from the *Anaconda Standard* was obliged to admit to being "victimized by a showman in search of publicity."

EDGAR WOULD BE IN TROUBLE if he stayed there for much longer. The newspapers were bound to start scrutinizing other aspects of his life, so he dragged Burtha from Butte to Great Falls, a city more than one hundred miles northeast, where people were unlikely to have seen the stories about him. Through the opening weeks of 1921, he performed at a movie theater there. Offering a fresh selection of songs and monologues, he featured in three different programs. Each of these constituted a familiar mixture of short supporting films, a comedy juxtaposed with a travelogue and an adventure serial, all leading up to the main attraction, marketed as "an exhilarating romance of the speediest two-gun wizard the West ever knew."

Burtha and her husband were then slated to move on to Seattle and appear at screenings of *Before the White Man Came*. But those plans were kiboshed by the failure of Greater Features to persuade any of Seattle's movie theaters to book it. News of this seems to have contributed to Burtha's mounting frustration with theatrical life, with constant work that left her feeling as if they'd made "little headway" in the joint show business career she'd envisaged.

Potential salvation was presented to her by the producer of the big-budget theater show about Native American history first pitched to her at the beginning of the previous year. "He says he is going to stage something that has never been produced before on the stage—and the entire program will be Indians," she wrote to Big Foot. "He will not tell us further than it's going to be an entire Indian play, and I imagine it is going to be something very good when one gets it organized and working—at least I am trusting that *some* dreams will come true."

Convinced the show would provide her and Edgar with a route into the big time—a glamorous tour of America and Europe—Burtha agreed to carry out unpaid preparatory work for it, which involved traveling across Montana to the Crow and Fort Belknap Reservations. Her task was to audition and then contract a half-dozen Native Americans who could begin rehearsals during late March. Though her mission proved a success, her resentment at the injustices perpetrated against Native Americans was deepened by the "rotten" conditions she saw on the reservations.

From Montana, she sent a letter to Big Foot in which she remarked, "I could tell some interesting things that happened in this free land of ours." Those things included witnessing groups of schoolchildren being forced to march "up and down with long heavy irons on their backs in the bitter cold." She added, "I expect to leave here in two or three days for Seattle. Won't be surprised if I spend a day in Yakima on my way in, because I want to see you and Mrs. McWhorter awful bad before I leave for the east with our troupe of Indians."

THIS NATIVE REDSKIN HAS A REMARKABLE VOICE, declared the advertisements for the show in which Edgar was meanwhile performing at the large new Winter Garden Theatre in rain-lashed Seattle. He featured on the same bill as a Buster Keaton comedy and music from a huge Wurlitzer organ.

Without Burtha's levelheaded presence, his income from working at the Winter Garden and subsequently at small venues around Puget Sound was outstripped by his spending, much of it probably on drink and drugs. As compulsive as he was, he'd developed a raging addiction to morphine and cocaine, which were plentiful in Seattle, though the cheaper sachets of morphine tended to be cut with chalk. Pay more and he'd get slightly less chalk.

Burtha—who had now rejoined Edgar—could only watch while he became, as she wrote, "a slave to the most terrible demon I know." But her pride discouraged her from talking about her husband's problem to anyone, even Big Foot, her discretion requiring what she described as "terrible willpower."

Edgar ended up owing money all over town. The situation grew so bad that Burtha felt compelled to place an ad in the *Seattle Daily Times* stating, "I will not be responsible for debts contracted by my husband, Dr. White Elk."

Burtha had the consolation of knowing that preparations for the as-yet-untitled all–Native American stage show were going well. Its producer had already plowed several thousand dollars into constructing scenery and purchasing equipment. To help Burtha bridge the financial gap until rehearsals got under way, he arranged to hire Edgar to perform in a series of small towns in Montana.

Before that tour commenced, she and her husband played some dates in Washington State. When they visited the town of Chimacum, they were provided with accommodation on the farm owned by the Native American state senator William Bishop, whom Burtha tagged "the best-educated Injun I have met in a long time." Spending a few days there lifted Burtha's spirits. "It does my heart good to see some Injuns really progressing," she wrote to Big Foot.

Yet her happiness had evaporated within a couple of weeks of returning to Seattle, where she and Edgar moved into a small house on West Barrett Street. In all likelihood alerted by Edgar's discovery that his would-be employer had not only unilaterally reduced his salary but also failed to land him the promised dates in Montana, she grew suspicious. She then consulted an attorney about the contract she'd signed with the show's producer. The attorney labeled it "the most one-sided affair" he'd ever read. He counseled her to renegotiate it or else "let the whole thing drop." By the first week of April she'd plumped for the second option.

"THE WAY THINGS KEEP TURNING OUT, I guess I am doomed to die a little tramp Injun," she confided in Big Foot. Close though her friendship with him had become, she withheld any reference to the financial and emotional damage wrought upon her by Edgar's drug taking, about which she was growing increasingly bitter. She believed it had "crushed out all the happiness" from her life, and that it was undermining Edgar's musical gifts.

He'd just gone back up to Washington State as part of a double act with Eugene Ferrio, a young French-Canadian who pretended to be his son, Eugene White Elk. Together they posed as representatives of a genuine Native American rights organization named the Society of American Indians. Onstage, the self-styled Dr. White Elk sang a few songs, told stories while playing the piano, and joined Eugene for a demonstration of what they called the "Bear Dance." Eugene also performed a solo routine, billed as the "Dagger Dance." But their act doesn't appear to have prospered. Worse still, Burtha probably discovered that his relationship with Eugene was not purely professional, which would have accounted for her dismayed reference to her husband's taste for "the strange and terrible vices" introduced to Native Americans by Europeans.

Fresh from giving up on the theater production in which she'd invested so much time, energy, and belief, Burtha wasn't about to do the same with her marriage, so she fixed up concert bookings for herself and Edgar in Vancouver. She was perhaps influenced by a desire to put some distance between her husband and Eugene, as well as to take her husband to a city where drugs would be impossible to obtain. If those were her objectives, then she appears to have succeeded in only one of them. She got him away from Eugene, yet drugs were much harder to evade. Cocaine and morphine turned out to be widely available across the border, especially in Vancouver. The big difference was that a sachet cost double the price Edgar would have paid on the streets of Seattle, easily absorbing whatever he earned and apparently compelling Burtha to sell her possessions to cover their other expenses.

Heavy cocaine use did nothing to diminish Edgar's flights of fancy. In Vancouver, he promoted himself as "Chief White Elk, the famous Indian movie star." From the beginning of May when he and Burtha were performing a vaudeville interlude at the theater on the corner of Dunsmuir and Granville Streets, they applied themselves to their work with unusual intensity. They hoped to catch someone's eye and secure a touring contract for the upcoming summer. Presumably on the basis of their earlier contribution to promoting the American release of *Before the White Man Came,* they got to know Jimmy Finch, a veteran Canadian movie huckster. On behalf of a film distribution outfit called Select Pictures, Jimmy was about to supervise the release throughout western Canada of that very movie. He gave Edgar and Burtha a six-month contract to perform at screenings of it.

Just five days after the movie previewed in Vancouver, Edgar and his wife—who was possibly motivated by a desire to rescue their now unhappy relationship—made a life-changing decision. It entailed them adopting a fair-haired, black-eyed fifteen-month-old Native American girl. They called their adoptive baby Ethel Lolita White Elk. And they gave her a Native American name that translated as "Silver Star."

In a letter to Big Foot, the jubilant Burtha broke the news. "Tell Mrs. McWhorter not to get too excited," she wrote, "for she is going to see a wonderful Injun baby one of these days, perhaps soon."

G etting from Vancouver to the quaint fishing town of Nanaimo could take as long as seven and a half hours. The ferry steamed out of the harbor, past the wreck of another ship and toward the blue, densely wooded mountains of Vancouver Island. Edgar and Burtha traveled with their baby daughter wrapped in a traditional papoose that earned her many admiring comments. Silver Star had a way of ogling people that led Burtha to joke that she was their "baby vamp"—a seductress.

Edgar and his family's tour started in Nanaimo. Coated in war paint, Edgar performed some Native American–style chanting as an overture to each screening of *Before the White Man Came*. He also gave a detailed talk, explaining significant yet potentially baffling aspects of the culture portrayed on-screen. Beneath the American Indian's "conventional covering of beads, feathers, and paint," he told his audience, were "highly spiritual" individuals, "possessed of a soul incapable of being conquered by the white man or any other race." In sketching a vivid and reverential picture of "the real American Indian," Edgar said they "saw something of the unseen forces of the universe in every tree, every animal, every bird and every inanimate creation."

To prevent the audience's attention from wandering, Edgar sprinkled his talk with humorous asides. Sometimes he even included a quiz about native life, "unique prizes" being awarded for the first correct answers.

He then sang "La Marseillaise" and other songs. When the last notes had faded, the movie began to roll. Now Edgar just had to kill time until he was due onstage to provide an epilogue. For that, he and Burtha performed an elaborately lit demonstration of Native American ritual dancing. Burtha recited a few of her poems as well, and she delivered a lucid, forceful lecture about her tribe.

Next on their itinerary was the genteel, attractive little city of Victoria, which necessitated a long but scenic journey down Vancouver Island's coastline. Jimmy Finch was there already, ballyhooing the imminent arrival of the "Chief of the Oklahoma Cherokee Indians" and "the last princess of the Klamath tribe."

Packed houses greeted each of their shows at the Victoria Theatre. Large throngs of disappointed people were turned away on a daily basis. Adding to the hullabaloo surrounding their tour, a local journalist remarked, "From the tip of the chief's feathered headdress to his heavily embroidered moccasins, White Elk is a superb picture of an Indian chief."

The customary relish with which the chief responded to the public may have been undercut by a sense of grievance. He and Burtha were, after all, chronically short of money, yet their work was netting sizable profits for Select Pictures and the movie theater owners.

All previous box office records at the Victoria Theatre broken, he and his family proceeded to the coal-mining town of Cumberland, where Jimmy had set up a three-day booking. Their visit to the town climaxed in what was advertised as "Ladies' Night." Scanning the women in the audience, Edgar picked the woman whom he regarded as the best-looking. Then he presented her with "a valuable and handsome souvenir."

Directly after the screening, he transferred to the movie theater's adjoining dance hall, where he moonlighted as an emcee and vocalist, fronting a four-piece band. His repeated boast that he could speak twenty-one languages spurred one of the townsfolk to inquire whether he spoke Scotch.

"No, but I can drink it," he wisecracked.

· · ·

EDGAR AND FAMILY HAD TO be back in Vancouver by Monday, August 1, 1921, when *Before the White Man Came* would be opening at the Columbia Theatre. To drum up attention for the movie, Jimmy started colluding with Edgar in portraying him as one of the stars of the film, and peddling him as "Chief White Elk with His All-Indian Drama." Jimmy also deployed a battery of other promotional gimmicks. The most flamboyant of these involved a local theater manager and sometime vaudevillian chauffeuring Edgar through downtown Vancouver that Saturday morning. Their vehicle joined a lengthy column stretching up Granville Street's gentle grade. Deep crowds stood along the sidewalks, ready for the parade to start. It was being held to celebrate the opening of the Caledonian Games—a big sports event saluting the city's ties to the Scottish highlands.

Just past noon, a military band started playing, the parade began to move, and the sunshine burned away the clouds. Around Edgar, who cut an imposing figure, were other vehicles carrying dignitaries, including the commander of the visiting U.S. fleet and the lieutenant governor of Washington State. Convoying down the road ahead were the military band, three companies of American infantrymen, a troop of cadets, and, in the far distance, a scarlet-uniformed horseback detachment from the Royal Canadian Mounted Police.

Edgar and the others glided past the Hotel Vancouver, where he'd stayed more than two years earlier. Then the parade wound its way across town, packed sidewalks flanking its route. Upward of ten thousand excited people had assembled at Hastings Park by the time Edgar was driven through the entrance. The spectators filled the grandstand and bleachers and spread across the grass, where the contestants in the Caledonian Games were waiting, a high proportion of them in kilts and other items of traditional Scottish costume.

FOR THE REMAINDER OF AUGUST and the first half of September, during which the rain scarcely let up, Edgar and Burtha performed at screenings in Vancouver and neighboring towns where Select Pictures had arranged brief runs of *Before the White Man Came.* But they were playing to dwindling audiences. Seeing so many empty seats only added to the gloom haunting the smile Burtha felt obliged to display.

"This traveling and show business when you have nothing but small-time is getting to be *hell,* and no getting around it," she wrote to Big Foot. She still hadn't confided in him—or anyone else—about Edgar's drug taking, yet she did admit to one thing: "I am awful homesick to see the good old USA again."

Speculation about the impending bankruptcy of Select Pictures didn't lift her mood. She took to crying herself to sleep and grieving over how far her husband had fallen, how he was a "Great Chieftain exiled as a tramp upon the face of the earth with his millions gone."

Despite everything, she felt that her marriage could be salvaged, assuming she and Edgar were able to escape from the prison of low-level vaudeville. If Select Pictures really did go bust, the pair of them resolved to quit show business and settle in Yakima, where three of Burtha's friends—Ben Olney, Big Foot, and his wife—lived. But Select Pictures *didn't* go bust, so Burtha and Edgar persevered with their tour.

It next took them to the town of Blairmore, Alberta, accessible via an epic train ride through the mountains. For the remainder of the fall, they accompanied the movie to a roster of small prairie cities across southern Alberta, the remoteness of these engendering in Burtha a feeling that she'd been exiled from the "world of opportunities." Her escalating depression fostered in her a sense of fatalism, a sense of being condemned to inhabit "the shore of darkness." She could hardly have been less equipped to contribute to the "jolly good time for all" promised to the audiences attending screenings at which she and Edgar performed.

With every venue they checked off their tour list and every sachet of cocaine Edgar snorted, his avowed attainments grew still more overblown. He became not just "a noted Indian tenor," "movie star," and "war hero" who spoke twenty-one languages, but also someone who had "entertained kings, queens, tsars and presidents."

. . .

ONE STEP FORWARD AND EDGAR would be dead. He was standing at the tip of a large expanse of flat rooftop, his arms outstretched. The roof belonged to the Hotel Selkirk in Edmonton. If he turned his head to the left, he could see the rear of a giant sign advertising the hotel. Right in front of him was a three-story drop straight down to the intersection of 101st and Jasper Streets.

The sidewalks below were clotted with passersby in hats and topcoats. So many people had gathered that they spilled onto the road as they waited, not for Edgar to jump, but for him to begin his widely advertised free noonday concert. He belted out his opening number without any accompaniment, his voice drifting over the city, where conditions were mild by Canadian standards.

His rooftop stunt had been scheduled to promote further screenings of *Before the White Man Came*. Billed as "A Real Indian Movie Star," he subsequently attracted lots of attention when he walked around the city and ran through some of his back catalog of tall tales. To these, he added a reference to being the "winner of the six-mile race in the Olympic Games at Greece." Yet there doesn't seem to have been even a flicker of skepticism in Edmonton, where he reassured the locals that he didn't "hold a grudge against the palefaces."

From Christmas into the new year, those palefaces flocked to his shows. Extra screenings at a movie theater in south Edmonton were hastily arranged to capitalize on his popularity. For the benefit of French Canadians, he performed one of these in French. On the basis, as he claimed, that "spiritualism was actually originated, practiced and demonstrated by the Indians long before the white man came," he supplemented the show with a mind-reading act. He'd likely mastered the duplicitous techniques of theatrical mind reading during his time on the vaudeville and medicine show circuits.

Only in the latter half of January 1921 did the Canadian winter assert itself. Braving the icebox conditions, Edgar and Jimmy Finch—minus Burtha and Silver Star—pressed on with the last few dates in their tour. It took them to Wainwright, a small market town over a hundred miles to the southeast. Edgar performed a string of sellout shows there before he and Jimmy lit out for the city of Winnipeg. Dubbed "the Chicago of Canada," it was the final stop on their tour. When they reached Winnipeg, Edgar appears to have bragged to the local press about having "royal Indian ancestry on both his father's and his mother's side." Edgar also seems to have claimed kinship to the fictitious Long Lance dynasty of Cherokee chieftains, little realizing that Sylvester Long Lance, famous Canadian-based survivor of the Princess Pat Regiment, would soon face accusations of being a racial impostor.

In Winnipeg that February, Edgar played as many as four shows each day to rapturously applauding capacity crowds at the plush 1,200-seat Starland Theater. Milking his popularity, he crammed in several unrelated engagements, including a concert in the gymnasium at the main police station and a sequence of spiritualist shows, during which he took the well-established role of the Native American spirit guide, acting as a conduit between this world and the next.

Even after he'd played his last date at the Starland, he remained in Winnipeg, luxuriating in the acclaim. Jimmy was meanwhile set to leave for Toronto, from where he'd be overseeing *Before the White Man Came*'s release across eastern Canada. Despite Chief White Elk's pivotal role in the success of the movie in the western provinces, Edgar was not going to have the opportunity to extend his collaboration with Jimmy, the two of them having probably fallen out. Prior to Jimmy's departure, Edgar appears to have obtained informal compensation by helping himself to the trunk that Jimmy kept at the Starland. Inside were possessions worth $500—enough to bankroll Edgar's next move.

Whatever he decided upon, he wouldn't be joined by Burtha. She'd come to what she described as "the terrible realization" that her "tired, worn mind and body" could no longer cope with her husband's drug addiction, that she must "submit herself to the inevitable," that she must leave him for the sake of their baby daughter. Only then did she unburden herself in a letter to Big Foot: "I stand ALONE! All alone, with a baby's clinging arms around my neck. Her tears were falling when I left—it broke my heart."

Finally she confessed to her friend about Edgar's drug addiction, describing it as the "secret that has practically ruined my whole life." Sadness colored her references to Edgar. "The dark gulf of silence rolls between us in this life, and through Eternity perhaps that same dark gulf will roll where his hands may reach out to mine and I to his, but they may never meet," she wrote. "I know not where his moccasined feet tread in the wilderness of despair and utter ruin."

PART II

Continental Grift

14

By November 1922 Edgar's moccasined feet were nowhere near "the wilderness of despair" where Burtha assumed he'd been exiled. Together with as many as thirteen hundred other passengers, he was aboard an ocean liner called the SS *Regina,* which had not long before peeled away from the quayside in Halifax, Nova Scotia. Looming over the harbor was a rocky outcrop crowned by a fortress that gradually shrank as the ship made her way out to sea, columns of smoke tumbling from her brown and black hooped funnels, livery of the White Star Dominion Line.

With Edgar on the *Regina* was Eugene Ferrio, the young French Canadian who had appeared alongside him onstage a little over eighteen months before. Until recently, Eugene had been working in one of Halifax's hotels, and lodging with an older male lover. Now he was passing himself off as Edgar's secretary. Of course, the threat of being arrested on a sodomy charge, which could lead to five years in a Canadian jail, offered a potent incentive to conceal the fact that Eugene's role was sexual rather than administrative.

At present the two of them were en route to England via Portland, Maine. Not much more than three years had passed since the first nonstop transatlantic flight, yet commercial aviation between the United States and England was still well over a decade away, so the journey had to be accomplished by sea. On the grounds that he was a Canadian Indian who didn't possess Canadian citizenship and could not therefore obtain a passport, Edgar was traveling under a Certificate of Identity, which named him as Dr. White Elk. He had lately talked the Canadian Immigration Officer into issuing it.

What prompted him to cross the Atlantic again was a desire to try his luck on the English stage. His decision followed the successful example of his theatrical model, Chauncey Olcott, and a host of other American performers who had made the trip. Knowing that his English adventure would've appalled his Francophile father, who detested Britain, may have made it more attractive still. Another consideration liable to have influenced Edgar was an awareness of the immediate circumstances. Salient among those was the European vogue for all things American. It had been kindled by the wartime presence of American troops who had introduced Europeans to their stylish lingo, as well as to catchy songs by Irving Berlin and others. Those troops had brought with them regimental bands, too— bands that played jazz and ragtime, the perceived idealism and youthful energy of their culture promising to revitalize a ravaged continent.

Skewing the odds further in Edgar's direction was the British fascination with Native Americans, so famously manifested by the popularity of Buffalo Bill's Wild West show. It had toured Britain three times, the last of these almost two decades earlier, whooping, war-bonneted Native Americans playing a prominent role. More recent encouragement for Edgar came from newspaper articles about the 1919 visit to the British Dominion of Canada by King George V's son, the Prince of Wales. Often they featured a photo of the prince dressed as a Native American. Edgar must have seen these and filed them away in his head for future use.

FIRST-CLASS TRANSATLANTIC TICKETS FOR BOTH Eugene and himself would have set Edgar back about $400. Such extravagance entitled them to their own cabins and to facilities that were inaccessible to the hoi polloi. Life aboard the *Regina* could scarcely have been further removed from the conditions under which Edgar had made his last transatlantic voyage.

Unless a one-in-a-million sequence of events culminated in another war breaking out before he completed the crossing, he wouldn't have to worry about U-boats this time. And he'd be able to avail himself of facilities alien to the U.S. Army Transport Service.

In the *Regina*'s communal lounge, dining saloon, and reading room, there were marble fireplaces, white tablecloths, and chintz-upholstered armchairs. Even the main stairway was adorned with decorative plaster-work and a mural depicting a lovely pastoral scene. These communal interiors might have been part of some classy East Coast hotel, their true location belied only by the movement of the ship, the hum of its engines, and the watery views from its windows.

After no more than a day at sea, the *Regina* docked at one of Portland's three undersized wharves. Next to these were a series of vast steamship sheds as well as several derricks and grain elevators.

During the *Regina*'s brief layover in Portland, Edgar gave an interview to a journalist from Reuters news agency, who was presumably attracted by his name's presence on the passenger list, accompanied by the phrase "Indian Chief." He told the Reuters correspondent that he was head of the Indian tribes of British Columbia, that he was a graduate of Carlisle, that he worked as a lecturer, and that he'd acted in the recent hit movie *The Sheik*—a movie starring Rudolph Valentino, among the world's most famous people. But Edgar didn't stop there. Succumbing to his compulsion to see how far he could take his lies, he spoke of being on his way to England to present his people's grievances to King George V, a concept perhaps inspired by Chief Red Fox's talk of riding across America to petition President Wilson. Edgar explained that he was seeking many reforms, mostly with regard to the education of Indians. He also mentioned that he'd already met the Prince of Wales and toured Canada with him. The prince had, he said, presented him with a diamond tiepin. Edgar pretended to have been puzzled by how he should wear it. He claimed that he'd tried wearing it on his clothes and in his hair, but he'd eventually opted to have a skilled dentist inset the diamond into his teeth. Ostensible evidence for his story was provided every time he smiled.

Over the following few days, newspapers in America, Canada, Britain, and France carried reports of his mission to speak to the British monarch.

Outlandish though the story of Chief White Elk's journey may have seemed, it was not short of precedents. Ever since the early seventeenth century, Native American political delegations had been traveling to England. By announcing that he was chief of the tribes of British Columbia, Edgar was, however, taking a giant risk. He might easily be rumbled by some knowledgeable journalist or newspaper reader.

THE PASSENGER LIST WOULD HAVE been slipped under the door of Edgar's cabin once the SS *Regina* left Portland. For those traveling first-class, this human inventory was essential reading. Careful perusal of its constituent names and associated titles yielded the key to a socially advantageous crossing. A word in the appropriate ear and Edgar could procure a seat at the dining table of anyone he wanted.

Etiquette dictated that Edgar's fellow first-class passengers wore evening dress to dinner, its approach signaled by a bugle playing "The Roast Beef of Old England." On the initial night of a transatlantic voyage, the dining saloon was traditionally sedate, even though alcohol could be dispensed immediately after the ship exited U.S. coastal waters, where Prohibition still held sway. Diners tended to devote all their energy to feigning nonchalance while their seasick companions bolted from the room.

A pageant of food and drink nonetheless formed the spine of the ship's routine, which gave Edgar an insight into the structure and wearying predictability that he'd gone to such lengths to exclude from his life. Breakfast was served between 8:00 and 10:00 a.m., cups of hot broth at 11:00, sandwiches at noon, lunch at 1:00 p.m., plus a selection of pastries and sorbets at 3:00. Those passengers who had not already lapsed into overstuffed lethargy, more closely resembling the product of taxidermy than cooking, could then look forward to sandwiches and cakes at 4:00 p.m., fruit compote at 5:00, dinner at 7:00, then coffee, tea, or liqueurs, rounded off by fresh fruit and ice cream at 9:00.

Invariably occupying the rest of the time were epic games of bridge, poker, whist, and backgammon. There were sporting tournaments, concerts, and dances as well. Additional distraction came from wagers on anything from the captain's age to the contents of the dinner menu. And professional entertainers were called upon to give performances. Much to his delight, Edgar wound up singing for the other passengers at a charity fundraising concert, the takings from which he probably pocketed.

"I'm the first Indian baritone," he told his fellow passengers, among whom he made himself very popular over the next eight days. Several of the other passengers felt relaxed enough in his company to get into bantering conversations with him. His excellent command of English, his cultured accent, and his features, "which might easily be taken for an Englishman, whose complexion was well-tanned by an open-air life," led them to tease him repeatedly about being an Englishman in disguise.

Perhaps having first spotted Major George Harrington, president of the Canada Club of Great Britain, on the passenger list, Edgar befriended the thirty-nine-year-old major, who was a pint-sized, warm-spirited raconteur. The two of them could trade war stories, because the major had served in France before becoming a deputy minister in the Canadian government. Harrington turned out to own Britain's earliest fur farm, to which he was exporting twenty silver-black foxes, whose pelts were destined for the garment industry.

But there was more to him than business and politics. He was a passionate campaigner for better conditions in Nova Scotia's mines, his work yielding apparent common ground with Edgar, who claimed to be a campaigner on behalf of the Cherokee. So spellbound was Major Harrington by Edgar that he offered to provide him with London accommodation as a guest of the Canada Club. Unlike many of the British capital's other historic clubs, which had their own guest rooms, Harrington's organization was a dining club without its own premises. When the ship docked, he'd have to book a London hotel room for Edgar.

AT 1:00 A.M. ON SUNDAY, December 17, 1922, the *Regina* entered the waters of the Mersey estuary. By then, Edgar and Eugene would have been surrounded by the ruckus that always preceded docking. Chambermaids helped the passengers pack their suitcases and trunks. Liveried cabin boys darted along the indoor corridors and outdoor gangways. Intensifying the commotion that night was the rapidly spreading news about one of Edgar and Eugene's fellow first-class passengers. The young man in question was found lying in a pool of blood. He'd slit his own throat with a razor. Barely alive, he was treated by the ship's doctor and then carried back to his cabin.

More unforeseen drama lay ahead of Edgar and Eugene prior to their arrival in Liverpool. As their ship skirted the righthand bank of the broad river, where chimneys and rooftops peeked over miles of dockside cranes and warehouses, several tugboats scurried back and forth through the icy waters. Only a few hours earlier, a freighter had sunk along this stretch of river. The tugs were conducting a fruitless search for several missing crewmen.

A few miles further upstream, the *Regina* docked at a vast floating quayside with customs offices on it and several bridges linking it to the shore. Edgar's outfit turned heads when he disembarked. He had on a turkey feather bonnet, a scarlet coat, and a beaded white apron that incorporated a green and blue floral pattern. Completing his get-up were wide-legged bright green pants with a pale stripe down them, stippled by yet more beads.

Thirty-four-year-old Edgar—in the guise of the impressively youthful-looking *fifty-eight-year-old* Dr. Ray Tewanna, Chief White Elk—was given a deferential welcome by a gaggle of reporters. They worked for newspapers as disparate as the London *Times* and the *Yorkshire Post and Leeds Intelligencer.* With them was a posse of press photographers. For their benefit, Edgar struck a suitably serious, purse-lipped pose.

Flashbulbs were not yet available, so the photographers brandished T-shaped holders loaded with explosive powder. Igniting at the press of a button that showered it with sparks, the powder emitted a loud, hollow *whoosh,* a powerful whiff of ammonia, and a glare dazzling enough to bleach Edgar's unsmiling face and make him squint.

He talked to the press corps about each component of his outfit. He said his feathered bonnet was part of his regalia as chief of the Cherokee. It was, he added, made sixty years ago for his grandfather. Each of its thirty-two plumes had, so his story went, been plucked from a different golden eagle. He even took the trouble to coin a name for his imaginary grandfather: "Chief Cuner Parker."

When speaking about the apron he wore, he liked to tell people that its dark blue maple leaf stood for war, its light green leaves opposite signifying the brighter days that would come afterward, its yellow threads symbolizing the ill health brought by the European invaders, its beaded white background standing for purity, "which we possessed before the advent of the white man." And when he moved on to the beadwork down the front of his pants, he said it depicted the mystic emblems of the Cherokee.

But his accent and comportment seem to have provoked a certain amount of distrust. His riposte was to assure the reporters that he wouldn't have been permitted to wear his headdress and associated attire unless he were an American Indian. To explain his Europeanized manner, he said he'd been educated at Yale University and the Rush Medical Institute, earning degrees in medicine, philosophy, and the arts. He also told the reporters that he'd served in the Royal Navy during the last war and that he'd come back to England as an emissary of the Cherokee people.

"I hope to have the opportunity of pleading with His Majesty the King for a more efficient education for all the members of my race in the Dominion of Canada," he explained. "We want better educational facilities so that we may become better citizens. The bulk of the Indians in the Dominion do not receive such chances and they are cooped up on reservations where they have no incentive to get the education which it is the privilege of the average Canadian citizen to obtain. It is the policy of the Canadian government to keep the Indians in their reservations, but not all of them have the instinct for the camp life now, and they are capable of something better. They are capable of becoming good and useful citizens and of living in towns and cities."

He went on to express optimism about his mission and spoke with ill-informed flattery about the British people: "They appreciate you for what you are, and it doesn't matter what color you are." Getting into his stride, he also spoke about his supposed tour of Canada with the Prince of Wales. Edgar now claimed to have been one of the five Indian chiefs who had awarded the prince an honorary title: "Chief Morning Star."

Soon Edgar's impromptu press conference was over. He then faced the same potentially nervous wait that followed the opening night of a vaudeville show. But he was in this instance awaiting reviews of a different nature, reviews that would have an even greater impact. If the press didn't buy his stories, he couldn't do what he did back home—just travel to the next city and go through the same routine. National newspapers in Britain, which did not yet exist in America, threatened to make that impossible. Any exposés of him would spread across the country with epidemic speed.

EDGAR MADE THE SHORT TRIP from the docks to the center of Liverpool, where—probably accompanied by his "secretary"—he checked in to the 550-room Midland Adelphi Hotel. Popular with rich transatlantic travelers, this was among the grandest of Britain's hotels, its marble-lined stairwell and much-vaunted atmosphere of refinement presaging exceptionally comfortable, centrally heated rooms.

Later that day, Edgar had the opportunity to adjust to the differences between North America and Britain, to the decorum of British waiters and desk clerks, to the way men didn't always remove their hats indoors, to the linguistic variations, to the guineas, half crowns, sovereigns, and other idiosyncratic coinage. Above all, he could forget about Prohibition and order a glass of wine to go with his lunch.

Wandering around the Midland Adelphi's maze of hallways, he entered what was once a ballroom and an adjoining lounge. The Voss Motor Galleries, open for business even on a Sunday, now filled these two rooms. A selection of twenty of the latest cars manufactured by Daimler, Napier, and other companies were parked there. Edgar paused to admire the brand-new vehicles, his feathered headdress and the rest of his outfit reflected in their paintwork. By passing appreciative comment on the skills of British coachbuilders, he curried favor with one of the sales staff, his perfect English and gentlemanly demeanor causing a certain amount of surprise. He added that the automobiles on display were far more beautiful than their American equivalents. When he remarked on how much smaller British cars were, he was ushered over to a soft-topped Austin Seven. The sight of this petite two-seater amused Edgar, who expressed doubt when he heard it was capable of carrying a full load at fifty miles per hour.

The owner of the dealership informed him that the Austin Seven—

"absurdly cheap to run"—was the smallest four-cylinder motorcar currently produced in the British Empire, but the dealer's patter failed to banish Edgar's mirthful incredulity. So the dealer asked if he'd care for a test-drive.

He accepted, though he must've had trouble folding his long limbs into the driver's seat. For a man of his size, the Austin Seven was more like a tight-fitting coat than an automobile. Its rudimentary instrumentation and interior certainly bore scant resemblance to those of the Studebaker he'd owned when he and Burtha were together.

From the Midland Adelphi Hotel, he piloted the car through the center of Liverpool, where the streets—yet to sprout pedestrian crossings or stoplights—would have been relatively quiet. Around him were lots of new buildings, which made it feel like an American city, though its air of modernity was diminished by the number of horse-drawn carts and cabs. Leafless trees emphasized the wintry bleakness as he drove through the city's parks.

Afterward he returned to the Midland Adelphi, an enormous, smooth, stone-jacketed building, outside of which a crowd awaited him. While he was still sitting in the Austin Seven, its soft-top folded down, a small child in a woolly hat approached him from the driver's side. Her face wasn't much higher than the steering wheel. She started crying when she saw Edgar in his regalia. Without getting out of the vehicle, he calmed her down. Then he removed his golden bracelet and placed it around the awestruck girl's wrist.

THE VERDICT ON EDGAR'S QUAYSIDE press conference was delivered by next morning's newspapers. If he had any worries about how the British press would portray him, these were rendered redundant by the uniformly supportive reviews he earned. He'd have been able to read and reread them, because he—and presumably Eugene, too—had a few hours to spare before they boarded a steam train down to London, the cars of which were divided into unfamiliar little compartments seating a maximum of eight passengers. Ahead of them was a journey timetabled at up to six hours. Parading across the window beside Edgar were the soot-blackened Liverpool suburbs, long stretches of farmland, and a sequence of small towns that soon dissolved in the encroaching darkness.

Night had fallen by the time he stepped onto one of the platforms at Euston Station, smoke from his train swirling beneath the low roof. Uniformed staff were ready to assist passengers with their luggage. Bewilderment registered on the porters' faces at the sight of Edgar's conspicuously colorful getup.

A reporter from the *Daily Express* likely chose this moment to corner Edgar, who spouted the usual stories about himself. "I have brought with me presents for the Prince of Wales from the Canadian Boy Scouts," he added. "These include a shield with a maple leaf in buckskin, inscribed with the names of all the subscribers."

Given that only a mile and a half of low-rise streets and antiquated buildings separated the train station from the Grosvenor Court Hotel, where he'd be staying, that final leg of the journey wouldn't have taken long. His hotel lay at the intersection of Oxford and Davies Streets, just across from a Lyons Corner House, part of a busy café chain. The realization that the Grosvenor Court was, for all its comforts, not among the city's most distinguished hotels may have been a source of dismay to Edgar. Yet the scenario wasn't without its consolations. Thanks to Major Harrington, his friend from the SS *Regina,* the Canada Club was paying for him to have a suite of rooms, which included the luxury of a private bathroom. The suite provided more than enough space for Eugene, too.

As Edgar and Eugene may have discovered since their arrival in Liverpool, the British tended to regard homosexuals with contempt. Particular scorn was reserved for the more visible of them—effeminate male homosexuals, or "nancy boys" in the pejorative slang of the era. Though sex between men was illegal in Britain at that period, hotels such as the Grosvenor Court were willing to accommodate male couples, so long as they didn't flaunt their sexuality. Despite this relative tolerance, Edgar and Eugene ran the risk that someone might report them to the police. Were that to happen, they could wind up being deported, sentenced to up to five years in jail, or even whipped.

Edgar lunched at the majestic Hotel Cecil, where the dining room looked across a wide stretch of the Thames, one of the world's busiest waterways, along which hefty barges were towed by steamers uncorking genies of smoke. On what was only his second afternoon in London, he'd been a guest of the British Association of Rotary Clubs. Even at this private event, Chief White Elk's celebrity attracted a reporter, who admired his "gorgeous" ensemble. Afforded the chance to talk about his mooted audience with the king, Edgar stressed the altruism of his own motives. "I want to convey to Great Britain first of all the renewal of our pledge of loyalty," he said. "At all times we shall be ready, as during the war, to follow the tracks of our forefathers and to guard and protect the colors in which we pledge our loyalty to His Majesty and to Great Britain."

Leaving the reporter with the impression that he was "one of the most picturesque personalities that has ever visited this country," Edgar exited the hotel, which had a taxi turnaround in front of it. Doormen wearing military-looking attire stood outside establishments such as the Cecil, waiting for departing customers. In what tended to be genteel accents that failed to disguise their Cockney origins, the doormen would say to the likes of Edgar, "Keb, sir?"

Probably utilizing this service, Edgar and Eugene boarded a cab. It would have taken them past the platoon of aging tin toy vendors who treated the sidewalk beyond the taxi turnaround as their counter. Little clockwork horses and errand boys hauling miniature trunks made erratic, darting movements that forced Christmas shoppers to improvise ungainly dance steps.

Seated in the taxi, Edgar and Eugene were driven over to the gentle arc of Regent Street. Pricey clothes stores, furriers, and jewelers dominated the early-nineteenth-century premises on either side. Interspersed with these were gutted buildings, vacant lots, and construction sites— something Edgar must have noticed on most streets in the city's West End, which vibrated with the hammering of demolition crews. A number of the surviving stores currently visible through the windows of Edgar's cab displayed the royal coat of arms, indicating that they had the honor of supplying goods to the royal household. If Edgar's plans worked out, he'd soon be a guest of that household.

He had already requested his much-trumpeted audience with King George V. To maximize the chances of having his request granted, Edgar couldn't risk being seen around town in anything other than his interpretation of Cherokee costume. Over his normal outfit, he was now wearing a black lamb's fur coat, necessitated by the plummeting temperature. Sharpening the chill was a wind fierce enough to wobble his taxi and jiggle the silver medallion that hung from his neck.

Hard to believe that the weather had been mild to the point of mugginess the day before. He hadn't needed a fur coat when he'd found his way over to Trafalgar Square, then clambered onto one of the huge stone plinths at the base of Nelson's Column. Sprawled across the plinth was a massive sculpture of a lion. Edgar had positioned himself in front of the creature's paws and then addressed the big crowd forming around him. Among the crowd was a press photographer, whose picture of Edgar ended up featuring in many of the newspapers that people were reading on the afternoon of his cab ride. Edgar might not have been too pleased, though, by the *Daily Sketch*'s decision to juxtapose his photo with a shot of a troupe of Russian midgets.

A little further down Regent Street, natural preserve of silk-stockinged window-shoppers, Edgar's cab pulled up. He and Eugene got out. Edgar—whose feathered headdress attracted the attention he craved—was instantly pounced upon by another reporter. She said she'd been hunting for him for the past couple of days.

He gave a hearty laugh. "Is that what women do in England?" he said, turning toward Eugene in a show of amusement. "Fancy *women* hunting men . . ."

Ditching his tone of jokey disbelief, he was soon talking about his favorite topic—himself. "I hope to have an audience with His Majesty, but please don't imagine I have any grievance to talk about." He added that his only son had died not long back, leaving him as the last hereditary chief of the Cherokee. "My people were the first real Canadians," he said, his fruity voice cutting through the street noise. "We are descended from the Iroquois, who inhabited North America long before any European races." Just in case he hadn't won over the newswoman, he deployed a burst of flattery. "London is a great surprise to me. It is larger and much more wonderful than I imagined. I don't think New York compares with it."

His sidewalk interview concluded, he and Eugene headed for their destination. This was likely the Café Royal, on the fringe of Soho, a neighborhood associated with homosexuality and drug dealing. Edgar would have been able to buy cocaine from the young women who pounded the streets carrying drawstring handbags that subtly advertised their wares. Purchasing drugs was risky, though. If caught in possession of them, he could be arraigned on felony charges. And there was a certain amount of risk associated with picking up young men, too. Many of the established cruising grounds were kept under surveillance by the police, who targeted them with agent provocateur operations.

Through the doors of the perennially fashionable Café Royal, where many of the regulars shared Edgar's taste for narcotics, were multiple bars and restaurants, all with red-plush-upholstered seating and tobacco-stained ceilings. Private dining rooms were also available, the tables swathed in crisp white damask and laid with floral-patterned Minton china and long-stemmed glasses brimming with vintage wines and champagne. Tall, gilt-framed mirrors reflected the movements of a disparate clientele. Aristocrats. Beautiful young women, employed as artists' models. Groups of Frenchmen, playing dominoes. Leading figures from the arts, not least the suave playwright and actor Noël Coward.

By throwing parties at chic venues like the Café Royal and at the kind of nightclubs where dance bands provided a watered-down interpretation of jazz, first popularized in Britain not quite four years previously, Edgar began to infiltrate the world of moneyed London. On the understanding that he was about to receive a stupendous windfall from King George V, who was set to return to him a million acres annexed by the British government, he appears to have been able to borrow money from his wealthy new acquaintances—money that could fund his self-aggrandizing extravagance.

EDGAR WAS IN THE AUDIENCE watching *The Private Secretary*—not his own nominal secretary, but a newly revived Victorian farce, staged at a handsome and capacious theater just down the street from Trafalgar Square. Creaky though the play turned out to be, its rollicking portrayal of two rogues assuming false identities in order to thwart their creditors tickled Edgar, whose merriment must have been rather more knowing than that of most other members of the audience.

When he left the Playhouse Theatre and crossed the West End, he'd have seen the animated electric advertising signs that had become a prominent feature of every main road. People would sometimes pause in front of these signs, mesmerized by the free show. One of these advertisements, composed of hundreds of lightbulbs, was near Edgar's hotel. The sign depicted a hand reaching toward a cabinet containing a gramophone and then placing the gramophone's arm onto a record, crimson musical notes floating out of the cabinet as the record spun.

But Edgar's chances of showing off his own musical talents on the London stage were not looking promising. He only had to talk to a theatrical agent or someone else in the business to discover how wrongheaded his original plan had been. Finding employment in the British equivalent of vaudeville, known as either "music hall" or "variety," wouldn't be easy, because he'd been unlucky enough to arrive when the business was in the middle of a protracted slump. Performers who once commanded sizable salaries had to accept a 50 percent pay cut. Others were reduced to selling combs and soap on the sidewalks. There were even tales of minor celebrities from the worlds of opera and movies working as buskers.

Suffice it to say it was no surprise that Edgar's attempt to obtain bookings on Sir Oswald Stoll's illustrious theater circuit met with disappointment. Edgar then turned his attention to what was, in the business, referred to as "the Gulliver Circuit." Headquartered in a warren of offices at the Holborn Empire, a large nineteenth-century building on High Holborn, this comprised sixteen theaters run by Charles Gulliver. Conveniently for Edgar, most of these were in and around London, though the problems afflicting the business left him with few grounds for optimism. There was a surfeit of other out-of-work novelty acts into the bargain. Up against him were Victor Niblo's Talking Birds; Chung Wang, the Chinese Magician; Zingaro, the Royal Gypsy Instrumentalist; to say nothing of Professor J. Raymond and His Electrically Controlled Automaton.

POSITIONED ONLY ABOUT A HUNDRED YARDS from the raggedy hem of southeast London, where houses gave way to fields, 60a Leyland Road was one of a row of large detached two-story Victorian properties. It had a bay window facing the broad, silver birch–lined road.

Homes were in short supply throughout the capital, so Edgar had been fortunate to be able to move into these five upstairs rooms not long after Christmas. He rented them using the name Dr. Tewanna. With him were Eugene and two other young men Eugene had befriended. Eugene's friends probably came from the city's flourishing yet unobtrusive gay subculture, which revolved around specific pubs, restaurants, parks, theaters, and public toilets (the latter known as "cottages").

Sharing the Leyland Road apartment, which backed onto a series of big, oblong gardens, was something of a comedown for Edgar after the luxury and metropolitan bustle of the Grosvenor Court Hotel. Still, he couldn't expect the Canada Club to keep paying his tab indefinitely.

Whenever he strode out of the house in full regalia, complete with feathered headdress, he was bound to provoke stares. After all, he wasn't just exotic—he was *famous,* thanks to yet more press coverage. Side by side with a picture of Britain's deputy commissioner of police, his photo had featured in the "Personalities of the Week" section of the *Illustrated London News.* And he'd appeared alongside Andrew Bonar Law—the country's prime minister—on the front page of the popular *Daily Graphic.*

Edgar's new apartment was more than seven miles from the West End, making his fondness for traveling by taxi expensive. The most direct route took him past a billiard hall and then through the squalid blue-collar neighborhoods on London's south side, row houses, pubs, small stores, and myriad businesses fringing the often-constricted streets, their sidewalks and slate roofs frequently coated by the chill sheen of winter drizzle.

In mid-January 1923—some two weeks after he'd taken the apartment—Edgar had his first taste of what locals called a "London particular," a phenomenon so well-known he'd likely have heard about it back home. Leyland Road and surrounding districts were swathed in smog. Not the soft, damp mist that sometimes hung over American cities, but a noxious, yellowish vapor that rendered day indistinguishable from night. Crossing town to a children's charity event, where Chief White Elk was the star attraction, would have been an unnerving and time-consuming experience for Edgar and Eugene. All over London, buses, cars, and trains were slowed to a nervous crawl. Watery eyes and coughing were other by-products of the smog. It lent the now-familiar sights and sounds an eerie unfamiliarity. Noises became strangely muted. People became ghosts, coalescing, then dispersing. And the steam-powered trucks that prowled the streets became sinister, fire-belching demons.

Mere smog wasn't sufficient, though, to prevent Edgar and Eugene from getting to Westminster for the children's charity event, where Eugene made himself useful. Not as a secretary, but as a minder, fending off scores of overexcited youngsters who were trying to pluck feathers from Edgar's headdress.

Leaving the party, Edgar and Eugene may have passed the railings in front of Buckingham Palace, the London home of the monarch with whom Edgar had solicited a meeting. Soon after the trip to Westminster, his request triggered an announcement from the king's offices at St. James's Palace. King George V would, according to the communiqué, be granting Chief White Elk an audience. Edgar could now start thinking ahead to the moment when some royal flunky presented him to the king. For everyone but Edgar, his encounter with the king would appear to be a meeting of equals, of two hereditary leaders of their people.

CANADIAN, AMERICAN, FRENCH, SWISS, New Zealand, and Australian newspapers had—unknown to Edgar in all probability—devoted space to the Cherokee chief's mission to see the king. St. James's Palace said the audience would take place as soon as His Majesty returned from his country estate at Sandringham. To ensure that the palace didn't let the arrangement slide, Edgar appears to have written to the Duke of Devonshire, asking for his assistance. Formerly viceroy of Canada, the duke had been installed as secretary of state for the colonies. He apparently replied that he thought he'd be able to get the palace to schedule the audience for the beginning of February.

Addicted not just to drugs and alcohol but also to audiences of any kind, Edgar found himself conversing with a *Daily Mail* reporter, whose questions took a potentially uncomfortable turn. "Are you a Canadian Indian?" the reporter inquired.

"I am a hereditary chief of the Cherokee," Edgar answered. "I am Cherokee royalty."

"People are wondering why, as you are not a Canadian resident or Canadian born, you should come over on behalf of the Canadian Indians."

Even that failed to catch out Edgar, who said quickly, "The Cherokee see no boundaries. We were there before the boundaries were made." He must have been grateful that the reporter was querying only his nationality, *not* his race.

"When are you making your first appearance on the music hall stage in this country?"

Annoyance coloring his response, he replied, "*Who* told you about this?"

"But isn't it true that you are starting a Stoll tour?"

"It certainly *isn't.*"

"Have negotiations fallen through?"

"Well, they have," he conceded. "I am opening at the Woolwich Hippodrome on Monday in 'Native Dances.' As a matter of fact, I am starting a Gulliver tour." He then asked how the reporter had got to hear that he was a music hall performer.

The reporter explained that there'd been a tip-off from a Canadian who remembered him performing in Vancouver.

"It's right," Edgar said with mock frankness. "I have been in the theatrical business since 1901 when I opened in *Antony and Cleopatra* as a fan-bearer."

"WE HAVE UNDERTAKEN EXTENSIVE INQUIRIES through Canadian correspondents," the ensuing *Daily Mail* article declared. "The results are given below. The Indian Department of the Canadian Government has no official knowledge of his visit. They say he is not a British Columbian Indian and has no authority to call himself one. Boy Scout headquarters in Canada say that he has not been entrusted by the general body of Canadian Boy Scouts to make any representations to the Prince of Wales.

"Certain English newspapers reported that White Elk accompanied the Prince of Wales on his visit to Canada, and escorted him when he was made Chief Morning Star. Prominent members of the Prince of Wales's train on that occasion cannot recall anyone by the name of Chief White Elk.

"In authoritative quarters he is believed to be an American Indian and not a Canadian Indian, and therefore not entitled to make any representations of Canadian Indians to the King."

Besides spawning similar pieces in newspapers across Canada, the article in the *Daily Mail* squelched Edgar's impending audience with King George V.

IMPOSTOR UNMASKED shouted the headline that appeared the day before Edgar's debut at the Woolwich Hippodrome. As an inveterate reader of newspapers, he may well have been confronted by it when he opened the

News of the World, a widely read Sunday scandal sheet. But the story was about someone else.

Characterized by the prosecutor as a "clever, persistent and plausible scoundrel," the man in question was being tried for the latest in a sequence of frauds that had seen him pose as an Irish freedom fighter and a lieutenant general in the Mexican army. His prosecution offered Edgar a reminder of the risks run by con men like them.

IN WOOLWICH THE NEXT MORNING, Edgar would have been required to attend a rehearsal known as "band call." To get there from his apartment entailed a four-mile journey through south London. Even though the smog wasn't as bad as it had been, it was still pronounced enough to make Edgar feel like he was peering through a dirty windshield.

Shoulder to shoulder with the domed, classical-style Town Hall, Woolwich Hippodrome was a bulky redbrick building. It would already have been advertising that week's show. Topping the bill was "White Elk, Chief of the Cherokee Indians."

Edgar would have been instructed to report to the Hippodrome's stage, which was separated from the steeply raked and multilayered late Victorian auditorium by an orchestra pit. Convention dictated that Edgar brought with him multiple copies of the score for his act's musical accompaniment. He and the rest of the cast were obliged to place their scores along the lip of the stage in sequence of arrival. Each act then rehearsed with the Hippodrome's band, the order of arrival dictating the order of rehearsal.

The main purpose of Monday morning band call was for the orchestra to master all the required musical cues. Joining Edgar would have been a juggler, a classical violinist, and a comedian who adopted the persona of a banjo- and ukelele-strumming vagrant. There was also a troupe of unicyclists, whose brisk and zany act involved performing tricks while playing drums, tambourines, and cymbals. Uncomplicated by comparison, Edgar's routine featured nothing more than a couple of songs and a demonstration of a Cherokee war dance.

Rehearsals would have alerted him to the stylistic differences between American vaudeville and British variety shows. Once he and the other artistes were done with their Monday morning ritual, they were free to while away the afternoon preceding their 6:30 p.m. debut—the dreaded "first house" when performers felt under the most strain. Meager audiences, a high proportion of them on free tickets, their jollity yet to be unshackled by alcohol, didn't make those shows any less taxing.

Being at the Woolwich Hippodrome rather than one of the higher-grade West End theaters, Edgar's twice-nightly performances failed to attract any reviewers from the London evening papers. He had to be satisfied with a brief write-up in the less-than-exalted pages of the *Woolwich Herald*. It lavished praise on his singing and remarked upon how his "war dance as danced by his forefathers on the North American frontier is well worth seeing."

After the final performance of his six-day engagement at the Hippodrome, Edgar had the chance to play the big shot. On those occasions, artistes were expected to tip the band, stagehands, and other employees at the theater, the size of the tips relative to the performer's position on the bill. If he could afford it, Edgar always dispensed generous gratuities.

Entrusting the Leyland Road apartment to Eugene and the two other young tenants, he set out a short time later on his theatrical tour, surely armed with a stash of drugs. His tour began in Birmingham, a little under two hours from London via the Great Western Railway's nonstop express. Toward the end of the journey, undulating farmland imperceptibly merged with factories and smoke-plumed chimneys, which served as a curtain-raiser to the drab industrial city beyond.

Before boarding the train, Edgar would have been issued with a list of Birmingham landladies who specialized in letting rooms to theatrical performers. Variety artistes customarily traveled on Sunday morning and spent that afternoon working through those addresses until they found accommodation. Trudging around wintry Birmingham in his Cherokee outfit, which had acquired a modish aura, similar costumes having been modeled in the British press by two of the figureheads of international fashion, he'd have been about as inconspicuous as a nudist strolling down a Manhattan street.

On Monday morning he'd have gone through the usual rehearsals prefacing his week at the Aston Hippodrome. Just to the north of the midtown area, this was another massive theater, at which he was head-lining a different lineup. Away from the supervision of his booking agent, he cheekily expanded his time onstage by supplementing his routine with a speech about himself, about qualifying as a doctor and earning several other university degrees. He added that he'd come to England to cam-paign for members of Canada's Indian tribes to be admitted to British universities.

While he was in Birmingham, he'd have been reminded of just how far removed provincial England was from everything that was coming to define the 1920s. Each mile from London carried him further into a world of rigid propriety that had barely been eroded by the atmosphere of youthful rebellion slowly transforming the capital. His indiscreet liaisons with younger men, whom he must have picked up during off-duty hours, scandalized the locals despite British show business's reputation for open-mindedness toward homosexuals.

Tittle-tattle bubbling in his wake, he moved on to the attractive ca-thedral town of Worcester, where he had a Monday-to-Saturday stint at a luxurious, recently refurbished theater. He shared the bill with the normal hodgepodge of journeyman performers, their talents magnified by the lens of promotional hyperbole. They featured a pair of ballroom dancers, an all-girl song-and-dance troupe, a conjurer, some gymnasts, a comedian, and a man bearing the dubious accolade of being "England's greatest sing-ing ventriloquist." Edgar's contribution was loudly applauded, the local press hailing it as "the most outstanding turn" in the show.

He didn't have far to travel to his next weeklong booking, which was at the Opera House and Hippodrome in the town of Dudley. There, he enthralled his audience with tales of his experiences, which purported to include playing one of the lead roles in *The Four Horsemen of the Apocalypse,* the movie that had swept Rudolph Valentino to celluloid stardom.

Almost unrelentingly wet weather providing little incentive for any-thing but indoor activities, Edgar's offstage existence demonstrated amo-rous gusto worthy of Valentino's persona as "the Latin Lover." The sight of Chief White Elk frolicking with a succession of compliant young men outraged many of the people he encountered during his tour. So flagrant was his behavior that the manager of one of his tour venues threatened to call the police, who would then be likely to prosecute him for "committing unnatural offenses."

Undaunted, he found himself yet another young male lover when he reached Leamington Spa, a town distinguished by its elegant, white-stucco-fronted Regency houses. Though he'd thus far avoided punishment by the British legal system, his casual promiscuity around that time led to him contracting syphilis, which appears to have gone untreated.

At Leamington's Theatre Royal, he and several of the other performers who had shared the bill with him earlier on his tour were reunited for a couple of shows, for which he was advertised as "the only living ruler over 16,000 Indians." Further ornamenting his persona, he was now pretending to be an Oxford man—someone who'd attended Oxford University.

In his dressing room, he was interviewed by a journalist from the *Leamington Spa Courier*. His "subtle magnetism," "quiet nobility," and apparent reluctance to talk about himself rapidly made an impression upon his visitor. The journalist was conned into believing that adroit maneuvering was required before the modest Cherokee could be persuaded to mention his mastery of twenty-one languages, his educational attainments, his three round-the-world trips, and his careers as a marathon runner, footballer, singer, pianist, and surgeon. Edgar said he'd arranged to meet King George V in June of that year when he'd be renewing his people's expressions of loyalty and allegiance to "the Great White Father," as well as petitioning the king for better educational facilities for Indians. "I want my people to have a chance in life," he explained. "I want them to have good schools."

The published interview praised his "well-nigh perfect" English and referred to his face being "a little more expressive than that of the average Red Indian." Edgar's interviewer also commented, "Though in his fifty-eighth year, this remarkable man does not look a day over thirty-five." He had, in truth, just turned thirty-five.

EDGAR RECEIVED A PITIFUL LETTER from Eugene, who announced he was starving to death. Eugene begged for money, but Edgar was surely too astute to fall for that. Far from being without food, Eugene was happily gadding about London with his two co-tenants. Edgar seems to have suggested that Eugene should join him for the next date on his tour.

By early April, Edgar and Eugene were sharing a bedroom at lodgings in the port city of Bristol, seventy-three miles southwest of Leamington Spa. The flow of illegal drugs through British ports likely enabled Edgar to restock with cocaine and morphine while he was there. Within a couple of weeks, though, he'd broken up with Eugene, who returned to the apartment they'd shared on Leyland Road.

From "a reliable source connected with the theatrical profession," a complaint about Edgar's homosexual dalliances had meanwhile been received by the Birmingham police. Since his home address was in the capital, they forwarded the complaint to Scotland Yard, headquarters of their London counterparts. Scotland Yard then launched an investigation of Edgar, placing the Leyland Road apartment under surveillance.

ON TUESDAY, APRIL 17, 1923, Edgar went back up to the northwest of England, apparently for a booking at the Salford Palace Theatre. That night he broke up his journey in Liverpool, where he registered at a downtown hotel as Chief White Elk. He then traveled the remaining thirty-two miles to the densely populated sprawl of Manchester, where the distinctive soundscape combined the clacking of millworkers' clogs, the *ding-ding* of streetcar bells, and the rattle of horses' hooves on the cobbled streets, down which they hauled wagons piled with freshly woven cloth.

Reverting to the name of Dr. Ray Tewanna, Edgar took lodgings in the tree-lined suburb of Levenshulme, exactly the sort of neighborhood that became an obstacle course for adults, who had to dodge packs of boys playing street soccer with anything from balls of twine to tennis balls. His new home was a large semidetached Victorian house at 65 Albert Road, where he seems to have struck up a warm relationship with his landlord and landlady. Both Cockneys in their late fifties, the couple comprised a salesman named Billy Holmes and Rebecca, his heavyset wife. Living with them was their thirty-seven-year-old daughter, Ethel, and her seven-year-old son, Leslie. He had a long, melancholy face and a ski-chute nose, inherited from his mother. Ethel's version of that nose came with high cheekbones, fashionably penciled-in eyebrows, an off-center smile, and dark, wavy hair. She fixed it in a short, center-parted style, sometimes hidden beneath a voguish cloche hat.

Like her parents, Ethel had been reared in the poverty-stricken East End of London. These days she worked on a telephone switchboard—a job that had become available to postwar women, now that their employment options extended beyond the confines of domestic service. Before long, she was romantically entangled with the lodger whom she addressed as "Ray," his high-alcohol-content cocktail of attractiveness blending charm, good looks, a life rich in anecdote, and a mellifluous voice, redolent of money and culture. Pepping up this already potent mix were slices of stardom and exoticism, sure to stand out from the prosaic, rainwashed surroundings.

For an unmarried mother with shaky financial prospects and a child to look after, Edgar's talk of how he was in line for a fabulous inheritance that was being blocked by the British government wouldn't have done any harm to his prospects as a suitor. Convenient endorsement of his talk about being a Cherokee chief was supplied by an official meeting with the city's Lord Mayor.

When his employment in Manchester tailed off, Edgar chose not to return to London. Instead of abandoning Ethel, toward whom he seems to have felt a powerful sexual attraction, he settled for some unglamorous work performing at the Star Picture House in the suburb of Stockport. During the Saturday children's matinee, dedicated to showing adventure serials featuring villains such as "the Hooded Terror," whose identity was concealed by a black hood and goggles, Edgar positioned himself in front of both the screen and the orchestra pit where the pianist played a medley of popular songs. Arms folded like a footballer posing for a team photo ("Tewanna, Thomas, Carlisle, 1909"), he maintained a posture of taciturn dignity. The children responded by clapping and cheering. Further endearing himself to his audience, which probably included Leslie, Edgar distributed complimentary candy and comics.

His rapport with children and his paternal affection toward Leslie, combined with his ready embrace of Ethel's parents, whom he called "Dad" and "Mother," must've made him seem still more of a catch for her. He told her that he was a widower, bereavement lending them an additional bond.

Ethel's handsome younger brother—photographed in a Royal Artillery uniform, a peaked cap pulled over his forehead and a bandolier stretched across his chest—had been wounded in Flanders and later died in a hospital. Edgar was well-rehearsed for talking about the experiences that he and her brother had shared in the mud and blood of wartime Europe.

Tightening the connection with her, Edgar said to her that Leslie reminded him of his own son, who had passed away two years earlier. Even though Ethel felt the intense social stigma of being an unmarried mother, she confided in Edgar that she'd given birth out of wedlock. Inside three months of becoming her parents' lodger, Edgar supplied the antidote to this stigma. At the pretty Wesleyan Methodist Church in Chorlton-cum-Hardy, a district not far from their home, they entered into a bigamous marriage one unseasonably cool, breezy June day when fat clouds skittered across the blue sky.

On the marriage certificate, Ethel described herself as a widow. Yet this falsehood was eclipsed by Edgar's contribution to the paperwork. Besides marrying under his assumed identity and presenting himself as a "doctor of medicine," he named his father as "Chief Wolfrobe" and his father's rank or profession as "ruler," the loftiness of that title contrasting with the mundane entry of "salesman" next to his father-in-law's name.

But marriage wasn't the only good thing that happened to Edgar. Not that he'd have been aware of the other significant piece of luck from which he benefited. It consisted of Scotland Yard's decision to drop their investigation of him, because "nothing of an improper nature" had been witnessed during the surveillance of his Leyland Road apartment. Of course, Edgar's perceived moral rectitude owed everything to his absence from that address.

Soon he'd be absent from his Manchester address, too. His ego, ambition, and wanderlust militating against any temptation to settle for an ordinary job and establish a conventional life there, he had—most likely through the booking manager at Charles Gulliver's firm—secured employment in France. He was due to appear at the casino in Étretat, a fashionable seaside resort where the summer season had just begun.

16

Together with his new wife and stepson, Edgar set out for France. Journeying there would have involved them going through London to the busy port of Southampton, where liners to Australia, South America, and the Mediterranean berthed. Tourists in that era were mainly restricted to the middle and upper classes, who could afford both the requisite time off work and the ticket prices. Among them were numerous people undertaking pilgrimages to the battlefields and cemeteries associated with the recent war.

Steamers took almost seven hours to complete the voyage from Southampton across the English Channel. In Le Havre, where the ships docked, Edgar would have had an opportunity to practice his French. He and his wife and stepson would've then had a sixteen-mile journey through the Normandy countryside, its grassy hills and cottage gardens exhibiting a carelessness more reminiscent of America than England.

Crouched at the foot of lofty bluffs that curved around a small bay, the waters of which had drilled through the rock face at one end to form a colossal arch, Étretat was a fishing village that had grown popular with English tourists. It had a pebbly beach, screened by an embankment and punctuated by upturned ships' hulls, pressed into service as fishermen's storehouses. For Ethel and Leslie, accustomed to the soot and drizzle of Manchester, it must have seemed like a magical place. And, for Edgar, it must have seemed a world away from the bustling vulgarity of Coney Island, where popcorn and frankfurters flavored the salty breeze, where thousands of lightbulbs outlined the minarets and domes after nightfall, where the rumble of the roller coaster was counterpointed by the whistling and drumming of a cluster of smallish, semi-naked brown men and women from Borneo, who formed a living exhibit.

Genteel in comparison, Étretat's Casino, at which Edgar was due to perform, occupied a wide terrace near the beach. Within the building were several ballrooms, a concert hall, and a theater. Edgar started work there as emcee for a troupe of acrobats. He also sang two or three numbers and gave his bewildered audience a demonstration of "the Great Scalping Dance."

As mid-September arrived and the end of the summer holidays approached, Edgar, Ethel, and Leslie—whom he treated as his son—lit out for the French capital, where he had an engagement at a new venue run by a couple of Charles Gulliver's business partners. Until the most hectic period of Paris's tourist season finished a month later, every hotel room in the city was taken, likely compelling Edgar and family to launch an immediate hunt for rental accommodation. Few of the Parisians they encountered would have spoken English, so Edgar's fluency in French, albeit of the French-Canadian variety, must have been useful.

Edgar would surely have been struck by how Paris differed from other big cities he'd known. Unlike any of those, it was shaped by a single architect, its straight, well-kept boulevards hedged by stores and apartment blocks that seldom topped seven stories, their symmetrical, tawny gray façades endowing the place with unusual coherence. Yet its architecture was just one of many things setting it apart. Its gleaming patisseries were another. So, too, were its drivers, who sped down its cobblestoned streets with homicidal haste, all the while toot-tooting horns. Even its sidewalks held an air of novelty for Edgar, particularly during rush hour when homeward-bound workmen in blue overalls instigated a bantering conviviality so dissimilar to London. Comparably alien were the dense plantations of tables and chairs that narrowed the sidewalks at frequent intervals. The customers at these cafés often gave off the candy-sweet aroma of L'Heure Bleue perfume, jostled by the smells of cognac, garlic, hot chocolate, and cigarette smoke far more pungent than the smoke from American tobacco. Edgar had, however, spent so much of his life on the road that he never took long to make himself at home someplace new.

He appears to have found an apartment for himself and his family on Passage Violet, an austere backstreet within earshot of two major train stations. Dotted with comfortable but not imposing hotels, this was in the crowded 10th arrondissement, sitting on the Right Bank of the Seine.

All such apartments came with a resident concierge, invariably a woman who did her best to sustain her profession's deserved reputation. Parisian concierges, feared by locals and out-of-towners alike, were notorious for prying into tenants' lives. Often that involved scrutinizing the postmarks and handwriting on tenants' mail before surrendering it to its rightful recipients. But Edgar was unlikely to have realized that concierges also provided a well-established information network for the police.

JUST FIVE BLOCKS SEPARATED PASSAGE VIOLET from where Edgar had been hired to perform. As a belated substitute for his elusive appointment at Buckingham Palace, he'd secured an engagement at a different palace—the Palace Theater.

Slotted into a cheerful stretch of the rue du Faubourg Montmartre, near to the cafés that were the favored haunt of the city's actors, the Palace's slender frontage didn't even hint at the scale or recently refurbished opulence of what lay beyond. In collaboration with Charles Gulliver, it was managed by Henri Varna and Oscar Dufrenne, Varna's willowy effeminacy and luxuriant hair contrasting with Dufrenne's cushioned torso, sagging features, and retreating locks.

Dufrenne and Varna formed a seasoned and exceptionally versatile theatrical team who codirected their own productions and even designed the lighting and scenery. Both of Edgar's new bosses, famed for the sumptuousness of their gargantuan shows, were gay. Indulgent though the French legal system was of same-sex relationships, Varna remained bashful about his own proclivities, which sometimes involved dressing as a schoolgirl and engaging in alfresco sex. No such reticence encumbered Dufrenne, a charming and outspoken socialist who possessed none of the blustering moralism of some of the provincial English theater managers Edgar had so outraged.

Toutes les femmes (*All the Girls*), the show with which Dufrenne and Varna had reopened the Palace Music Hall, had been playing for several triumphant months when Edgar started working for them. Mildly scandalous, it filled the Palace's thousand-seat auditorium every night, and it helped install Edgar's new workplace on the list of must-see attractions for the camera-toting American tourists who were making themselves conspicuous. They flocked to the city in such numbers that the only other people around at that time of year were said to be the working class and Parisians seeking "to improve their English accent." Driving this transatlantic tourist boom was the bargain exchange rate between American and French currency. A contributing factor was the number of American ex-servicemen who had visited Paris during the Great War and wanted to return.

Part of what lent the city its appeal to Prohibition-era Americans was its bars, cabarets, and music halls. These made Paris a synonym for sexual license, for the type of louche entertainment epitomized by Dufrenne and Varna's productions. Besides supervising *Toutes les femmes,* they ran Au Canari, a high-profile cabaret reached by a staircase leading down from the lobby of the Palace Theater. Edgar—or, rather, Chief White Elk—was booked as its star turn. The cabaret didn't get under way until midnight, so Edgar could feed his theatrical interests by watching *Toutes les femmes,* which kicked off three and a half hours earlier.

Nothing he had seen during rehearsals at the Woolwich Empire or in the vaudeville houses of America would have prepared him for Dufrenne and Varna's show, portrayed by the French press as "Nude Music Hall." Unfolding in a sequence of more than thirty tableaux, it was a camp extravaganza that passed in a swirl of feathers, artificial snow, sparkling costumes, precariously tall headdresses, and bare-breasted young chorus girls. Nominally at least, the darkly handsome Harry Pilcer—America's most famous dancer before Fred Astaire—functioned as the headline attraction.

He gave a virtuosic display, clad at one point in a dappled body stocking while he danced and mimed to Claude Debussy's "Prélude à l'après-midi d'un faune" ("Prelude to the Afternoon of a Faun"), in which muted wood-wind and strings combined to create a sinuous and erotic melody.

Backstage, surrounded by dozens of chorus girls wriggling into costumes, many of these designed by the illustrious couturier Paul Poiret, Edgar probably met Harry Pilcer. A New York–born near-contemporary of Edgar's, Harry had risen from prostitution to international celebrity, working with such venerated artistic figures as the writer Jean Cocteau and the composer Francis Poulenc. Harry and his lover, the enormously successful French singer Mistinguett, currently performing at a nearby theater, may have been present for one of Edgar's appearances at the downstairs cabaret, where the management joked that smoking was obligatory.

Au Canari pulled in customers from the cream of the Parisian artistic, literary, and theatrical worlds, who were all there to dine, drink, and dance as well as enjoy the show. Warming up the audience for Edgar was a selection of support acts. They included "the Beautiful Zoulaïka," a thickly made-up young belly dancer with black eyebrows that looked like they'd been drawn on with the aid of a ruler. As she danced, her dark, wavy, center-parted hair and beaded metallic bra must have swayed in time to her gyrations. These were deemed so sensual that she'd been the target of an unsuccessful prosecution for obscenity earlier that year.

Another of the support acts was the Crastonians, an eccentric British trio, comprising the lively son and fetching young daughters of the celebrated clown Joe Craston. Together they sang, danced, and larked around, extracting comedy and something akin to music from their unconventional instruments.

Edgar would have benefited from both of these warm-up acts. He'd also have been assisted by the receptivity of French audiences to American popular culture, which had grown ever more fashionable since the Great War. So he received frantic applause when he performed his song-and-Cherokee-dance routine, which earned him as much as five hundred francs a night. He supplemented this with the cash he made from peddling postcards, more than likely comprising signed photos of himself in full costume. Often his stock of promotional materials depicted him in dramatic settings. In one of the most popular of his postcards—photographed when he'd visited Stanley Park, Vancouver—he loomed out of a dark tree hollow, the deeply grooved trunk of which parted around him like tied-back drapes.

His earnings from selling postcards and performing at Au Canari were sufficient to buy himself a car. He invested in a new Native American costume from the nearby Galeries Lafayette department store, too. As ever, money slipped through his fingers when he wasn't onstage.

Outside working hours he was fêted in aristocratic salons. He paid recurrent trips to the city's movie theaters. He attended official receptions. He got acquainted with princesses in pink evening gowns. And he strutted down the city's boulevards in full costume and war paint, his clothes impressing one journalist with their "simplicity and majesty." Frequently, he was accompanied by his stepson, Leslie, who eagerly embraced him as a substitute father.

Every two or three blocks, Edgar and Leslie found themselves on a different boulevard, the boulevard de la Madeleine flowing into the boulevard des Capucines and so on. What remained constant, however, was the exuberant street life. Edgar's unusual getup, which received a thorough eyeballing from locals and tourists alike, would surely have attracted the innumerable grifters who trawled the boulevards. The more furtive of those grifters touted pornographic postcards and trips to brothels and blue movie shows. Others tried to sell Algerian or Tunisian rugs, which were unrolled across the sidewalk at the faintest encouragement.

As Edgar and Leslie explored the boulevards, they must have encountered the other routine components of those neighborhoods. There were the street fairs and sidewalk toy stalls, where Edgar could play the doting stepfather by buying gifts for Leslie and treating him to rides on the merry-go-rounds and roller coasters. Then there were the wheezing barrel organs, the buskers, the wiggly-assed, flashily dressed prostitutes, and the snatches of megaphoned commentary from "charabancs"—long, open-topped trucks that were the precursors of today's tour buses. Along with Leslie, Edgar would also have passed some of the city's ornate six-sided metal newspaper kiosks, more often than not tended by brisk little women, each of them with a yapping dog that patrolled the adjoining sidewalk. From these kiosks, Edgar probably purchased copies of *Le Temps* and other newspapers in search of references to himself. But the coverage of his visit was limited to just a few small stories, as well as ads for his performances at Au Canari.

Fame addict that he was, Edgar tried to rectify the situation by detouring into a photo studio where he and Leslie had their picture taken by what appears to have been an American press photographer. When they posed for the portrait, Edgar—who had·on a tasseled buckskin shirt and a neckerchief—let his eight-year-old stepson borrow his headdress. It came down over the boy's eyebrows. The picture wound up in newspapers in Detroit, San Francisco, and elsewhere in the States. Quoted alongside the photo was his claim that Leslie would be inheriting his title as chief of their tribe.

In the course of one of his walks through central Paris, Edgar strayed from the boulevards onto the rue de la Paix, where fashion houses stood cheek-to-impeccably-powdered-cheek with jewelers displaying giant emeralds, huge pearls, and diamonds so big they had their own names. He was soon accosted by what Parisians called a "midinette." These vivacious young seamstresses and shopgirls from the fashion houses were a familiar sight promenading the streets during their short lunch breaks. Style-conscious like all midinettes, she'd probably seen the recent French magazine image of the celluloid heartthrob and trendsetter Rudolph Valentino, wearing an outfit just like Edgar's. She might even have mistaken Edgar for the man himself, who was visiting Paris at the time.

With cheerful nonchalance, she asked Edgar for a kiss. He graciously obliged.

BESIDES WANDERING THE BOULEVARDS, he strayed north into Montmartre. That neighborhood, huddled around the steep hill leading to the white triple-domed cathedral of Sacré-Coeur, had an international reputation as the center of Paris's gaudy nightlife; as the home of the Moulin Rouge, Folies Bergère, and other famous music halls; as somewhere every visitor should see. It also had a reputation both as a stronghold of street gangs, and—not unconnectedly—as somewhere you could buy cocaine and other drugs.

Edgar, who must have needed to feed his narcotic addictions, took to spending a lot of time there. Only coming to life after dark, its lightbulb-strung streets harbored bars, shabby hotels, extortionate cabarets, sidewalk cafés with their own little orchestras, and jazz joints from which syncopated rhythms leaked, rhythms incompatible with the music Edgar sang. Pacing those streets were tourists, middle-class Parisians, and refugees from Russia's communist revolution. There were also African American jazz musicians, enjoying freedoms denied them in the Jim Crow south. And there were small-time hoodlums, easily recognized by their proprietorial swagger and the colored silk neckerchiefs they wore. They were known as "apaches," due to their wild, flailing style of dancing, which Parisians imagined to be analogous to the tribal rites of their Native American namesakes. Most of Edgar's time in Montmartre was presumably spent with the local apaches, because his French became infused by their slang.

Through his forays into "the Butte," as Montmartre was nicknamed, he'd have seen that it no longer merited its reputation. Over recent years, the nucleus of Paris's bohemian life had shifted across the river to Montparnasse. By the penultimate week of September, Edgar had found his way there, presumably drawn by its fashionable status, along with its fame as a refuge for transgressors and as a magnet for American expats.

It was just a short drive from Passage Violet, though even short forays into the city's anarchic traffic must have tested Edgar's nerve and skill behind the wheel. He had to be alert for both other drivers and the carts that interspersed them, some towed by bicycles, others hauled by a combination of a man and a harnessed dog.

Straddling the boulevards Saint-Germain, Raspail, and Saint-Michel, where the university was located and where several thousand students lived, Montparnasse was fondly referred to as "Montparno" or "the Quarter," short for "the Latin Quarter," so named because Latin had been the language spoken by the university's first scholars. On its streets Edgar would have glimpsed students of many nationalities—from fair-skinned

Swedes to American girls in horn-rimmed glasses. Similarly conspicuous were the number of fashionable cafés, restaurants, and nightclubs.

Edgar swiftly installed himself as one of the "Dôme-ites," regulars at the Café du Dôme. By some distance the Quarter's preeminent meeting place, it presided over the intersection between the boulevards Montparnasse and Raspail, its tables and chairs spilling over the sidewalk. These were so tightly packed that the scurrying waiters had difficulty weaving through them.

Around noon the Dôme was crowded with artists' models and girls from the local mail-sorting depot, but it didn't tend to get busy again until midevening. If Edgar arrived any time between 9:00 p.m. and 2:00 a.m., he would've had trouble finding a seat. He'd have then had to settle for a noisy, smoky spot at the zinc-topped bar, where English was the prevailing language among the customers but not the staff. From behind the cash register, the owner's wife nodded affably to regulars like him. At the bar, he could buy tobacco and order what was jokily known as a "perpendicular" drink. He'd also have been able to sample Perroquet, Cinzano Cassis, and other cocktails and liquor not readily available outside France. Glass in hand, he'd have had the chance to assess the comparably varied clientele, who led one somewhat pretentious visitor to coo, "The Dôme is not a place: it is an atmosphere."

Side by side were the impoverished and the affluent, the modish and the mangy, the young and the old, the unknown and the famous. Excited customers pointed out visiting stars, who justified the café's longtime renown as a rendezvous for artists and writers. Edgar's Dôme-ite peers included the poet Ezra Pound, sometimes joined by the prose writer James Joyce. The painters then frequenting the Dôme were Fernand Léger, Jules Pascin, George Braque, André Derain, and Moïse Kisling, their loud shop-talk audible across the café. Maurice Utrillo, Henri Matisse, and Pablo Picasso dropped by once in a while, too.

Edgar's new haunt was equally renowned for offering a vivacious floor show. It enticed limousines that pulled up at the curbside and disgorged rich American sightseers, keen to ogle its cultural celebrities, its mannish mademoiselles and mademoiselle-ish men, its smattering of outlandishly attired showboats like Edgar, who faced tough competition from fellow Dôme-ite exhibitionists.

Prominent among those was the painter and raconteur Nina Hamnett, given to brandishing a guitar and accompanying herself as she sang tuneful renditions of "Bollocky Bill, the Sailor" and her other favorite ballads. Also there was the amiable Ukrainian artist Sam Granowsky, dressed as if he were competing in a rodeo—neckerchief, Stetson, flannel shirt, the full rig—though people said he was incapable of riding even a seaside donkey. Then there was the black model Aïcha Goblet, so extroverted that she'd been known to dance in the street. And there was the pretty and effervescent Flossie Martin, an orange-haired former New York chorus girl–turned–occasional movie actress, who endeavored to sweep newcomers into her circle, hailing everyone with loud hilarity, often punctuated by her trademark expression, "I never laughed so much since Mother caught her breasts in the wringer."

For the Dôme's staff and clientele, the impact of Edgar's costume was, in any case, diluted by the recollection of a recent, similarly attired Montparnasse visitor who claimed to be a Cherokee chief as well. The other man, named Gitche Manitou, appears to have been a genuine Native American. Knowing that his exotic presence attracted customers, the owner of the Dôme had, over a two-year period, employed him to sit there, eating and drinking. In a dismal precedent for Edgar, Chief Gitche Manitou now tended bar at a nearby nightclub.

Diluting Edgar's impact still further was the current presence in Montparnasse of Willie Malies, a burly young African American jazzman and eccentric from the Deep South. Willie had reinvented himself as a Sioux chief, complete with buckskins, beaded moccasins, and ebony cheeks slathered in bright war paint. "This sure am a good town for Indians," Willie later declared. Some of the people gawping at both Willie and Edgar may have wondered whether they were hallucinating, the potency of their hallucinations conjuring a *third* Native American chief. Prowling many of the same streets at the same time was Chief Deskaheh, an authentic Cayuga leader who, as he explained to the press, had come to Europe on a mission.

From Chief Deskaheh, Edgar stole the notion of being in Paris to air the grievances of his tribe at the scheduled December meeting of the Council of the Geneva-based League of Nations, forerunner of the United Nations. Always drawn to roles that imbued him with the heroism he lacked, Edgar started telling people about the mission he was undertaking on behalf of his people. He even had his employers at Au Canari bill him as a "Delegate to the League of Nations."

During the closing days of September, however, the French newspaper *L'Humanité* ran an article poking gentle fun at Edgar. It mentioned that one of its readers had seen Chief White Elk performing at the casino in Étretat. "Times are hard for the Last of the Mohicans," it added before mischievously speculating on whether the man at the casino was merely someone *pretending* to be Chief White Elk.

17

A round the start of October when cooler weather and heavy down-pours heralded the end of the long, hot Parisian summer, Edgar was reunited with the charming Polish globetrotter who called himself Captain Walter Wanderwell. The reunion probably came about through a showbiz agent friend of Walter's, who provided free access to cabarets such as Au Canari.

Since meeting Edgar three years earlier on the Flathead Indian Reser-vation in Montana, Walter had discarded his previous alias. He was now pretending to be an English officer named Captain G. Armstrong. His world tour had moreover evolved into a competition, which he and his wife liked to present as a "million dollar wager endurance race." Journey-ing in separate cars, each supported by a team of passengers, the two of them were competing to see which of them could visit the most countries and clock the most miles on their way to the 1926 Philadelphia Exposi-tion. Walter's wife was still in America while Walter and his team had traveled to Europe that summer. His team comprised three young women, one of them Canadian, the others French and Peruvian.

Edgar began keeping company with Walter and his headstrong, convent-educated sixteen-year-old Canadian passenger, who, like Walter, wore a pseudo-military khaki costume with leggings and riding breeches. She'd recently joined his team. Her real name was Idris Hall, though Walter had jokily renamed her Aloha Hall after a building in San Francisco. Tall yet graceful, she had an attractive button-nosed, blue-eyed face and blond hair that brushed the shoulders of her jacket. She spoke fluent French and had a handshake as powerful as a prizefighter's.

Walter's showbiz agent buddy introduced her—and, in all likelihood, Edgar and Walter as well—to Rudolph Valentino. Starstruck though she was, Aloha managed to sustain a conversation with him about Italy, which she and Walter had visited not long before. Edgar may have been able to chime in, because he'd inevitably have seen the reports from Italy that had provided a conspicuous component of many Canadian and British newspapers over the past fourteen months. Those reports detailed the factory sit-ins; the riots; and the bitter, socialist-sponsored general strike, which had presaged the previous fall's march on Rome by thousands of fascist paramilitaries. Exploiting the situation, Benito Mussolini, leader of the fascists, had railroaded the elected government into stepping down. He'd since taken the post of prime minister, consolidated his power through what was euphemistically dubbed "electoral reform," and established a reputation for himself outside Italy as the man who had saved his country from a blood-soaked, Russian-style communist revolution.

Aloha and Walter funded their travels to Italy and elsewhere by selling photos and regularly screening silent films shot en route. When Walter presented his film show, to which he gave the unimaginative title *Journey Round the World,* he supplied a live commentary. His footage included New York City from the air, Niagara Falls, and the Native American wedding in Montana where he and Edgar had crossed paths and where Edgar made a cameo appearance on film. In the commentary, Walter described Edgar as "the great Indian chief White Elk, who is a doctor of medicine and speaks twenty-one languages."

Despite the affirmation offered by such screenings, Edgar was having to fend off skeptics by confessing to anyone who would listen that he was not "a purebred Red Indian," that he was born in North Carolina five years after his tribe made peace with the U.S. government, that he was "the son of a redskin, Yellow Root, and a French mother." In a flash of rare honesty, pervaded by a rueful acceptance of at least one aspect of the truth, he added, "If I didn't have my outfit, I'd look like everyone else."

THOUGH THE PARIS CORRESPONDENT OF the London-based *News Chronicle* questioned Edgar's persistent claim that he was a delegate to the League of Nations, the advertisements for his midnight performances at Au Canari still carried that empty boast. By mid-October he was sharing the bill with Roseray and Capella, enticingly billed as "nude dancers." They consisted of a lean, muscular man in a loincloth whose female partner—attired in just panties, a headband, and nipple tassels—struck balletic poses while balancing on his shoulder or being scooped off the stage by him.

In the theater upstairs, *Toutes les femmes* made way for a new, similarly spectacular girlie show called *Oh! Les belles filles* (*Oh! The Beautiful Girls*), which starred the Dolly Sisters. Well-established as American vaudeville stars and leading figures in "the Jazz Age"—a phrase lately popularized by the novelist F. Scott Fitzgerald—they were identical twins from Hungary, who went in for a style of heavy, pert-lipped makeup that heightened their doll-like features. They wore identical clothing and performed a ballroom dancing routine in which they mirrored each other's movements.

Very likely through his former Palace Theater colleague Harry Pilcer, who had worked for the Famous Players–Lasky film company, part of Paramount Pictures, Edgar snagged a job with the company. His new work, slated to begin after his engagement at Au Canari, was linked to the imminent release in Paris of *The Covered Wagon*. Easily the biggest budget Western to date, the film had already scored a huge success in London. It was being shown in Europe as a "road show"—the same strategy used for *Before the White Man Came*.

Famous Players–Lasky had hired a touring party of Native Americans to publicize *The Covered Wagon,* which—by a cruel irony—celebrated the westbound migration of the mid-nineteenth-century European settlers who drove those Native Americans' ancestors from their homelands. The well-remunerated touring party, made up of Arapaho who featured in the movie, was also contracted to take part in a live prologue before each screening.

Half the Arapaho were set to travel from London to Paris during mid-December, ready for the French premiere. Since their chaperone couldn't speak French, Edgar would be assisting him and functioning as emcee at screenings and press conferences.

Edgar met the Arapaho on the quayside as they disembarked from the Dover-to-Calais ferry. The party consisted of five long-haired men and four women. They had seven babies with them, each swaddled in multicolored, beaded blankets. Watching over this reticent group was their chaperone, Ed Farlow. He figured that the man calling himself Chief White Elk had no more than "a little Indian blood in him." On the quayside Edgar complained to him about being broke. Farlow promptly doled out a modest loan.

Farlow was a beefy and jovial Midwesterner in his early sixties. He had a long face, heavy-lidded eyes, and a graying mustache, shaped like an upward-pointing arrowhead. To keep out the cold, he had on a dark topcoat, gloves, and cowboy hat. Before being employed by Famous Players–Lasky, he'd worked as a gold prospector, and as a rancher in Wyoming, where he had befriended members of the Arapaho and gotten to know their sign language.

Disdainful expressions registered on their faces when they saw that Edgar's feathered bonnet was a cheap turkey feather replica. But he wasn't the first fake Native American they'd seen on their tour. In London they'd attended a fairground sideshow where one of the performers was billed as "White Buffalo, an American Indian." The man turned out to be a very light-skinned African American. Like Edgar, he had sported a turkey feather bonnet. The Arapaho had subjected White Buffalo to such derision that he wound up quitting his job. Edgar was now in danger of meeting the same fate.

WAITING AT THE TRAIN STATION on the evening of Wednesday, December 12, 1923, was a large crowd. Press photographers clutching flash-lamps were loitering on the same platform as reporters from publications as varied as *Le Figaro* and the European edition of the *Chicago Tribune.* Rumors about the arrival of a delegation of Native Americans had further swelled the crowd at the Gare du Nord. In muddled tribute to the visitors, many people were wearing moccasins, leather gauntlets, sombreros, and red neckerchiefs.

At nine o'clock that night, Edgar stepped from the express train that had just pulled into the station. He was decked out in a poncho, elbow-length suede gloves, and a broad-brimmed hat that looked as if it had been part of the wardrobe from *The Covered Wagon.* To make room on the platform, he shooed back the throng.

Dazzling light from the flashlamps perforated the nocturnal gloom as the Arapaho, one of them armed with a tomahawk, followed him onto the platform. Edgar then introduced them to the crowd. Included among the Arapaho were Lone Bear, Black Weasel, and Yellow Bird, as well as Old Eagle, the group's leader. Edgar explained that a combination of seasickness and a grueling journey had left them feeling weary.

Blue-tinted sunglasses screening his eyes, the elderly yet straight-backed and glossily black-haired Old Eagle presented the most striking figure. He wore a dark robe gussied up with red and white beads, a shell-studded belt, and a necklace strung with buffalo bones. Forming a mismatched fringe was a shaggy tussock of someone else's scalp, held in place by a thin gold chain. Alongside Old Eagle was his much younger wife. From her back hung a papoose with the head of a bobble-hatted baby protruding from it.

Once the introductions had been completed, Edgar announced to the crowd, "My friends are accompanying the film *The Covered Wagon,* which will soon be opening in Paris. Their tribe has used this opportunity to send them to France, the land synonymous with the freedom, equality, and fraternity that is denied Indians in their own country." He said his friends would be contacting the League of Nations—the governing council of which had just held its scheduled meeting in the city. "It is the Arapaho delegation's plan to submit a proposal to the League that the Utah Indians should be granted their freedom," Edgar added, unaware that they were from Wyoming rather than Utah, where *The Covered Wagon* had been filmed.

"So you want an independent state of Utah, then?" asked one of the crowd.

"More humane treatment would be enough for the American Indians, who would like to be treated like other citizens—at the same time as maintaining their traditions and way of life."

"Hopefully they'll also maintain their picturesque style of clothes, which would be a great loss if they disappeared."

"There's nothing to worry about in that respect. You can count on that being preserved on film."

Near the latter stages of the press conference, one of the reporters said, "Your countrymen will find the Parisian weather hard at this time of year."

With a knowing chuckle, Edgar replied, "At the moment there's three feet of snow in the Arapaho hunting grounds, which are in the northern part of the United States. Paris will feel as pleasant to them as the Riviera feels to you."

Some fifteen minutes after Edgar and the others had arrived, the press conference came to an end. But not before chaperone Ed Farlow had spoken to the reporter from the *Chicago Tribune*. Farlow mentioned that none of the Arapaho possessed U.S. citizenship, so he was under strict orders from the American government to be sure they returned—in handcuffs, if necessary—to the Wind River Indian Reservation once their tour was over.

As Edgar ushered the Arapaho toward the roomy automobile that had been provided for them, someone in the crowd asked Old Eagle whether he'd be part of the delegation to the League of Nations.

"We'll go," he replied. "We'll go. It was fun being an actor, but it'll be nice to be a politician, too."

On that note, he and the others climbed into the car and departed. For their first night they'd have to make do with the temporary beds set up for them at the offices of Famous Players–Lasky. After that, they'd be staying in a hotel on one of the boulevards until their tipis were shipped from London.

Sleeping under a roof wasn't to their tastes, though. In New York—as Farlow may have explained to Edgar—they'd pitched their tipis on the grounds of the Museum of Natural History. And in London they'd camped in the park at suburban Crystal Palace.

OVER THE NEXT THREE DAYS, Edgar was expected to become properly acquainted with the Wind River contingent. He also had to master his duties as chaperone. These included keeping the hard-drinking Arapaho sober enough to appear onstage. Neither Ed Farlow nor Famous Players–Lasky knew Edgar well enough to realize that he, too, had a powerful thirst for liquor, rendering him ill-suited to the task.

The plan was for Farlow to hand over supervisory responsibilities to Edgar by that Sunday. All being well, Farlow would then go back to London, where he could rejoin the other half of the Arapaho touring party, which was still appearing at West End screenings of *The Covered Wagon*.

Early on the morning after the press conference at the Gare du Nord, Old Eagle and the rest of the group were taken on the first of a series of tourist trips around Paris—trips that had the dual purpose of potentially attracting press coverage. These began with a visit to an exhibition of telescopes at the giant, glass-roofed Grand Palais. When Edgar's flock emerged from the exhibition, they strolled down the Champs-Élysées, where the leafless trees added to the wintry ambience and where the traffic characteristically ranged from horse-drawn hansom cabs to Rolls-Royces, Hispano-Suizas, and other luxury vehicles. Along this immensely broad street, glorious vistas across the adjoining parks and over the river toward the gilded dome of Les Invalides clicked into place like images from a slideshow. Lining the park were donkey rides, as well as Punch and Judy shows that now attracted only the youngest children, the older ones having been lured away by movie theaters.

On the Champs-Élysées, the Arapaho were approached by a journalist. Old Eagle used the opportunity to declare, "The Indians are victims of serious wrongs. The whites want to annihilate what is left of once rich and powerful nomadic tribes."

• • •

ED FARLOW ARRANGED FOR OLD EAGLE and his companions to be shown the other tourist sights, presumably by Edgar. Bored though the Arapaho were by this enforced dose of Gallic culture, they were dragged around the Arc de Triomphe, Napoléon's tomb, and the cathedrals of Notre-Dame and Sacré-Coeur. Plus, they were taken up the Eiffel Tower. Near its upper platform, just over nine hundred feet off the ground, a number of the Arapaho complained about the cold. Another confessed to feeling scared. Uniting them was their impatience to ride the elevator back down. One of them expressed surprise that anyone would want to build a tower like that, because it might fall over and kill people.

Dining with Old Eagle and the others in cafés or restaurants presented Edgar and his boss with problems also. Foremost among those was the tendency of the Arapaho to ignore their utensils when served meat. In breech of European-style etiquette, they'd simply pick up the meat and gnaw it. Or they'd grip it between their teeth and start hacking at it. Then they'd lick their fingers.

Elaborate French cuisine didn't, in any event, comply with their idea of good food. To them, meat was thick and juicy and cooked over an open fire. It wasn't thinly sliced and doused with creamy sauce, or reduced to the gray and tasteless consistency it had been at the London boarding-house where they'd moved after the damp English winter forced them to quit their tipis.

As contemptuous as the Arapaho were toward turkey feather head-dresses of the type he wore, Edgar redeemed himself by talking with them in their own language. He'd probably picked this up from the Native American woman who had traveled with him back when he used to sell snake oil. Hearing Edgar speak Arapaho impressed his wife. Ethel was also impressed by how well he got on with Old Eagle and the rest of the troupe. In her eyes, Old Eagle treated Edgar as "a fellow tribal chief." Often, though, it was hard to be certain whether the Arapaho were being serious or just teasing.

EDGAR AND HIS ARAPAHO FRIENDS were due to attend the French premiere of *The Covered Wagon,* scheduled for the Friday before Christmas.

As an indication of just how exclusive an occasion this would be, a strip of carpet had been laid across the sidewalk leading into the Madeleine Cinema, where the premiere was being held. Above the carpet, an awning had been rigged up. En route into the movie theater, stars of the city's art, cinema, and political worlds posed, resplendent in elegant evening dress. Glamorous girls handed bouquets to the women as they sailed through the entrance, across the lobby, and into the auditorium, which was garlanded by carnations and roses.

By nine o'clock, all the seats in the stalls and balcony were taken— a good omen for future screenings. Punctuality was not a strong suit of Old Eagle and his compatriots, yet they arrived with time to spare. No instructions had been issued to them about what to wear onstage. They'd just been told "to show the white man audience how they looked when they felt beautiful." Wearing a joyous, multicolored array of eagle feather headdresses, gold earrings, fringed buckskin shirts, medallions, beaded trousers, seashell chokers, and embroidered moccasins, they prepared to stride in front of the audience.

At these live prologues, a painted wilderness backdrop covered the screen and a tipi stood near the side of the proscenium arch. Leaves, branches, and the remains of a pretend campfire meanwhile embellished the stage.

With what one witness regarded as "great finesse," Edgar announced the arrival of the Arapaho onstage. A tremendous ovation greeted the men and papoose-laden women, who communicated among themselves with sign language. Edgar gave a humorous speech, in which he claimed to have used the lure of the dollar to recruit the Arapaho from the plains of the Far West.

Led by an accomplished conductor, an orchestra was on hand to provide the accompaniment as *The Covered Wagon*'s opening sequence appeared on-screen. The film that unspooled over the next ninety-eight minutes told the story of a wagon train making the two-thousand-mile trek across America in 1848. Many of the story's ingredients—its fights, its chases, its battles—were familiar from the Western serials that were a staple of movie theater programs. Yet it possessed a newfound scale and epic seriousness that lived up to its advance publicity, which highlighted its use of three thousand actors, one thousand covered wagons, six hundred cattle, and one thousand mules and horses.

A wave of applause swept through the auditorium when the closing titles appeared. If Edgar needed reminding of how movies and the experience of watching them had been transformed since the first movie theater opened in the neighborhood where he was raised, then that night's screening of *The Covered Wagon* provided it. Strictly speaking, the first movie theater in Central Falls was what was known as a nickelodeon, a slightly disreputable storefront with space for almost two hundred hard kitchen chairs and a musical accompanist competing against the barker or record player out front booming "It's only five cents! See the moving picture show!" As a work-shy sixteen- and seventeen-year-old, Edgar would surely have idled away many hours there with his friends, yakking, smoking, flirting, singing along to the verses periodically projected onto the screen, and watching the ten- or fifteen-minute films, which the projectionist would sometimes speed up or run backward just to get a laugh.

Writing about the entirely different experience afforded by the French premiere of *The Covered Wagon,* one of the Paris newspapers the next morning proclaimed, "Nobody should miss this sensational spectacle." The similarly rhapsodic response of most of the other critics teed up the movie for its first public screenings at the Madeleine Cinema, where Edgar and the Arapaho were paid to appear three times daily. On the third night of this hectic rotation, Edgar took a couple of the Arapaho out drinking after their final performance of the evening. They went to a nightclub, probably in Montmartre, little more than a mile from the movie theater. For expatriate American and English artists such as Edgar, the preferred all-night hangout was Kiley's, known as "Jed's" in homage to its congenial Chicagoan owner, Jed Kiley. Located on the rue Fontaine, sometimes dubbed "the 42nd Street of Montmartre," it had classy, Art Deco furnishings, a large dance floor, and a roster of bands blaring hot jazz. Its clientele always featured a surfeit of desirable girls, ensconced at tables where sweating champagne buckets stood on pristine white tablecloths. Stop by at Jed's for a nightcap and you'd find time accelerating. Before you knew it, the band was packing up and the remaining customers were breakfasting on ham and eggs.

Still drunk, Edgar and his two Arapaho friends stumbled into the Madeleine Cinema around lunchtime the following day. Their boss was appalled. If anything, Edgar was in worse shape than the Arapaho whom he was meant to be keeping an eye on. Farlow had trouble sobering them up and maneuvering them into their fanciest clothes in time for their matinee performance. That afternoon Farlow wrote to the London office of Famous Players–Lasky, bellyaching about the choice of Edgar to chaperone the Arapaho on their continental tour. Unable to count on Edgar looking after them in his absence, Farlow elected not to go back to London as planned. Instead, he'd remain in Paris.

CROWDS CONTINUED TO FLOCK to screenings of *The Covered Wagon* and, in his off-duty hours, Edgar continued going to the Café du Dôme. But his attempts at rivaling its troupe of exhibitionists had been so unsuccessful that he no longer bothered showing up in his Native American outfit.

Lately the Dôme had been further enlivened by a gregarious chain-smoking twenty-two-year-old who styled her hair in a severe bob, her eyes and lips accentuated by dramatic makeup that stood out against her heavily powdered face. She modeled for prominent artists and fellow Dôme denizens Maurice Utrillo, Tsuguharu Foujita, Moïse Kisling, and her two-timing photographer boyfriend, Man Ray. Her name was Alice Prin, though everyone knew her as Kiki. And everyone *did* seem to know her, Edgar probably included.

Kiki had just come back from New York City, where she'd hoped to land a movie contract and begin a new life. After a few weeks in America, however, she had wired a request to Man Ray for money to buy her a ticket back to France. She'd celebrated her homecoming by visiting the Dôme and her other favorite haunts. Her return heightened the Dôme's atmosphere of predatory female sexuality, typified by the recent incident when another young woman had drunkenly shouted after two passing sailors, "I love seafood!"

About the time Kiki reappeared at the Dôme, Edgar received some important news. Old Eagle and the other Arapaho disclosed that they wanted to return to Wyoming instead of going with *The Covered Wagon* on the rest of its European tour. Despite Farlow's damning letter about Edgar, Famous Players–Lasky hired him to substitute for the Arapaho. When the tour moved on to Belgium and then the South of France, Edgar would perform the prologue and, with the assistance of a publicity manager, help to whip up press coverage.

18

"entlemen, this isn't an official visit to Belgium, but I wanted to express to your country the admiration that the Indians feel for it," Edgar said in his most formal French. He was addressing a group of reporters, who had been invited to the room at the luxury hotel where he and his family had registered after alighting in Brussels at noon on Thursday, February 14, 1924. The instant he'd emerged from the train, bright-eyed with excitement, his Chief White Elk costume rendering him unmistakable, he had been mobbed by photographers and journalists.

Later that day, he said to the reporters assembled in his hotel room, "The Indians are a people for whom loyalty, nobility of heart, and courage are the virtues we value above all others. Therefore I would remind you that it was thanks to our tribes that the first food-relief train was sent to Belgium after the outbreak of the Great War. We raised $75,000 to pay for this. During your king's visit to the United States, we had the honor— several tribal leaders and I—to be presented to him as the *true* American citizens. He was keen to acknowledge our gesture and thank us."

"We'd like some information about your claims," asked a journalist, rightly dubious about what was, in truth, one of Edgar's flights of fantasy.

Like a politician dodging a tricky question, Edgar countered with another barrage of invention: "There are now 2,672 million Indians, divided into 124 tribes, each speaking its own dialect. These tribes all speak the same sign language. I, for my part, am the hereditary chief of the Cherokee tribe that originally lived in North and South Carolina. After the Civil War, we moved down to Virginia, Texas, and finally the state of Oklahoma, where we and other tribes were confined on reservations by the U.S. government.

"We ask one thing—U.S. citizenship. Though it has been offered to us, it has only been offered under unacceptable terms. To obtain it, we'll have to give the government our land, yet those terms aren't applied to black people, Japanese, or Chinese residents in America. Why is this the case when *we* are the true Americans? Why should we give our land, which is all we have, to people who are already millionaires?

"Do not believe that we are tempted. Do not be deceived by our feathers, our necklaces, our rings, and our clothing, which seem to you so strange. Instead, look at the depths of our hearts, our ardent desire for friendship. We have a large and beautiful civilization. Why should we be enslaved? We once had Indian universities, but the government has withdrawn its subsidy for them under the pretext that there was no money to spare. Do they want to kill us? Our schools have been closed down and 12,000 children are reliant on being taught at home."

"Were you well received in Paris?" one of the reporters inquired.

"Beautifully." He underlined his own elevated status by casually adding, "The Council of the League of Nations was very interested in our delegation. They gave us a lovely welcome."

Edgar wrapped up the press conference by telling a lighthearted story. He said that a woman had asked him if it's true that feathers grow out of Indians' heads, to which he'd replied, "Certainly, madam, I need to pluck them every week." At this, he gave one of his deep, childishly uninhibited laughs, which may have owed more to cocaine or alcohol than to what one of the listening reporters interpreted as his "sincere and friendly" disposition.

· · ·

THE INDIAN CHIEF WHITE ELK IS IN BRUSSELS, the headline declared. It graced the front page of the next morning's edition of *La Nation Belge,* among Belgium's foremost newspapers.

In the wake of this, boxed gifts started being delivered to the hotel room Edgar was sharing with his wife and stepson. The boxes contained jam and candy, as well as lavish presents such as an electric toy train and a miniature cinema projector for Leslie. Edgar also received five hundred invitations to dinner parties, trips to the theater, and other social occasions. He was even offered honorary membership in the city's exclusive shooting clubs.

Between his appearances at the Brussels movie theater where *The Covered Wagon* was playing, he strolled around the city, its patisseries, glowing electric signs, swirling street life, and handsome architecture showing why it had earned its reputation as "the miniature Paris." He visited the vast Palais de Justice, received complimentary dinners at restaurants, signed autographs for adoring girls, gambled using free chips, and attended parties thrown by diplomats and members of Belgian high society. Deploying his well-tested line about how King George V was about to return to him millions of acres of tribal land in Canada, he hustled large sums of money from many of the people he met.

His main victims were wealthy old women, overawed by his courtly manners and exotic stories. One of his marks was an elderly dowager who bankrupted herself by lending him a million Belgian francs. He supplemented this with money cadged from a midwife he'd befriended. The aggregate take from these two scams was equivalent to around $220,000, more than 20 percent of the entire budget of *The Covered Wagon.*

Among the other people who succumbed to his spiel were several unsuspecting and glamorous young women. In exchange for worthless checks, they gave him their jewelry, which he said he wanted as a souvenir of his trip. Under the influence of the moneyed crowd with whom he was mixing, Edgar started spending on a scale worthy of the tribal potentate he was pretending to be. As he walked around Brussels, he scattered handfuls of money to street urchins—a habit that reinforced the impression of him being boundlessly rich. Cheerful flocks of impoverished children followed him. But the police soon ordered him to desist.

Greedy for acclaim, he wasn't simply passing himself off as a wealthy Cherokee. He was selling people his old line about being a war veteran. And somehow he even duped the local press into believing he was "a poet of rare sensitivity." His poetic output—illusory, of course, unless his regular displays of poetic license were taken into account—garnered him an invitation to speak at a public meeting organized by a student literary circle based at the Free University of Brussels. Known as La Lanterne Sourde (the Deaf Lantern), the group hosted talks by cultural figures as significant as the writer Stefan Zweig, the composer Erik Satie, the painter James Ensor, and the architect Le Corbusier. Edgar accepted the group's invitation to lecture on the evening of Tuesday, February 19, 1924.

Just the day before Chief White Elk's widely promoted lecture, the Belgian daily newspaper *Le Peuple* announced that the event had been canceled. "Indeed, serious doubts have been raised about the claims of the alleged Indian chief," the article disclosed. "Knowledgeable people state that, contrary to what he said, he never addressed the League of Nations, and he has never been asked to represent anyone." Concluding the article was the pronouncement "Human credulity is a wonderful thing."

OVERNIGHT THE SITUATION CHANGED. Edgar's powers of persuasion were probably behind La Lanterne Sourde reversing their earlier decision to cancel his lecture. It would now be going ahead at the advertised time and place—8:30 p.m. in the Free University's main auditorium, which had a capacity of one thousand, provided everyone packed in tightly.

With an hour and a half to spare, fifteen hundred people flowed through the entrance on the rue des Sols, jostling their way into the auditorium. Two thousand more who wanted to hear Edgar were shut outside, where they expressed their frustration by shouting and screaming.

Fresh waves of raucous people kept turning up over the next hour, yelling, singing, pushing, trampling on other people's feet, and crushing their ribs. Half an hour before the show, some four thousand of them were gathered in front of the auditorium, the pressure splintering its doors, which eventually gave way. Other members of the riotous crowd ripped the windows off their hinges and climbed across the shoulders of the people inside. Someone was soon swinging from a light fixture. Elsewhere fights broke out.

When Edgar showed up, he found the hallways leading into the auditorium clogged with people. Though he wasn't wearing his chief's costume, he was recognized by at least one of those people, who made threats against him, which precipitated his hasty departure. And his lecture was called off for a second time. Then the authorities began to evacuate the dense crowd. All told, this took an hour, during which the police rolled up and the casualties were taken to a hospital.

THE ARTICLE THAT APPEARED IN one of Belgium's most prominent newspapers the next morning was not calculated to appeal to Edgar's vanity. In describing the previous night's chaos at the Free University, *Le Vingtième Siècle* stated, "White Elk, who never flinches at the sight of a buffalo on the prairie, had a moment of heroic inspiration—frightened for the first time in his life, he fled."

With the connivance, perhaps, of the publicity manager from Famous Players–Lasky, who had been detailed to promote his tour, Edgar endeavored to restore his tarnished public image among the city's French-speaking population. No sooner had the article appeared in *Le Vingtième Siècle* than someone posing as his secretary contacted its rival French-language newspaper. At the request of Edgar's fictitious secretary, *La Libre Belgique* agreed to publish what purported to be a letter from Chief White Elk to Spotted Eagle, an equally fictitious Comanche chief. Supposedly translated from White Elk's native language into French, his self-aggrandizing letter sought to ingratiate himself with the Belgian people. It also offered a face-saving corrective to the previous account of his cowardice in the face of the unruly mob.

"Spotted Eagle, oh great leader!" it began.

> *Having been summoned by telegram, I'm now in the main village of the Belgian tribe, where the people are very pleasant. I've had huge success. I've attracted sympathy and curiosity. All the major newspapers marked my arrival with enthusiastic*

biographies of me, accompanied by photographs of me in my war bonnet. This was organized very well by my manager. I've only one worry, that the press hasn't paid sufficient attention to the number of languages I know. In different articles these vary from five to seventeen, but the public was generous enough not to notice. And, in any case, I'm learning a sixth, or perhaps an eighteenth language, thanks to a tutor who was found for me by the porter at the hotel where I'm staying. This tutor is teaching me Flemish, the main language of the people here.

Edgar's letter went on to refer to "the wisdom and perfection of Belgian institutions" and the economic hardships being endured by many people in Brussels. "A student body had bestowed on me the great honor of inviting me to speak one evening at a hall in the university," his letter continued.

I was planning to get there at about nine o'clock, but my manager warned me not to go because I could lose my feathers, which are worth a lot of money in this country. Curiosity drove me there, however. I quickly acquired a traditional Flemish costume and, in this disguise, went to the university. It was awful yet moving! Moving because the show strongly reminded me, in this faraway land, of scenes from home, of victorious warriors taking part in a frenzied scalp dance.

A COUPLE OF DAYS AFTER the publication of his letter, Edgar headed through Brussels to the venue for his rescheduled lecture. Despite being staged on a Monday afternoon, the event sold out. No trouble broke out this time, though. Instead, the enthralled audience listened politely to Edgar's long talk about the language, customs, religion, outlook, and aspirations of Native Americans.

To illustrate aspects of what he was saying, he reminisced about his imaginary grandmother who, he claimed, was 108 years of age. He told his audience that people had a garbled notion of what American Indians were like, a notion based upon the misrepresentations of popular nineteenth-century novelists such as James Fenimore Cooper, author of *The Last of the Mohicans.* "I heard kids on the boulevards say that I was not a real Indian because I did not have a scalp on my belt, a knife in my teeth, and a tomahawk in my hand," he added. "Indians today have taken on the customs of their white brethren. They have shown themselves capable of the same qualities of heart and mind, but nobody has written about this."

Enthusiastic applause was unleashed when his talk ended. The ovation persisted for so long that he was able to bow three times before it faded away.

In the audience was a reporter from a newspaper based in the city of Charleroi. Edgar persuaded the reporter that any lingering rumors about him being an impostor were the product of malice. He also went some way toward mending the damage to his reputation caused by the story about him fleeing from the crush at the Free University. After hearing his lecture, the reporter wrote, "We have no doubt that he is a very brave man—very intelligent, too."

AROUND THE STATIONARY BUS WERE some two hundred children. They belonged to the Boy Scouts of Belgium. Edgar had earlier that morning treated them to a talk and a selection of songs. He'd also enlisted his stepson's assistance in demonstrating an Indian war dance.

Now—at lunchtime on Sunday, March 9, 1924—he was sitting on the bus with Leslie and Ethel. A disabled Belgian war veteran and close to a dozen other people were aboard as well. Through the windows they could see the Boy Scouts assemble into formation, like a troop of miniature infantrymen. Soon the formation was escorting the bus as it crawled north down the boulevard Adolphe Max, one of the most fashionable shopping streets in Brussels. On either side were tall, flamboyantly ornamented nineteenth-century buildings. When Edgar's bus reached the T-junction at the far end, it made a right onto a broad road that skirted a park and a hospital. Dominating the park was a domed hothouse. Beyond that, Edgar's procession turned onto the rue Royale, home of the midwife he'd bamboozled. No fewer than twenty minutes after setting out, he and the others approached the Colonne du Congrès, a giant monument that resembled Nelson's Column.

They stopped near the terrace on which the monument stood. It overlooked the city, lit by bright spring sunshine. A stone balustrade separated the terrace from the street, where a policeman guarded the entrance. Startled by the procession's sudden arrival, the policeman went up to the bus and said "people in carnival-style costumes" weren't permitted to enter the area around the Colonne du Congrès.

On being informed that what appeared to be a carnival costume was, in fact, Chief White Elk's national dress, the policeman's officiousness mutated into flustered embarrassment. Edgar couldn't hide his own amusement at this turn of events.

The policeman apologized and then allowed the procession onto the graveled terrace that formed an apron around the monument. At its base, a pair of bronze lions stood sentinel. Belgium's Unknown Soldier had been interred there eighteen months previously, his burial a symbolic acknowledgment of the many unidentified combatants who had perished in the Great War. A mound of wreaths lay on his tomb. It had already become a pilgrimage site for visiting monarchs, presidents, and generals. Edgar was keen to buttress his perceived regal status by taking part in a ceremony there. More than likely notified by his publicist from Famous Players–Lasky, a press photographer was on hand to record the occasion.

Row upon row of Boy Scouts watched as Edgar advanced toward the tomb, carrying a wreath. Alongside him was the Belgian war veteran who had been on the bus. Two walking sticks were required for the veteran to hobble across the terrace. In deference to his fallen comrades, he removed his hat.

Leslie joined the Boy Scouts in saluting as Edgar placed the wreath on the tomb. Affixed to the wreath was a card reading, "From Chief White Elk, on behalf of the North American Indians."

Minus their Boy Scout escort, Edgar and Leslie—and presumably Ethel, too—were then treated to a sightseeing tour by a journalist. Their car took them past the Belgian parliament, the sumptuous mansions of the avenue Louise, and the remains of the city's fortifications. Many of the streets were chockablock even though it was a Sunday. Naturally, the tour encompassed the Manneken Pis fountain, a small statue of a naked boy from whose penis water traced a gentle arc. Leslie broke into wild laughter as soon as he set eyes on it. Edgar kidded about lending the naked statue a feather, which could be deployed in lieu of a fig leaf.

From the Manneken Pis, their driver chauffeured them the short distance to the Grand Place. In this cobbled, gently sloping plaza, bounded by remarkable medieval buildings with spires, turrets, and pointed gables, was a market selling flowers, small animals, pigeons, and other birds. The journalist tagging along with Edgar ushered him into a tavern on the plaza, where he sampled several bottles of *kriekenlambic,* the local specialty beer, made from Morello cherries. Edgar pronounced it "a first-rate drink." It primed him for an evening at one of the city's cabarets.

EDGAR HAD CAUSE TO FEEL PLEASED because his wreath-laying at the Tomb of the Unknown Soldier earned him a place on the front page of two of Belgium's national newspapers. Over the following days, he also visited a military hospital, where he gave injured war veterans a performance of his tribal songs and dances. And he attended a high-society masked ball, organized by the city's Jewish community.

Several fellow guests at the ball were surprised to see Edgar in a tuxedo rather than his familiar garb. When someone commented upon his more ordinary getup, he came out with a mischievous reply: "I thought, 'Good, since this is a Parisian-style ball, I'll disguise myself as a European.'"

Moving in such deep-pocketed circles, his earnings from promoting *The Covered Wagon* and scamming the locals failed to keep pace with his high-rolling expenditure, which probably featured not just alcohol and drugs but also costly souvenirs that he'd either lose or give away in a display of princely largesse. Though he swallowed his pride and supplemented his income by working as a dishwasher, he was still unable to support his wife and stepson. Other problems meanwhile threatened to bushwhack him before he and his family headed back to France for the final leg of his tour.

Until now, his victims' sense of shame had insulated him from the legal repercussions of his activities in Brussels. Most of his wealthy Belgian victims couldn't bring themselves to admit they'd been fool enough to fall for such baloney. Even the dowager bankrupted by Edgar balked at pressing charges against him. Yet the midwife who had lent him seven thousand francs could afford no such inhibitions. Belatedly cottoning on to the fact that he wouldn't be repaying her, she complained to the Brussels police, whose interest in him was magnified by an allegation that he'd recently robbed a chorus girl. Edgar could now look forward to being grilled by the authorities, slung into a jail cell, and ultimately deported to the United States, where he still faced a number of outstanding charges. The way things were going, he was looking at years in jail, exiled from the luxury and the deluge of praise to which he'd become so accustomed.

W ithout settling what was probably a colossal hotel bill, Edgar and his family left town near the end of March. From Brussels, they returned to Paris, its streets yet to feel the warm hand of spring. Instead of keeping Edgar company on the last stretch of his tour, Ethel and Leslie stayed in the French capital while he journeyed four hundred and ten miles south to the Mediterranean. He didn't endear himself to his wife by providing her and Leslie with next to nothing on which to live, their penury leaving them well-placed to test the adage about Paris being "the cheapest city in Europe to starve in."

Edgar was now in the cosmopolitan port of Marseilles, famed for its menacing backstreets, bustling quayside, quaint-looking commercial sailing vessels, and crowded main thoroughfare. Once he'd completed his contribution to a brief series of screenings of *The Covered Wagon,* he traveled along the coast to the Riviera, a narrow, flower-scented ribbon of countryside sandwiched between the bleak Maritime Alps and the rocky promontories jutting into the ever-tranquil blue sea. Long established as a byword for wealth, glamour, titled privilege, and the type of moneyed decadence that attracted the drug dealers on whom he depended, the

Riviera was in those days at its busiest during the winter. Its mild climate enticed an annual tide of well-heeled foreign visitors, many of them from England and America.

The holiday season had already started to wane by the first week of April when Edgar—going under the moniker of Prince Tewanna Ray, Chief White Elk—arrived in Nice. A huge crowd greeted him. With them was a newsreel cameraman who filmed Edgar as he stepped into a specially decorated carriage, waiting to transport him across the beautiful, polyglot city.

He took up residence at one of Nice's most lavishly appointed hotels. The majority of these stood on the shoreline, where the wide, palm-fringed Promenade des Anglais paralleled the long, graceful curve of the pebbly beach and the bay beyond. Strolling past the giant hotels, the adjacent mansions, and the Jardin Albert Premier, its flower beds frothing with brightly colored blooms, were some of the most ravishing women in Europe, arrayed in the latest Parisian creations. Not to be outdone, Edgar wore his pastiche Cherokee costume, now incorporating numerous fake jewels that winked in the crisp, spring light.

Stories about Edgar and his League of Nations mission meanwhile appeared in the local papers. Though the Riviera press carried recurrent warnings about the confidence tricksters who preyed upon the city's tourists by posing as retired bankers, affable priests, or wealthy philanthropists, Edgar exuded such charm and plausibility that he was taken at face value.

LATE EACH MORNING AND EVENING, the balmy sunshine eventually giving way to a nocturnal chill, Edgar had to report to the Maison Berger. A downtown property spanning a full block, it housed a photographer's studio, a tobacconist, and other small businesses. It also housed the Mondial Cinema, where *The Covered Wagon* was making its Riviera debut. Luckily for Edgar, who hadn't lost his thirst for alcohol, the movie theater had its own bar—next to a small dance floor.

He gave politely applauded talks in French before each screening and then collected donations from his audience, who were urged to help impoverished "little Indian children." (In truth, the money went toward helping a certain impoverished Rhode Islander who qualified as neither a Native American nor a child.)

Between his modest work commitments, Edgar insinuated himself into the world of tea dances, soirées, and grand receptions, frequented by aristocrats such as Prince Aga Khan, Grand Duke Cyril of Russia, and Prince Haidar Fazel of Cairo. Within that refined milieu, Edgar fell in with many of the visiting blue bloods. And he befriended the officers from the USS *Pittsburgh,* a visiting American warship, jokily dubbed a "playship" because its function was to tour foreign ports where the crew was expected to schmooze with civilian and military dignitaries. Edgar would, of course, have had no difficulty trading seafaring reminiscences over a few glasses of cognac.

Among the people he chanced upon in Nice was the fittingly surnamed Dr. Perry Chance, a rich, middle-aged dentist from Ohio, whose past patients included the German royal family. For more than two decades Dr. Chance had been living in Europe. He and his wife had a combined dental surgery and home just up the street from the Promenade des Anglais.

One of his treasured possessions was an improbable keepsake from the United States—an authentic Native American feathered headdress, for which he'd paid a lot of money. Edgar sweet-talked the doctor into letting him borrow it. He donned it whenever he gave his presentations at the Mondial Cinema, where, on at least one occasion, he arrived in such a soused condition that the bartender refused to serve him.

AFTER HIS THIRD LUNCHTIME SHOW in as many days, Edgar headed into the Mondial's lobby. Together with his publicity manager, who masqueraded as his secretary, he began hobnobbing with a gaggle of VIPs. In so doing, he received an introduction to Contessa Antoinette Khevenhüller-Metsch, who had come to the Mondial with another young contessa. Antoinette, known by friends and family as "Atta," was a beautiful, dark-eyed twenty-seven-year-old Viennese brunette with a pale, broad face. She favored heavy lipstick and a fashionable hairstyle, cut just below her ears, gentle, permed waves rolling out from a side part. Sympathetic toward the supposed plight of Edgar's people, Atta handed him a very generous donation of three hundred francs. Naïvely, she thought the money would go toward "the needs of Indian orphans."

Next evening she visited him at the movie theater. She told him that her mother would like the honor of his company for dinner at their hotel the following day. Edgar accepted her invitation, which necessitated a short excursion down the meandering coast to Monte Carlo, where the mountains reared up behind the city's low-slung casino, extravagant hotels, outsize modern mansions, deluxe stores, jungly gardens, and sea-view terraces. For all the talk of the holiday season being pretty much over, a full cast of visiting merrymakers still crowded the stage of this sunlit amphitheater, gilded youth coexisting with tarnished old age. Not many of the visitors were more recognizable than the ballet impresario Serge Diaghilev, who was there with his Ballets Russes troupe.

In company with a smattering of French, British, and Romanian aristocrats, plus a princess from Diaghilev's homeland, Atta and her mother, Contessa Milania Khevenhüller-Metsch, were staying at the Grand Hotel des Étrangers. Dinner with them was an impressive affair.

Habitually referred to by Atta as her mother, the older woman was, in reality, her *stepmother*. Yet the two had a close relationship befitting a mother and daughter. Milania—a onetime lady-in-waiting at the Hapsburg court—was a tall, high-cheekboned sixty-three-year-old Hungarian, widowed by Atta's father more than a decade earlier. Atta's stepmother had distinctively Slavic features, a frail voice, and the bearing of someone much older, her independent and adventurous youth but a distant memory. Like many visitors to Monte Carlo, Milania had been wintering there for health reasons. Despite feeling a bit off color, her stylish dress sense was undiminished. That evening she wore an elegant black ensemble, accessorized by a long pearl necklace and two chunky diamond earrings that caught Edgar's attention.

Though he wasn't in his Native American getup, Milania addressed him as "Chief." Much of the subsequent dinner-table talk centered around Edgar, who charmed his somewhat needy hostess. On prominent display were his suitably regal manners. These must have distracted from the oddity of his request to examine one of her earrings. Presumably making a joke of what he did next, he rubbed it against some glass to test whether it was a genuine diamond, in the process confirming that Milania was as wealthy as she appeared.

At the end of their meal, he excused himself. He said he needed to go back to the Mondial Cinema to change into the clothes he'd be wearing for the quarter-to-nine performance. But his hostess wanted to continue their chat. She insisted on him having tea with them after his show, yet there was no sign of Milania when he returned to the Grand Hotel later in the evening. Her sweet-natured stepdaughter explained that she was "indisposed with a severe headache." Edgar let Atta talk him into remaining there a smidgen longer.

As the time for his eventual departure approached, the young contessa said she could do with some fresh air. She and Edgar then took a protracted and expensive carriage ride to his hotel in Nice. Along the way, Atta presented him with a package from Milania. Inside were five thousand francs, which Milania had won at the casino in Monte Carlo on the night he and Atta first met. The cash was intended as a gift for the Native American children he'd mentioned. Atta regarded this as only "a small payout," though it would have funded a fourteen-week stay at a top Riviera hotel.

EDGAR'S CONTRACT WITH FAMOUS PLAYERS–LASKY was due to end about a week later. Until that moment, he lavished most of his free time on Milania and Atta, whose Monte Carlo base offered plenty to keep them amused during the afternoons and late evenings. They could saunter around the city's upscale stores, eat homemade pastries and candied fruit at the café near the English church, travel down the coast, attend mid-afternoon classical concerts, or listen to the Black and White Jazz Band playing in the ballroom at the casino.

Overlaying the time Edgar spent with the two contessas was the insistent drone of a single airplane etching the sky immediately overhead. Its daredevil exhibitions of spiraling, looping, and nose-diving aerobatics, which recalled the stunt flying at the Montana State Fair, encouraged everyone to speculate about the pilot's identity. She was soon named as Adrienne Bolland, already the most celebrated French aviatrix.

When the contessas were with Edgar, they competed to demonstrate which of them could be more attentive toward him. Dazzled by the publicity he'd sparked and by his apparent exotic glamour and regal status, not to say his well-honed powers of persuasion, they swallowed his tall stories. He told them about his "fabulous wealth" deposited in Vancouver bank accounts, which had been frozen by the British government—hence his present dependence upon paychecks from Famous Players–Lasky. He also said the British were preventing him from exploiting the oil fields discovered on his land.

Cunningly projecting an impression of candor that lent weight to what he'd just said, Edgar confided in the contessas about being married. He then stoked their fast-ripening romantic interest by adding that he wanted a divorce from his British wife. As he admitted to Milania, his disillusionment with his marriage was fueled by his spouse's nationality. Within the scenario he'd sketched, Britain was, after all, responsible for both his current money problems and the hardships endured by his people.

Probing the full extent of the contessas' trusting, sensitive, and unworldly natures, he fed them a description of the wonders of his tribal homeland. He claimed there was a cold stream on one side, where you could go fishing. On the other side, he said, was a stream so hot that the water could be used to cook the fish you'd caught in the cold stream. Verification of the contessas' heaven-sent gullibility came when they fell for this yarn. He went on to obtain a loan from Milania using the bogus collateral of his inherited wealth. She presented him with upward of five thousand francs. Meanwhile, her stepdaughter showered him with gifts.

He started dropping references to how he'd like to travel to Italy, where they lived. By going there, he said, he could extend his campaign to alert the people of Europe to the conditions afflicting his tribe. In response, Milania suggested he should visit her family home near Trieste.

Edgar's promising relationship with the contessas was, however, truncated by their departure for the island of Corsica, from where they were scheduled to return home.

20

There was nothing to detain him. Following the contessas' departure, he headed back to Paris—the better part of a day's train ride away. In the capital, where the nights remained chilly yet the days were bathed in spring warmth, he rejoined Ethel and Leslie, who had endured dire poverty while he was enjoying the high life on the Riviera.

He quickly slipped into his old habit of visiting the Café du Dôme. One of its regulars joked that without his feathered headdress and the rest of his costume, he looked "like any of the other elks."

Talk at the Dôme and elsewhere in Montparnasse revolved around the Olympic Games. Not around the official event that was opening in Paris in less than two weeks, but around the Latin Quarter's own facetious version of it. The Montparnasse Olympiad pitted bohemians of numerous nationalities against one another in unconventional athletic events of the sort that probably included a sprint from café to café, a glass of booze gulped down at each of them. Cash had already been staked on the outcome of every contest.

Edgar's tendency to spend on a scale appropriate to his self-anointed eminence meant that by now he likely retained little of the money he'd been given by Milania. Rather than attempt to tap her for yet another loan, he trained his charm on her stepdaughter, who wired him eight thousand lire—a substantial sum that reached Edgar during the penultimate weekend of April.

Alerted to the susceptibility of the younger of the contessas, that Sunday he sent her another request for money. Since she was in Italy by then, he helpfully translated the desired figure into Italian currency.

JUST RECEIVED THE MONEY, he wrote, BUT SORRY TO SAY I WON'T HAVE ENOUGH. PLEASE ASK YOUR MOTHER. YOU SEE, I HAVE TO PAY FOR MY CAR, WHICH IS LIABLE TO 2,000 LIRE IN CUSTOMS DUTIES. TELL HER SHE WILL RECOUP THIS FROM THE 20TH OF THIS MONTH. He closed the telegram with a line that tweaked their burgeoning emotional bond: NOW, CONTESSA, YOU ARE JUST LIKE FAMILY TO ME.

ATTA SEEMS TO HAVE FALLEN for Edgar's latest ruse. Yet that didn't stop him from trying to extract more money from her stepmother just four days later. He asked Milania to wire him an immediate loan of another five thousand francs. In a psychologically deft, confidence-building play, he sought her permission to arrange for the British government to recompense her from the vast sum it owed him.

She urged him to address her as "Aunt Milania" whenever he sent her telegrams or letters. She also cautioned him to sign himself as her nephew. It was a fiction cooked up by her and Atta in case her meddlesome stepson, Count Georg Khevenhüller-Metsch, whom she treated with extreme wariness, discovered their correspondence. To deprive him of ammunition for any xenophobic grousing about the unseemliness of her and Atta's relationship with an American Indian, she and Atta conspired to tell Georg that Chief White Elk was a distant cousin—that he was the child of an Austrian relative who had run away to Cuba and then North America a generation earlier.

As gullible as ever, Milania probably responded to the telegram from her "nephew" by coming through with the five thousand francs he wanted. The influx of money would have given Edgar a chance to exercise his spendthrift proclivities, with which his wife—who still hadn't pegged him as a crook and an impostor—was losing patience. He didn't have time to bankrupt himself, though, before he and his family made the sharp transition from Paris to the Manchester suburb of Levenshulme.

Relative to the life he'd been leading with his two aristocratic admirers, cold, wintry Manchester, where he and Ethel were once again squeezed into her parents' house, must have felt drab and constrained. No wonder Atta thought he "sounded suicidal" when he next wrote her. And Ethel wasn't much happier. She got the impression that his only interest in her now was sexual.

WITHIN THREE WEEKS OF HIS RETURN to Ethel's family home in Levenshulme, Edgar wrote to Milania soliciting an additional loan. So hefty was the specified figure that it would've covered five years' rent on a house in London. Edgar made the request on the spurious grounds that he needed to pay £150 to the British government. This was, he explained, being demanded as surety, without which the British refused to return $75,000 worth of Canadian property they'd confiscated from him.

Milania, who was falling in love with Edgar, obliged by transferring the required Italian currency to the London outpost of her bank.

Edgar then jettisoned his wife and stepson and traveled down to the capital, where the cold weather suddenly gave way to unrelenting, sticky heat more commensurate with New York City in high summer. Walking even a few yards in London that day was tiring. Edgar nonetheless schlepped over to the financial district and called on the offices of the Credito Italiano, to which Milania had wired the money. He went over to Whitehall, too. A thoroughfare associated with government ministries and the attendant bustle of men carrying attaché cases and stacked documents, it was lined with elephantine, soot-grimed buildings flying Union Jack flags. Toward the south end of the street, Edgar neared the Cenotaph, London's equivalent to the Colonne du Congrès, where two months earlier he'd laid a wreath. Whenever men—be it government staff or teenage delivery boys—hurried past, they'd raise their hats in tribute to this cream-colored slab of solidified national grief, the base of which was always moated by flowers.

Through a door opposite the Cenotaph, Edgar went into the Home Office and headed for the Immigration Directorate. He was there to speak with someone from the directorate's Aliens Branch, the government department charged with keeping track of visiting foreign nationals. Before he could travel to Italy to see Milania and Atta, he had to obtain a Document of Identity, enabling him to enter France without either a passport or his previous (now-redundant) paperwork.

In his application, he cited his wife's address in Manchester as his current residence. He stated that his name was "Tewanna Ray or Chief White Elk" and that he wanted to go to Italy, France, Switzerland, and what used to be known as Austria-Hungary. With the application, he furnished a black-and-white identity photo of himself. It showed him in three-quarter profile, wearing a suit and necktie, light reflecting off his greased-back hair. Though he remained handsome, the boyishness evident just a few years previously had been eroded not only by age but also by hard living and the unremitting strain under which con men existed. His features were now patinaed by middle-aged toughness.

The chief inspector at the Aliens Branch rubber-stamped Edgar's application multiple times, further ratifying it with a scribbled signature. Edgar afterward contacted Milania to let her know that he'd be setting off to visit her soon. He also wired a message to his stepson. DEAR LESLIE, he wrote, dripping with what may have been genuine emotion (or, more likely, self-dramatizing theatricality). YOUR FATHER MUST LEAVE AND NEVER COME BACK.

ELEVEN DAYS AFTER HIS TRIP to the Immigration Directorate, he spent part of the weekend composing another telegram to Milania, this time from Paris. CONTESSA, COULD YOU WIRE ME 15,000 FRANCS? his message began. He informed her that he required the loan because A FRIEND OF MINE IS COMING OVER. The loan would, he assured her, be settled when he met her in Italy that Thursday. Paying no heed to her request that he should, if he wrote to her, pretend to be her nephew, he asserted his power over her by signing himself as CHIEF.

His confidence in the emotional grip he already had on her was such that he was willing to risk not showing up that Thursday at the planned rendezvous. He even had the self-assurance to go one stage further in his quest to subdue her. I'M LEAVING TONIGHT FROM PARIS TO MILAN, he wrote. THERE TELEGRAPH MY ARRIVAL. WITH ALL RESPECTS. CHIEF. He sent the wire to Venice, where Milania was staying. Despite finagling a British Emergency Certificate that would, in lieu of a passport, get him into Italy, he failed to board the train that night. Instead, he carried on enjoying himself in gray, showery Paris, where he had the opportunity to look up friends at the Café du Dôme. Nothing much had changed there, save for the industrious presence behind the bar of the owner's son, just back from military service.

Edgar soon received a telegram from Milania. She wanted to know why he'd been delayed.

PLEASE SEND ME MONEY BECAUSE I AM SICK IN BED, he fired back.

For once Milania didn't accede to his request. Virtuoso manipulator though he was, he'd plainly misjudged the situation. He'd gone too fast. And now he'd blown his shot at pocketing more of the Khevenhüller-Metsch dynasty's riches.

BUT EDGAR WAS IN NO MOOD to quit. Five days after sending his request to Milania, he tried a different angle. His new approach involved wiring a brief message to her stepdaughter. It reiterated his story about falling sick. He also used the telegram to ask Atta to persuade her stepmother to send him the money he required.

Under the impression that he was seriously ill and in need of costly medical attention, Milania dispatched eighty thousand francs to him via a French bank. The money corresponded to a full year's wages for a leading French civil servant. Even by Edgar's profligate standards, he now had more than enough to make the most of his remaining time in Paris.

Somewhat over 150 miles away, the Brussels police had meanwhile indicted him for fraud and sent warnings about him to their counterparts in numerous countries. News of the hunt for Chief White Elk thus spread to the press in Australia, Britain, New Zealand, Belgium, and Switzerland. According to one such newspaper, the wanted man was "sufficiently distinctive" for the manhunt "to yield immediate results." In a waggish conclusion, it added, "You can't travel with impunity when you have feathers on your head."

Traveling with impunity was, however, what he was about to do. One morning around the start of June, he went over to the Gare de Lyon and joined the people filing onto the Simplon-Orient-Express. Its passengers, many of them accompanied by cosseted pooches, were largely drawn from the ranks of aristocrats, stockbrokers, Greek shipping magnates, famous opera singers, Viennese bankers, drug smugglers, Balkan landowners, and Middle Eastern businessmen, as well as pairs of diplomatic couriers, a valise always chained to the wrist of one of them. Staff in old-fashioned, high-collared military-style uniforms looked after Edgar and the other passengers, each of whom had a separate compartment. Punctuating these were washrooms, accessible only from the two adjacent compartments, thus offering privacy for aficionados of casual sex like him.

As his train left Paris and sped through France, farmhands usually glancing up from their labors in time to gape at this flickering emblem of wealth and glamour, Edgar was surely ignorant of the danger awaiting him at the Swiss border. Customs officers stationed there had been instructed by the Brussels police to detain him. The officers would have boarded the train when it drew up at the frontier, but they always treated passengers on the Simplon-Orient-Express with negligent deference. Their examination of passports, visas, and identity papers was cursory at best, so Edgar didn't find himself being escorted off the train before it resumed its journey.

It stopped in Lausanne, then wove its way through mountainous scenery that may have reminded Edgar of Colorado. His train entered Italy via the Simplon Tunnel. Peering out of the window at the fields, villages, and towns between there and Milan, he would probably have seen little evidence of the seismic political change that had occurred there. Just over eighteen months earlier, Mussolini and his Partito Nazionale Fascista (PNF) had formed Europe's first fascist government. Yet black shirts, the prime component of the PNF uniform, were an infrequent sight, as they were regarded as too sacred for everyday use. Members reserved them for parades and other official events. In place of uniforms, fascists communicated their allegiances by wearing discreet metal badges. Edgar was at the outset unlikely to have understood the significance of these depictions of an axe protruding from a bundle of tightly bound sticks, known collectively as the "fasces."

From Venice, where his train made a brief stop, he wired Milania to let her know he'd be in Trieste late that evening. When he disembarked in this handsome old Austro-Hungarian port city, which had been seized by the Italians toward the close of the Great War, he headed along its grand waterfront. He ended up at the Savoia Palace Hotel. Without question the most expensive hotel in town, it had a wide, bulging stone frontage, corseted by columns. At large Italian hotels like this, he could get away with communicating in only English or French. He registered as Prince Chief White Elk. His concocted title secured him the hotel's Royal Suite, even though his title was a mismatched hybrid, part European, part Native American. The lyrics to a song from his repertoire, proclaiming "There's a long, long trail a-winding into the land of my dreams," might have been written especially for the moment he took possession of his suite.

He was still in residence at the Savoia Palace when Milania came to chauffeur him back to her villa. First, though, she settled his hotel tab and took him to the Trieste branch of her bank. She withdrew a large sum of money—about 12,000 lire. She handed the bulk of it to Edgar and begged him not to tell her stepson, whom he'd be meeting at the villa.

In advance of their departure from the city, she and Edgar also went shopping. They visited a jewelry store, where Milania bought two gold watches. And they called at a tailor's. Knowing that Edgar didn't have many clothes with him, Milania arranged to have him fitted for several custom-made suits. These cost her 4,800 lire.

Edgar and his hostess were not through with their shopping spree, however. Milania accompanied him to an automobile dealership, where they admired the new models. Ever since attending the Paris Motor Show almost two decades earlier, she'd been a keen driver. On her visit to the Motor Show, she'd purchased a Mercedes Simplex 28/32, only the second vehicle manufactured by the German company. She had gone on to compete in road races, twice winning the race from Klagenfurt to the Glocknerhaus in Austria. In the second of those victories, she defeated Ferdinand Porsche, founder of the eponymous car company.

While Edgar and Milania were at the automobile dealership, Edgar test-drove an inordinately expensive Lancia. Milania ended up buying it. Her intention was that Edgar would present the vehicle to Georg when they first met, thus currying favor with her stepson and complying with the tradition of gift giving between aristocrats.

PRINTED ON THE VISITING CARD was a crown. Beneath were the words "His Highness, the Prince, Chief White Elk." Upon arriving at the Khevenhüller-Metsch's large villa in the town of Fiumicello, nineteen miles to the northwest of Trieste, Edgar handed his card to all the hired help.

At the villa he was introduced to Milania's twenty-five-year-old stepson, a onetime officer in the Austrian army. Georg had just returned from a hunting trip to Africa. So admiringly had Milania spoken about Chief White Elk that Georg was keen to meet someone he believed to be a "distinguished redskin prince."

Georg commemorated their meeting by giving Edgar a diamond, emerald, and sapphire ring. Edgar reciprocated with the Lancia, which was a perfectly chosen gift because Georg shared his stepmother's enthusiasm for cars. The extravagance of this gesture, compounded by Edgar's antsy entreaties that Milania should permit him to store his jewel-encrusted national costume in her safe, appeared to validate everything he subsequently told Georg about the oil fields he owned and the riches he was destined to receive.

For about the next month, during which Atta got back from a trip to Austria, Edgar wallowed in the hospitality Milania often lavished upon visitors. She treated him as one of the family. He knocked back bottle after bottle of her scotch, which must have tasted a whole lot better than the moonshine served stateside. He took advantage of the doting contessas' offer to allow him to ride their horses and drive their cars. He tagged along with them on jaunts to local beauty spots. He repeatedly accompanied them to the swimming baths. And he went with Atta to the nearby town of Aquileia, where they joined the army veterans, grieving families, and tourists visiting the military cemetery that lay in the shadow of a

Roman basilica. With familiar theatrical solemnity, Edgar laid a wreath at the war memorial.

During a trip to Trieste, he visited a bank to which he pretended that some of his wealth was being transferred. Presumably with at least one of the contessas present, he complained vocally about the failure of his money to materialize.

He must also have mentioned to his hostess that Ethel and Leslie were short of cash, because she wired no less than fifty thousand lire—almost the amount she'd spent on the Lancia—to a bank in Manchester. Surreptitiously, Edgar then channeled the money to an Italian account he'd opened—money that would have allowed him to maintain his twin drug habits. (Despite the regime's efforts to stamp out the drug trade, which fascist propaganda depicted as a communist plot to erode the nation's moral fiber, cocaine and morphine were available to him.)

Around that time he received a letter from Ethel, urging him to come back to her. She floated the idea of opening a small hotel together and added, "Everyone at home thinks this is a wonderful idea, because you would have the chance to sing and attract lots of people to the hotel." She suggested they name the place "the Hotel Indian Chief."

Edgar didn't bother answering his wife's letter. Next to the deluxe life furnished for him by Milania, Ethel's pipe dreams clearly held no appeal.

Cognizant of the threat Georg posed to this hedonistic existence, Edgar began cultivating Milania's stepson. In that regard, Edgar was so successful that he left Georg in no doubt as to his status as "a semi-royal relation." Georg even felt comfortable enough in his presence to talk him through the photographic souvenirs of his recent safari. From Africa, Georg had brought back a young elephant and donated her to Schönbrunn Zoo in Vienna.

Another time, Edgar held forth to Georg about the invention of radio, how it had revived the venerable art of storytelling, how English radios were the finest in Europe. Georg asked Edgar to choose one for him. Edgar was handed eight thousand lire to buy the latest model, though he spent only half the money and pocketed the balance.

· · ·

WITH A VIEW TO UNDERTAKING an Italian tour, ostensibly aimed at increasing awareness of the parlous conditions under which his people lived, Edgar went on to wring another 65,000 lire or thereabouts out of Milania. She joined him in Trieste, where she chartered the *Cimarosa*—a small, late-nineteenth-century steamship—to take him around the Italian coast.

Before his ship motored out of Trieste harbor on Saturday, July 12, 1924, Edgar spoke to an Italian news agency reporter, who wired ahead to the many places on his itinerary. Big crowds were consequently waiting for him at the quayside when, over the next seventeen days, the *Cimarosa* made hasty stops at the lovely Adriatic ports of Venice, Fiume, and Ancona.

Often as not Edgar's disembarkation was marked by music from a brass band. Sometimes they played the Italian national anthem. Sometimes they played the "Giovinezza"—a military march that doubled as the Italian fascist anthem. And sometimes they played a tune mistakenly held to be "the Red Indian national anthem."

Stepping ashore, Edgar would be greeted by an excited crowd, its excitement symptomatic of the same vulnerability to outsize personalities, charisma, mythmaking, and ostentatious theatricality that lay behind Mussolini's success. Many of the people on the quayside had likely grown up reading about Native Americans in Italian writer Emilio Salgari's popular Wild West novels. Also there to greet him would be members of the municipal fascist hierarchy. Being a talented linguist, he soon picked up a smattering of Italian, deployed in combination with French and English phrases.

On the first three stops of his tour, he was lionized at official receptions. He received honorary membership in the local PNF. He was introduced to regional dignitaries, one of whom appears to have been Gabriele D'Annunzio, the eccentric poet and libertine who had led a fascist coup in Fiume. Edgar was taken on visits to places such as the shrine at the Basilica della Santa Casa, just south of Ancona. And he played the role of a wealthy royal benefactor by distributing gifts, be it money to the PNF, photographs of himself, banknotes to the poor, or objects he had himself been given by Milania, among them a platinum ring with a small pearl inset.

His politics as fluid as his sexuality and so much else about him, Edgar professed—whenever the occasion required—a hatred of "anarchists and reds." For deferential fascist grandees, whose quasi-religious ideology glorified wartime bloodshed, Edgar's visit afforded a valuable opportunity. It gave them the chance not only to associate with a representative of what tended to be portrayed as a warrior culture, but also to distract public attention from what promised to be a terminal scandal enmeshing the PNF.

That scandal had its roots in a parliamentary speech made the previous month by Giacomo Matteotti, one of the country's socialist leaders. Ceaselessly vocal in his opposition to Mussolini's would-be dictatorship, Matteotti lambasted the voter intimidation tactics perpetrated by the PNF during its recent election victory, achieved while Edgar was still in Nice. Ten days after the speech, Matteotti was assaulted in the street by a gang of thugs. Other political opponents of Mussolini's had suffered the same fate, but this was different: Matteotti's five assailants dumped him in a car and drove him away at high speed.

Inside forty-eight hours, the police had identified the perpetrators and found the vehicle used in the kidnapping. Enough blood was spattered over its upholstery to suggest that Matteotti must have been murdered. Its license plates had meanwhile been traced to the editor of a fascist newspaper controlled by Mussolini.

Correctly reading the incident as an assault on constitutional government, both the Italian press and public opinion turned sharply against Mussolini. So, too, did some of the non-fascist politicians who had previously supported him. If his involvement in the kidnapping and suspected murder could be verified, then he faced the prospect of being put on trial.

More immediately, he had to deal with a political crisis that threatened to unseat him. A coalition of 150 Italian parliamentarians—everyone from communists to right-wing Catholics—were striving to bring down his government. In protest at what had happened to Matteotti, they boycotted parliament, their gesture attracting immense popular support. Edgar now had cause to wonder whether he'd staked Milania's money on the wrong horse.

. . .

A PLATOON OF SOLDIERS MARCHED down the quayside toward Edgar. He could have been forgiven for assuming that his devotees from the PNF had been ousted from government, and that the soldiers were coming to take him away. On Tuesday, July 29, 1924, at 4:00 p.m., the platoon marched aboard the *Cimarosa,* which had docked at the sun-bleached southern city of Bari four hours previously. But they weren't there to arrest him. They were escorting two of the city's most prominent fascists—a politician and one of the leaders of the *Milizia Volontaria per la Sicurezza Nazionale* (MVSN), the fascist militia.

Other fascist notables soon joined "Prince Chief White Elk Tewanna, son of Chief Yellow Robe" aboard the *Cimarosa.* His face had over recent weeks become quite bronzed, which chimed conveniently with his chosen identity. Bolstering this were his current clothes—white suede pants, brightly hued appurtenances, an orange shirt, and a cloak embellished by a thick mink tail. His practice of wearing a feathered headdress, tucking a dagger into his belt, and puffing on a traditional, long-stemmed ceremonial pipe in between cigarettes also boosted his credibility. So, too, did his frequent talk of the land he owned.

In what remained of the afternoon, his newly acquired entourage went with him on a drive around Bari, the sights of which included a castle and a cathedral. Edgar and his retinue stopped at the opera house and the Barion Canoe Club, where he signed the visitors' books. At the Barion, a young woman presented him with a bouquet. He responded by gallantly ripping the mink tail from his cloak and handing it to her.

Continuing to foster the illusion of fabulous wealth, Edgar wired two thousand lire to the PNF's offices in Fiume. And he gave a generous donation when he dropped by the headquarters of its provincial federation. He was rewarded with membership, together with the title of honorary corporal in the militia, a title about which he was inordinately proud. Only Mussolini, who had been granted the rank of first honorary corporal, trumped it.

After a swift pit stop at a crowded restaurant where he bought hard liquor for the other customers, Edgar went for a stroll through the Old Town's narrow and mazelike medieval streets. These sheathed the uneven contours of a spit of land that projected into the sea. He pandered to his hosts by expressing admiration for the fascist movement. He also dispensed more money to the poor, mainly to children and the elderly.

Numerous urchins from the Old Town, forming part of a substantial group, were still trailing behind him as he made his way back to the *Cimarosa*. Some of the crowd even followed him onto the ship. They included an amputee, lots of children, and a sailor who saluted him. Edgar rewarded their determination with bountiful handouts. And when a little ragamuffin showed off to him by diving into the sea, he tossed a fifty-lire bill in his direction.

As the *Cimarosa* prepared to cast off from the wharf where it was docked, Edgar pledged to return to Bari in forty days and distribute more cash. Lining the wharf were his fascist hosts, along with large numbers of impoverished women and children who waved enthusiastically as the vessel slipped its moorings.

He came away feeling impressed by the "fantastic" reception he'd enjoyed. Surely not unrelated to the warmth with which he'd been welcomed by the people of Bari was the fact he had given away close to fifty thousand lire of Milania's fortune in the two and a half hours he'd spent there. Beneath headlines such as A REDSKIN PRINCE IN BARI, his grandiose munificence received acclaim from the Italian local and national press. Stories about his generosity then spread to newspapers in countries as distant as Australia, the details often exaggerated, the whole affair accruing the quality of a fable, albeit a fable whose moral had not yet been unveiled.

Rich though Edgar's benefactress was, she'd had to sell a handsome tract of land in order to bankroll his antics. The revelation that she'd parted with this upset Georg, whose late father had formerly owned it. His resentment comingling with his burgeoning suspicion regarding his stepmother's beloved Canadian cousin, Georg got in touch with one of the network of British consulates. He asked the consulate for information about Prince Chief White Elk. The countdown to Georg discovering that his so-called relative was an impostor had now begun.

By all indications oblivious to the impending catastrophe unleashed upon him by Milania's stepson, Edgar was steaming down the Italian coast aboard the *Cimarosa*. He went from Bari to Brindisi, a pleasant little town sitting on the rim of a wide bay, where he stopped for only a day before heading to Catania. Just three and a half hours after the *Cimarosa* reached this crowded Sicilian city, he and a group of fascist officials embarked upon an overnight train journey to Rome, a journey that would have felt even longer because Italy's trains were notoriously decrepit and dirty.

For the opening leg of the trip, Edgar's train crossed dramatic vistas strewn with orange groves, jagged mountains, and scorched hillsides. He had abundant time in which to savor how much his life had changed since the days when a vacation meant something entirely different. It used to mean nothing more exotic than Sockanosset School for Boys's annual day trip, which would begin with him and three hundred other cadets pouring out of their dormitories and lining up outside, their sense of anticipation intensified by the sight of a procession of trucks bumping across the school grounds.

When kindly Superintendent Eastman, who ran the school, would ask Edgar and the others if they were ready, they'd all shout, "Yes, sir!" Then they'd give him three rousing cheers. And he would tell them to do the same for the school.

Lungs fresh from this vocal workout, Edgar and the rest of the cadets would pile onto the trucks, which would take them on the slow journey to Gaspee Point, where the shore overlooked the estuary of the Providence River. Under the command of Deputy Superintendent Butterfield, Edgar and his fellow cadets would be ordered to change into their bathing costumes and line up along the beach's grassy fringe.

Teasingly, the deputy superintendent would keep them waiting before shouting "All in!" Edgar could then show off his athletic skills during the mass sprint toward the sea, where the boys would spend until lunchtime splashing about and hollering. After a meal of sandwiches, ice cream, cake, and coffee, they'd swim some more. They'd also play baseball, collect seashells, and dig for clams, the school band's rendition of "Yankee Doodle" enhancing the carnival atmosphere.

More than two decades, three thousand miles of ocean, and several lifetimes' experiences separated Edgar's current self from those trips to Gaspee Point. They probably felt so remote and intangible that they might as well have happened to someone else. In a sense, they *hadn't* happened to him. They'd happened to Edgar Laplante, who was long gone.

EARLY ON THE MORNING AFTER boarding the train in Catania, Edgar and the fascist officials arrived in Rome, its tan skyline fretted with spires and domes. There, Edgar became the houseguest of an Italian aristocrat who had a villa close to the sprawling, sparsely ornamented Palazzo del Quirinale, home of King Vittorio Emanuele III, now the focus of widespread speculation. Mussolini's opponents, still boycotting parliament, hoped to persuade the king to exercise his constitutional prerogative and fire Mussolini as prime minister.

Newspaper coverage of the ongoing tour by the king's Cherokee counterpart having already made Edgar famous in Italy, passersby pointed out "the prince" as he swanned around the capital. While he was there, he made an ostentatious display of consulting an attorney about his avowed problems with the British government. And he kept up to date with what had become a regular correspondence with Milania, during which he'd gotten into the habit of mailing her some of the commemorative photos, gifts, and other trophies he was collecting.

Milania's replies were colored by a maternal tone that sought to protect him from what she regarded as his tendency to be "too generous and a bit disorganized." Her stepdaughter, who penned fond and admiring letters to him, shared this slight frustration, and even ventured to reprimand him gently about his behavior.

Writing to Milania from Rome, Edgar claimed he'd taken the liberty of speaking on her behalf to members of the fascist government. They were, he informed her, sympathetic toward her family's long-running struggle to obtain compensation for the damage to their property inflicted during the Great War.

Due to rejoin the *Cimarosa* following almost a week away, Edgar soon afterward quit Rome. He then made the 117-mile journey along the coast to Naples, a city unlike anyplace he had visited. Its celebrated beauty, backed by the busty silhouette of Mount Vesuvius and fronted by the blue waters of the harbor, was at odds with the teeming squalor of its pungent streets. Many of these, heaped with trash and spanned by clotheslines, echoed with the hooves of goats and cows. Others were haunted by tenacious beggars. Among Edgar's colleagues in the con game, it was held that giving money to a beggar—"a plinger," in grifters' slang—would always be rewarded by good luck. But Edgar couldn't go on handing out so much cash without getting the ever-pliable Milania to make another bank transfer.

From Naples, he sent a telegram requesting that she wire money to Genoa, three stops further along his itinerary. As bait for Milania, who made no secret of her and her stepdaughter's desire to see him flourish, he explained that the money would bring him an appointment as a colonel in the Italian military. Secure in her conviction that Edgar was an eminent person who possessed ample finances, Milania needed scant encouragement to lend him however much he requested.

Back on the *Cimarosa*, he left Naples and traveled to Palermo, then Cagliari, an atmosphere of excitement prevailing ahead of each stop. People even rented windows overlooking streets where they might glimpse Prince Tewanna Ray, whose generosity earned him comparisons to the virtuous heroes from fairy tales. Accounts of him dishing out large sums of money spawned obsequious begging letters, addressing him as "Your Highness."

ITALIANS SOMETIMES USED THE PHRASE *la superba* when referring to the city of Genoa. As Edgar discovered in late July when he landed there to a familiar tumultuous reception, Genoa merited that label by virtue of its spacious parks, sweeping views, and seaward slopes barnacled with marble palaces and dusty yellow houses. He cabled Milania a request for another loan. The money would, he said, cover newfound expenses, incurred as the upshot of being appointed to a senior position within the PNF. Milania transferred twenty thousand lire—a figure on a par with the annual salary of a top Italian sportsman—to an account in Genoa.

Edgar was, however, penalized for his greed when he called at the bank. Weighed down perhaps by Milania's cash, he appears to have tripped while collecting it. His ankle was so badly sprained that he had to retreat to the *Cimarosa* and have his injury examined by a doctor.

Instead of setting off for Milan, as previously planned, Edgar stuck around in Genoa while he waited for his injury to mend. He was visited aboard his ship by both of the contessas, who appear to have consoled him with scotch, a bunch of roses, and a further fifty-five thousand lire. They also probably let slip that Georg had been making inquiries about him.

Now Edgar developed a sudden desire to leave the country. But the Document of Identity that he'd obtained in London didn't entitle him to do so, meaning he was trapped in Italy, a country well on its way to becoming a dictatorship, a country where anyone who fell foul of the fascist regime was in line for a beating or worse—*far* worse, as Giacomo Matteotti had discovered.

And you could guarantee the fascists wouldn't be too happy when they cottoned on to the fact that Edgar had played them for suckers.

DESPITE HIS SORE ANKLE, Edgar went to see Britain's acting consul general on the morning of Saturday, August 9, 1924. Keeping up the fiction that he was a Canadian Cherokee, he took with him the Document of Identity. He filled in the acting consul general about his travel plans, which received the go-ahead.

"No objection to bearer proceeding to Spain," the British official wrote on the back of the Document of Identity. He also signed and rubber-stamped it, leaving Edgar free to instruct the captain of the *Cimarosa* to plot the envisaged course for Barcelona via Marseilles. In the minutes before departing, he doled out a few hundred lire to the stevedores loading the ship with provisions, to a homeward-bound widow, and to the chief customs officer. But the latter handed back the money, saying that he and his staff weren't permitted to accept gifts. He was ultimately persuaded by Edgar to keep the five hundred lire and donate it to charity.

Slipping out of the harbor around noon, the *Cimarosa* headed west along the low, sandy coastline of the Italian Riviera, Edgar's sprained ankle probably aggravated by the swaying deck. Through the daylight hours, he'd have seen brown-sailed trawlers, wheezy-motored cargo vessels, and—when the wind let up—schooners towed by boats that were powered by swarthy, semi-naked oarsmen, perspiring like the galley slaves who had preceded them hundreds of years earlier. After nightfall Edgar would have seen the tremulous light from acetylene flares. These were used to lure fish toward the trawlers, whose crews then tossed dynamite into the shoals, its dull concussion reminiscent of the depth charges dropped during his wartime voyage to France.

Edgar had the *Cimarosa* make for Porto Maurizio. From some distance out at sea, the pale dome of the town's cathedral was visible, protruding from the jumble of buildings that clung to the sloping promontory. On the streets of this bucolic little burg, through which old women carried baskets on their heads, dark-eyed girls in richly colored shawls sauntered, and farmers led donkeys, foreigners of any description—never mind an American attired in his idea of a Cherokee chief's costume—were a novelty.

He remained there just long enough for his extravagance to yield gossip and for him to elicit a fifty-thousand-lire loan that Milania sent to the local branch of the Credito Italiano. Yet the bank was so dubious about Edgar that it declined to release the money. Both Milania and her stepdaughter soon rendezvoused with him in Porto Maurizio, presumably so Milania could vouch for him at the bank. She or Atta may also have mocked Georg's suspicious nature and talked about his detective work to Edgar.

Georg had, in the meantime, secured an appointment with the head of one of Britain's consulates. At the meeting, he followed up his inquiry about Prince Tewanna Ray. The consul—who obviously hadn't troubled to question the relevant officials in Britain or Canada—had soothed Georg's anxieties by saying, "This man is worth ten million."

THE THREAT FROM GEORG'S INVESTIGATION LIFTED, Edgar gave up on the idea of going to Spain. Once he'd distributed another wad of Milania's money, some of it in high-denomination bills, he hired a car and was driven a short way down the coast to the adjoining town, where he'd arranged to meet Atta and Milania a day or two later.

Set amid woods and olive groves as characteristic of the region as its azure sea and sky, Diano Marina was a modern seaside resort. Edgar checked in to the highly recommended Hôtel du Paradis, which faced a palm tree–dotted strip of park and the ocean beyond. His recovery monitored by a doctor, he passed the second half of August there with Milania and her stepdaughter. In surreptitious exchange for the money that continued to be given him by Milania, he appears to have assumed a grudging role as her lover.

Years of cocaine and morphine dependency had by then left him with a fixed stare that contributed to his vague manner. To exacerbate his problems, he was also drinking heavily enough to unveil a coarse and argumentative disposition that Milania had not hitherto witnessed. She heard him rail against the British authorities, which had, he said, stolen £200 million from him. Probably influenced by the regional leader of the PNF's decision to grant him a two-soldier escort whenever he wanted, he spoke in support of Mussolini's beleaguered government. He said it was the only one capable of comprehending the plight of the Italian people. Edgar also dropped hints about how he wanted to sell his oil fields and seek Italian citizenship.

Atta endeavored to pull some strings on his behalf by writing to Tullio Tamburini, the Florentine fascist leader.

"Noble Contessa," Tamburini replied. "I am trying to obtain what the chief desires—citizenship. Tell him to forward his documents to me right away."

Edgar's desire for Italian citizenship was surely less about switching nationality than about posing as an ardent admirer of Mussolini's regime. The fact was, Edgar never got around to mailing Tamburini his somewhat meager documentation.

OVER DINNER WITH THE CONTESSAS on the terrace of the Hôtel du Paradis, where they'd likely have been able to enjoy such regional specialties as *bouillabaisse* and *zuppa di pesce,* Edgar was introduced to Count Ludovico Barattieri di San Pietro. A suave twenty-three-year-old, serving as a senior officer in the fascist militia, he had dark hair atop a face dominated by close-set eyes and an aquiline nose.

Milania presented herself and her stepdaughter as the aunt and cousin of Prince Ray Tewanna, Chief White Elk.

"Don't call me 'Prince,' but simply 'Ray,'" a falsely modest Edgar told the count.

Ludovico quickly demonstrated his exalted connections by introducing Edgar to a series of aristocratic women from his native Turin, who were on vacation there. Promising Ludovico the gift of a villa situated near some hot springs in Canada, Edgar wound up hiring the count as his secretary.

Through Ludovico, Edgar angled to secure a meeting with Mussolini, known by the reverential title of Il Duce—the Leader. PRINCE WHITE ELK WISHES TO DISCUSS SERIOUS MATTERS WITH YOUR EXCELLENCY, announced Ludovico's initial wire to the Italian prime minister. It precipitated an exchange of telegrams between Edgar and Mussolini—telegrams from one leader to another. Edgar sought to get in Mussolini's good graces by warning him that he was suffering from a stomach ulcer. "As a medical practitioner, I recognize these ailments," Edgar wrote. "I can tell from the way you breathe and your eyes and how you hold your hands and how you move."

Sure enough, Edgar bagged an appointment with Mussolini, whose political position remained precarious. The naked corpse of the abducted socialist politician Giacomo Matteotti had just been found in a shallow grave near Rome, giving the king even greater justification for dismissing Mussolini as prime minister.

Before leaving the contessas and setting out for Rome, where the meeting was due to take place, Edgar told Milania that he'd use his time in the capital to try to persuade the British government to return his confiscated assets. Partnering him for the trip was Ludovico. On the morning of Thursday, August 28, 1924, they headed for the busy Piazza Colonna. Across from the massive Roman column in the center was the Palazzo Chigi, to which Edgar and Ludovico reported. Decorating its interior were Renaissance statuary and painted ceilings. Soon Edgar would be talking with Il Duce, whose pugnacious profile may have been familiar to him from grainy newspaper photos.

But Edgar eventually discovered that Mussolini couldn't see him. Il Duce had needed to hurry to Tuscany to deal with a miners' strike. Were Edgar to admit the truth about his futile visit to the Palazzo Chigi, he'd have risked losing credibility with Milania. When he next wrote to the contessa, he made a point of saying how well his Roman trip was going. He added that the British government remained obstructive, so he wondered whether she'd mind lending him some extra money to tide him over. This time he didn't ask for 50,000 lire. He asked for 110,000.

More convinced than ever about the lofty social and economic realm inhabited by Chief White Elk, Milania transferred the money to him via Ludovico's bank account. Edgar preyed upon her seemingly unshakable belief in him by swiftly submitting further requests—for 15,000 and then 125,000 lire, which she sent him by the same route.

There was still time for Edgar to transform his second visit to Rome into more than just a financial success. In hope of getting Edgar an audience with the pope, Ludovico—whose network of connections embraced the Vatican—paid a substantial bribe to a Roman Catholic cardinal. For once, though, Edgar was the chump. His money bought nothing beyond a pair of signed photos of the pope.

To save face, Ludovico appended forged papal inscriptions to both pictures. "The Holy Father," read one of those inscriptions, "bestows an apostolic blessing to Your Highness, the Prince Tewanna Ray and your Indian brothers."

While in Rome, Edgar also tried his luck with the Italian queen mother. As a pretext for contacting her, he mailed a beaded necklace to her, accompanied by a request to visit the Pantheon and lay a commemorative crown there. She responded with a dismissive note explaining that nobody but princes and monarchs was entitled to lay crowns in the Pantheon. With her message, she enclosed the necklace and one hundred lire to cover Edgar's postal expenses.

TOGETHER WITH LUDOVICO AND THE SPANISH CONSUL, Marquis José Alli Maccarani, Edgar drove from Rome to Florence on Sunday, August 31, 1924. He moved into a top-floor suite at the Grand Hotel Baglioni, a historic mansion that had become one of the city's costliest hotels. It looked onto the giant obelisk that skewered the broad expanse of the Piazza dell'Unità Italiana, down the side of which streetcars rattled. Local newspaper stories about the arrival of the famously generous "Canadian prince" ensured that a crowd quickly formed there. To prevent the crowd from getting into the Baglioni, police manned every entrance.

Bellhops and miscellaneous flunkies beat a path to Edgar's door, carrying packages, telegrams, flowers, and letters from Italians who'd heard about him. No matter whether the author of those letters offered the gift of two brand-new motorbikes or pleaded for three thousand lire to avoid disgrace and the consequent necessity to commit suicide, Edgar opened many of them with a contented smile. Geographically and in every other respect, he'd come a long way since the days when he was laboring amid the stifling heat and toxic fumes of a zinc smelting plant in Bartlesville, Oklahoma.

Alongside his fan mail, which made it increasingly hard to distinguish the con man from the conned, mounds of pricey gifts accumulated. To safeguard his assorted booty and his jewel-spangled chief's robes, supposedly of "incalculable value," the manager of the Baglioni arranged for an extra police officer to be stationed outside Edgar's suite.

Edgar treated his robes with the offhand carelessness of someone who had grown up with priceless possessions. His jeweled getup drew admiring comments when he donned it for his second evening in Florence. By claiming his birthday was that day, he gave himself an excuse to throw a big dinner party. Dining with "His Royal Highness" at the Baglioni were José Alli Maccarani and wife, plus representatives from the city's fascist leadership. Edgar found favor with the fascists by toasting Il Duce, who clung to power despite the parliamentary boycott, the threat of intervention by the king, and the flood of adverse comment from press and public.

Sufficient champagne flowed to ensure that the dinner table atmosphere was relaxed and the speeches earned a warm response. Edgar appeared moved by the occasion, his alcohol and drug intake surely contributing to his audacious duplicity, to the escalating scale of the lies he'd been telling. Now it was no longer about the money—if it ever had been. The money was just a means of calibrating the risks he was taking.

BUNDLES OF TEN- AND FIFTY-LIRE BILLS filled the pockets of his chief's costume next morning. He wore it as he walked past the police guard and out of the Baglioni's main entrance.

Waiting for him in the piazza was a parked car. Between him and the car, a crowd had assembled in hope of receiving cash handouts. The crowd surrounded him before he could narrow that gap. He dipped into his pockets and started doling out wads of currency to those closest to him. As he did this, the crowd congealed around him, impeding his progress still more.

He'd exhausted his supply of bundled banknotes by the time he was approached by a man on a buggy, hauled by a skeletal horse. The man begged him for money. Assuming an expression of sympathy, Edgar handed the man a hundred-lire bill and then got into the parked car.

With some difficulty, the car nosed through the scrimmage. Once it escaped from the piazza, it took Edgar on a rapid tour of the city's main landmarks, the majority of them grand Renaissance buildings, their terra-cotta rooftops superimposed over the mountains beyond. Conspicuous among the tourist sights was the Duomo, a cathedral with a lofty, symmetrical façade, inset with varicolored marble and seething with statuary.

Edgar called on the headquarters of the fascist militia. Like all such buildings, it had what was known as a Sanctuary of the Fallen, where visitors could venerate the concept of national regeneration through violent sacrifice. When Edgar met with the thickset, shaven-headed Tullio Tamburini, whom Atta had earlier contacted on his behalf, he could wheel out his make-believe military reminiscences. One of the principal organizers of the March on Rome, the coup d'état that had installed Mussolini as prime minister, Tamburini presented Edgar with a militia uniform and a fascist armband.

That afternoon Edgar further flaunted his supposed allegiances by visiting the Fiesole neighborhood's local fascist headquarters, where he spent enough time to charm the women, voice his admiration for their movement, and pledge to send them a donation. He also joined a collection of senior military men for a wreath-laying at the Porte Sante cemetery, just south of the river that split the city. His companions included Tamburini's sixty-two-year-old friend and fellow fascist Major General Sante Ceccherini.

Surpassing even his normal flights of fancy, Edgar enriched his performance as a visiting grandee by telling people that he was descended on his mother's side from the Bourbons, the former ruling dynasty of France. He backed up this story by adding sufficient detail to distract from the manifest implausibility of it all. In an erudite display of contrivance, he said he was a kinsman of the Duke of Bourbon, who had revolted against King Francis I of France and then fought for Charles V—ruler of the Holy Roman Empire—at the sacking of Rome in 1527. He even dispensed a scholarly footnote about how the duke had been killed by a musket-ball, which the artist, writer, and soldier Benvenuto Cellini boasted about firing.

Under the gaze of numerous police officers, a small crowd was loitering outside the Baglioni's austere frontage when Edgar returned that evening. Most of the people in the crowd were relatively young. His long-awaited return prompted cheering. A number of the women standing in the piazza clutched bunches of flowers, yet they didn't get a chance to present them to him. Smiling, he bustled straight through the police cordon and into the hotel. Then he went up to his suite, which was linked to the lobby via a sweeping staircase.

From his rooms, he could probably hear the noisy throng that lingered in the piazza despite attempts by the police to disperse it. Several times during what remained of the evening, the crowd looked as if it was about to storm the hotel. And on each occasion the police moved into position, ready to parry the assault that never came.

The situation nonetheless encouraged the authorities to arrange for Edgar to switch hotels. When he heard about his enforced departure, he let his displeasure show. Compelling him to flee the crowd was akin to dragging an actor offstage during the middle of a sellout performance.

As a preamble to Edgar quitting the Baglioni, the police sealed the building. Not very effectively, though. For the second time in recent days, one of the people in the crowd somehow sneaked into the hotel. A woman had last time found her way up to the fourth floor where Edgar's suite lay, but she'd been dragged away before she could reach him. In this instance, however, the intruder managed to buttonhole Edgar, who handed over a few hundred lire.

Outside the hotel, Edgar was picked up by his driver. The police were unable to hold back the raucous crowd, which surged around him. One of the boys in the crowd sparked hollering and applause by climbing onto Edgar's car for a few moments. Gradually the vehicle accelerated and broke free. A pack of young boys chased it down the street.

Edgar was driven through the nocturnal city, where his car may have passed one of the torchlit funeral processions so commonplace in Florence, the coffin bearers headed by a crucifix-wielding priest. Someone—likely

Edgar himself—must have leaked his destination, a quayside piazza on the other side of the river. When his car got there, a crowd had already convened outside the Grand Hotel de la Ville. Before he could step out of the car, he had to wait for the police to arrive and keep the crowd under control. Only then did he enter his new hotel—a thoroughly modern establishment.

After he'd taken possession of the suite reserved for him, sundry fascist dignitaries came to pay their respects. This was presumably the occasion when he met one of the party's rising stars, Roberto Farinacci, a pudgy-faced thirty-two-year-old with dark, lugubrious looks, their lugubriousness invariably accentuated by a fastidious little triangular mustache that belied his taste for violence. Edgar made sure to cultivate Farinacci by offering to pay the funeral costs of two fascists who'd recently been killed when a hand grenade had accidentally exploded.

Chatter about Edgar's whereabouts was meanwhile spreading across the city and causing the crowd in front of his hotel to multiply. As the night wore on, the mob grew more unruly. Extra police—reinforced by the carabinieri, their military adjunct—eventually had to be summoned to drive the crowd from the piazza.

THE TROUBLE OUTSIDE EDGAR'S HOTEL presaged trouble of a different nature. First thing the next morning one of the country's leading news-papers, its overtly anti-fascist stance rendering it unsympathetic to anyone so visibly, if superficially, associated with the regime, *Corriere della Sera* ran a succinct yet scathing item about "the Canadian Prince Elk." Rehashing the contents of the piece that had appeared in the London-based *Daily Mail* all but two years previously, the article queried his self-professed role as an official representative of his tribe. *Corriere della Sera* also dropped a sly, uncorroborated reference to him being employed at a theater in Vancouver, thus implying the whole thing might be a hoax.

Such open skepticism seems to have led a reporter from the Florentine newspaper *Il Nuovo della Sera* to probe him about the reasons behind his Italian tour. He responded by cooking up a story about promising his dying mother that he'd travel to Italy and undertake charitable work.

Press interest of this sort lent urgency to the moves Edgar was making to secure an Italian passport. He'd already hired an attorney and, to speed up the application process, given him the huge sum of 100,000 lire, a high proportion of which must have been required for kickbacks to government officials. The moment he obtained the passport, he could reactivate his earlier plan to abscond before the Italian newspaper stories blossomed into something more dangerous.

ANY CYNICISM PRESENTLY FELT ABOUT EDGAR by the people congregating outside his hotel was offset by their desire to obtain some of the cash he regularly distributed with such largesse. Surely encouraged by a report disclosing his whereabouts to the readers of Wednesday's edition of *La Nazione,* another Florentine newspaper, the crowd had grown substantial. Emerging from his hotel at ten o'clock that morning, Edgar received a round of applause.

His pockets were once again stuffed with banknotes. In the few days since his arrival in Florence, he'd sent Milania three requests for loans. The scale of those requests keeping pace with the scale of the lies he was telling, Edgar sought 40,000, 70,000, and then 100,000 lire. Each time he cited delays in releasing his Canadian fortune as the reason for his request. And each time the contessa—who signed her replies with a heartfelt LOVE, MILANIA—sent the bank transfer via José Alli Maccarani. For the Spaniard, the sudden appearance of such large amounts ratified Edgar's status as a prince, accustomed to playing with vast sums of money.

Striding across the piazza facing his hotel, Edgar plucked banknotes from his pockets and handed them to people. He beamed with delight as a succession of women reciprocated with bunches of flowers. Plentiful though his stock of banknotes was, it soon ran out. When that happened, he quickly climbed into the car standing by for him.

The car drove west out of the city and down the winding roads that led through the rolling, famously attractive Tuscan countryside. At several of the villages dotting his twenty-four-mile journey, Edgar insisted on stopping. Whenever he pulled over, villagers rapidly surrounded him, eager to grab the money he doled out.

Edgar had been invited to the town of Ponte a Egola, where José Alli Maccarani and his poetry-writing Italian wife had a villa. In Edgar's honor, they gave a lavish lunch. He remained at their home until late afternoon when he drove back with them to Florence, where they and a select band of friends reconvened. Milania and Atta, who had just arrived in Florence, appear to have been part of their group.

They gathered at a midtown restaurant on the Via de' Tornabuoni, a long and relatively narrow road, synonymous with expensive restaurants and punctuated by palazzi—not palaces, but Renaissance mansions. Seeing them may have been what instigated a conversation Edgar had with a local aristocrat. His casual reference to how he was thinking of buying a Florentine palazzo led the aristocrat to inquire whether he wanted to purchase theirs.

"How much?" Edgar asked.

"Eight million."

A note of incredulity entering his voice, Edgar replied, "Eight million? It's too little. I offer you fifteen."

Reluctant to exploit Edgar's ostensible unselfishness, the aristocrat pushed him toward a compromise figure.

In front of the restaurant where Edgar and friends were dining, another crowd formed. As the dinner progressed, the crowd became rowdier. Soon the carabinieri showed up to maintain order.

The people in the street were still there when Edgar and his entourage left the restaurant at 11:00 p.m. and went back to his hotel, where they could continue the party. Edgar had by then conned José into getting the Spanish government to release funds to him. These were styled as an "investment," likely in his mythical Canadian oil fields.

Playing an increasingly hazardous game, Edgar gave Milania the comforting impression that her loans to him, now totaling somewhere in the region of 780,000 lire, equivalent to twice the annual wage of the U.S. president, were secured by the Spanish government. Additional reassurance was provided when he elaborated on the story of his Bourbon lineage. He told Milania that his father, Chief Yellow Robe, had married the Contessa di Rocca Guglielma, daughter of Prince Ludovic Mario of

Bourbon, through whom Edgar claimed to be related to the former empress of Austria-Hungary. The empress had, he mentioned, been extremely short of money after she'd been ousted from the throne, so he had lent her a million lire. If he was prepared to bail out someone with a loan of that magnitude, then *he* surely merited comparable generosity in *his* time of need.

22

Within a few hours of Edgar's return to the Grand Hotel in Florence, the consequences of his interview with the reporter from *Il Nuovo della Sera* became apparent. No sooner had the resulting article been published than his reference to being in Italy for charitable purposes unleashed some three thousand letters pleading for assistance. Penned by a cross section of the population, they provided entire family histories—tales of luck turned sour, of homelessness, poverty, romance, and attempted revenge. Edgar even received a cheeky letter from a racing cyclist who wanted fifty lire to fix his bike.

Fortunately, Ludovico Barattieri seems to have been on hand to sift through the mail and allocate donations to the most deserving candidates. Edgar, meanwhile, continued to enjoy his regal perks. That day he took up an invitation to visit the famous Richard Ginori porcelain factory in Sesto Fiorentino, not far beyond the city limits. At the factory, he was presented with a specially commissioned three-foot-tall ceramic sculpture portraying him in his full regalia. He also mingled with the workers in the canteen, posed for a photo with them, handed each of them a hundred-lire bill, and splurged another thirty thousand lire on six vases. When he got back to Florence, he gave these away. One of them went to José Alli Maccarani's wife. Another went to Tullio Tamburini. And he gave another to Tamburini's friend Major General Sante Ceccherini, who had been organizing a show at the Alhambra Garden Theater in commemoration of Edgar's visit.

After the performance that evening, Edgar thanked the major general and his associates by hosting a sumptuous dinner for him—and, it seems, the contessas—at the adjoining restaurant. Edgar wasn't confronted with the sizable bill until next day. Maybe because he was out of cash, he refused to pay. He said there must be some mistake, as he was merely a *guest* at the dinner.

His atypical reluctance to part with Milania's cash extended to the Florentine palazzo he'd undertaken to purchase. Though he kept making promises to its aristocratic owner, these failed to crystallize into hard currency. For now at least, he was able to elude both his aristocratic acquaintance and the repercussions of his unpaid restaurant bill by departing on a day trip.

In the company of the contessas, Tullio Tamburini, José Alli Maccarani's wife, and various other aristocrats—plus several officers from the fascist militia—he took the train to Bagni di Montecatini, a nearby spa resort favored by wealthy Italians. When his party rolled up at the Hotel Locanda Maggiore, they were met by the local big shots. "His Royal Highness" and the rest of his entourage were then shown around the thermal baths, the town hall, and the headquarters of the Montecatini chapter of the PNF. They were also taken out to a neighboring village, where Edgar gave generously to the children of the poor.

Upon returning to the Locanda Maggiore that evening, he and the others were treated to dinner. It functioned as the prologue to a visit to the theater for a performance of Giuseppe Verdi's opera *Rigoletto,* starring the world-famous soprano Luisa Tetrazzini. Her singing of the higher notes was a marvel of crisp phrasing ornamented by perfectly executed trills, yet she sang the middle notes in a breathy style that would have been alien—even comical—to an American such as Edgar. Closing his eyes, he might have assumed her singing emanated from a young girl rather than the sixty-three-year-old barrel of flesh to whom he was introduced. He left her under the illusion that she'd just met someone important, someone who had lately received an audience with Il Duce.

At midnight he and his party returned to Florence, where his problems were about to deepen. Intrigued by the stubborn presence of crowds outside Edgar's hotel, a foreign correspondent from the *Daily Mail* had written a piece about him, which was published in Britain the morning after his trip to Montecatini. The correspondent's distrust of "the man calling himself 'White Elk'" infected the hitherto supportive Florentine press. Its rapid change of heart perhaps also owed something to gossip about him swindling the owner of the restaurant next to the Alhambra Garden Theater. *La Nazione* soon published an article lamenting the gullibility of the city's inhabitants and remarking on how "the shining fur of White Elk" had acquired "gray undertones."

AMONG THE MAIL ADDRESSED to Edgar was another letter from his wife Ethel. Most likely it had been inspired by a British newspaper story that described him wading through the Florentine crowds and dishing out money. The piece quoted his boast that he'd given away a vast amount in just two months.

"Do you think I want to stay in England while you are in Italy being treated like a god?" Ethel wrote. Her patience with Edgar exhausted, she added, "You treat me like a streetwalker."

She was so mad at him that she also mailed a letter to Milania and Atta. This contained documents proving he wasn't the millionaire he claimed to be. Even allowing for his powers of persuasion, he'd have trouble getting the contessas to disregard these.

HIS DAYS OF PRODIGAL SELF-INDULGENCE drawing to a close, Edgar left Florence with Milania and Atta. Together, they started out for the Khevenhüller-Metsch family's castle in southern Austria. Edgar—now deprived of the services of Ludovico Barattieri—was driven by the contessas to Bologna, a prosperous city sixty-three miles to the north. He and his companions spent nearly a day and a half amid its ubiquitous redbrick, its amalgam of the medieval and the modern, its Gothic-arched arcades and canted towers. Though his chief's costume was beginning to look suspiciously shabby, he was given an official reception and awarded honorary membership in the local chapter of the fascist militia. He also had time to hand out money to the poor, visit a hospital, and accept another invitation to a theater show, in the wake of which he squandered an astronomical sum on champagne for a café full of freeloaders. But he required more than just a few glasses of bubbly to maintain his precarious equilibrium.

Horrified by the occasional boorishness brought out in him by heavy alcohol consumption, Milania asked Edgar to quit drinking. For all the liquor in his bloodstream, he remained clear-sighted enough not to rile the woman who was financing his current extravagance. He responded to her pleas by promising to go on the wagon—all too appropriate in view of the covered wagon that had played such a fateful role in bringing the two of them together.

As if to remind him of what he'd lose if he fell out with Milania or ended up being exposed as a fraud, Italy's most fashionable and luxurious beach resort provided their next homeward-bound layover. From the Riva degli Schiavoni, a spectacularly beautiful Venetian quayside, the three of them only had to take a short boat trip across the lagoon to get there.

Beaches, luxury hotels, and villas fringed the sliver of land that comprised the Venice Lido. Even in late September, its tourist season was in full swing, Germans predominating among the wealthy visitors who came to broil themselves on the sand. In these swank surroundings, the contessas could show off their royal guest. Over the next two days, Edgar shelled out another ten thousand lire of Milania's money on hosting a dance. It threatened to be his final taste of the high life. Any day now Milania and Atta would receive the letter from his wife. He'd need a miracle to avoid winding up in prison for years.

But what sometimes seemed an inexhaustible supply of good luck came to his rescue. His wife's letter never reached the contessas. It was either lost in transit or else he had the chance to intercept it surreptitiously when he spied its Manchester postmark.

. . .

THE CUSTOMS OFFICIAL AT THE FRONTIER between Italy and Austria examined Edgar's Document of Identity. Edgar and the contessas were at the checkpoint in the village of Rosenbach, to which they'd traveled after a brief visit to the Khevenhüller-Metsch family's villa in Fiumicello. Probably because Edgar was in such august company, the customs official stamped his invalid Document of Identity and let him through. Edgar and his friends then sailed through waves of rich farmland bounded by a distant mountain range. Hochosterwitz Castle, built in the sixteenth century by an ancestor of Atta's father, was their destination. Rumored to be the inspiration for the castle in *Sleeping Beauty,* it draped itself over a rocky spur that made it visible from almost twenty miles. To get inside, Edgar and his companions had to drive up a zigzagging road that took them through more than a dozen fortified gates, the first of these bearing the family coat of arms.

At Milania's insistence, Edgar slept in her late husband's bedroom. Further symbolic clarification of Edgar's role was provided by her willingness to let him ring the bell in the family's private chapel—something that, as she readily conceded, no other man had done since her husband passed away. So besotted was Milania that she took to leaving valuable gifts on Edgar's pillow. He played along with her by going for regular walks through the castle grounds, picking flowers and placing them in her bedroom. These gestures may have helped to offset the displeasure she felt with him for his failure to keep his promise to abstain from alcohol.

Edgar and the contessas had only been at the castle for a few days before Atta's brother Georg arrived. Later that week, Edgar, Milania, and Georg took a trip to Klagenfurt, a pretty old town ten miles to the southwest. In the middle of its main plaza, a verdured bronze statue stood atop a bulky marble plinth. When Edgar spotted the statue, he hesitated beside it and stared at it with contemplative intensity. The voluminously gowned statue, which depicted Maria Theresa, eighteenth-century archduchess of Austria and queen of Hungary and Bohemia, had a crown on its head and a scepter in its hand. Affecting a quavering voice, Edgar said she was a kinswoman of his.

While they were in Klagenfurt, Milania purchased some white deerskins, which could be used to make Edgar a new Cherokee outfit. Re-signed to his drinking, she also stocked up on the better part of ten pints of scotch for him. Its exorbitant cost provoked an argument between Milania and her stepson.

By the end of her weeklong visit to the castle, her hard-drinking guest had accumulated so many new possessions they wouldn't fit in the trunk that had previously held all his luggage. Miscellaneous family heirlooms he'd purloined from the castle, not least an ornate silver tea service carrying the Khevenhüller-Metsch crest, seem to have been among his acquisitions. Two additional trunks were now required to transport Edgar's things when he returned to the villa in Fiumicello with Milania and her stepchildren.

About that time, he entertained them with mind-reading and hypnotism routines, which he must have picked up during his days on the vaudeville and medicine show circuits. Yet he didn't let on that these were only tricks, mere variants of the mind games he used on his victims. Instead, he presented his tricks as "occult experiments" of the type "popular in India."

READY FOR THE RESUMPTION of his Italian tour, Edgar decamped to Trieste in early October. He moved back into the Savoia Palace Hotel, where stacks of mail awaited him, thanks to press coverage of his previous sojourn there. Mainly consisting of several hundred charity-seeking letters, the mail also included three telegrams inviting him to Venice. Before taking up the invitation, he finessed Milania into lending him another 157,000 lire. She also paid for his chief's costume to be repaired, for some imitation jewels to be transferred onto it from her wedding dress, and for some ermine fur to be added to the black cloak he wore these days.

All of her loans to him would, he pledged, be repaid on Sunday, December 28, 1924. That was, he explained, the date on which his Canadian fortune would be released by the British government. With those words, his impulse to keep upping the ante had brought him to the moment when he was impetuous enough to stake everything on a losing hand.

Coinciding with his return to Trieste was a visit by the USS *Pittsburgh,*

whose officers he'd come to know while the vessel had docked on the
French Riviera. He threw a large party for the ship's diminutive, silver-
haired commander, Admiral Philip Andrews, and the other officers. They
returned the favor by arranging a reception in his honor aboard their ship.

But Edgar's time in Trieste was blighted by protracted bouts of fatigue.
These were diagnosed as a symptom of alcohol-related cirrhosis of the
liver.

Were he able to peruse the French press, he'd have had something else
to worry about. He'd just made front-page news, having been indicted on
a charge of theft. The charge pertained to the valuable feathered headdress he'd stolen from Dr. Perry Chance, the American dentist he had
befriended in Nice. Despite the failure of the French authorities to track
him down and compel him to appear in court, he'd been sentenced to one
year in jail.

A WELCOMING COMMITTEE FOR EDGAR had already gathered around the
entrance to the deluxe 310-room Venetian palazzo that housed the Hotel
Royal Danieli. He was walking toward there, autumnal sunlight bathing
his ermine-trimmed costume, which included an ebony cane, topped by
what purported to be hippopotamus horn. When he was sighted by the
fascists outside the hotel, they started cheering. Obviously they hadn't
heard about the recent French newspaper coverage of his sentencing.

He proceeded to butter up the welcoming committee by speaking enthusiastically about the PNF and hinting that he'd be making a donation
to it. Once he'd settled into the Danieli, which offered views of the lagoon, he rejoined the little troop of fascists, who were set to escort him
to their party headquarters. At his slightly petulant request, they'd be
presenting him with a fascist pennant of the sort he had been awarded
elsewhere in Italy.

Marching alongside him to the beat of an accompanying drummer,
the fascists guided him away from the Danieli. Their route took them into
the Piazza San Marco, always dense with a mix of tourists and pigeons, the
cooing, murmurous sound from these frequently pierced by the shouts of

the birdseed vendors—*"Grani, grani, grani, pei piccioni!"* ("Grain, grain, grain, for the pigeons!"). As he and his escort bisected the crowd, he would've had a chance to snatch glimpses of the peripheral braiding of arches, the brick clock tower, the shadowy arcades, the pavement cafés, and the little souvenir stores, as well as the cathedral's tan, mosaic-gilded façade.

Through a labyrinth of tight streets and diminutive bridges, Edgar and the fascists wove their way from the piazza to the Casa Farsetti, a large building where the Venetian chapter of the PNF was headquartered. Banners carrying fascist insignia decked its exterior. A similarly unambiguous display could be seen inside the building, where the walls were hung with framed photographs of Mussolini.

Edgar marked his visit by donating a large amount of money to the PNF. At a formal ceremony afterward, he gave a fascist salute and was handed the promised pennant. Unable to resist indulging in ham theatricality, he planted a solemn kiss on the pennant. Then he began a speech in his usual collage of English, French, and broken Italian, praising Il Duce and the fascist movement. Reference to the press, which had been fanning persistent speculation about Mussolini's role in the assassination of Matteotti, prompted him to affect a show of anger. He raised his voice and waved his cane emphatically in support of Mussolini. Such backing must have been doubly welcome to his hosts, because their party remained vulnerable. All that was keeping it in power was King Vittorio Emanuele III's current unwillingness to demand its leader's resignation.

RUNNING A HIGH FEVER, Edgar returned to his hotel for a siesta before reemerging in time to keep an afternoon appointment with the fascists who'd welcomed him to the city. He went with them to a mooring place near the Casa D'Oro, a busily decorated Gothic building located toward the north end of the Grand Canal, which functioned as Venice's principal thoroughfare. On that segment of its serpentine route, it was approximately two hundred feet wide. Regularly crisscrossing it were fast motorboats, slower steam-powered water-buses, and even slower gondolas, the latter almost noiseless bar the soft plash of the gondoliers' oars.

Edgar hired several gondolas for his guests. Sharing his boat were a leading city official and three prominent fascists, including Angelo Birenzi, an army officer–turned–journalist.

With the other boats following, their gondola glided south, Edgar's improbable outfit rendering it conspicuous. They hadn't gone far, though, before their boat collided with one of the regular ferries traversing the canal. Edgar's gondola capsized, pitching him and the others into the deep water.

The group that had gone overboard swam across to the ferry and scrambled up its flank. Initial consternation among its passengers was caused by the sight of Edgar boarding it in his sodden regalia.

Safely returned to the quayside, Edgar and his companions were found a fresh gondola. As a replacement for his now-soggy headdress, someone also found him a red fez. He and his convoy then continued their journey. They passed a series of palazzi that gondoliers routinely commented upon, the water's edge pincushioned by clusters of colorfully striped wooden mooring posts. Edgar's purring verdict on the city was "Venice exceeds all dreams."

From his wobbling but thus far upright gondola, he pointed at people walking along the canal-side streets and tried to impress his companions with his powers of observation. Sometimes he declared, "That must be a communist." Other times he said, "That must be a fascist." He did the same with the pedestrians on the covered bridge that gradually came into sight.

His convoy moored close to the bridge—the famous Ponte di Rialto. Gesturing toward the bar opposite, which was called the Birreria Sport, he said it looked like a hotbed of communism. He then turned to his companions and suggested they should go in and spread fascist propaganda.

Inside the teeming bar, he revealed his idea of propaganda. It merely consisted of handing out money and offering to purchase beer for other customers, many of them dirt-poor. Soon he was the focus of much shouting and excitement, which he acknowledged with a sequence of regal bows and smiles. He was offered some celebratory champagne, but he asked the bartender for a bottle of scotch instead. To pay for it, he proffered a large banknote, the change from which he distributed among the people flocking around him.

A still larger throng had gathered outside by the time he and his companions, full of food and liquor, came out of the bar. Chorused shouts of "Viva Italia!" greeted them as they headed back to their gondolas and resumed their progress down the Grand Canal, balconied and soft-hued façades sliding past like stage scenery.

Some way beyond the low arch of another bridge, Edgar's convoy navigated into a stopping place for water-buses. Poised to board one of these steam-powered vaporettos was a young woman who waved hello to Angelo Birenzi, part of Edgar's retinue. The woman turned out to be Birenzi's sister. When Edgar said he'd like to meet her and buy her tea at his hotel, Birenzi treated this as a royal command. Birenzi's sister was by then aboard the vaporetto, which had just left the quayside. He shouted, "Stop! Stop!"

Request stops by a vaporetto were prohibited, so its driver ignored Birenzi. Enraged by what was happening, another of the drunken fascists pulled out a revolver. He then took aim at the receding vaporetto, his gunshot causing pandemonium among the quayside crowd.

By a stroke of luck, the bullet didn't hit anyone. It didn't even persuade the driver of the vaporetto to return to the wharf.

Under Birenzi's bellicose leadership, Edgar's gondola and attendant craft took off in pursuit. Their quarry was already puffing its way along the canal. Just beyond a magnificently domed church on the far bank lay its next stop. It was still there when the flotilla of gondolas caught up.

Over the chugging of its engine, Birenzi screamed insults at its driver for being disrespectful to His Highness, Prince Tewanna Ray. A colleague of Birenzi's jumped onto the vaporetto, slapped the driver, yanked him away from the steering wheel, and forced him to his knees. In deference to Edgar, the pilot was made to remove his cap. Then he was compelled to beg for the prince's forgiveness.

It was sundown when Edgar returned to the Grand Hotel Danieli. He was accompanied by Birenzi and three of the fascists. Edgar introduced them to the contessas and made a show of being grateful to them for the way they had "defended him."

He persuaded Birenzi to accept a job as his secretary on a weekly wage of 1,000 lire. Reprising an old trick of his, which made him appear to be an exceptional specimen of Native American manhood, he told Birenzi that he was sixty years old, pushing two and a half decades older than he really was.

After an evening at the Malibran Theater, where Edgar received a standing ovation from both the audience and the cast when he took his seat in one of the private boxes, he returned to Trieste with Birenzi and the contessas. In the space of only about two days there, Milania lent him another 157,000 lire, followed by further loans of 140,000 and 150,000 lire. She remained confident that he'd soon be making good on the entire debt.

His new secretary meanwhile heard that the police were investigating the assault on the vaporetto driver. Edgar told Birenzi not to be afraid, grandly adding that he'd sort out the problem with the help of the ambassador he'd appointed to represent his tribe in Italy.

SWAPPING TRIESTE FOR THE CHIC tourist destination of Brioni, a famously attractive island not far down the Adriatic coast, Edgar and his entourage checked in to a large seafront hotel beside its own nine-hole golf course. He took a suite formerly occupied by the abdicated German monarch, Kaiser Wilhelm II. For the ensuing week, part of which he spent with a cheerful group of hunters stalking hares and pheasants, he operated on a suitably regal budget.

The promised date of his debt repayment bearing down on him as inexorably as a Rhode Island winter, he began to think about finding an escape route. In desperation, he wired Ethel, whose last letter to him had been so furious. He ignored that, preferring to reply to her earlier telegram in which she'd urged him to go back to her and open a hotel with her. Now he implied that he'd belatedly come around to the idea. He pleaded with her to travel to London and find a means of getting him back there.

Even if Ethel forgave him for everything and decided to help, fleeing to London was not a viable option. Unknown to Edgar, his exploits in Brussels had convinced the British government to bar him from reentering its country. "This man is a scoundrel," warned a letter circulated to immigration officials at all British ports.

IN THE AUSTRIAN CAPITAL—270 MILES from Brioni—Milania's stepson was poised to clinch a business deal. When he arrived at the Viennese branch of his bank and asked to withdraw 300,000 lire from his family's current account, he was informed that the account was empty. Certain that he'd been the victim of nothing more than a clerical error, he headed straight back to Trieste, where he planned to discuss the matter with someone at the branch he normally used.

Edgar meantime blew an additional 70,000 lire or more of Milania's money on hosting a party to mark his last evening on Brioni. No ordinary cocktail party, this was to be a masked ball, staged in the lounge of his hotel. He invited the officers from the USS *Pittsburgh* and an Italian warship, both anchored nearby. Also among the guests was the younger of the contessas, whom he started referring to as his fiancée.

While everyone was dancing, he rode a horse into the room, his familiar getup making him look as if he'd stepped straight out of the Wild West. Frenzied applause greeted him. The clapping kept on when he dismounted and walked out of the hotel's lounge. He went down to the sea, where he boarded a waiting seaplane. It accelerated across the water and eventually took off en route to the town of Chioggia, only a short distance south of the Venice Lido.

Perturbed by his erratic behavior yet seemingly oblivious to the cocaine and morphine consumption that nourished it, Milania penned him a letter, doting attentiveness suffusing her writing. "Dear Chief," the letter began. "You are lost in the world, bouncing all over the place like a ball.

"You are too good, and sometimes you lose your head. You've never needed money, and your generous manner means you give it all away and are left with nothing. I am very sorry that you are not keeping your promise not to drink." She later added, "I only wish you peace and happiness, but you have to listen to me at some point, so you can be happy and calm, and then everything will end well.

"My opinion of Indian honor has never wavered."

When he and Milania were reunited at the villa in Fiumicello, he must have known this was likely to be his final visit. He had good cause to cherish memories of the experiences he'd enjoyed since he'd first stayed there some five months earlier. Over that period, he had amassed a treasured collection of photos, fan letters, and other keepsakes. The photos included autographed portraits of Italian dignitaries such as Gabriele D'Annunzio and Major General Sante Ceccherini. The latter's picture bore the inscription "To His Highness Chief White Elk, noble Italian soul."

But Edgar's current visit to Fiumicello didn't go the way he might have hoped. It wound up being soured by the arrival of Georg, fresh from calling at the bank in Trieste and being informed once more that his family's account was empty. Shock and distress coloring his demeanor, Georg confronted Milania and Atta. He wanted to know where the money had gone, though he must've had his suspicions. Edgar was now only a phone call away from becoming the target of an Italian police investigation.

WHAT HAPPENED NEXT SEEMED TO corroborate the belief that giving money to beggars brought good luck to the giver. Instead of sharing her concerns about Chief White Elk, Milania told Georg there was nothing to worry about. She and Atta stressed the chief's honesty and said the money had only been lent to him on a short-term basis. Yet Edgar must have realized that Georg would be less than forgiving when the December 28 deadline—now a little under ten weeks away—passed without the promised repayment. At that point even Milania and Atta would surely get wise to the massive swindle perpetrated against them.

Putting some distance between himself and the Khevenhüller-Metsch family, Edgar recommended his Italian tour by traveling to Turin, a modern, industrial city that had the attraction for him of being conveniently close to the Swiss border. He then moved into the fanciest midtown hotel, set in a rectilinear street pattern.

Edgar began holding court at his hotel in a manner appropriate for a visiting monarch. His aura of authority was promoted not only by the attentive and ubiquitous presence of Angelo Birenzi and two of the other Venetian fascists, but also by the large black ring he proudly displayed. He'd tell people it had been presented to him by Il Duce. In truth, the ring—which resembled a famous item of jewelry worn by Mussolini— was just a cheap lookalike, given to Edgar by a Florentine admirer. The word "cheap" could not, however, be applied to the wreath that Edgar, in a well-practiced bid for statesmanlike gravitas, made a point of laying at the local war cemetery.

Happy to accept the florid fiction he was peddling, the city embraced Edgar with familiar zeal over the next several days. Newspapers fêted him. The military assigned him a guard of honor. Photographers took his picture. Aristocratic families were drawn into his orbit. Honorary memberships of organizations such as the regional association of disabled war veterans were bestowed upon him. And fan mail was sent to him, each letter, each photograph, each certificate, each fawning accolade furnishing tangible affirmation of the vast scale on which he'd reshaped reality to suit his self-image.

One of the letters was from Mussolini's Musketeers, the prime minister's troop of unpaid bodyguards. With the letter, they enclosed a ceremonial dagger. "To His Excellency Chief Elk Tewanna, drunk with joy and enthusiasm, we have in our hearts the faith to drown our hate and revenge in the blood of our adversaries," the accompanying message read. "We offer our symbol, our dagger."

Invitations to the usual receptions and other official functions came his way, too. Thus he spent an evening at the city's Trianon Theater, where a grand gala was being held to celebrate the second anniversary of the March on Rome. Not wanting to waste such a good opportunity to show off, he procured a spot on the roster of speakers. He was asked by the organizers to come in full costume and to wear his ceremonial dagger. Rounding off his outfit was a gaudy selection of necklaces and pendants.

His speech, venerating Mussolini, was delivered in a persuasive replica of impassioned sincerity. When he proceeded to castigate Il Duce's opponents, he underscored the speech with a touch of professional stagecraft by brandishing a knife and saying *that* "represented the best medicine for traitors to their homeland."

The audience responded with fervent approval.

IN THE RECENT PAST he'd have endorsed his spurious credentials as a Native American prince and a supporter of Mussolini by making a hefty donation to the PNF, but he could no longer afford that. His habitual profligacy had ensured that he could now only distribute alcohol-scented promises of future donations, because little remained of the seven to eight thousand lire he'd possessed when he arrived in Turin.

Georg had been exaggerating when he'd accused Edgar of borrowing the entire Khevenhüller-Metsch fortune, yet Edgar was reluctant to ask for more money—a request that would only hasten the impending trouble. His already precarious relationship with the family hadn't been helped by the letter he received from Atta, who had heard about him referring to her as his fiancée. "You hurt my feelings because I care about my honor," she scolded him.

As if he didn't have enough to contend with, he was taken sick with abdominal pains and another high fever. He nonetheless smuggled his souvenir collection out of his hotel, where he'd run up a massive bill. Quitting the hotel without paying what he owed, his failure to settle this debt probably contributing to the sudden removal of his honor guard, he was admitted to the private San Vito Hospital, southeast of the city. There, he was cared for by a nursing staff of nuns, the sight of whom may have been sufficient to send childhood recollections of Catholic parochial school wafting through his fever-stricken mind. Physicians at the hospital subsequently diagnosed the source of his condition as syphilitic hepatitis, a rare yet treatable manifestation of secondary syphilis.

WHISPERS ABOUT HIM HAD REACHED MILANIA. Not about his true identity, his criminal past, or the reason for his hospitalization. Instead, the talk concerned his excessive spending, about which she'd previously reproached him. Yet when he contacted her from the hospital, clearly angling for help with the cost of his medical treatment, she assured him that she'd be glad to pick up the tab.

Even though Dr. Angelo Viziano, one of the physicians at the hospital, spent a full night taking care of him, Edgar wrote a letter to Atta, beefing about the treatment he was receiving and about how cold the place was. Anything short of deluxe accommodation was these days insufficient for the self-styled prince.

"Please don't criticize the hospital where you're being looked after with great devotion. It's the only place where you'd be taken in without payment," Atta chided him in her reply, which went on to display a belated psychological insight into his personality. "You don't treat real friends the way they deserve, real friends being people who aren't interested in what you can do for them. You only value those who suck your blood."

Afforded time to brood on his predicament, Edgar's characteristic nonchalance was replaced by an air of desperation, surely aggravated by his present feverish state. When Atta swung by the hospital in early November, bringing him a selection of edible treats, she asked for him to be dosed with something to calm him down, because she feared he might attempt suicide. She also asked the hospital authorities to place him under observation.

Her stepmother, who shared her concern for Edgar's well-being, visited the hospital, too. Edgar introduced Milania as his aunt. Milania felt sorry enough for him to pay ten thousand lire to cover his hospital bill. She also handed over another large loan. And she gave him a couple of warm topcoats to keep out the wintry chill fast engulfing that part of the country. She even had him transferred to his own private room on the top floor. When he began to recover, Milania expressed her gratitude to Dr. Viziano with the gift of an expensive cigarette case, along with a hair clip for the doctor's sister.

Among the hospital staff, Edgar had become such a celebrity that he put on his chief's outfit and posed for a group photo with them. Further validation of the enduring strength of his assumed identity came in the form of a letter from the bishop of Trieste, to whom he'd earlier promised a donation. "I regret I have just learned that Your Highness is ill," the bishop wrote, "and I will pray for a speedy recovery."

Lying in bed, Edgar was often surrounded by well-known locals, who included his former secretary, Count Ludovico Barattieri. The current incumbent of that post, Angelo Birenzi, came to see him as well, though Birenzi's time at his bedside was truncated by the arrival of the police.

EDGAR MUST HAVE BEEN BOTH surprised and relieved that the police didn't arrest him. They served a warrant against Birenzi instead. For all Edgar's previous assurances about using diplomatic channels to get the case dropped, Birenzi was charged with complicity in the attack on the vaporetto driver. Led away in handcuffs, Birenzi had an opportunity to reflect upon the worthlessness of Edgar's promises.

Someone with even more reason to do that was, of course, Milania, whose faith in Edgar was finally beginning to ebb. Under pressure from Georg, who seems to have persuaded her that the chief had made a bad business decision by spending more than a million lire on forcing the British government to release the same amount, she asked a Turin attorney to contact him. The attorney informed Edgar that she was growing apprehensive about the money he owed her. Consequently, the attorney requested a formal document acknowledging the debt.

But Edgar ignored the request, and tried to fob Milania off with a set of expensively produced photographic portraits of himself. She employed these as the pretext for a thank-you letter in which she wrote, "I certainly have faith in you, Chief." Then she added, "Do not forget to write to me and send the document that has been requested from you." She endeavored to make this seem casual by referring to how such a document was "normal even among relatives." Georg had suggested it, she explained, because it was in everyone's best interests. She added that it was necessary in order to give her priority during the financial settlement accompanying Edgar's planned divorce.

Though she signed her letter "with love," Edgar must have realized he'd struggle to chisel any more loans out of Milania, who had arrived at the painful realization that he only contacted her when he needed money, which he then frittered away. "I do hope you are not going to spend any more money because, by doing so, you're going to ruin yourself and us," she cautioned.

Edgar kept her dangling for going on two weeks before mailing her a letter confirming that he owed her more than a million lire—well over double the jackpot in the Italian national lottery. Alcoholic bravado sweeping him across the frontier between the risky and the downright reckless, he promised that his debt would be settled by Sunday, January 25, 1925, at the latest. On top of the capital repayment, he generously pledged 6 percent interest, his generosity facilitated by the knowledge that he'd never have to hand over the money.

His bid to placate Milania and family was, however, put in severe jeopardy by the next day's edition of the Turin newspaper *Gazzetta del Popolo*. It carried a piece headlined THE TRUTH ABOUT THE REDSKIN PRINCE.

The piece about Edgar that appeared in *Gazzetta del Popolo* tagged him as an impostor, though it otherwise mirrored his sketchy relationship to the facts. He was portrayed as someone who had acted in hit movies such as *The Four Horsemen of the Apocalypse* and who had directed *The Covered Wagon*. His work in the movies had purportedly enabled him to imitate "the customs, habits and rituals" of Native Americans. To minimize any loss of public trust in the PNF, which was so closely associated with him, the newspaper informed its readers that previous stories about Chief White Elk being awarded honorary membership in numerous chapters of the party were just a product of his fantasies.

Milania and Atta can't have been aware of the article, because they clung to the regal fiction Edgar had wrought. Their residual faith in him even survived his failure to reply to their recent letters—something that may have motivated Atta's next visit to San Vito Hospital. About that time, Edgar proposed marriage to her, seemingly as a means of ensuring she remained on his side.

She accepted the engagement ring that came with his proposal. From both a romantic and a pragmatic point of view, it made sense for her. If everything he said about his Canadian assets were true, becoming his wife would provide a *boost* for her in terms of finance and status.

Brimming with pride, he presented his fiancée—the glamorous Contessa Antoinette Khevenhüller-Metsch—to Dr. Viziano. The doctor appears to have taken this as the cue to warn Atta about the Turin police's planned deportation of her husband-to-be. Atta expressed amazement that the Italian government could even contemplate doing that to a foreign dignitary.

Manifestly skeptical about Edgar, Viziano went further by counseling her to go to London and try to find out more about Chief White Elk.

VERIFICATION THAT CHIEF WHITE ELK was an impostor and possessed no authority to represent American Indians reached the Italian government via the U.S. Embassy in Rome. On Friday, November 28, 1924— five days after the exposé in *Gazzetta del Popolo*—Edgar received another visit from the police. They informed him that he'd have to leave Italy once he was fit to travel.

Erroneous newspaper reports of what was described as his arrest spread rapidly. Within a week, there were headlines about it in France, Belgium, Holland, and the United States. One of these declared WHITE ELK IS A CROOK. Another of them, suffused with condescending preconceptions about Native Americans, depicted him as "an Indian chief" who had gotten into the movies and "learned much of the white man's ways," notably the art of "fleecing wealthy women."

In the absence of press coverage of the loans Edgar had obtained from Milania, there was much speculation across Italy as to how he'd funded his tour of the country. Some said the Russian communist government— staunch ideological opponents of the Italian fascists—had underwritten it. Others said it had been financed by the Italian opposition. Either way, people agreed that the purpose of his tour had been to make Mussolini's regime look ridiculous. Self-deprecating humor not being a characteristic of fascism, Edgar couldn't count on getting any help from the PNF, formerly so assiduous in its courtship of him.

The newspaper stories about his arrest, which fed widespread gossip, probably contributed to Atta's sudden change of attitude toward him. She revealed her mounting anxiety in a letter she sent him from Fiumicello. "You have to try to come back here," she wrote. "It's the only place you can rest." She explained that Georg was insistent upon the notion that the chief should stay at their villa until his debts had been cleared. "I have the highest regard for Indian honor, and all who have met you see in you an honorable person," she added, her need to mention this hinting at her doubts as to just how honorable he really was. If "for whatever reason" he left the country without repaying what he owed her family, she reminded him, he'd bring shame upon his people. "My mother has done all she could for you. We are more or less ruined because of you."

HEEDLESS OF ATTA'S APPEAL to his honor and conscience, Edgar discharged himself from the hospital, went to the Swiss consulate in Turin, and applied for a two-month visa. It would allow him to enter Switzerland and resume his medical treatment at the hospital in Bellinzona, capital of the Swiss province of Ticino. Staffing the hospital were nuns from the same religious order as the sisters who had looked after him for the past couple of weeks. The Turin nuns, sensing further generous donations to their order, had arranged for their Swiss counterparts to accept him as a patient.

Just in case Edgar had second thoughts about going to Switzerland, the Italian police escorted him on the train ride there. Beyond the modern industrial city of Milan lay a route through a string of much smaller towns and cities, through countryside studded with villas and factories, through landscape dominated by mountains, one of them pierced by a tunnel, which took Edgar and his escort to the border with the Italian-speaking sector of Switzerland. They reached the bleakly inhospitable Swiss customs post on the afternoon of Saturday, December 13, 1924.

Edgar had with him two battered trunks. The remainder of his possessions, comprising his chief's outfit and a collection of black shirts that had presumably been given to him by his onetime fascist friends, would be mailed to Bellinzona.

As the Swiss frontier guards checked his travel documents, he showed them some of the autographs and other souvenirs he'd accumulated. He also name-dropped the pope and other famous people. And he bragged about what a big spender he was. Though his expenditure these past seven months had been staggering, he may have been striving to impress the frontier guards by inflating the figure. He said he'd spent in excess of five million lire while he was in Italy—more than $247,000.

Waved through the border, he continued his train journey, skirting Lake Lugano before crossing a narrow section of the lake via a half-mile causeway. More mountains, tunnels, and wooded ravines preceded his late-night arrival in the ancient, Italian-looking city of Bellinzona, which stretched across a valley that had once been dominated by three now partially ruined castles.

Someone from the local hospital was waiting for him when he alighted at the train station. He presented a large gratuity to the porter who carried his luggage. Then he was chauffeured to the hospital, where he registered around midnight. He gave his name as His Excellency Prince White Elk, Tewanna Ray, and told the staff that he was a former physician.

Allocated a private room, he lent credence to his self-declared status by exhibiting his impressive hoard of autographed photos and other memorabilia, notably the ceremonial dagger awarded by Mussolini's Musketeers. Among the photos was a shot of him with what appeared to be his tribe but which must have been the troupe of Arapaho he'd met while he was promoting *The Covered Wagon*.

His photo collection would have tracked the physical changes wrought upon him over the past year. Dense and dark though his hair remained, alcoholism, sickness, drug addiction, and time had diluted his good looks. He was fuller in the face than he had been, his jawline betraying signs of incipient jowliness, his cheekbones coated by sufficient flesh to lose their camera-friendly contours. Now he'd no longer provoke admiring disbelief if he pretended to be a lot older than his thirty-six years.

Word of his arrival swept through the hospital. Nurses and doctors flocked to his room to meet him. Amiable, exquisitely polite, and suitably regal-looking in floral-patterned pajamas and a pair of delicate slippers, he sprawled across a chaise longue and addressed his audience with the self-assurance of a visiting monarch. Over the next few days, he embellished his regal aura by telling stories about the fabulous wealth he possessed in Canada, promising colossal donations, giving a gold watch to the woman who was nursing him, disbursing lavish tips to other members of the staff, and handing out candy to fellow patients and toys to children who had been hospitalized, too.

Swiss journalists had not thus far recycled the scathing press coverage of him in Italy, France, and elsewhere, so there was no obvious reason for skepticism. Even the hospital's director, Dr. Emilio Sacchi, bought the line that Edgar was "a prominent and very wealthy man, who is also a physician."

Talk of the prince generated flattering stories in the Swiss newspapers. And a parade of local worthies trooped into the hospital to pay homage to him. These visitors included numerous distinguished women, quite a few of whom seemed keen to bag him as a husband. Less than a week ago, his life had been beset with problems, yet now it was ripe with encouraging possibilities.

24

Edgar's continued munificence left him so short of cash that he could only afford to dispense tips amounting to ten lire or less. These did little to buttress either his references to his own wealth or his airy talk of the extravagant gifts he aimed to bestow.

People began to wonder whether he was suffering from some form of mental illness alongside his physical ailments. In a sign that the symptoms of those ailments were fading, Edgar's libido reasserted itself. When he propositioned a male nurse who strayed into his room, the nurse was disgusted. But even that setback failed to diminish his belief in his powers of persuasion.

Shortage of money encouraged him to write a begging letter to Milania, the letter inevitably giving away his whereabouts. He stressed that Milania shouldn't worry about the loans he was set to repay her next month, and that everyone would be happy in the end. As the prelude to him seeking an emergency loan, he also dished up a catalog of excuses.

In previous months his request would have precipitated a bank transfer, but this time it triggered a visit from Atta, who showed up a week after his admission to Bellinzona's hospital. She was in an exceptionally agitated state, apparently handing back her engagement ring.

Her arrival overlapped with a visit from a left-wing attorney named Mario Ferri. Edgar appears to have engaged Ferri's professional services in order to lend substance to his long-running yarn about being embroiled in a legal dispute with the British government. Daunted by his tales of being related to the Bourbon dynasty and owning a large property in Fiumicello, as well as oil wells and extensive land in Canada, Ferri addressed him with groveling courtesy as "Your Most Serene Royal Highness."

To quell Milania and Atta's growing fretfulness about the money owed their family, Edgar composed a note to the governor-general, Britain's senior representative in Canada. His note sustained the conceit that the British colonial authorities were denying him access to his own money. But there was a slight snag. He didn't know the governor-general's name. Plucking a name from his imagination, he called the governor-general "Mr. Larkin," this seeming familiarity with such a high-ranking official emphasizing just how well-connected he was.

"I hereby authorize the Contessa Khevenhüller-Metsch to handle my affairs, for I am sick and unable to come in person," he wrote. "And I hope to get justice as a Canadian." He signed the note, "Chief White Elk." When he handed it to Atta, he must have known it would secure him nothing more than temporary remission.

Atta still felt sympathetic enough toward him to foot his medical bill, yet her suspicions about him had grown dramatically. Unnerved by the situation, she left Bellinzona right away and started out for London, where she could find out about his estranged wife and talk to people responsible for Britain's dealings with Canada and its governor-general. The journey would take a minimum of three days, on top of which another week or two would be required to arrange the necessary appointments. By the early part of January 1925, she was bound to obtain incontrovertible proof that Edgar had swindled her family.

EDGAR'S PLAN WAS WELL-ADVANCED. Likely utilizing Mario Ferri's legal know-how, he hoped to escape the consequences of his fraud by obtaining citizenship from the microstate of San Marino, just over sixty miles to the east of Florence. With his intended departure looming, he met Milania in Bellinzona on Christmas Eve—four days after his encounter with her stepdaughter.

Over lunch he capitalized on Atta's absence by soft-soaping Milania into lending him about twenty-five thousand lire. When he introduced Milania to Dr. Sacchi, the hospital's director, he referred to her as his aunt. In awe of Edgar, Sacchi invited them both to dinner at his home that evening.

Sacchi's attitude toward Edgar would have been very different if he'd had access to that morning's edition of one of Belgium's most prominent newspapers. Dominating its front page was a less-than-reverential cartoon about Edgar. It depicted three young girls, one of whom gestured toward another and said, "Look at the fun she's having—and she hasn't even seen White Elk."

There was barely time for Edgar to sleep off the aftereffects of the dinner party before his departure for Lugano, hometown of Mario Ferri, who had recommended the city to him. An eighteen-mile ride on the St. Gotthard railroad, featuring sharp grades and a passing cavalcade of alpine peaks and car-free valleys, provided the easiest means of taking up Mario's suggestion. Perched upon the rim of an expansive lake typically swarming with motorboats, steamers, and rowboats, Lugano was cradled by forested mountains, their lower slopes sheathed in vineyards and gardens. Its tightly packed buildings, arcades, and granite-paved streets, where horse-drawn carriages coexisted with streetcars, felt as if they belonged to an Italian city. Enhancing this was the sound of Italian on the sidewalks, and the presence of many refugees from Mussolini's government, which had against all odds weathered the Matteotti scandal. If Il Duce could get away with murdering a key political opponent, then maybe Edgar could also evade justice.

EDGAR TOOK OVER A PLUSH SUITE at the Hotel Centrale, from where he made repeated forays around the city. In the window of a tobacco store, he caught sight of a display of foreign cigarette packs bearing the head of a Native American. He went in and bought several packs from the woman who ran the store. They had, he informed her, been manufactured at a plant he owned in the United States. And he got talking with other people to whom he said he meant to purchase one of the local hotels or even a castle.

His billfold shrinking with familiar speed, he felt the need to scam Milania out of some more money before her stepdaughter alerted her. "We should be happy, because I understand from Atta that everything is going well in England," his deceitful letter to Milania announced. He explained that the British government had confirmed they'd be releasing all his assets, this imminent bonanza offering security against whatever Milania lent him.

She was then duped into coughing up an additional eighteen thousand lire. Edgar converted it into large bags of one-franc Swiss coins. He carried these with him on regular strolls along the quayside, which grew busy during the evenings when the streetlamps illuminated the lakefront. With ostentatious bravado, he skimmed coins across the surface of the water. Eventually tiring of that, he gave handfuls of them to aging strangers.

Among the people he buttonholed was a long-faced fifty-six-year-old woman with dark, curly hair. When he tried to hand her a five-franc piece, she looked surprised and refused it. She turned out to be Princess Victoria, the waspish, unmarried sister of King George V of England.

Despite Edgar's habit of flaunting the ring he'd been given by a Florentine admirer—the ring that he liked to say Il Duce had presented to him—Mario Ferri took him to the Red Ball, the local socialist party's New Year's Eve shindig. Edgar had on his full getup, along with the dagger donated by Mussolini's Musketeers. Sensibly, he'd removed the fascist insignia beforehand, though that didn't deter several of the other guests from criticizing Mario for inviting such a well-known supporter of the Italian fascist regime.

Inside forty-eight hours of the Red Ball, Edgar seems to have been broke again. Compounding his problems was the news that he hadn't obtained the San Marino citizenship he'd been counting on.

. . .

UNDER THE PRETEXT THAT HE couldn't access his bank account due to the public holiday, Edgar sponged four hundred Swiss francs from the owner of the hotel where he was staying. Another two hundred came from Mario. But these borrowings fell way short of the cost of the boozy banquet he laid on for a couple of hundred freeloaders, who wound up smashing glasses, bottles, and dishes.

With his hotel bill and other debts still outstanding, he appears to have used a hired car to skip town, not before telling his admirers that he'd been summoned back to America, where he was planning to sell some of his oil wells. His creditors must have been embarrassed about being fleeced by him, because the majority of them never reported him to the police.

Early in the first week of 1925, he returned to Bellinzona, checked in to the Hotel Metropole, and swiftly renewed his friendship with Dr. Sacchi. In addition to being the director of the city's hospital, Sacchi was the president of Bellinzona Municipal Council. Falling for Edgar's showy talk about how he'd like to fund the construction of a new hospital, Sacchi invited Edgar to use the Municipal Council's private box at the theater that Wednesday evening.

The invitation led Edgar to pay someone to paste red STOP PRESS strips onto the posters advertising the show, which featured the Maieroni Theater Company. "This evening His Excellency Tewanna will honor the artiste Maieroni by attending the show wearing his ornate national costume," the announcements declared.

Sacchi was not alone in succumbing to Edgar's charm. It also captivated a local woman who ran a hairdressing business. She soon developed a crush on him. Persuaded that he hadn't budgeted for the cost of visiting the country's central region, she withdrew 250 Swiss francs from her savings and lent this to him. Edgar said he'd repay her in just a few days, the promise of 1,000 francs interest yielding a potent incentive.

On the evening of the show, he hired a carriage that enabled him to make a grand entrance to the similarly grand nineteenth-century Teatro Sociale, which had attracted a sellout crowd. He was initially refused entry to the Municipal Council's private box. When the theater staff at last permitted him to enter the wooden cubicle, one of many such cubicles that formed a horseshoe arrangement around the stage, his feathered headdress and the rest of his ensemble snagged people's attention. The audience acknowledged him with a standing ovation.

"ATTA IS SUCH A NICE GIRL," Milania wrote on January 4, 1925. "She will help you and I am sure she will sort out everything for you."

Edgar was, however, under no illusion that Atta's trip to England would do anything except deepen his problems. These were multiplying despite his triumphant evening at the theater. It gave rise to an article in the local press, questioning his regal status. Many people defended him and were angry that such disrespect should be shown to a foreign dignitary, yet he chose that moment to make his surreptitious exit. He left behind the familiar compendium of unpaid loans and bills.

In his hotel room, he also left some of the charity-seeking letters he'd received. But he wasn't prepared to relinquish the bulk of his trophies. Crammed into his suitcases was a chaotic collection of paperwork. He kept some two thousand letters. He kept newspaper stories about himself. He kept posters advertising shows held in his honor. He kept official invitations. He kept PNF membership cards. He kept letters from Milania and Atta and other female admirers, among them Alda Borelli, one of the most famous Italian stage actresses of that era. He kept numerous photos, now arrayed in a leather-bound volume decorated with an embossed image of Dante and Beatrice. He even kept a copy of a satirical magazine that had made fun of him.

Journeying out of the Italian-speaking section of Switzerland, he made brief stops in Bern and Lausanne. On Friday, January 9, 1925, he breezed into the city of Neuchâtel. More than a hundred miles from Bellinzona, it faced a large lake. Neuchâtel's often quaint streets, which played host to European students of all ages, marched away from its long, tree-lined quayside and then up a steep gradient, capped by a church and a castle.

Now that he was in Switzerland's Francophone region, Edgar had no difficulty communicating with people. As Prince Tewanna Ray, he registered at the fifty-room Grand Hôtel du Lac, a starchy, midtown establishment looking onto the docks and the lake beyond. He told the owner that he was the holder of a diplomatic passport, that the local police had been ordered to protect him, and that his Canadian assets were worth millions of dollars. Alcoholism as well as drug addiction doing nothing to sustain his once-unerring facilities as a smooth talker, Edgar's self-important blather merely succeeded in arousing the hotelier's distrust. The subsequent behavior of the supposed Canadian prince only intensified that.

Each day Edgar made a point of having at least one and three-quarter pints of cognac sent up to his room. He got into a row with a boy—probably a bellhop—who worked there. He likely availed himself of the surfeit of cocaine that had long been on the streets of Neuchâtel. And he began flirting with the waiter assigned to serve him in the hotel restaurant. Not such a good idea. For a start, it risked antagonizing the hotelier and maybe even drawing the attention of the police, since male homosexual liaisons were against the law in Switzerland.

Between his arrival in Neuchâtel and the next morning, Edgar was welcomed by a half-dozen university students. With generosity in keeping with the man he pretended to be, he invited them to lunch at his hotel, where he furnished them with gifts (one of which appears to have been the ceremonial dagger he received from Mussolini's Musketeers). During the meal, he and his guests downed six bottles of champagne, the full cost of the party added to Edgar's tab.

Sad and disenchanted, Atta rolled up in Bellinzona that day, intent on confronting Edgar, who had already decamped to Neuchâtel. In the twenty-one days since their last meeting, she'd discovered that his Canadian oil wells were as fictional as his Bourbon ancestry. She had also visited the Manchester address to which she'd written the previous summer. There, she'd met his wife and stepson, the two women striking up an improbable friendship, borne out of their shared ordeal. Her attitude toward Edgar transformed, Atta now regarded him as "a madman and a con man." From England, she had wired her stepmother about the results of her investigation. NOTHING GOOD, her wire proclaimed. HE MUST BE ARRESTED.

. . .

MILANIA REFUSED TO GO to the police and acknowledge her foolishness in falling for Edgar's preposterous stories, her sense of shame enabling him to carry on hustling the citizens of Neuchâtel. He passed the next three days borrowing money, seducing women, and drinking heavily to compensate for his inability to obtain cocaine or morphine. He also insinuated himself into the city's Italian community.

Twice within that short space of time, he attended meetings of the local Italian Circle, each time making a speech. He pledged to donate twenty-five thousand lire to assist impoverished members of their community. Yielding to the effects of having more cognac than hemoglobin in his circulatory system, one of his speeches lurched into embarrassing incoherence.

His reputation in Neuchâtel was not helped by his behavior at the Grand Hôtel du Lac. Besides unsuccessfully propositioning a member of the staff, he succeeded in luring up to his bedroom the waiter with whom he'd been flirting.

Increasingly censorious of Edgar, whose seduction of the waiter scandalized the other staff, that Tuesday the hotel's owner presented him with a bill totaling three hundred Swiss francs. As Edgar had no means of paying, the owner threw him out and confiscated his treasured souvenirs and the rest of his luggage, even the bulk of his ostensibly valuable Native American costume. Other than his feathered headdress, which he managed to take with him, Edgar retained nothing but the warm, far-from-exotic clothes he had on: a thick shirt and matching tie, plus a tweed jacket and a pale homburg with a dark band around it. In defiance of his dire situation, he wore the homburg at a jaunty angle that concealed his mussed hair but failed to distract from the shadows under his tired-looking eyes.

Weak and malnourished after several days during which he had evidently prioritized alcohol over food, he traipsed through the city in search of accommodation. He tried somewhere cheaper—the cumbersomely named Hôtel des Alpes and Terminus, situated beside the train station. But when the hotelier saw that he possessed neither luggage nor money, he was given just five minutes to leave the premises.

If Edgar thought the situation couldn't get any worse, then he was in for a nasty surprise. At the insistence of her stepson, Milania had been

Portrait of Edgar Laplante and his wife Burtha Thompson,
taken by Emma B. Freeman in Washington State, 1918.

The Newberry Library

Poster for the 1920 silent movie in which Edgar Laplante, aka Chief White Elk, claimed to have acted.

Poster for the big-budget 1923 epic whose European release Edgar Laplante helped to promote.

The front cover of a December 1923 monthly guide to Parisian nightlife.
The Dolly Sisters, among the Jazz Age's biggest stars,
were performing at the same venue as Chief White Elk.

Bibliothèque nationale de France

The Café du Dôme, the famous Left Bank bohemian haunt where Edgar Laplante became a regular.

The Estate of André Kertész, Museum of Fine Arts, Boston

Chief White Elk sold signed souvenir postcards like this one when he was living in Paris.

Aloha Wanderwell, ca. 1924.

National Automotive History Collection, Detroit Public Library

The troupe of Arapaho who helped to promote *The Covered Wagon* posing before a screening of the movie in 1924. Ed Farlow, who supervised their tour, is pictured center stage.

Fremont County Pioneer Museum

CÉLÈBRE CHEF ÉLAN BLANC
(WHITE ELK) délégué de la S.D. N.
chante, danse à minuit

AU CANARI 8, faubourg Montmartre

La Belle Zoulaïka -:- Célèbres Crastonians
- AU CANARI PARIS RIT

Advertisement for the Parisian cabaret in which "the famous Chief White Elk" appeared, October 1923.

Travel poster promoting Venice, 1920. *Library of Congress*

Roseray and Capella, the gymnastic duo who appeared in the same Parisian cabaret as Chief White Elk, 1923. *Bibliothèque nationale de France*

"The Beautiful Zoulaïka," the scandalous belly dancer who was part of the same Parisian cabaret as Chief White Elk, 1923. *Bibliothèque nationale de France*

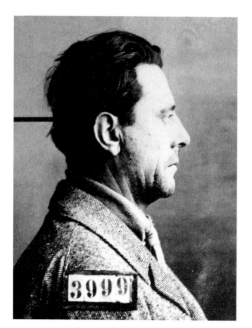

Mug shots of Edgar Laplante, taken by the Swiss police, January 1925.
National Archives, UK

View of the Grand Canal, Venice, September 1920.
Library of Congress

Cover of the magazine section
of the August 23, 1925,
issue of *New Orleans States*.
Library of Congress

The fifty-four-year-old
Edgar Laplante in a
1942 press photo.
Library of Congress

persuaded to press charges against him. Edgar was also the subject of a complaint to the Neuchâtel police by the owner of the Grand Hôtel du Lac. The police responded by wiring their counterparts in Ticino, the region within which Bellinzona was located. From Ticino, they received word that the "prince" had already been the subject of unfavorable reports about his "questionable morals."

LATER THAT DAY, Edgar knocked on the door of the hospital run by the Catholic Brothers of Providence, though he and providence were no longer on speaking terms. He was not only seeking sanctuary but also probably hoping the doctors would take pity on him and give him a series of cocaine and morphine injections. Without those, he'd continue to suffer the menu of withdrawal symptoms from which he was being treated to a five-course banquet. Stomach cramps, fatigue, sweating, nausea, anxiety, vomiting, and nightmares were just a few of its constituent delicacies.

Once he'd been admitted to the hospital, he somehow got his hands on enough cognac to offer him a route to either alcoholic oblivion or suicide. While he was holed up that evening, the Ticino police issued a warrant against him on fraud charges. Their equivalents in Neuchâtel promptly launched a search for him.

Accompanied by the commissioners of both police departments, the search party found him at the hospital shortly after midnight on Wednesday, January 14, 1925. He looked very surprised when he saw them, yet his expression of astonishment faded quickly. He must have known he'd finally landed in a jam from which no amount of talking could extricate him.

"The comedy's over," he said as the police arrested him. They led him out of the hospital and into the midwinter darkness. Except for his feathered headdress, a droopy memento of happier times, he had nothing with him, not even a few coins left over from the huge sums of money that had slithered through his fingers like one of the imaginary trout in his imaginary kingdom.

At the police headquarters in Bellinzona, he was fingerprinted, weighed, and measured. His dejection temporarily alleviated by the prospect of stepping in front of a camera, he was also photographed for a sequence of mug shots. And he was given a physical examination, which revealed two scars on his chest. He said that one of them had been caused by shrapnel during an explosion on the ship he'd served aboard. The other had, he explained, come from "a rather barbaric Indian rite." Fourteen-year-olds from his tribe were obliged to prove themselves, he claimed, by undergoing ritual wounding with a flaming spear.

When the time came for him to be questioned, the local police chief broke the ice by handing him a cigarette and saying he wasn't sure how to address him.

Edgar must've felt cornered, drug and alcohol withdrawal leaving him desperate enough to try to appease the police chief by answering at least one question truthfully. So he told the man to make inquiries in Rhode Island. "Look for an Edgar Laplante and you will find the precise facts about me," he said. But he proceeded to tell a string of such improbable stories that his *real* name was assumed to be an alias.

Asked whether he had a criminal record, he replied, "When I was a boy I used to steal cherries and potatoes. I never stole anything else."

His response was contradicted by the speed with which he adjusted to his routine behind bars, speed indicative of prior acquaintance with the inside of a jail cell. Sharing his new home was a man arraigned on petty theft charges and placed there as a stool pigeon. Too melancholy for conversation, though, Edgar spent much of the time slumped in the corner. Only the prospect of someday writing his autobiography perked him up. He even used this to buttress his sense of his own importance by chattering about it to a visiting journalist. In an article for *Corriere della Sera,* the journalist salivated over the thought of Edgar telling "the story of his great life."

The Swiss police meanwhile retrieved Edgar's possessions from the Lugano hotelier who had impounded them. Included in his luggage was the Document of Identity he'd obtained in London, establishing him as Tewanna Ray, Chief White Elk. To ascertain whether this really was his name, the police contacted the American and British authorities.

His true identity took several weeks to confirm. In that time, his case generated widespread European press coverage, much of it veined with amused incredulity. "How and where was he born?" asked *Corriere della Sera.* "Nothing is certain, not even his age. . . . He has said he is forty, fifty, and sixty-two on various occasions. From his travel papers, he should be only thirty-seven. From his face, experts say they can only tell he has led a full life."

Even the showbiz trade paper *Variety* ran a piece on him. It quoted a conversation with his father, who was scraping out a living in a basement carpentry shop. Quizzed about the oil wells that Edgar had said he owned, his father wisecracked, "*Banana* oil."

DOZENS OF LETTERS from female admirers started arriving at Bellinzona police headquarters. Edgar never got to read these, because the police withheld them. Otherwise he was well treated, something Atta did her best to ensure. In the misguided belief that he still had the money he'd stolen from her family, she figured such good treatment would make him more inclined to divulge the whereabouts of their cash. Playing to his better nature, she and Milania paid off the Swiss debts he'd run up, and Georg helped to fund his defense by presenting him with a large sum of money and a diamond ring.

Atta, Milania, and Georg even visited him in jail. Milania remained so susceptible to his charm that she invited him to join her in San Marino once he was freed from prison. Every time she and her stepdaughter saw him, Edgar put on a show of mournful penitence, which vanished the moment they left the room. Bumming cigarettes off the guards then became his priority. "You'll laugh when you hear about my adventures in Brussels," he said to them.

His self-congratulatory delight hidden behind a necessary mask of contrition, he wrote to Atta: "I am very sorry that everything has taken a bad turn." On this note of inadvertently comic understatement, he assured her that he'd borrowed the money from her mother only because it gave him "an opportunity to do good." Angling for her family's assistance in returning to the United States, he promised to find employment and repay them at the rate of one hundred dollars a month. "Please ask your mother to forgive me," his letter concluded. He must have been hoping that his plea for forgiveness would distract Atta and her mother from scrutinizing the practicalities of his mooted repayment schedule. Clearing his entire debt to them would take a mere 465 years.

But forgiveness was not uppermost in the minds of Atta and family, their posture toward Edgar probably altered by some recent information from Ethel. She revealed that the Canadian authorities had notified her that Edgar was "not an Indian," and that there was no record of anyone named Chief White Elk. So Atta, Georg, and their stepmother filed charges against Edgar in Italy. As an excuse for their own gullibility, they accused him of defrauding them by using his powers as "a hypnotist" and "master of magic."

Their case against him was vastly more serious than its Swiss counterpart, because the Swiss could prosecute him only for crimes committed in that country. Proceedings were initiated to extradite Edgar to Italy, but the Swiss rebuffed these and slated him to stand trial in Lugano that June.

He faced five counts of fraud against the Khevenhüller-Metsch family and others.

Uninhibited by feelings of shame, Edgar sought help from Ethel of all people. "I know I have done wrong," he admitted before floating the idea of them getting back together after he'd shaken off his current problems. She and Leslie should, he proposed, go back with him to America, where the three of them could "start life anew." The potent lure of a fresh start blinding Ethel to all the suffering he'd inflicted upon her, she was soon penning letters of support for him and soliciting the assistance of the U.S. consular service.

His chosen defense against the fraud charges was "partial insanity." Arrangements were made by his attorney for him to be examined by Dr. Bruno Manzoni, director of a psychiatric hospital not far from Lugano. Dr. Manzoni's ensuing, remarkably insightful report diagnosed Edgar as "a psychopath," who could "only tell the truth by mistake." It was a diagnosis that had nothing to do with the latter-day meaning of that word. For the psychiatrists of that era, psychopaths were people prone to a range of compulsive behavior—from alcoholism and prodigality to lying and swindling. Within those parameters, Edgar was a textbook psychopath, so Dr. Manzoni argued that the charges against him should be dropped on grounds of diminished responsibility.

NEITHER ATTA NOR MILANIA were in the courtroom when the trial opened. Georg was there, however. Populating the gallery were journalists from across Europe, not to mention some of Edgar's voguishly attired female fans. His enduring popularity with women delighted him.

Dressed in ordinary clothes instead of his Cherokee costume, now draped across the evidence table in front of him, Edgar cut a diminished figure. For the journalists, whose retrospective wisdom alerted them to the shoddiness of that costume, the sight of his current incarnation was hard to reconcile with the prosecutor's portrait of him as "the biggest swindler of all-time."

Under cross-examination in French, he endured a succession of uncomfortable moments, none more so than when the prosecutor said, "Do you remember that you told the authorities that you had a medical diploma from Carlisle?"

"I *don't* remember," he answered.

"Do you not often claim to have attended Carlisle?"

"I just went there to play football."

"A letter from that college has just been received by the authorities. It states that they don't know you—even as a football player."

Waves of laughter from the gallery greeted his evasive and often patently ridiculous responses to other questions. "Did you say that you owned a lot of land in Canada?" the prosecutor asked him.

"Well, I certainly *hope* to own a lot of land."

Challenged about his reference to being sixty years of age, he fobbed off the prosecutor with an ingenious reply: "According to the Italian calendar, I am thirty, but according to the Arabic calendar, where a year equals six months, I am sixty."

He plumbed similar depths of absurdity when asked about his bigamous marriage to Ethel. "In the States," he explained, "you can marry twice—once under your baptismal name and once with another name."

But all this was subsidiary to the most important question. How did he come to obtain so much of the contessas' money?

"They just forced it on me," he said.

Gleeful coverage across America as well as Europe commented on each day of his trial. THE INCREDIBLE REAL-LIFE MOVIE one of the Italian headlines blared.

During the trial's summing-up phase, the defense attorney argued that Edgar shouldn't be convicted of fraud, because he'd given away the money. The attorney also highlighted Edgar's psychological abnormality and emphasized that he wasn't responsible for his actions. If anyone was to blame for what happened, Edgar's attorney stated, it was the public, who treated him as a genuine prince. Loud applause emanated from the gallery when the attorney's closing remarks culminated in an appeal for clemency.

On its fifth day, the trial concluded with the judge ruling that Edgar couldn't be absolved from "the hideousness of his misdeeds" because he possessed "a lively intelligence and a deep intuition." He was sentenced to one year's imprisonment—minus time served—and ordered to pay a heavy fine, though his penniless state rendered that purely theoretical. As he was led down the courthouse steps, two glamorous young women stepped out of the crowd and handed him packs of cigarettes. An Italian reporter, who witnessed his blank-faced acceptance of these, later quipped, "It's all smoke."

Edgar was transported from the courthouse to the psychiatric hospital in Bellinzona and placed under observation, because there must have been a suspicion that he'd try to commit suicide. Chances were, he had no idea that his case had meanwhile become the subject of another flurry of newspaper articles in cities from Vienna to New Orleans. His case also spawned an American movie that borrowed from his life as freely as he had once borrowed from the contessas. Released by Universal Studios as *The Open Trail,* it told of a white man who believed himself to be a Native American named White Elk.

After two months, Edgar was transferred from the psychiatric hospital to Lugano's prison, where he'd been held in the run-up to his trial, conditions prompting him to complain, "It's worse than Siberia." He remained there until the fall, by which time the Swiss authorities had announced that they'd soon be freeing him. In preparation for his anticipated return to America, the steadfast Ethel and her now eleven-year-old son appear to have moved from England to Pawtucket, Rhode Island, where they could set up home with Edgar. The prospect of them becoming a family again came a lot closer to fruition when he walked out of jail shortly before 9:00 a.m. on Tuesday, October 20, 1925.

26

The order had already been issued. From the prison, he was taken to Switzerland's southeast frontier and handed over to the Italian authorities. They conveyed him to the jail in Trieste, ready to stand trial on the charges that Milania and family had filed.

For just short of a year, Edgar—who bore his captivity with stoicism, enlivened by sparks of skittish humor—was held in Trieste and then Turin while he awaited his next court appearance. At a preliminary hearing, the prosecutor asked, "Have you ever spoken to the contessa about owning fabulous wealth in Canada and having large sums of money deposited in English banks?"

"I cannot answer 'yes' or 'no,'" Edgar said, "because when I was with the contessa I was often drunk on the whiskey she made me drink."

Near the end of the summer of 1926, Edgar received a letter from England, written by the devoted Ethel, who informed him: "We are looking forward every day to your release from prison." She went on to write:

> *I enclose two small photographs, one of Leslie and one of me,*
> *taken in Blackpool. I wrote to the American consul, asking him*

to let me have a full account of the case. You must not be sorry
if Leslie does not write to you, because he is not even at home for
two minutes and spends all his time on his bicycle. But, dear, he
always asks about you.

I close here, dear, because there is no other news to give you.
All the people in my family say hullo.

With the greatest love and kisses from me and Leslie.

Yours forever,
Ethel

Yet her long-awaited reunion with Edgar could not occur until he'd stood trial in Turin during the fall. His latest spell in the dock generated still more international newspaper coverage and courthouse hilarity. Unlike the previous trial, though, Atta, Georg, and their quivery-voiced stepmother gave evidence against Edgar, who, as one reporter observed, wore a low-key outfit that included "large glasses made of tortoise shell—fake, of course." The testimony of the Khevenhüller-Metsch family helped to ensure another guilty verdict. It led to a jail sentence of seven years, five months, and fifteen days. With that came a 9,000-lire fine and an order to repay 1,018,657 lire to Milania, though there was scant possibility of Milania ever recouping this substantial amount of money.

Edgar was placed in solitary confinement at the city's prison. Deprived of an audience for his posturing, depression overwhelmed him. He also fell sick, the poor prison diet hastening his descent into emaciated frailty, yet he mustered the energy to find a new attorney to draft an appeal against his conviction. The attorney, Girolamo Bevinetto, was struck by Edgar's "truly pitiful state" when the guards escorted him into the interview room for their first meeting. Edgar gave the impression that he'd been abandoned by everyone, so Bevinetto started bringing him food, sending him English and French magazines, and giving him money to buy cigarettes and milk. Other donations soon reached him from Ethel, as well as from the director of the prison, the U.S. consul, the local nunnery, and elsewhere. These consisted of money, along with shoes and warm clothing to fend off the encroaching winter.

Bevinetto drew up an appeal citing nearly a dozen reasons why the verdict of Edgar's trial should be overturned, or at the very least why the sentence should be reduced. Partnering the appeal was a rambling, floridly archaic statement by Edgar. In this, he pretended that his earlier accounts of his relationship with Milania and Atta were mere "Mother Goose stories." Quoting a self-penned ode to chivalry, he claimed to have concocted these to spare the contessas' embarrassment, because they'd hired him as a gigolo and an entertainer. He even had the gall to protest that they still owed him part of the prearranged fee. "Blame me for folly, but not for knavery," his statement concluded.

Hopeful of overturning the outcome of the trial, Bevinetto submitted the appeal in late December. Edgar then had a worrisome wait for his case to be heard. His life nonetheless improved over the ensuing month and a half. At last removed from solitary confinement, he reverted to playing the role of the gracious benefactor. When another prisoner asked him for a smoke, he took the last of his cigarettes out of his mouth, snapped it in two, and handed half to the man. Edgar also gave away his socks— "I gave them to a guy who needed them." But altriusm wasn't what motivated him. As he explained to Bevinetto, "Cotton socks are not suitable for those who are accustomed to silk ones."

Textiles were soon to become more than just a badge of status for Edgar, who was put to work in the prison's knitwear shop, where he rapidly learned how to hand-stitch embroidery and operate a weaving machine. His minuscule income from that work averaged less than a lire a day.

He wasn't short of cash, though, due to a generous monetary gift from one of his female fans, which must have contributed to his cheerful disposition the next time Bevinetto visited him. The gift came from an aristocratic Belgian writer, who believed in Edgar's self-proclaimed cause as an Indian rights campaigner. Half the money was credited to him at the prison commissary and the other half went toward the cost of having a daily lunch brought in from a local restaurant. His Belgian benefactress also offered him a job as her chauffeur, secretary, or bodyguard when he was released from jail. But he declined her offer because he wasn't, as he informed her, certain what he wanted to do with the rest of his life.

The court of appeal's examination of his case would go a long way toward clarifying his immediate future. All over Europe there was press coverage of what one leading Italian newspaper billed as this "latest episode in the now-famous courtroom comic drama." With lip-smacking relish, the front page of *Paris-soir* led with THE RISE AND FALL OF WHITE ELK. And another French newspaper ran a story claiming that Edgar was a Frenchman from the working-class Parisian suburb of Belleville.

Both the court's original verdict and the sentence ended up being upheld by the presiding judges. On the assumption that "no one in this world is completely normal," their ruling spurned the notion that Edgar's abnormal psychology was a mitigating factor in his crimes.

His personality had, however, come to fascinate the attorney who represented him during the appeal process. Bevinetto afterward dashed off a short and sympathetic book about Edgar's dealings with the Khevenhüller-Metsch family. Entitled *Le Avventure di Edgardo Laplante* (The Adventures of Edgar Laplante), it was released in a small edition by an obscure Italian imprint. Bevinetto's book hailed him the "con man supreme."

ACROSS THE ATLANTIC, where references to Edgar had long since evaporated from the newspapers, a fellow con man and pale-skinned publicity hound by the name of Charles Smith obtained inspiration from his shenanigans. Smith posed first as the son of Chief White Elk and then as the chief himself. Over a five-month period, this counterfeit of a counterfeit fronted promotional events at Californian car dealerships, addressed schoolchildren about Indian tradition, and crowed to the press about his power to influence sports contests by performing ritual dances. He also grabbed his own sliver of notoriety by getting himself picked up as a suspect in the murder of a twenty-year-old woman, later identified as a typhoid victim.

Edgar was meanwhile transferred to Civitavecchia prison, only a short distance from Rome. Broke once again, he was reduced to paying for cigarettes by selling the gold crowns on several of his teeth.

Good behavior earned him parole just two and a half years into his sentence. But the Italian fascist regime, which had lately completed its evolution into a dictatorship, branded him "a dangerous character" and refused to release him until he could be repatriated at his own expense. Edgar was probably behind the failed bid to persuade his father—whom he hadn't seen for fifteen years—to put up the $118 fare home.

He had to endure another two months at Civitavecchia until the local U.S. consul secured employment for him as a mess steward on the SS *Executive,* an American cargo vessel, scheduled to steam from Genoa to New York City in mid-August 1929. Before that, Edgar was moved to Le Nuove prison in Turin, where he shared a cell with the nineteen-year-old antifascist Massimo Mila, who would go on to become an eminent music critic.

In readiness for the SS *Executive*'s departure, the Italian authorities then moved Edgar to Genoa, a city he'd last visited during his triumphal tour of the country. He was turned loose from prison only just prior to embarkation, at which point he exchanged his jail uniform for the uniform of a mess steward. Dapper though he looked in his latest costume, made up of a white mess jacket, matching shirt, dark trousers, and wavily striped necktie, his once-photogenic features bore the heavy boot print of life in jail. His skin had grown coarse, his mouth was bracketed by deep grooves, and his teeth were badly discolored and punctuated by gaps. Only his hair, which he wore in a fashionable greased-back style, remained unaltered, still dark and dense.

American and Italian journalists seized the opportunity to quiz him before he departed. He told the Italians that prison had transformed his personality, revived his love of hard work, and cured him of what he called his two vices—alcohol and morphine. Any mention of his parallel cocaine addiction was omitted.

When Edgar spoke with a representative from the Associated Press, he announced that he bore no ill feeling toward the country where he had been imprisoned for so long. His comments, together with reports of his imminent homeward voyage, were carried by numerous American newspapers. At least Edgar had the consolation of knowing he hadn't been forgotten.

27

Save for a dog-eared copy of the transcript of his Italian trial, fifteen dollar bills, and a wooden spoon, used for the duration of his imprisonment, Edgar had no luggage when his ship docked in Greenpoint, Brooklyn, on Friday, September 20, 1929. He wore the rest of his possessions: a neat gray suit, a matching necktie, a white shirt, and a pair of tan oxfords. The one thing distinguishing him was the unconventional absence of a hat.

He'd been at sea for the better part of a month, during which he had impressed his commanding officer with his efficiency as a mess steward. Mundane though his duties had been, Edgar had transformed them into a theatrical performance, balancing a circular tray on the tips of his fingers with the aplomb of a waiter at some elegant Manhattan restaurant.

From the deck of the SS *Executive,* he had a view across the East River toward the city, where pale wisps of smoke typically meandered across the bar chart of its skyline, which had sprouted many more skyscrapers since he last saw it. As the river's choppy waters slapped against the rotting wooden pier that constituted the Greenpoint Terminal, Edgar strode down the gangplank. Below him, a rat swam frantically along the narrow channel between the ship and the wharf.

Edgar's noonday arrival, which overlapped with a shrill blast from a factory whistle, could scarcely have been more different from his arrival in so many Italian ports only five summers back. There was no cheering crowd, no brass band, no government welcoming party, no ripple of fascist salutes. There were no picturesque buildings, either. Just a strip of grimy waterfront, lined with enormous factories, one of which had ROPE & TWINE written across the front in huge letters. But for a mangy dog, two blue-coated dockworkers, and two reporters and their attendant press photographers, waiting in the fall sunshine, the waterfront was deserted.

His swagger unimpaired by his European ordeal, Edgar posed for the photographers, a pair of dark glasses accentuating his casual panache. He also sold the *New York Times* some hokum about how he'd be "quite content" to settle down in Rhode Island and become "a plain factory worker." Perched on an upturned oil drum, he then spoke to a female feature writer from the *Brooklyn Daily Eagle,* who was interested in his recent past. "And to think that it was all because of a woman." he mused. "Originally I came from Pawtucket, Rhode Island. I am partly Indian. My mother was a member of the Tuscarora tribe. While I was out in California, the Paramount Film Company hired me to go to London with the production *The Covered Wagon,* as an interpreter to the Indians who were acting in it. While we were over there, the publicity man had the bright idea of billing me as 'Chief White Elk,' a delegate to the League of Nations, representing the American Indian. As luck would have it, at the same time there was an Indian chief who had come over to plead with the king on behalf of his people. One day a man from Paramount asked me to make a speech and the crowd sort of . . . got me confused with the visiting chief and that's how it all started."

Edgar proceeded to unfurl a distorted account of being sent to the continent and meeting the younger of the Contessas Khevenhüller-Metsch in Nice. He said she'd insisted on going for a coffee with him, and the two of them had afterward shared a cab home. "Well, the next thing I knew, the contessa had burst into tears and was telling me how much I looked like the fiancé that her family had not allowed her to marry. The only way

I could make her stop was to accept the pearl ring that she took off her finger and thrust into my hand—and the diamond bracelet, too."

He talked about how she'd obtained his address from the management of the movie theater where he worked. "Before I could say a word, she took out a blue silk bag and tossed it into my lap. In it was $10,000! When I refused to accept it, she insisted that it was my half of the winnings at Monte Carlo, as she had worn the lucky feather that I had given her out of my headdress the night before.

"Things began to get so deep that I thought I had better pay a visit to my wife, an English girl whom I married four months before I signed up with the Paramount Company. I told the contessa and her mother good-bye and went home to her in England. Everything went along fine for a couple of days, but pretty soon cables began to arrive and one day along came a cable from the Bank of Manchester with a draft for £1,500 from the contessa. There was nothing to do but to go back and try to straighten things out with her. I joined her in Trieste, at the Savoia Hotel, where I was given the Royal Suite No. 14. Picking up the pen, I wrote on the register 'Chief White Elk' but was told to change it to 'pasha,' as 'chief' was very confusing because of its use among the military attachés in Italy. So I wrote 'pasha' and went on up to bed.

"The next morning—bright and early—somebody knocked. When I yelled 'Come in!' in walked a bellboy so full of gold braid that he was all bent over. 'What does your Highness require this morning?'

"I answered, 'Sleep!' so he went out and closed the door.

"In a few moments in rushed the contessa all excited and said, 'Come, put on your pants—the ones with the beads on and your hat with the feathers. They will soon be here!'

"Soon, in they came. Dozens of them. All in gold-braided uniforms like a musical comedy. Generals and the mayor and everybody. They led me onto the balcony where they presented me with a silver key to the city, and down in the courtyard the band played the National Anthem, and everybody was shouting.

"When they had gone, the contessa sprung the real surprise. She had chartered the top deck of a steamer and we were to leave in the morning for a trip."

He added that there was no way he could get out of the arrangement. "Every port that we pulled into gave us the royal salute. Life was a dream." Back in Trieste, he explained, four cars and a seaplane were placed at his disposal. "In a way, this bearing of gifts isn't new to me. You see, it is an old Indian custom with my people, so why shouldn't I accept them? How did I know that brother Georg was out to get my scalp? It seems that he didn't like to see me getting all that money and those gifts, so he did some enquiring here and there. When we got back from the cruise, I was all slated for another little trip—this time to Civitavecchia prison, just outside Rome."

The reporter asked about the younger contessa's reaction to him landing in jail.

"Oh, she went insane the day that I was convicted," he replied. "Night after night I used to try to go to sleep thinking of the United States and what a fool I was to ever leave. All I ever had to eat was thin soup and half-steamed spaghetti. I used to starve myself so that the doctor would order milk and eggs, just to get off that diet for a few days."

Well-stocked now with material for her story, the reporter and her photographer offered Edgar a ride to a nearby subway station. Their car drove through bustling though not especially prosperous Greenpoint and into the Navy Yard District, tenements abutting cobblestoned streets not dissimilar to where Edgar was raised. What must have been alien to him, though, were the new clothes and hairstyles that had appeared since he left the United States almost seven years earlier.

Through the windshield, Edgar would have seen the swelling silhouette of the Brooklyn Bridge. "Say, this is Sands Street, isn't it?" he said as the car reached a narrow, dingy thoroughfare, where trolley buses skirted coffee shops and stores selling naval uniforms. The car pulled up just across from a drugstore near the bridge. Almost blocking the sidewalk outside was a covered stairway up to the huge, elevated train station above.

"D'you know, I am just like a kid about being back in the States again?" Edgar remarked. "I stayed up all night to see the Statue of Liberty." His attention was suddenly hijacked by a passing young woman. "Look at that girl's skirt," he added. "Why, when I left in 1923, girls would have been ashamed to show their knees like that." Thoughts of women coaxed his mind in another direction. "As soon as I can get enough money together, I am going to send for my wife who is still in England. She's my second wife—my first wife was an Indian from the Klamath tribe in California. She died during the flu epidemic. I can't do enough for the girl I have now. She has been true blue all the way through. What worries me is just what I'll do with my future, as $15 isn't so much."

"Well, maybe the contessa will . . . ?" the reporter ventured.

But Edgar cut in. "The contessa!" he exclaimed with dismissive vehemence. "She's a regular Indian giver. Now she claims that I stole the jewels and the money. Well, maybe my lawyer will be able to . . ." He let the sentence fizzle out, then shook hands with the reporter before they parted. Anyone who glimpsed Edgar walking along Sands Street would have pegged him as an average commuter, maybe a shift worker on his way into Manhattan. Had they struck up a conversation with him in a subway car or at a lunch counter, they would have taken him for a madman if he'd dropped so much as a cursory reference to the swank hotels he'd stayed in, the Italians who had addressed him as "Your Highness," the vast sums of money he'd squandered, the aristocrats who had once fawned over him, the huge crowds that had greeted him, the banquets staged in his honor, the women who had loved him.

EPILOGUE

Edgar's once impeccable sense of timing had deserted him. A shade over four weeks after he said goodbye to the woman from the *Brooklyn Daily Eagle,* the Wall Street Crash of 1929 occasioned a protracted and savage economic depression. Even without that, circumstances were against him.

Over the preceding few years, his homeland had been subject to changes that were certain to make life difficult for him no matter whether he stayed on the right side of the law or resumed his former life. If he chose the latter, he'd have to contend with the still understaffed yet increasingly effective Bureau of Investigation, forerunner of the FBI. Most threatening from Edgar's point of view was the creation of an Identification Division, entrusted with collecting fingerprints from police forces across the nation and searching that collection upon request. The nationwide distribution of wanted posters, featuring details of criminal suspects on the run, posed another impediment to Edgar's old habit of moving to a fresh city whenever doubts about his identity surfaced. Recent improvements in communications between cities didn't help with that, either, those advances being in telephone technology, the birth of national radio networks, and the highways starting to branch across the country.

If he wanted to pursue a law-abiding career, though, Edgar would have faced other obstacles that had sprung up while he was away. Performing in chautauqua might have tempted him, but such a choice was unrealistic because these tours had gone into steep and terminal decline. Vaudeville was in trouble, too. And the arrival of talking pictures had sounded the death knell for combined theater and movie shows. Further decreasing Edgar's chances of resuscitating his stage career was the toll that years of drinking, drug taking, and hard living had taken on his appearance, now gaunt, gap-toothed, and less than alluring. He also found himself hamstrung by changes in musical fashion, the availability of sensitive electronic microphones facilitating the emergence of a hushed and intimate style of singing that left baritones like him sounding risibly passé.

Where he went and what he did in the months subsequent to his return from Europe remain mysterious. But his archival trail reappears in March 1930 when he was living at a hotel in Boston. Counter to what he'd told the reporters who had greeted him when he returned to America, he hadn't mended his ways, embarked upon a conventional life, or engineered a reunion with Ethel and Leslie. He had, instead, surrendered to compulsion by donning the familiar identity of Chief White Elk. Under that name, he advertised for performers to accompany him on a touring radio show. HELP WANTED, the ad stated. TWO GIRLS, PROFESSIONAL DANCERS AND SINGERS, AND ONE MUST KNOW HOW TO PLAY THE PIANO.

By the onset of summer, his tour—if it ever happened—was over. He then went back to Rhode Island, which he'd left more than a decade previously. His reappearance there courted the anger of his Pawtucket-based father, who had lately told a reporter, "If Edgar knows what is good for him, he will steer clear of Pawtucket."

Disregarding his father's warning, Edgar headed for that city, and moved in with his widowed forty-seven-year-old French-Canadian cousin and her five children. One of them worked as a theatrical agent, possibly helping Edgar obtain salaried employment selling perfume at a vaudeville venue. Yet he or whoever filled out that year's U.S. Census still provided the defiant reply "theatrical performer" in the section about his profession.

Itinerant by nature, he was back on the road and in the guise of Chief White Elk just a few months later. Passing through New Jersey, Massachusetts, and New York City, he spoke at a Kiwanis Club lunch, sang at a movie theater, and gave a couple of newspaper interviews about his experiences in Europe. "For a year and a half I was a prince and lived like one," he told a reporter from the popular *New York World*. "Twenty-two servants, I had. A general for my secretary, perfumed baths, a maid to scrub my back. Well . . . now I haven't had anything to eat for three days. I don't know where I'm going to sleep tonight. I can't get a job. All that trouble in Europe has ruined my prospects."

With mingled pride and regret (pride quickly gaining ascendancy), he reminisced about his time in Europe, about "the magnificent ball" he'd hosted, about "the splendid gifts" he'd presented, about what he'd said to Mussolini and what Mussolini had said to him. At one point Edgar gave a grand, sweeping gesture. When he caught sight of his rough, dirty skin, arthritic fingers, and broken nails, he sighed disbelievingly and said, "Ah, the women who have kissed that hand." He went on to feed the reporter the biggest of all his self-serving lies about his royal tour of Italy. "I really began to feel it was true. I actually came to think I *was* a prince."

WHITE AMERICA'S ABIDING FASCINATION with the Wild West, sustained both by Hollywood and by the enormous popularity of *Western Story* and other such magazines, worked in Edgar's favor. Cashing in on this pervasive interest, he returned to his well-tested trick of lecturing on Native American culture. His lectures were juxtaposed by demonstrations of traditional dances and chants, together with his song repertoire, which—somewhat incongruously—expanded to include "Ol' Man River," the show tune synonymous with the African American singer Paul Robeson.

Edgar also campaigned to improve the conditions and legal rights of what passed for his brethren. Despite citizenship being granted to all U.S.-born Native Americans while he was in Europe, voting rights were still being withheld in certain localities, where state law took precedence.

Calling himself Chief Louie Tewanna, his tribal affiliation fluctuating between the Choctaw, Tuscarora, and Sioux, he once again characterized himself as a figure worthy of veneration—a war hero, football star, surgeon, linguist, and Olympic athlete. He even juiced up his already overstuffed résumé by claiming to be the brother of the Hollywood actress Laura La Plant. Not content with all that, he awarded himself a PhD from Cornell University, a senior position within the American Indian Association, plus a list of acting credits in prominent movies starring the likes of Charlie Chaplin, Rudolph Valentino, and the young John Wayne.

Between the closing months of 1930 and the summer of 1932, a grim period of widespread homelessness and poverty, Edgar swung through the Deep South on a coast-to-coast tour. He performed at screenings of Westerns. He addressed civic clubs, school classes, college students, and Boy Scout troops. He gave lessons in beadwork and other traditional Native American crafts, among them basket weaving, which Burtha must have taught him. He yarned about traveling through Europe and meeting King George V and the pope, as well as spending time with Valentino. All of this garnered him a modest level of hospitality and acclaim.

Temporarily reverting to his Chief White Elk persona, he broadcast from a Kansas City radio station and sang the "Tantum Ergo"—a medieval Latin hymn—during mass at a Catholic church in Sedalia, Missouri. He also suckered a newspaperman into believing he planned to return there with his symphony orchestra as part of its world tour. The same journalist even fell for Edgar's story of how he'd played football for Carlisle under a different name—Man Afraid (the name of a genuine Native American footballer, mentioned in the serialized reminiscences of the team's coach).

By July 1932 Edgar had pitched up in Oregon, where he began pulling a fresh con. He was now a sixty-year-old Native American and former Olympic star, who had run out of money en route to Los Angeles to attend the latest installment of the Olympics. His plight spurred residents to set up a fundraising campaign to help him get there.

In a strange footnote to an already strange life, another grifter was meanwhile touring the country, posing as Chief White Elk's younger brother. Edgar's bogus sibling, who went by the name of Chief Eagle Feather, billed himself as the "world's greatest American Indian tap dancer" and pretended to have played a starring role in *The Covered Wagon*. Stranger still, these two impostors wound up working together in Canada through the winter of 1932–33. They were part of an ostensibly all–Native American road show, featuring an amplified band and a troupe of salesmen, each pitching a specific product—soap, in Edgar's case. And not just *soft* soap.

From this period onward, the hitherto abundant documentation about Edgar grows scarce. The next recorded reference to him doesn't appear until May 1934 when he cheated a family in Hopewell, Maryland. In exchange for a loan that enabled him to catch the bus out of town, he promised to arrange for some Native American friends to visit the family and drop off "two fine riding ponies."

As he faded from the public record, another impostor calling himself Chief White Elk came to national prominence. Likely galvanized by Edgar, Herbert R. Davis—a resident of Wilmington, Delaware—started dressing in Native American garb and masquerading variously as a member of the Sioux, Nanticoke, and Chinook peoples. Davis used this new identity to promote everything from a toy shop to a boat show. He even made a brief foray into the big leagues, formerly the province of Edgar.

During the summer of 1936, by which time the ravages of the Depression had been alleviated by the New Deal, President Franklin D. Roosevelt's economic rescue program, Davis was in the front row of the 100,000-strong crowd attending a rally in Philadelphia. The rally marked the president's acceptance of the Democratic Party's nomination for a second term. Before the speeches began, Davis stepped onto the platform and spoke to Roosevelt's mother. His remark, supposedly made on behalf of the North Dakota Sioux, would attract substantial press coverage. "Your son has given our people a New Deal," he assured her. And when the president later commenced the speech that declared "This generation has a rendezvous with destiny," Davis removed his feathered headdress and waved it supportively in the air.

THROUGH THE PUBLICATION IN 1935 of *Getting Rich Quick*, which anthologized history's greatest con tricks, a modest number of readers were introduced to the story of Edgar's Italian rendezvous with destiny. His health deteriorating, he was by then back in Pawtucket, where he eked out a living as—of all things—a church organist.

He then surfaced in Montana in December 1937. Presenting himself as Dr. Dillon White Elk, a part–Native American, part-Inuit member of an Alaskan delegation traveling to Washington, DC, to protest illegal Japanese fishing in American territorial waters, this former embodiment of Roaring Twenties excess hustled several individuals, extracted money from a charity, and left behind an unpaid hotel bill.

Perhaps as a legacy of long-term cocaine use, which damages the heart and cardiovascular system, he suffered a heart attack while passing through Flint, Michigan, just short of a year later. He was hospitalized in a ward for people without means to pay for their own treatment. Illness left his once-athletic frame so wizened that he was described as a "little Indian." His cadaverous features topped by an enduringly dark shock of hair, which lent him the appearance of a sinister manservant in a horror movie, he moved on to Detroit. There, he was hospitalized again.

Another heart attack struck him as he journeyed through Northern California in August 1939. He was found sprawled beside the Sacramento-to-Vallejo highway. The motorist who came to his rescue took him to Sacramento County Hospital, where he was admitted to the paupers' ward. Incorrigible even under these circumstances, this pauper who had once lived like a prince entranced people with the story of how four years previously he'd led a team of nine dogsleds through the Alaskan wilderness. He said his objective had been to reach the crashed airplane in which the columnist, broadcaster, and Hollywood star Will Rogers had been flying. The Associated Press wire service picked up Edgar's story, providing a conduit into newspapers up and down the West Coast.

On being discharged from the hospital, there were reports of Edgar visiting Oregon, where he morphed into Dr. E. Warren La Plante, Chief White Elk, an inhabitant of Prince Patrick Island in the Canadian Arctic. His latest variation on his tried-and-untrustworthy persona involved him claiming to be a representative of "the Sons of the Land of the Midnight Sun," a genuine organization open to the descendants of Norwegian settlers, its exotic-sounding name presumably taking his fancy.

When he headed south into California, there's a possibility that he achieved reconciliation with his twenty-two-year-old adopted Native American daughter, whom he had abandoned early in her childhood. After Burtha's premature death, she'd been adopted yet again, this time by Edgar's in-laws. They, too, had since passed away. Now she was living in the large Native American community within the Hoopa Valley, not far from Sacramento.

Riding a bus through New Orleans in the summer of 1942, Edgar's cardiac problems brought on what appears to have been his third heart attack. It was followed by a brief period of recuperation in the city's Charity Hospital. Afterward he gave a long interview to the *Times-Picayune,* in which he reflected upon the vast amount of cash he'd given away during his Italian tour. But he didn't even mention the cash he'd blown while he was in Belgium that year. The combined total, which had disappeared from his leaky pockets in the course of only twelve months, was as much as $58.9 million in 2018 terms. "I could use some of it now," lamented Edgar, whose unbridled extravagance and audacious self-reinvention carry echoes of Jay Gatsby, F. Scott Fitzgerald's most famous character.

To thicken his empty billfold, Edgar conceived a scam that entailed selling shares in new and nonexistent oil companies. Whatever money he pocketed from this had been frittered away by December 1943 when he found himself in the desert city of Phoenix, Arizona, where he passed himself off as Dr. White Eagle, native of the nearby town of Gila Bend and by implication a member of the Papago tribe, many of whom lived on the Gila River Indian Reservation. He'd probably gone to Phoenix with the intention of conning some of the thousands of tourists flocking there over the winter, during which the downtown streets acquired a cohesive flavor. While the storefronts displayed Native American blankets, silver, and turquoise jewelry, the busiest sidewalks served as market stalls for Native American women selling handmade pottery.

Yet Edgar's glory days as a grifter were far behind him despite him being just fifty-five years old. Flat broke and deprived of the attention and acclaim that had propelled him through life, the dual onslaught of pneumonia and bronchitis landed him in the Schmidt Haven of Rest, a south-side hospital catering not just to the impoverished elderly but also to the demented, their presence rendering questionable its credentials as a haven of rest. As he lay there over Christmas, memories of his glorious past offering some measure of insulation against his *in*glorious present, he may have realized that he wouldn't be able to escape from the hospital as easily as he'd escaped from so many hotels. The unavoidable truth was, he had less than a month to live. If he'd been able to see into the future, though, he would surely have found solace in the knowledge that he *hadn't*—contrary to present indications—been forgotten, and that his Italian adventures would decades later be commemorated in a collection of poetry, three novels, and a Swiss television drama.

Weakened by illness, he succumbed to a fatal heart attack on Sunday, January 23, 1944. His demise went unreported by the press that had once upon a time contributed to his worldwide celebrity. Death ratifying the doctorate and Native American identity he'd long coveted, the Arizona bureaucracy registered him as "White Eagle, Dr., Indian male." A subsequent inspection of his personal effects, which must have included some form of false ID, gave the authorities the impression that he was also known as Edward La Plante.

For someone determined to live at other people's expense, it was apt that the self-styled Dr. White Eagle should be buried on the Phoenix taxpayers' dime. After nearly thirty-four rootless years, his wanderings carrying him from blue-collar Central Falls to the sumptuous hotels of Venice and Florence, the charismatic Edgar Laplante finally found a permanent home in the desiccated bleakness of the paupers' burial ground at Maricopa County Cemetery.

NOTES

Abbreviations: NAL (National Archives, London); WSU (Washington State University).

EPIGRAPH

vii   **"Through others we":** L. S. Vygotsky, *The Collected Works of L. S. Vygotsky: Child Psychology,* Volume 5, p. 170.

CHAPTER 1

3   **had a reputation:** *San José Mercury News,* January 16, 1916, p. 4.

3   **"I'm sorry":** *San José Mercury News,* March 5, 1917, p. 6.

4   **"the big Indian":** Ibid., p. 2.

4   **he liked to:** *San José Mercury News,* March 4, 1917, p. 20.

4   **"This is the":** *San José Mercury News,* March 5, 1917, p. 2.

4   **"I never heard":** *San José Mercury News,* March 4, 1917, p. 8.

5   **Tom said he'd:** *San José Mercury News,* March 5, 1917, p. 2.

5   **For him, the:** *San José Mercury News,* March 6, 1917, p. 3.

5   **"The thing to do":** *San José Mercury News,* March 5, 1917, p. 2.

5   **Tom suspected:** *San José Evening News,* March 6, 1917, p. 3.

5   **he'd been drawn:** *San José Evening News,* March 16, 1917, p. 2.

6   **smoking cigarettes:** *San José Mercury News,* March 5, 1917, p. 2.

6   **seducing young women:** *San José Mercury News,* April 27, 1917, p. 12.

6   **seducing young men:** *Spokane Press,* November 27, 1909, p. 4.

6   **He would have been horrified:** *San José Evening News,* November 3, 1917, p. 1.

7   **sure to be withdrawn:** *San José Mercury News,* April 27, 1917, p. 12.

7   **To publicize his show:** *San José Evening News,* March 5, 1917, p. 7.

8   **which led one:** *San José Mercury News,* March 6, 1917, p. 3.

8   **he was happy:** Ibid.

8   **Now he started:** *San José Evening News,* March 6, 1917, p. 3.

CHAPTER 2

11   **Snazzy hotels:** Maurer, *Big Con,* p. 166.

12   **he gave his new:** *San Diego Evening Tribune,* March 17, 1917, p. 1.

12   **Risk and reward:** His well-documented behavior demonstrates his addiction to risk-taking, which is, to a lesser extent, prevalent among con men. See Maurer, *Big Con,* pp. 131–32.

12   **He told the journalist:** *San Diego Union,* March 9, 1917, p. 8.

12   **For all his storytelling:** *L'Ouest-Éclair* (Rennes, France), October 12, 1923, p. 2.

13   **where his debonair:** *San Diego Union,* March 17, 1917, p. 2.

13   **"temporarily embarrassed":** Ibid.

13   **Flimflam merchants:** Maurer, *Big Con,* p. 1.

13   **he began saying:** *Washington (DC) Times,* March 12, 1917, p. 10.

14   **he pledged to:** *San Diego Union,* March 19, 1917, p. 4.

14   **"Hopscotching":** Maurer, *Big Con,* p. 263.

15   **Edgar was asked to:** *San Diego Union,* March 17, 1917, p. 2.

16   **"souvenir fiend":** *Bisbee (AZ) Daily Review,* January 17, 1917, p. 2.

16   **"newsies":** Blanke, *1910s,* p. 42.

16   **"Although still":** *San Diego Weekly Union,* March 15, 1917, p. 6.

16   **Reading multiple:** Maurer, *Big Con,* p. 166.

18   **Edgar made a:** *San Diego Union,* March 15, 1917, p. 9.

19   MAN POSING: *San José Evening News,* March 15, 1917, p. 1.

CHAPTER 3

20   **which advertised:** *Official Guide and Descriptive Book of the Panama-California Exposition.*

21   **After the concert:** *San Diego Union,* March 17, 1917, p. 1.

21   **"The man who":** *San José Evening News,* March 15, 1917, p. 1.

21   **Edgar told the:** *San Diego Evening Tribune,* March 16, 1917, p. 1.

22   **Highland Brewery:** This was managed by the father of Theodor Seuss Geisel, better known by his nom de plume, Dr. Seuss. Edgar and his family were provided with a company house on the grounds of the brewery.

22   **motormaniacs:** *Los Angeles Times,* March 7, 1917, p. 12.

22   **"The Utmost":** *Evening Public Ledger* (Philadelphia), March 16, 1917, p. 3.

22   **It covered:** *Los Angeles Herald,* March 16, 1917, p. 24.

23   **The suspicion that:** *Los Angeles Times,* March 18, 1917, p. 13.

23   **Chief Harry Johnson:** *Salt Lake Tribune,* March 21, 1918, p. 1.

His choice of name may have been inspired by the Native American baseball pitcher George Johnson, who had recently made the Pacific Coast League's all-star team. People knew George Johnson as "Chief Johnson," not because he was a tribal chief, but because that title was a derogatory nickname commonly applied to Native American men.

23   **the eighteenth century:** In the eighteenth century, rival British and French settlers wore Native American costumes while staging raids on each other's communities, their aim being to foist blame for these attacks onto the indigenous population. A comparable disguise was favored by campaigners for American independence, who used Native American clothing to conceal their identities and intimidate anyone who might try to obstruct their protests. Most famously, members of a clandestine group called the Sons of Liberty dressed as Mohawks when they boarded three British ships and decanted a huge quantity of valuable imported tea into Boston Harbor. Just as tea had become symbolic of hated British taxation and colonial rule, Mohawk apparel came to symbolize the white American struggle for self-government—a link infused with venomous irony by the imposition of white American rule over the Mohawks.

This form of cultural cross-dressing continued during the 1780s. At annual parades mounted in Philadelphia and New York City by two self-defined patriotic clubs named the Tammany Societies, members donned Native American–style costumes as their uniform. It was a gimmick also adopted by the Society of Red Men, a quasi-Masonic group founded in 1812. For its private ceremonies—touted as "Indian mysteries"—members wore similar clothing. The practice proliferated after 1833 when the group morphed into the Improved Order of Red Men and spread across America.

24   **"Great Disease Detective"**: Undated postcard, sold by WorthPoint auctions.

24   **"genuine Indians"**: *Easton (MD) Gazette,* December 19, 1908, p. 4.

25   **"The Great Indian"**: Medicine bottle, private collection.

25   **"Ladies and gentlemen"**: McNamara, *Step Right Up,* pp. 105–6.

26   **Unlicensed pitchmen like:** Anderson, *Snake Oil, Hustlers and Hambones,* p. 103.

26   **Edgar said his oil:** *L'Impartial* (Neuchâtel, Switzerland), March 12, 1945, p. 1.

26   **His career as:** *St. Louis Post-Dispatch* magazine, October 20, 1929, p. 4.

27   **The chief would, according:** *Eau Claire (WI) Leader,* June 5, 1917, p. 2.

27   **"the great white chief":** *Detroit Free Press,* June 11, 1917, p. 3.

27   **he now proclaimed:** *Eau Claire (WI) Leader,* June 5, 1917, p. 2.

He also resorted to fabrication when he strove to demonstrate the patriotism of Native Americans, plenty of genuine evidence of which existed. As proof of their commitment to the United States, he announced that Princess Lola, "among the wealthiest of the Indians," had launched a campaign to raise $1 million from the Oklahoma Cherokee and Osage peoples, money used to help finance the war. Edgar had most likely excavated this wealthy benefactress's name from the recesses of his memory—Princess Lola was the stage name of a fellow vaudevillian who claimed to be a Sioux.

28   **he said it:** *Eau Claire (WI) Leader,* June 6, 1917, p. 2.

28   **There, he gave a:** *Eau Claire (WI) Leader,* June 7, 1917, p. 5; June 29, 1917, p. 5.

29   **To lend weight:** *Eau Claire (WI) Leader,* June 9, 1917, p. 4.

29   **the owner of:** *Eau Claire (WI) Leader,* June 29, 1917, p. 4.

29   **He took to:** *Eau Claire (WI) Leader,* June 6, 1917, p. 2.

29   **So persuasive:** Ibid.

30   **"extensively acquainted":** *Eau Claire (WI) Leader,* June 9, 1917, p. 4.

30   **At the interview:** Ibid.

30   **Each of them:** *Eau Claire (WI) Leader,* June 29, 1917, p. 4.

30   **Admittedly, he *was*:** *Eau Claire (WI) Leader,* June 7, 1917, p. 5.

31   **new silent movie:** He had taken part in a similar show five months earlier when he was in Abilene, pretending to be Tom Longboat. On that occasion he had set out to magnify his celebrity by saying he was "the brother of the famous Indian motion picture actress, Princess Mona Darkfeather." (If he'd known the truth about the princess, he would never have said that. Born

Josephine M. Workman, she had no more Native American blood than him.) *Abilene Daily Reporter* (TX), January 2, 1917, p. 6.

31 **and Native Americans:** The most successful of the Native American impersonators was Arthur B. Burk, a second-string performer otherwise known as Chief Little Elk. Styling himself as the "Sioux Indian Baritone," he had a song, dance, and cello-playing routine that he and his wife, "the Chiefess," performed in front of a wigwam, a campfire, and a simulated waterfall.

31 **"mechanics of emotion":** Butsch, *Making of American Audiences,* p. 116.

31 **He described the:** *Eau Claire (WI) Leader,* June 7, 1917, p. 5.

32 **In any case, he:** This is evident from the well-documented trajectory of his life.

32 **Headlined** BIG CHIEF: *Detroit Free Press,* June 11, 1917, p. 3.

32 **"blind pigs":** Johnson, *Detroit Beer,* p. 22.

CHAPTER 4

34 **level of the pickpockets:** Maurer, *Big Con,* p. 152.

34 **And he circulated:** *Fort Wayne (IN) News,* June 22, 1917, p. 1.

35 **"a flash act":** Haupert, *Entertainment Industry,* p. 34.

35 **Even mild:** Lloyd, *Vaudeville Trails Thru the West,* p. 29.

35 **"drew blood":** Butsch, *Making of American Audiences,* p. 116.

36 **He added that:** *Fort Wayne (IN) Journal-Gazette,* June 22, 1917, p. 21.

37 **And wisecracks:** *Evening World* (New York City), August 4, 1917, p. 3.

37 **the kind of people:** *St. Louis Post-Dispatch* magazine, October 20, 1929, p. 4.

37 **They formed:** Markham, *Financial History of the United States,* p. 6; Shackleton, *Book of New York,* pp. 53–54.

38 **port of embarkation:** "Hoboken in World War I," Hoboken Historical Museum, http://www.hobokenmuseum.org/.

38 **Young soldiers:** Shanks, *As They Passed Through the Port,* pp. 138, 226; *Laramie (WY) Republican,* January 1, 1918, p. 1.

39 **asked the nearsighted:** "Chief White Elk," Investigative Case Files of the Bureau of Investigation 1908–1922, Old German Files, 1909–1922. Original data from US National Archives; accessed through Fold3.com. Hereinafter cited as "Chief White Elk," Fold3.com.

39 **"slam-bang, knock-'em-down":** *New York Tribune,* July 29, 1917, p. 4.

40 **Kit bags slung:** Schauble, *First Battalion,* pp. 45–49, provides a detailed account of the embarkation and voyage.

41 **Edgar knew that:** Gleaves, *History of the Transport Service,* pp. 37–38.

42 **terrier named Smoke:** The dog survived in France for more than a year,

but died when he was hit by a dispatch rider. "There were real tears shed as Company 'E' buried him near a pine woods just north of Neufchâteau," wrote the Battalion historian. Schauble, *First Battalion*, p. 32.

42   **"heaven, hell":** Ziegler-McPherson, *Immigrants in Hoboken*, p. 196.

43   **The officers dismissed:** Schauble, *First Battalion*, p. 49.

43   **"Soon after":** *Brooklyn Daily Eagle*, August 8, 1917, p. 14.

43   **Staff at the:** *Brooklyn Daily Eagle*, August 14, 1917, p. 20.

43   **Most of them:** *Brooklyn Daily Eagle*, August 16, 1917, p. 20.

44   **the storm abated:** Schauble, *First Battalion*, pp. 45–49, provides a detailed account of the voyage.

44   **MY CONVOY:** Fry, *War Record of the U.S.S.* Henderson, p. 9.

47   ***"Vive les Américaines!":*** Schauble, *First Battalion*, p. 49.

CHAPTER 5

48   **Craig accused:** *Laramie (WY) Republican*, January 1, 1918, p. 1.

48   **Edgar began by:** Ibid.

49   **With vivid:** *Syracuse (NY) Post-Standard*, October 18, 1917, p. 24.

50   **He captivated:** *Schenectady (NY) Daily Gazette*, October 18, 1917, p. 12.

51   **"you could hear":** Anderson, *Snake Oil, Hustlers and Hambones*, p. 145.

51   **Klein signed the:** "Chief White Elk," Fold3.com.

51   **"a shill":** Maurer, *Big Con*, p. 270.

51   **The talk was:** "Chief White Elk," Fold3.com.

52   **"I was over":** *Cincinnati Enquirer*, October 28, 1917, p. 4.

53   **Half the proceeds:** "Chief White Elk," Fold3.com.

53   **Over that weekend:** Ibid.

54   **For his next:** *Laramie (WY) Republican*, January 1, 1918, pp. 1, 5; "Chief White Elk," Fold3.com.

55   **Mingling with:** *Laramie (WY) Daily Boomerang*, December 18, 1917, p. 4.

55   **One thing:** "Chief White Elk," Fold3.com.

55   **Satisfied that:** *Laramie (WY) Daily Boomerang*, December 10, 1917, p. 8.

55   **Grifters like him:** Maurer, *Big Con*, p. 254.

56   **but napping on:** Baedeker, *United States*, p. xvi.

56   **war pretender:** *Rock Springs (WY) Miner*, December 21, 1917, p. 10.

56   **When questioned:** *Laramie (WY) Republican*, January 1, 1918, p. 1.

56   **He confessed that:** Ibid., pp. 1, 5.

57   **In his defense:** Ibid.

57   **county attorney charged him:** "Chief White Elk," Fold3.com.

57   **He'd been playing:** *St. Louis Post-Dispatch* magazine, October 20, 1929, p. 4.

58   **The county attorney released him:** *Salt Lake Tribune,* March 20, 1918, p. 1;
      March 21, 1918, p. 1.

CHAPTER 6

59   **He only had:** James E. Hansen II, "Moonshine and Murder: Prohibition in
      Denver," *Colorado Magazine,* 1973, pp. 8–10.

60   **Fresh acquaintances of:** *Pueblo (CO) Chieftain,* January 25, 1918, p. 3.

61   **On suspicion of:** *Deseret Evening News* (Salt Lake City), March 21, 1918
      (second edition), p. 1.

61   **He expressed:** "Chief White Elk," Fold3.com.

61   **When Special Agent Craft:** Ibid.

62   **After the interview:** *Pueblo (CO) Chieftain,* January 31, 1918, p. 4.

63   **"We have no":** "Chief White Elk," Fold3.com.

63   **officers from the:** *Pueblo (CO) Chieftain,* January 31, 1918, p. 4.

63   **Edgar devoted:** "Chief White Elk," Fold3.com.

64   **counterfeit candor:** Ibid.

64   **He gave his:** *Chickasha (OK) Daily Express,* March 21, 1918, p. 1.

65   **"The boys want":** *Pueblo (CO) Chieftain,* February 13, 1918, p. 7.

65   **On Tuesday:** *Pueblo (CO) Chieftain,* February 14, 1918, p. 5.

65   **He tried to:** *Chickasha (OK) Daily Express,* March 21, 1918, p. 1.

CHAPTER 7

67   **Edgar announced:** *Salt Lake Tribune,* March 20, 1918, p. 1.

68   **NEW SPRING HATS:** *Salt Lake Tribune,* March 6, 1918, p. 2.

68   **An impending:** *Salt Lake Telegram,* March 7, 1918, p. 2.

69   **he referred to:** *Salt Lake Herald,* March 8, 1918, p. 8.

69   **Edgar led the:** Ibid.

70   **what they labeled:** Thompson, *To the American Indian,* p. 151.

70   **helped prepare a:** Burtha's father transcribed this book, which was dic-
      tated to him by her illiterate stepmother, Lucy Thompson. Entitled *To the
      American Indian,* the book—privately printed, courtesy of a donation from
      the spouse of a local lumber baron—enjoyed a very limited readership, yet
      it has since gained recognition as a significant cultural artifact.

70   **"Talth":** Thompson, *To the American Indian,* p. 115.

70   **Burtha nevertheless:** *San Francisco Chronicle,* February 20, 1915, p. 1.

70   **"New Woman":** Blanke, *1910s,* pp. 5, 10.

70   **"liberty torches":** Drowne and Huber, *1920s,* p. 41.

70   THE GREATEST: *Goodwin's Weekly* (Salt Lake City), March 9, 1918, p. 7.

70   **The rich odor:** During the summer of 1910 when Edgar worked for Bostock's Animal Arena, the show featured a group of lions and bears being provoked by two men armed with spears. The other acts included a snake charmer, an illusionist, and a three-round boxing bout between a kangaroo and its trainer.

71   **"a girl show":** Blanke, *1910s,* p. 212.

71   **"on the masthead":** *Goodwin's Weekly* (Salt Lake City), March 9, 1918, p. 10.

71   **fixing to:** *Salt Lake Herald,* March 10, 1918, p. 12.

71   **So impressed:** Mrs. White Elk to Lucullus V. McWhorter, September 9, 1922, WSU.

      All quotations from the letters of Mrs. White Elk to Lucullus V. McWhorter are by permission of the Manuscripts, Archives, and Special Collections section (Lucullus V. McWhorter Papers) at Washington State University Libraries.

72   **"the race of":** *San Francisco Chronicle,* February 20, 1915, pp. 1, 3.

72   **highly critical:** Mrs. White Elk to Lucullus V. McWhorter, February 5, 1921, WSU.

73   **Edgar liked to:** *Salt Lake Herald,* March 14, 1918, p. 9; *Salt Lake Telegram,* October 4, 1918, p. 13.

73   **He urged:** *Salt Lake Tribune,* March 20, 1918, p. 1.

74   **"the incarnation":** *Salt Lake Telegram,* March 12, 1918, p. 10.

75   **He goaded:** *Deseret Evening News,* March 9, 1918 (first edition), p. 8.

75   **The telegram:** *Deseret Evening News* (Salt Lake City), March 21, 1918 (second edition), p. 1.

CHAPTER 8

77   **"best Cherokee dress suit":** *Deseret Evening News* (Salt Lake City), March 13, 1918 (first edition), p. 1.

77   **Several misguided:** *Salt Lake Tribune,* March 13, 1918, p. 5.

77   **flaunted his patriotism:** *East Oregonian* (Pendleton, OR), March 13, 1918, p. 8.

78   **Edgar had the privilege:** *Salt Lake Herald,* March 13, 1918, p. 2.

78   **A story about his wedding:** *Salt Lake Telegram,* March 13, 1918, p. 8.

78   **given to him by President Wilson's daughter:** *Salt Lake Tribune,* March 13, 1918, p. 5.

79   **He passed approving:** *Deseret Evening News* (Salt Lake City), March 16, 1918 (first edition), p. 14.

80 THOUSANDS OF: *Salt Lake Tribune,* March 8, 1918, p. 4.

81 **Jails were dangerous places:** Maurer, *Big Con,* p. 152, 184.

82 **five thousand Indians serving:** *Salt Lake Tribune,* March 14, 1918, p. 9.

"Perhaps 12,000 to 12,500 Native Americans served in the military during World War I. . . . In response to popular stereotypes that depicted Indians as born warriors, Native Americans often received dangerous assignments as scouts, snipers and messengers. Their casualty rate, consequently, was significantly higher than other Americans in the American Expeditionary Force." Britten, "American Indians in World War I," p. v.

82 **"be permitted to proceed":** "Chief White Elk," Fold3.com.

83 **Edgar grew resentful:** *Salt Lake Tribune,* March 21, 1918, p. 1.

CHAPTER 9

84 **At the suggestion:** *Salt Lake Tribune,* March 21, 1918, p. 1.

85 **Rumors reached:** *Salt Lake Tribune,* March 20, 1918, p. 1.

85 **Early on the evening:** *Salt Lake Tribune,* March 20, 1918, p. 1; March 21, 1918, p. 1.

85 **"propaganda campaign":** *Oregonian* (Portland, OR), July 20, 1919, p. 8.

85 **Edgar phoned Newman later:** *Salt Lake Tribune,* March 20, 1918, p. 1.

86 **The front page:** Ibid.

86 **When they got there:** *Salt Lake Telegram,* March 20, 1918, p. 1.

88 **"Courtesy is to business":** *Howard (RI) Times,* April 11, 1903, p. 1.

88 **"Do not try to pass":** *Howard (RI) Times,* April 6, 1903, p. 1.

88 **who retained her belief:** Mrs. White Elk to Lucullus V. McWhorter, September 9, 1922, WSU.

88 **Edgar started by pledging:** *Deseret Evening News* (Salt Lake City), March 21, 1918 (second edition), p. 1.

88 **so he turned them down:** *Salt Lake Herald,* March 21, 1918, p. 10.

89 **Edgar assured the audience:** Ibid.

89 IMPOSTOR HAD MANY ALIASES: *Salt Lake Tribune,* March 21, 1918, p. 1.

89 **he seems to have confided:** Mrs. White Elk to Lucullus V. McWhorter, September 9, 1922, WSU; *Salt Lake Tribune,* March 21, 1918, p. 10.

90 **"Well, what you have printed":** *Salt Lake Tribune,* March 21, 1918, p. 10.

90 **In what remained:** *Salt Lake Tribune,* March 22, 1918, p. 2.

91 **Uncharacteristically flustered:** *Salt Lake Telegram,* March 21, 1918, p. 2.

92 **a reporter working:** *Deseret Evening News* (Salt Lake City), March 21, 1918 (second edition), p. 1.

92 **"Is Chief White an elk":** *Salt Lake Telegram,* March 22, 1918, p. 7.

93 **who had completely bought the idea:** *Oregonian* (Portland, OR), July 20, 1919, p. 8.

CHAPTER 10

95 **As Burtha waited:** *San Francisco Chronicle,* April 11, 1918, p. 4.

96 **Or renaming sauerkraut:** *Bemidji (MN) Daily Pioneer,* March 19, 1918, p. 2.

96 **Yellow paint:** *Daily Herald* (Grand Forks, ND), March 28, 1918, p. 6; *Evening Times-Republican* (Marshalltown, IA), April 1, 1918, p. 3; and others.

97 **"refined dancing":** *Oakland Tribune,* April 13, 1918, p. 9.

97 **He'd positioned:** *Oakland Tribune,* April 18, 1918, p. 5.

98 **a waggish local singing star:** Ibid., p. 18.

98 **When the time came for him:** Ibid.

99 **Two hundred members:** *Berkeley Daily Gazette,* April 17, 1918, p. 2; April 18, 1918, pp. 1, 8.

100 **the scuttlebutt:** *Walnut Valley Times* (El Dorado, KS), May 8, 1918, p. 1; *Muskogee (OK) Times-Democrat,* May 11, 1918, p. 18.

100 **who developed a taste for how the drugs:** Mrs. White Elk to Lucullus V. McWhorter, September 9, 1922, WSU.

100 **"Singing Sailor Spaulding":** *Red Bluff (CA) Daily News,* July 27, 1918, p. 1.

101 **a flag-raising ceremony:** *Red Bluff (CA) Daily News,* June 29, 1918, p. 1.

101 **There was a sequel the next day:** "Chief White Elk," Fold3.com.

101 **When he stepped:** *Red Bluff (CA) Daily News,* June 29, 1918, p. 1.

102 **her husband's drug taking:** Mrs. White Elk to Lucullus V. McWhorter, September 9, 1922, WSU.

102 **In the attractive little city:** *Oregonian* (Portland, OR), July 12, 1918, p. 6.

102 **stories about meeting the general:** *Pueblo (CO) Chieftain,* January 25, 1918, p. 3.

102 **BULLY FOR YOU:** *Morning Oregonian* (Portland, OR), July 12, 1918, p. 6.

102 **Edgar claimed he:** *Sacramento Union,* July 12, 1918, p. 6.

103 **"sexual perverts":** Shneer and Aviv, "Classifications on Homosexuality," *American Queer, Now and Then,* p. 8.

103 **Quizzed about Chief White Elk:** *Red Bluff (CA) Daily News,* July 27, 1918, p. 1.

103 **Ingram and Clinch next went round:** *Sacramento Union,* July 6, 1918, p. 6.

104 **"joy dust":** Kohn, *Dope Girls,* p. 35.

104 **"a deck" or "a bindle":** *Seattle Star,* October 18, 1919, p. 1; *New York Sun,* July 27, 1919, p. 25.

105   **the Death Trail:** Cullen, *Vaudeville Old and New,* p. 4.

105   **"split weeks":** Haupert, *Entertainment Industry,* pp. 21–22, 26.

105   **"all-star":** *San Diego Union,* December 15, 1918, p. 25.

105   **none of his victims:** Among Edgar's mortified San Diegan victims was Judge George J. Leovy. The judge had fielded a series of waggish phone calls inquiring whether he'd "received any information concerning the present whereabouts of Tom Longboat." *San Diego Union,* March 18, 1917, p. 4.

106   **Nowhere was his:** *Salt Lake Telegram,* October 4, 1918, p. 13; *Salt Lake Tribune,* October 10, 1918, p. 9.

CHAPTER 11

108   **Burtha's biological mother:** About a year before Burtha came into the world, her mother, Nora, left Jim Thompson and moved in with a Native American named Pecwan John. Burtha appears to have been the product of a brief reconciliation between Nora and Jim.

108   **"haunts me like Satan in hell":** Mrs. White Elk to Lucullus V. McWhorter, September 9, 1922, WSU.

108   **Close friends knew her as "Toots":** Palmquist, *With Nature's Children,* p. 17.

109   **"Nature's monarchs of the wild":** Ibid., p. 19.

109   **"official government photographer":** Ibid., p. 65.

109   **In his familiar role:** Ibid., p. 67.

110   **For Burtha and Lucy:** Thompson, *To the American Indian,* pp. 138–40.

110   **"ruthlessly handled":** Ibid., p. 139.

112   **"the Beautiful Broadway Song Birds":** *Santa Ana (CA) Register,* January 4, 1919, p. 4.

112   **"a whole show":** *Oxnard (CA) Courier,* January 9, 1919, p. 4.

112   **invited to a dinner party:** *Los Angeles Times,* January 19, 1919, p. 32.

      Muddling Edgar with his fellow vaudevillian, Chief Little Elk, one of his hostesses thought she'd met him at a Woman's Christian Temperance Union conference in Portland when he was playing the prestigious Orpheum vaudeville circuit. Hard-drinking Edgar seems to have reinforced her misapprehension by talking about how he'd campaigned for Prohibition among the Indians of Oklahoma.

112   **They asked the desk clerk:** *Morning Oregonian* (Portland, OR), April 14, 1919, p. 2.

112   **Comparable disbelief:** Ibid.

113   **"From the experience we've had":** Ibid.

114   **Later that morning:** Ibid., p. 12.

114   **The article in the *Morning Oregonian* caught:** *Morning Oregonian* (Portland, OR), April 15, 1919, p. 17.

114   **Soon the district attorney:** Ibid.

115   **At one of those, he posed:** *Bellingham (WA) Herald,* April 23, 1919, p. 5.

115   **who contemplated launching herself:** Mrs. White Elk to Lucullus V. McWhorter, February 5, 1921, WSU.

115   **She got her big break:** *Seattle Times,* August 7, 1919, p. 11.

116   **"the greatest summer school":** *Lyceum Magazine,* August 1919, p. 33.

116   **were tales of how he'd campaigned:** *Vancouver Daily World,* May 22, 1919, p. 20.

117   **When passing isolated farmsteads:** Lloyd, *Vaudeville Trails thru the West,* pp. 5, 13.

118   **"the Chinese Mark Twain":** *Lyceum Magazine,* January 1915, p. 55.

118   **And when he'd finished:** *Lyceum Magazine,* August 1919, p. 24.

119   **The carriages rocked:** *Lyceum Magazine,* December 1919, p. 23.

119   **He visited a local children's club:** *Edmonton Bulletin,* June 18, 1919 (city edition), p. 3.

119   **In an article about the Liberty Loan:** *American Indian,* Summer 1919, pp. 104–5.

120   **long, chatty letters she liked to write:** Witnessed by her correspondence with Lucullus V. McWhorter, WSU.

120   **"the Bare-Footed Nature Dance":** *Seattle Star,* August 2, 1919, p. 5.

120   **"a wonderful talker":** Mrs. White Elk to Lucullus V. McWhorter, February 5, 1921, WSU.

121   **But his many Native American friends:** Evans, *Voice of the Old Wolf,* p. 51.

121   **Edgar and Burtha took a great liking:** Mrs. White Elk to Lucullus V. McWhorter, July 30, 1920, WSU.

121   **what real Native Americans would decades:** Green, "The Tribe Called Wannabee," p. 35.

The Wannabe, whose racial identity represents a triumph of wishful thinking over genetics, have been consistently overlooked by the U.S. Census, though they boast several other once-famous but now largely forgotten members. Among those is Princess Chinquilla (ca. 1865–1938), who graduated from being part of a banjo-playing and juggling vaudeville duo to being a lecturer on Native American history and crafts. Bizarrely, in 1926 she and Red Fox founded the American Indian Club, a New York City social club for Native Americans.

Other previously celebrated Wannabe include the Italian American actor Iron Eyes Cody (1904–99) and the English-born conservationist Archibald Stansfeld Belaney, aka Gray Owl (1888–1938). Perhaps the most intriguing member of the Wannabe was the man calling himself the Reverend Big Chief White Horse Eagle, who claimed the nonexistent title of "Chief of Chiefs" and followed Edgar's example by touring Europe. In 1931, White Horse Eagle brought out an autobiography titled with inadvertent humor, *We Indians.*

121   **Yet both Edgar and Burtha took a shine:** Mrs. White Elk to Lucullus V. McWhorter, July 30, 1920, WSU.

121   **"Supreme Most High Chief":** *Tomahawk,* October 4, 1917, p. 1.

122   **Red Fox wound up inviting Edgar:** Mrs. White Elk to Lucullus V. McWhorter, July 30, 1920, WSU.

122   **"One Hour of Laughs":** *Gazette-Times* (Heppner, OR), March 11, 1920, p. 8.

123   **"Unique Indian Concert":** *Olympia (WA) Daily Reporter,* May 7, 1920, p. 6.

123   **Edgar wired Big Foot:** Mrs. White Elk to Lucullus V. McWhorter, July 30, 1920, WSU.

124   **No matter how committed she was:** Ibid.

124   **"going bughouse":** Mrs. White Elk to Lucullus V. McWhorter, August 28, 1920, WSU.

125   **Red Fox warned him:** *Lincoln (NE) Evening Journal,* July 21, 1920, p. 1.

CHAPTER 12

126   **"working for the benefit of Indian children":** *Daily Inter Lake* (Kalispell, MT), July 24, 1920, p. 5.

127   **"Memories! Fond memories":** Included in the Mrs. White Elk–Lucullus V. McWhorter correspondence, WSU.

128   **who addressed each:** *Columbian,* July 29, 1920, p. 2.

129   **But Edgar, despite all his father's chivying:** *St. Louis Post-Dispatch* magazine, October 20, 1929, p. 4; U.S. Census, 1910.

129   **"to start out again as entertainers":** Mrs. White Elk to Lucullus V. McWhorter, August 28, 1920, WSU.

129   **Its organizer was delighted:** *Helena (MT) Daily Independent,* September 5, 1920, p. 2.

130   **"Panhandle Pete":** *Independent Record* (Helena, MT), September 12, 1920, p. 2.

130   **Fittingly, Edgar's contribution:** *Helena (MT) Daily Independent,* September 16, 1920, p. 1; *Independent Record* (Helena, MT), September 17, 1920, p. 3.

130 **Mrs. Georgia Prest:** *Anaconda (MT) Standard,* September 13, 1920, p. 1; September 18, 1920, p. 2.

131 **addressed as "Cap":** "Aloha Wanderwell: Life Story," alohawanderwell .com; Wanderwell, *Call to Adventure,* p. 28.

131 **Its bodywork bore the names:** *Oregon Daily Journal* (Portland, OR), August 15, 1920, p. 50.

131 **"Wanderwell World Tours":** Ibid.

132 **She also published:** "The Owl and the Yellow Pine Roots," *Anaconda (MT) Standard,* December 26, 1920, p. 5.

132 **"awful busy":** Mrs. White Elk to Lucullus V. McWhorter, December 8, 1920, WSU.

132 **Edgar even substituted:** *Anaconda (MT) Standard,* October 19, 1920, p. 13; *Great Falls (MT) Daily Tribune,* May 8, 1919, p. 14.

132 **When Edgar and his wife hit the town:** Mrs. White Elk to Lucullus V. McWhorter, December 8, 1920, WSU.

133 **His wife was also given prominent billing:** *Anaconda (MT) Standard,* December 15, 1920, p. 9.

134 **Burtha gloated:** Mrs. White Elk to Lucullus V. McWhorter, December 15, 1920, WSU.

134 **"full-blooded Indians":** *Anaconda (MT) Standard,* December 27, 1920, p. 5.

135 **Burtha had come to resent:** Mrs. White Elk to Lucullus V. McWhorter, March 13, 1921, WSU.

135 **"The White Elk Show":** *Anaconda (MT) Standard,* December 30, 1920, p. 2.

135 **Edgar was nonetheless:** *Anaconda (MT) Standard,* December 31, 1920, p. 10.

137 **The next morning's edition:** *Anaconda (MT) Standard,* January 4, 1921, p. 11.

137 **"an exhilarating romance":** *Great Falls (MT) Daily Tribune,* January 13, 1921, p. 7.

138 **Burtha's mounting frustration:** Mrs. White Elk to Lucullus V. McWhorter, February 5, 1921, WSU.

138 **her resentment at the injustices:** Mrs. White Elk to Lucullus V. McWhorter, December 8, 1920, WSU.

138 **From Montana:** Mrs. White Elk to Lucullus V. McWhorter, March 5, 1921, WSU.

139 **a raging addiction:** Mrs. White Elk to Lucullus V. McWhorter, September 9, 1922, WSU.

139 **the cheaper sachets:** *Seattle Star,* May 24, 1920, p. 3.

Cocaine and morphine were being imported illegally from Canada. Seattle also suffered from being the main point of departure for the legal export of these drugs. Within just five months that year, fifteen tons of narcotics were shipped to China and Japan.

139 **could only watch:** Mrs. White Elk to Lucullus V. McWhorter, September 9, 1922, WSU.

139 **The situation grew so bad:** *Seattle Daily Times,* April 17, 1921, p. 28.

139 **"the best-educated Injun":** Mrs. White Elk to Lucullus V. McWhorter, March 28, 1921, WSU.

140 **She then consulted:** Ibid.

140 **"The way things keep turning out":** Ibid.

140 **about which she was growing:** Mrs. White Elk to Lucullus V. McWhorter, September 9, 1922, WSU.

140 **Together they posed:** *Lynden (WA) Tribune,* April 14, 1921, pp. 5, 10.

140 **"the strange and terrible vices":** Mrs. White Elk to Lucullus V. McWhorter, September 9, 1922, WSU.

141 **"famous Indian movie star":** *Vancouver Daily World,* May 10–11, 1921, p. 7.

141 **They hoped to:** Mrs. White Elk to Lucullus V. McWhorter, May 7, 1921, WSU.

141 **"Tell Mrs. McWhorter":** Mrs. White Elk to Lucullus V. McWhorter, August 22, 1921, WSU.

CHAPTER 13

142 **Silver Star had:** Mrs. White Elk to Lucullus V. McWhorter, June 20, 1922, WSU.

142 **"conventional covering of beads":** *Winnipeg (MB) Evening Tribune,* February 18, 1922, p. 29.

143 **included a quiz:** *Cumberland (BC) Islander,* July 23, 1921, p. 7.

143 **imminent arrival:** *Daily Colonist* (Victoria, BC), July 19, 1921, p. 13.

143 **Adding to the:** Ibid.

143 **Their visit to the town:** *Chilliwack (BC) Progress,* August 18, 1921, p. 5.

143 **Scanning the women:** *Cumberland (BC) Islander,* July 23, 1921, p. 7.

143 **His repeated boast:** *Cumberland (BC) Islander,* July 30, 1921, p. 8.

144 **portraying him as one of the stars:** *Vancouver (BC) Daily World,* August 3, 1921, p. 7.

145 **Seeing so many empty seats:** Mrs. White Elk to Lucullus V. McWhorter, September 9, 1922, WSU.

145 **"This traveling and show business":** Mrs. White Elk to Lucullus V. McWhorter, August 22, 1921, WSU.

145   **She took to crying:** Mrs. White Elk to Lucullus V. McWhorter, September 9, 1922, WSU.

145   **Despite everything:** Mrs. White Elk to Lucullus V. McWhorter, August 22, 1921, WSU.

145   **"world of opportunities":** Mrs. White Elk to Lucullus V. McWhorter, September 9, 1922, WSU.

145   **"jolly good time":** *Redcliff (AB) Review,* October 29, 1921, p. 5.

145   **"a noted Indian tenor":** *Blairmore (AB) Enterprise,* September 22, 1921, p. 1; *Redcliff (AB) Review,* October 27, 1921, p. 5.

146   **If he turned:** Photographs (NC-6-7060) in the Glenbow Museum Archives, Calgary, Alberta.

146   **"A Real Indian Movie Star":** *Edmonton Bulletin,* December 23, 1921 (city edition), p. 10; December 24, 1921 (city edition), p. 18.

146   **"spiritualism was actually originated":** *Edmonton Bulletin,* December 30, 1921 (city edition), p. 6.

147   **"the Chicago of Canada":** Baedeker, *Dominion of Canada,* p. 276.

147   **Edgar appears to:** *Edmonton Bulletin,* December 23, 1921 (city edition), p. 10.
       Confronted with imminent publicity about him being an impostor, the Hollywood actor–turned–journalist Sylvester Long, known as Chief Buffalo Child Long Lance—who had claimed to be a chief of the Cherokee and Blackfoot tribes—committed suicide. By the standards of racial classification accepted in later decades, Long Lance *was,* however, a Native American.

147   **"the terrible realization":** Mrs. White Elk to Lucullus V. McWhorter, September 9, 1922, WSU.

CHAPTER 14

152   **He had lately:** Bureau de Police Centrale to Commissioner of the Police, January 23, 1925, MEPO 3/1180, NAL.

152   **What prompted:** *Register* (Adelaide, South Australia), March 14, 1923, p. 14.

152   **Knowing that his English:** Edgar's father had been the treasurer of a Rhode Island organization that had campaigned energetically against an alliance between the United States and Britain. For French Canadians like Edgar's father, who disapproved of the British Empire and the way it had suppressed nationalist movements in Ireland and elsewhere, Britain was "the arch criminal of the world." *Pawtucket Times,* February 6, 1899, p. 9.

152   **More recent:** *Lewiston (ME) Daily Sun,* December 8, 1922, p. 35.

153   **During the *Regina*'s brief layover:** *Times* (London), December 9, 1922, p. 9; *Le Populaire* (Paris), December 12, 1922, p. 2.

153   **his name's presence on:** *L'Impartial* (Neuchâtel, Switzerland), March 12, 1945, p. 1.

154   **Etiquette dictated:** Donzel, *Luxury Liners: Life on Board,* pp. 68, 108; Reynolds, *Paris with the Lid Lifted,* p. 125.

155   **Much to his delight:** *Yorkshire Evening Post,* December 18, 1922, p. 5.

155   **So spellbound was:** Ibid.

156   **a pool of blood:** The incident may have aroused in Edgar long-dormant recollections of a comparably gruesome episode when he was eleven years old. Early one evening, the bullet-riddled body of George D. Saxton, brother-in-law of the soon-to-be-assassinated President William McKinley, was found crumpled next to the sidewalk just down the street from where Edgar and his family lived.

156   **He talked to the press corps:** *Manchester (UK) Guardian,* December 18, 1922, p. 7.

157   **When speaking about the apron:** *Liverpool (UK) Echo,* December 18, 1922, p. 7.

157   **His riposte:** *Daily Mail* (London), December 18, 1922, p. 7; *Times* (London), December 18, 1922, p. 11; *Yorkshire (UK) Evening Post,* December 18, 1922, p. 5.

158   **accompanied by his "secretary":** *Daily Graphic* (London), December 21, 1922, p. 4.

158   **Wandering around:** *Liverpool (UK) Echo,* December 18, 1922, p. 7.

158   **By passing appreciative:** Ibid.

159   **"absurdly cheap":** Austin Seven sales brochure, 1922.

160   **Bewilderment registered on the porters' faces:** *Daily Express* (London), December 19, 1922, p. 5.

160   **"I have brought with me":** Ibid.

160   **hotels such as:** Houlbrook, *Queer London,* p. 122.

CHAPTER 15

161   **admired his "gorgeous":** *Evening Standard* (London), December 20, 1922, p. 10.

161   **Afforded the chance to talk:** Ibid.

161   **In what tended to be genteel:** Morton, *Spell of London,* p. 34.

163   **instantly pounced upon:** *Daily Graphic* (London), December 21, 1922, p. 4.

165   **There were even tales:** *Performer,* February 21, 1922, p. 6.

165   **in the business:** *London Palladium,* p. 53.

165   **public toilets:** Partridge, *New Partridge Dictionary of Slang and Unconventional English,* p. 486.

166   **his photo had featured:** *Illustrated London News,* December 23, 1922, p. 1,025.

166   **And he'd appeared:** *Daily Graphic* (London), December 27, 1922, p. 1.

166   **"London particular":** Hilaire Belloc and A. H. Pollen, *Land and Water,* vol. 15, p. iii.

166   **a phenomenon so well-known:** The Chronicling America newspaper archive (http://chroniclingamerica.loc.gov/) shows numerous references to "London fog" in the years prior to 1922.

166   **Soon after the trip to Westminster:** *Lichfield (UK) Mercury,* January 19, 1923, p. 8.

167   **St. James's Palace:** Ibid.

167   **Edgar found himself conversing:** *Daily Mail* (London), January 23, 1923, p. 5.

168   **"We have undertaken extensive":** Ibid.

168   IMPOSTOR UNMASKED: *News of the World,* January 28, 1923, p. 10.

169   **Edgar would have been required:** Wilmut, *Kindly Leave the Stage,* p. 133.

169   **Topping the bill:** *Woolwich (UK) Herald,* January 26, 1923, p. 1.

170   **the dreaded "first house":** Wilmut, *Kindly Leave the Stage,* p. 134.

170   **"war dance as danced":** *Woolwich (UK) Herald,* February 2, 1923, p. 1.

170   **Edgar always dispensed:** *Corriere della Sera* (Milan), August 10, 1924, p. 6; *La Stampa* (Turin), June 24, 1925, p. 3.

171   **he cheekily expanded:** Chief Constable of Birmingham to Commissioner, Scotland Yard, April 4, 1923, MEPO 3/1180, NAL.

171   **Tittle-tattle bubbling:** Ibid.

171   **"England's greatest singing ventriloquist":** *Worcester (UK) Daily Times,* February 26, 1923, p. 2.

171   **Edgar's contribution:** *Worcestershire (UK) Echo,* February 27, 1923, p. 2.

171   **There, he enthralled:** *Dudley (UK) Chronicle,* March 22, 1923, p. 4.

171   **So flagrant:** Commissioner of Police to the Bureau de Police Centrale, January 3, 1923, MEPO 3/1180, NAL.

172   **"the only living ruler":** *Worcester (UK) Daily Times,* February 26, 1923, p. 2.

172   **In his dressing room:** *Leamington (UK) Spa Courier,* April 6, 1923, p. 5.

172   **Edgar received a pitiful letter:** Chief Constable of Birmingham to the Commissioner, Scotland Yard, April 4, 1923, MEPO 3/1180, NAL.

173   **"a reliable source":** Sergeant Kelly, Inspector Barnes, Superintendent McCoy to C.I.D. "A" Division, January 28, 1925, MEPO 3/1180, NAL.

174 **she addressed as "Ray":** Bevinetto, *Le avventure di Edgardo Laplante,* p. 128.

174 **Edgar's talk of:** *Brooklyn Daily Eagle,* February 2, 1927, p. 17.

174 **toward whom he:** *La Stampa* (Turin), June 26, 1925, p. 5.

174 **whom he called "Dad" and "Mother":** Dr. Tewanna to Mrs. Tewanna, February 4, 1925, quoted in Bevinetto, *Le avventure di Edgardo Laplante,* p. 78.

174 **He told her that he was a widower:** *La Stampa* (Turin), June 26, 1925, p. 5.

175 **Leslie reminded him of his own son:** Bevinetto, *Le avventure di Edgardo Laplante,* p. 124.

175 **Even though Ethel:** Her feelings are evident from her declaration of herself as a "widow" on the certificate for her marriage to Edgar. It's also apparent from her statement quoted in Bevinetto, *Le avventure di Edgardo Laplante,* p. 124.

175 **On the marriage certificate:** Certificate, June 27, 1923, MEPO 3/1180, NAL.

175 **Scotland Yard's decision:** Metropolitan Police report, April 20, 1923, MEPO 3/1180, NAL.

CHAPTER 16

177 **gave his bewildered:** *L'Humanité,* September 29, 1923, p. 2.

That audience probably included Caresse Crosby, a decadent and irreverent thirty-two-year-old American expat vacationing in Étretat with friends. Yet to establish herself alongside her spouse, Harry, as an avant-garde publisher and fixture in the Parisian literary world, she liked to go to the Casino.

178 **Oscar Dufrenne:** Almost a decade later, Dufrenne would be brutally murdered, his death spiced with sexual and political intrigue that made it one of France's best-known interwar crimes.

179 **They flocked to:** Phillips, *Gay City,* p. 1.

179 **"Nude Music Hall":** *Le Journal* (Paris), October 8, 1923, p. 4.

180 **the management joked:** *Paris-soir,* December 21, 1923, p. 5.

180 **"the Beautiful Zoulaïka":** *Le Journal* (Paris), October 18, 1923, p. 5.

181 **his clothes impressing one journalist:** *Cyrano* (Paris), December 7, 1924, pp. 16–17.

181 **which received a thorough eyeballing:** *Le Petit Parisien,* September 14, 1923, p. 2.

183 **They were known as "apaches":** Phillips, *Gay City,* pp. 154–55; *Days and Nights in Montmartre and the Latin Quarter,* p. 203.

183 **his French became:** *Le Temps* (Paris), December 12, 1923, p. 4.

183   **across the river to Montparnasse:** Phillips, *Gay City,* p. 123.

184   **"Dôme-ites":** Ibid., p. 127.

184   **order what was jokily:** "Bars and Cabarets," *Jazz: A Flippant Magazine,* June 1, 1924, p. 10.

184   **"The Dôme is not a place":** Ford, *Left Bank Revisited,* p. 14.

185   **Sam Granowsky:** His penchant for dressing as a cowboy apparently dated back to when he'd been employed as an extra in a Western being filmed on a Parisian movie lot. "He put such soul into his work that the director gave him the costume, which he promptly adopted as his habitual outfit." Wilson, *Paris on Parade,* p. 220.

185   **though people said:** Phillips, *Gay City,* p. 127.

185   **who endeavored:** McAlmon, *Being Geniuses Together,* p. 109; "Dusting Off the Old Ones," *Jazz: A Flippant Magazine,* June 15, 1924, p. 11.

185   **Knowing that his exotic:** Kohner, *Kiki of Montparnasse,* pp. 44–45.

185   **Willie had reinvented:** *Chicago Tribune* (European edition), September 2, 1923, p. 14.

186   **Edgar started telling people:** *Le Journal* (Paris), October 12, 1923, p. 4.

186   **"Times are hard":** *L'Humanité,* September 29, 1923, p. 2.

CHAPTER 17

187   **He was now pretending:** *La Siècle* (Paris), October 11, 1923, p. 1; *Oakland (CA) Tribune,* November 18, 1923, p. 19.

187   **which he and his:** "Aloha Wanderwell: Life Story," alohawanderwell.com.

188   **"electoral reform":** *Times* (London), June 7, 1923, p. 13.

188   **In the commentary:** *Prager Tagblatt* (Prague), April 2, 1925, p. 3.

188   **Edgar was having to fend off:** *L'Ouest-Éclair* (Rennes, France), October 12, 1923, p. 1.

189   **enticingly billed as "nude dancers":** *Paris-soir,* October 18, 1923, p. 5.

189   **"the Jazz Age":** The phrase, propagated via the publication in 1922 of F. Scott Fitzgerald's *Tales of the Jazz Age,* was already in circulation by July 1921 when it featured in the *Yale Expositor.*

190   **He figured that:** Farlow, *Wind River Adventures,* pp. 201–2.

190   **In London they'd attended:** Ibid.

191   **At nine o'clock:** *Chicago Tribune* (European edition), December 13, 1923, p. 14; *Le Figaro* (Paris), December 13, 1923, p. 3; *L'Ouest-Éclair* (Rennes, France), December 5, 1923, p. 5; *Le Temps* (Paris), December 12, 1923, p. 4.

193   **The plan was for Farlow:** Farlow, *Wind River Adventures,* pp. 201–2.

193   **"The Indians are victims"**: *La Presse* (Montreal), December 13, 1923, p. 1.

194   **Near its upper platform**: Farlow, *Wind River Adventures*, p. 202.

194   **Dining with Old Eagle**: McCoy, *Tim McCoy Remembers the West*, p. 192.

194   **Edgar redeemed himself**: Bevinetto, *Le avventure di Edgardo Laplante*, p. 96.

195   **No instructions**: McCoy, *Tim McCoy Remembers the West*, p. 193.

195   **"great finesse"**: *Camoedia* (Paris), December 22, 1923, p. 3.

195   **A tremendous ovation**: *Le Petit Parisien,* December 22, 1923, p. 4; *Paris-soir,* January 5, 1923, p. 5.

196   **a musical accompanist**: Nasaw, *Going Out,* p. 162.

196   **"Nobody should miss this"**: *Le Petit Parisien,* December 22, 1923, p. 4.

196   **For expatriate American**: Phillips, *Gay City,* p. 114; *Jazz: A Flippant Magazine,* April 15, 1924, p. 26.

196   **"the 42nd Street of Montmartre"**: Reynolds, *Paris with the Lid Lifted,* p. 160.

197   **Their boss**: Farlow, *Wind River Adventures,* p. 201.

197   **the recent incident**: "Bars and Cabarets," *Jazz: A Flippant Magazine,* May 15, 1924, p. 6.

CHAPTER 18

199   **"Gentlemen, this isn't"**: *La Nation Belge* (Brussels), February 15, 1924, p. 1.

201   THE INDIAN CHIEF: Ibid.

201   **"the miniature Paris"**: *Traveller's Handbook for Belgium,* p. 59.

202   **"a poet of rare sensitivity"**: Unidentified Belgian press cutting, Archives et Musée de la Littérature, Brussels.

202   **Just the day before**: *Le Peuple* (Brussels), February 18, 1924, p. 2.

203   **"White Elk, who never flinches"**: *Le Vingtième Siècle* (Brussels), February 21, 1924, p. 2.

203   **At the request of**: *Le Libre Belgique* (Brussels), February 23, 1924, p. 1.

204   **Edgar's long talk**: *Journal de Charleroi,* February 29, 1924, p. 2.

206   **"people in carnival-style costumes"**: *Le Vingtième Siècle* (Brussels), March 11, 1924, p. 1.

206   **Edgar couldn't hide**: Ibid.

206   **Affixed to**: Ibid.

207   **Leslie broke into wild laughter**: Ibid.

207   **"a first-rate drink"**: Ibid.

207   **When someone commented**: *La Meuse* (Liège, Belgium), April 6, 1924, p. 1.

CHAPTER 19

209   **their penury leaving them:** Phillips, *Gay City*, p. 28.

210   **He gave politely:** *La Stampa* (Turin), June 27, 1925, pp. 3–4.

211   **jokily dubbed a "playship":** Shenk, *Playships of the World*, p. 208.

211   **known by friends:** Bevinetto, *Le avventure di Edgardo Laplante*, pp. 81, 98.

212   **"the needs of Indian orphans":** Ibid., p. 127.

212   **that caught Edgar's:** *La Stampa* (Turin), June 27, 1925, pp. 3–4.

212   **Milania addressed him as "Chief":** Bevinetto, *Le avventure di Edgardo Laplante*, p. 134.

213   **he rubbed it:** *Corriere della Sera* (Milan), June 27, 1925, p. 4.

213   **At the end of their meal:** Ibid., pp. 28, 94; *St. Louis Post-Dispatch* magazine, October 20, 1929, p. 4.

214   **He told them about his "fabulous wealth":** Bevinetto, *Le avventure di Edgardo Laplante*, pp. 94–95.

214   **Edgar confided in the contessas:** Ibid., p. 122.

214   **he fed them a description:** *Observer* (London), October 17, 1926, p. 12.

214   **He started dropping:** Bevinetto, *Le avventure di Edgardo Laplante*, p. 94.

214   **Milania suggested:** Ibid., p. 34.

CHAPTER 20

215   **One of its regulars joked:** "Down the Latin Quarter," *Jazz: A Flippant Magazine*, May 15, 1924, p. 15.

215   **Talk at the Dôme:** "Montmartre and Montparnasse," *Jazz: A Flippant Magazine*, May 1, 1924, p. 14.

216   **he helpfully translated:** Bevinetto, *Le avventure di Edgardo Laplante*, p. 127.

216   **He asked Milania to wire him:** Ibid., p. 129.

216   **She urged him to address her:** *St. Louis Post-Dispatch* magazine, October 20, 1929, p. 4.

217   **Atta thought he "sounded suicidal":** Bevinetto, *Le avventure di Edgardo Laplante*, p. 133.

217   **Edgar wrote to Milania:** *La Revue* (Paris), October 9, 1926, p. 3.

217   **Milania, who was falling in love:** Bevinetto, *Le avventure di Edgardo Laplante*, p. 63.

218   **In his application:** "International Public Safety," January 31, 1925, MEPO 3/1180, NAL.

218   YOUR FATHER MUST LEAVE: *Il Manifesto* (Rome, online edition), April 26, 2013.

218   CONTESSA, COULD YOU WIRE ME: Bevinetto: *Le avventure di Edgardo Laplante,* p. 127.

219   I'M LEAVING TONIGHT: Ibid., p. 34.

219   PLEASE SEND ME MONEY: Ibid., p. 127.

219   **Five days after sending:** Ibid.

219   **According to one such newspaper:** *Journal de Charleroi,* May 31, 1924, p. 5.

220   **aficionados of casual sex:** See police reports, MEPO 3/1180, NAL.

221   **From Venice:** Bevinetto, *Le avventure di Edgardo Laplante,* p. 34.

222   **Her intention was that Edgar:** *St. Louis Post-Dispatch* magazine, October 20, 1929, pp. 4, 7.

222   **Printed on the visiting card:** *La Stampa* (Turin), June 27, 1925, pp. 3–4.

222   **So admiringly had Milania:** Ibid.

222   **compounded by Edgar's antsy:** Ibid.

223   **he complained vocally:** Bevinetto, *Le avventure di Edgardo Laplante,* p. 129.

223   **Around that time:** Ibid., p. 128.

223   **"a semi-royal relation":** *Brooklyn Daily Eagle,* February 2, 1927, p. 16.

223   **Edgar held forth to Georg:** Bevinetto, *Le avventure di Edgardo Laplante,* pp. 138–39.

224   **"the Red Indian national anthem":** Dilnot, *Getting Rich Quick,* p. 203.

225   **Edgar professed:** *Evening Capital News* (Boise, ID), January 3, 1920, p. 3.

226   **Other fascist notables:** *Gazzettino di Puglia* (Lecce), July 30, 1924, p. 4.

      The name was borrowed from Chauncey Yellow Robe, a leading educator and Native American rights campaigner.

226   **He pandered to:** Ibid.

227   **He came away feeling impressed:** Bevinetto, *Le avventure di Edgardo Laplante,* p. 43.

227   A REDSKIN PRINCE: *L'Epoca* (Rome), July 31, 1924, p. 1.

227   **The revelation that she'd parted:** *La Stampa* (Turin), June 27, 1925, pp. 3–4; *Journal Suisse,* October 12, 1926, p. 4.

CHAPTER 21

229   **When kindly Superintendent Eastman:** *Howard (RI) Times,* September 12, 1903, p. 2.

229   **passersby pointed out "the prince":** *Corriere della Sera* (Milan), October 9, 1926, p. 2.

230   **"too generous":** *Corriere della Sera* (Milan), June 28, 1925, p. 4.

230   **Writing to Milania from Rome:** Bevinetto, *Le avventure di Edgardo Laplante,* p. 129.

230 **Among Edgar's colleagues:** Maurer, *Big Con,* p. 185.

230 **he explained that:** *Corriere della Sera* (Milan), June 27, 1925, p. 4.

231 **Italians sometimes used the phrase:** Muirhead and Bertarelli, *Northern Italy: From the Alps to Rome,* p. 45.

231 **Now Edgar developed:** Bevinetto, *Le avventure di Edgardo Laplante,* p. 46.

232 **He filled in the acting consul general:** Document of Identity, May 14, 1924, MEPO 3/1180, NAL.

233 **Georg had, in the meantime:** *Journal Suisse,* October 12, 1926, p. 4; *Journal de Geneve,* October 12, 1926, p. 8.

234 **Atta endeavored to pull some strings:** *La Stampa* (Turin), June 27, 1925, p. 3.

234 **Milania presented herself:** Bevinetto, *Le avventure di Edgardo Laplante,* p. 122.

234 **"Don't call me 'Prince' ":** Ibid., p. 125.

234 **Promising Ludovico the gift:** Ibid., p. 126.

234 **PRINCE WHITE ELK WISHES:** Ibid., p. 47.

235 **Edgar told Milania:** Ibid., p. 84.

235 **When he next wrote to the contessa:** Ibid.

236 **Ludovico appended forged papal inscriptions:** *La Stampa* (Turin), June 26, 1925, p. 5.

237 **robes, supposedly of "incalculable value":** Bevinetto, *Le avventure di Edgardo Laplante,* p. 50.

237 **Waiting for him:** *La Nazione* (Florence), September 3, 1924, p. 3.

238 **Edgar enriched his:** *Daily Mail* (London), September 6, 1924, p. 7; Bevinetto, *Le avventure di Edgardo Laplante,* pp. 125–26.

240 **Edgar made sure:** *Greensboro (NC) Daily News,* August 30, 1925, p. 21.

240 **"the Canadian Prince Elk":** *Corriere della Sera* (Milan), August 10, 1924, p. 6.

241 **who signed her replies:** *Corriere della Sera* (Milan), June 27, 1925, p. 4.

242 **a conversation Edgar:** *Cyrano* (Paris), December 7, 1924, pp. 16–17.

242 **Edgar gave Milania the comforting impression:** Bevinetto, *Le avventure di Edgardo Laplante,* p. 129.

242 **Additional reassurance:** Ibid., p. 126.

CHAPTER 22

245 **He said there:** *Nieuwe Zeeuwsche Courant* (Netherlands), February 14, 1925, p. 2.

245 **He left her:** *Richmond (VA) Times-Dispatch,* November 8, 1925, p. 65.

246 The correspondent's distrust: *Daily Mail* (London), September 6, 1924, p. 7.

246 *La Nazione* soon published: *La Nazione* (Florence), September 10, 1924, p. 3.

246 "Do you think I want to stay": *La Stampa* (Turin), June 26, 1925, p. 5.

247 Horrified by the occasional boorishness: Bevinetto, *Le avventure di Edgardo Laplante,* p. 135.

248 the displeasure she felt: Ibid.

248 When Edgar spotted the statue: *Corriere della Sera* (Milan), June 27, 1925, p. 4; *La Stampa* (Turin), June 27, 1925, pp. 3–4.

249 Yet he didn't: Bevinetto, *Le avventure di Edgardo Laplante,* p. 99.

249 All of her loans: *Corriere della Sera* (Milan), July 1, 1925, p. 4.

250 which included an ebony cane: Bosworth, *Italian Venice: A History,* p. 125.

251 *"Grani, grani"*: Schoonmaker, *Come with Me Through Italy,* p. 82.

251 Then he began a speech: Bosworth, *Italian Venice: A History,* p. 125.

252 Edgar's purring verdict: Ibid., p. 126.

252 "That must be a communist": *La Stampa* (Turin), March 29, 1925, p. 4.

252 Gesturing toward the bar: Ibid.

254 made a show of being grateful: Ibid.

254 Edgar told Birenzi not to be afraid: Ibid.

254 he began to think: *Corriere della Sera* (Milan), July 1, 1925, p. 4.

255 Unknown to Edgar: W. Haldane Porter to the Immigration Officer, May 30, 1924, MEPO 3/1180, NAL.

255 Certain that he'd been the victim: Bevinetto, *Le avventure di Edgardo Laplante,* p. 64; *Corriere della Sera* (Milan), June 27, 1925, p. 4.

255 "You are lost in the world": *Le avventure di Edgardo Laplante,* p. 135.

256 The latter's picture: *Corriere della Sera* (Milan), June 27, 1925, p. 4.

256 Shock and distress: Bevinetto, *Le avventure di Edgardo Laplante,* p. 64.

257 He'd tell people: *L'Express* (Neuchâtel, Switzerland), January 19, 1925, p. 4.

257 One of the letters: *Corriere della Sera* (Milan), June 28, 1925, p. 4.

257 His speech, venerating Mussolini: Bevinetto, *Le avventure di Edgardo Laplante,* pp. 66–67.

258 "You hurt my feelings": *La Stampa* (Turin), June 27, 1925, pp. 3–4.

259 "Please don't criticize the hospital": Ibid.

259 she asked for him to be dosed: Bevinetto, *Le avventure di Edgardo Laplante,* p. 133.

259 "I regret I have just learned": *Corriere della Sera* (Milan), July 1, 1925, p. 4.

260 Milania, whose faith in Edgar: *La Stampa* (Turin), June 27, 1925, pp. 3–4; Bevinetto, *Le avventure di Edgardo Laplante,* p. 134.

260   **But Edgar ignored:** Bevinetto, *Le avventure di Edgardo Laplante,* p. 134.

261   **he promised that his debt:** *La Stampa* (Turin), June 27, 1925, pp. 3–4.

261   **the next day's edition:** Bevinetto, *Le avventure di Edgardo Laplante,* p. 66.

CHAPTER 23

262   **The piece about Edgar:** Bevinetto, *Le avventure di Edgardo Laplante,* p. 66.

263   **Brimming with pride:** *Brooklyn Daily Eagle,* February 2, 1927, p. 16; *Corriere della Sera* (Milan), June 27, 1925, p. 4.

263   **One of these declared:** *Le Peuple* (Brussels), November 30, 1924, p. 4.

263   **Another of them:** *San Francisco Chronicle,* December 2, 1924, p. 24.

264   **"You have to try to come back home":** Bevinetto, *Le avventure di Edgardo Laplante,* pp. 135–36.

264   **he showed them:** Ibid., p. 103.

265   **He gave his name as:** Ibid.; *La Stampa* (Turin), June 24, 1925, p. 3.

266   **Even the hospital's director:** *L'Express* (Neuchâtel, Switzerland), January 24, 1925, p. 4.

CHAPTER 24

267   **People began to wonder:** *La Stampa* (Turin), June 24, 1925, p. 3.

267   **When he propositioned:** *Corriere della Sera* (Milan), January 18, 1925, p. 3.

268   **Daunted by his tales:** *La Stampa* (Turin), June 24, 1925, pp. 3–4.

268   **Edgar composed a note:** Bevinetto, *Le avventure di Edgardo Laplante,* p. 130.

268   **Atta still felt sympathetic:** *Journal Suisse,* January 16, 1925, p. 4.

268   **he hoped to escape:** *Corriere della Sera* (Milan), January 21, 1925, p. 4.

269   **Over lunch he capitalized:** *La Stampa* (Turin), June 24, 1925, p. 4; Bevinetto, *Le avventure di Edgardo Laplante,* p. 75.

269   **Dominating its front page:** *La Nation Belge* (Brussels), December 24, 1924, p. 1.

269   **In the window:** *La Stampa* (Turin), June 27, 1925, pp. 3–4.

270   **And he got talking:** *Corriere della Sera* (Milan), January 23, 1925, p. 3.

270   **he felt the need to scam:** Bevinetto, *Le avventure di Edgardo Laplante,* p. 130.

271   **Falling for Edgar's showy talk:** *L'Express* (Neuchâtel, Switzerland), January 24, 1925, p. 4.

271   **The invitation led:** *Corriere della Sera* (Milan), January 18, 1925, p. 3.

271   **Edgar said he'd repay:** *Corriere della Sera* (Milan), January 21, 1925, p. 4; Bevinetto, *Le avventure di Edgardo Laplante,* pp. 101, 107.

272   **"Atta is such a nice girl":** Bevinetto, *Le avventure di Edgardo Laplante,* p. 135.

272 **He told the owner:** Ibid., p. 104; *Gazette de Lausanne,* January 20, 1925, p. 2.

273 **And he began flirting:** *La Stampa* (Turin), January 21, 1925, p. 4.

273 **In the twenty-one days:** *Corriere del Popolo* (San Francisco), February 20, 1925, p. 2; Bevinetto, *Le avventure di Edgardo Laplante,* pp. 96–97; *Corriere della Sera* (Milan), June 27, 1925, p. 4.

274 **he succeeded in luring:** *La Stampa* (Turin), January 21, 1925, p. 4.

275 **From Ticino:** *Gazette de Lausanne,* January 20, 1925, p. 2.

275 **He was not only seeking sanctuary:** *L'Impartial* (Neuchâtel, Switzerland), June 25 1925, p. 5.

275 **"The comedy's over":** *Corriere della Sera* (Milan), January 21, 1925, p. 4.

CHAPTER 25

276 **caused by shrapnel:** *Corriere della Sera* (Milan), January 21, 1925, p. 4.

276 **When the time:** *Corriere della Sera* (Milan), January 18, 1925, p. 3.

277 **Too melancholy for conversation:** *Corriere della Sera* (Milan), January 21, 1925, p. 4.

277 **Even the showbiz trade paper *Variety*:** *Variety,* February 18, 1925, p. 5.

278 **"I am very sorry":** Bevinetto, *Le avventure di Edgardo Laplante,* pp. 78–79.

278 **As an excuse for their own gullibility:** Ibid., p. 85.

279 **Edgar sought help:** Ibid., p. 78.

279 **His chosen defense:** Ibid., p. 103.

279 **For the journalists:** *Davenport (IA) Democrat and Leader,* July 3, 1925, p. 11.

279 **Under cross-examination:** *La Stampa* (Turin), June 26, 1925, p. 5.

280 **Challenged about his reference:** *La Stampa* (Turin), June 24, 1925, p. 3.

280 **He plumbed similar:** *La Stampa* (Turin), June 26, 1925, p. 5.

280 **How did he come to obtain:** *Davenport (IA) Democrat and Leader,* July 3, 1925, p. 11.

280 THE INCREDIBLE REAL-LIFE MOVIE: *La Stampa* (Turin), June 26, 1925, p. 5.

280 **On its fifth day:** Bevinetto, *Le avventure di Edgardo Laplante,* p. 111.

CHAPTER 26

282 **Near the end of the summer:** Bevinetto, *Le avventure di Edgardo Laplante,* p. 118.

283 **The attorney, Girolamo Bevinetto:** Ibid., p. 158.

284 **In this, he pretended:** Ibid., p. 147.

284 **But he declined her offer:** Ibid., p. 161.

285 **"latest episode":** Ibid., p. 172.

285   THE RISE AND FALL: *Paris-soir,* February 7, 1927, p. 1.

285   **On the assumption:** Bevinetto, *Le avventure di Edgardo Laplante,* p. 175.

285   **"con man supreme":** Ibid., p. 141.

286   **"a dangerous character":** *Boston Herald,* August 18, 1929, p. 21.

CHAPTER 27

287   **Save for a dog-eared copy:** Margaret Burrows, *Brooklyn Daily Eagle,* September 20, 1929, p. 9.

288   ROPE & TWINE: Photo from the collection of Brian Merlis of Brooklynpix .com.

288   **"quite content":** *New York Times,* September 20, 1929, p. 26.

288   **"And to think":** Margaret Burrows, *Brooklyn Daily Eagle,* September 20, 1929, p. 9.

EPILOGUE

293   **Under that name:** *Boston Herald,* March 4, 1930, p. 33.

293   **His reappearance:** *St. Louis Post-Dispatch* magazine, October 20, 1929, p. 4.

293   **Yet he or:** U.S. Census, 1930.

294   **"For a year and a half":** David Loth, *Milwaukee (WI) Journal,* October 12, 1930, p. 33.

295   **He also suckered:** *Sedalia (MO) Democrat,* January 24, 1932, p. 8.

295   **"world's greatest American Indian":** *Mason City (IA) Globe-Gazette,* November 1, 1930, p. 4.

296   **The next recorded reference:** *Daily Mail* (Hagerstown, MD), May 14, 1934, p. 1.

296   **Before the speeches began:** *Chicago Sunday Tribune,* June 28, 1936, p. 5.

Until his death in 1960, Herbert R. Davis would continue posing as Chief White Elk. Occasionally assisted by his wife, Loraine, aka Princess White Star, he made guest appearances at theme parks, school fairs, zoos, banquets, and other events in his home state of Delaware. For these, he donned his feathered headdress, performed his interpretation of Native American war dances, and told anecdotes about his fictitious Sioux heritage.

297   **"little Indian":** *Santa Ana (CA) Register,* August 15, 1939, p. 2.

297   **He said his objective:** *San Diego Union,* August 16, 1939, p. 3.

297   **His latest variation:** *Corvallis (OR) Gazette-Times,* August 20, 1939, p. 6.

298   **a long interview:** *Times-Picayune* (New Orleans), July 26, 1942, p. 27.

299   **his Italian adventures would:** With the publication of the Milanese poet

Delio Tessa's posthumous collection *Alalà al pellerossa* (Howdy to the Red-skin), which cast Chief White Elk in the central role within an anti-fascist satire, he launched a career as an artistic inspiration. Next came *Cervo Blanco* (White Elk), a 1980 novel by the prominent Italian literary figure Ernesto Ferrero, who fictionalized Edgar's royal progress through Italy. After a gap of more than twenty years, Ferrero published *L'anno dell'indiano* (The Year of the Indian), a second novel based on Edgar's escapades. But Edgar's potential as a character in fiction had not yet been exhausted. In Switzerland in 2004, Renato Martinoni released a novel about Edgar's time in that country. Entitled *Il tramonto degli dei* (The Sunset of the Gods), it provided the basis for a 2006 Italian-language Swiss television drama entitled *L'enigma Tewanna Ray* (The Enigma of Tewanna Ray). Danny Quinn, the handsome Italian-born son of Hollywood star Anthony Quinn, played the title role.

299   **fatal heart attack:** Edgar's death deprived him of the opportunity to see his old adversary, Chief Red Fox, receive his comeuppance. It arrived gift-wrapped in what seemed to be the venerable chief's supreme triumph—the publication of Red Fox's autobiography, which ascended the bestseller charts at home and abroad. But the popularity of *The Memoirs of Chief Red Fox* placed the old rogue under a disastrous level of scrutiny. Large chunks of his self-professed reminiscences were exposed as the product of plagiarism. And residents of the Pine Ridge Indian Reservation in South Dakota, where he claimed to have been born, said they'd never heard of him.

299   **Maricopa County Cemetery:** This has since been renamed the Cementerio Lindo.

SELECTED BIBLIOGRAPHY

Anderson, Ann. *Snake Oil, Hustlers and Hambones: The American Medicine Show.* Jefferson, NC: McFarland, 2000.

Baedeker, Karl. *The Dominion of Canada with Newfoundland and an Excursion to Alaska: Handbook for Travellers.* Leipzig, Germany: Karl Baedeker, 1922.

———. *Switzerland Together with Chamonix and the Italian Lakes.* Leipzig, Germany: Karl Baedeker, 1922.

———. *United States, with Excursions to Mexico, Cuba, Porto Rico* [sic] *and Alaska.* Leipzig, Germany: Karl Baedeker, 1909.

Bailey, Almira. *Vignettes of San Francisco.* San Francisco: San Francisco Journal, 1921.

Bertarelli, L. V. *Southern Italy, Including Rome, Sicily, and Sardinia.* London: Macmillan, 1925.

Bevinetto, G. *Le avventure di Edgardo Laplante, Capo Cervo Bianco (Chief White Elk).* Turin: Graziano and Giuliani, 1927.

Blanke, David. *The 1910s.* Westport, CT: Greenwood, 2002.

Bosworth, R. J. B. *Italian Venice: A History.* New Haven, CT: Yale University Press, 2014.

———. *Mussolini's Italy: Life Under the Dictatorship, 1915–1945.* London: Allen Lane, 2005.

Bronski, Michael. *A Queer History of the United States.* Boston: Beacon, 2006.

Brook, Harry Ellington. *Los Angeles, California: The City and the County*. Los Angeles: Los Angeles Chamber of Commerce, 1918.

Browder, Laura. *Slippery Characters: Ethnic Impersonators and American Identities*. Chapel Hill: University of North Carolina Press, 2000.

Brown, Robert Craig, and Ramsay Cook. *Canada, 1896–1921: A Nation Transformed*. Toronto: McClelland and Stewart, 1974.

Bruguière, Francis Joseph. *San Francisco*. San Francisco: H. S. Crocker, 1918.

Butsch, Richard. *The Making of American Audiences: From Stage to Television, 1750–1990*. Cambridge: Cambridge University Press, 2000.

Charters, James. *This Must Be the Place: Memoirs of Montparnasse, by Jimmie, the Barman*. London: Herbert Joseph, 1934.

Chauncey, George. *Gay New York: The Making of the Gay Male World, 1890–1940*. New York: HarperCollins, 1995.

Clifton, James A., ed. *The Invented Indian: Cultural Fictions and Government Policies*. New Brunswick, NJ: Transaction, 1990.

Crowell, Benedict, and Robert Forrest Wilson. *The Road to France: The Transportation of Troops and Military Supplies, 1917–1918*. 2 vols. New Haven, CT: Yale University Press, 1929.

Cullen, Frank, *Vaudeville Old and New: An Encylopaedia of Variety Performers in America*. New York: Routledge, 2007.

Davis, Mary B., ed. *Native America in the Twentieth Century: An Encyclopedia*. New York: Garland, 1994.

Deloria, Philip Joseph. *Playing Indian*. New Haven, CT: Yale University Press, 1998.

Dévoluy, Pierre, and Pierre Borel. *The French Riviera*. London: Medici Society, 1924.

Dilnot, George. *Getting Rich Quick: An Outline of Swindles Old and New, with Some Account of Manners and Customs of Confidence Men*. London: Geoffrey Bles, 1935.

Donzel, Catherine. *Luxury Liners: Life on Board*. New York: Vendome, 2005.

Drowne, Kathleen, and Patrick Huber. *The 1920s*. Westport, CT: Greenwood, 2004.

Evans, Steven Ross. *Voice of the Old Wolf: Lucullus Virgil McWhorter and the Nez Perce Indians*. Pullman: Washington State University Press, 1996.

Ford, Hugh. *Left Bank Revisited: Selections from the Paris Tribune, 1917–1934*. State College, Pennsylvania State University Press, 1974.

Farlow, Edward J. *Wind River Adventures: My Life in Frontier Wyoming*. Glendo, WY: High Plains, 1998.

Fry, Lieutenant Henry J. *The War Record of the U.S.S. Henderson*. New York: Brooklyn Eagle, 1919.

Gibbons, Herbert Adams. *Riviera Towns*. New York: Robert M. McBride, 1920.

Gleaves, Vice Admiral Albert. *A History of the Transport Service: Adventures and Experiences of United States Transports and Cruisers in the World War.* New York: George H. Doran, 1921.

Graham, Stephen. *London Nights: Studies and Sketches of London at Night.* New York: George H. Doran, 1926.

Green, Nancy L. *The Other Americans in Paris: Businessmen, Countesses and Wayward Youth, 1880–1941.* Chicago: University of Chicago Press, 2014.

Grieve, Robert. *An Illustrated History of Pawtucket, Central Falls and Vicinity.* Pawtucket, RI: Pawtucket Gazette and Chronicle, 1897.

Handbook to Belgium and the Battlefields. London: Ward, Lock, 1921.

Haupert, Michael John. *The Entertainment Industry.* Westport, CT: Greenwood, 2006.

Henderson, Helen W. *A Loiterer in Paris.* New York: George H. Doran, 1921.

History of the United States Twenty-Second Infantry, 1866–1922. New York: Privately printed, 1922.

Houlbrook, Matt. *Queer London: Perils and Pleasures in the Sexual Metropolis, 1918–1957.* Chicago: University of Chicago Press, 2005.

Johnson, Stephen C. *Detroit Beer.* Mount Pleasant, SC: Arcadia Publishing, 2016.

Kohn, Marek. *Dope Girls: The Birth of the British Drug Underground.* London: Lawrence and Wishart, 1992.

Konnikova, Maria. *The Confidence Game: Why We Fall for It . . . Every Time.* New York: Viking, 2016.

Kophner, Frederick. *Kiki of Montparnasse.* London: Cassell, 1968.

Kyvig, David E. *Daily Life in the United States, 1920–1939: Decades of Promise and Pain.* Westport, CT: Greenwood, 2002.

Laughlin, Clara E. *So You're Going to Paris! And If I Were Going with You These Are the Things I'd Invite You to Do.* Boston: Houghton Mifflin, 1924.

Lloyd, Herbert. *Vaudeville Trails thru the West: By One Who Knows.* Chicago: Herbert Lloyd, 1919.

Mander, Raymond, and Joe Mitchenson. *British Music Hall.* Rev. ed. London: Gentry, 1974.

Markham, Jerry W. *A Financial History of the United States.* Armonk, NY: M. E. Sharpe, 2011.

Maurer, David W. *The Big Con: The Story of the Confidence Men and the Con Trick.* Armonk, NY: M. E. Sharpe, 2002.

McAlmon, Robert, and Kay Boyle. *Being Geniuses Together, 1920–1930.* Garden City, NY: Doubleday, 1968.

McCoy, Tim, with Ronald McCoy. *Tim McCoy Remembers the West: An Autobiography.* Garden City, NY: Doubleday, 1977.

McNamara, Brooks. *Step Right Up.* Jackson: University Press of Mississippi, 1995.

Morton, H. V. *The Heart of London*. London: Methuen, 1925.

———. *The Spell of London*. London: Methuen, 1926.

Moses, L. G. *Wild West Shows and the Images of American Indians, 1883–1933*. Albuquerque: University of New Mexico Press, 1996.

Muirhead, Findlay, ed. *England*. London: Macmillan, 1920.

———. *London and Its Environs*. London: Macmillan, 1922.

———. *Switzerland with Chamonix and the Italian Lakes*. London: Macmillan, 1923.

Muirhead, Findlay, and L. V. Bertarelli. *Northern Italy: From the Alps to Rome*. London: Macmillan, 1924.

Muirhead, Findlay, and Marcel Monmarché, eds. *Belgium*. London: Macmillan, 1924.

———. *Normandy*. London: Macmillan, 1925.

———. *Paris and Its Environs*. London: Macmillan, 1924.

Nasaw, David. *Going Out: The Rise and Fall of Public Amusements*. New York: Basic Books, 1993.

Nelson, Michael. *Americans and the Making of the Riviera*. Jefferson, NC: McFarland, 2008.

Nevill, Ralph. *Days and Nights in Montmartre and the Latin Quarter*. London: Herbert Jenkins, 1927.

Official Guide and Descriptive Book of the Panama-California Exposition. San Diego: The Exposition, 1915.

Olson, James S., and Raymond Wilson. *Native Americans in the Twentieth Century*. Urbana: University of Illinois Press, 1984.

Palmquist, Peter E. *With Nature's Children: Emma B. Freeman (1880–1928): Camera and Brush*. Eureka: Interface California, 1976.

Partridge, Eric, Tom Dalzell, and Terry Victor. *The New Partridge Dictionary of Slang and Unconventional English*, Volume 1. New York: Routledge, 2006.

Phillips, Arthur. *The Gay City: Being a Guide to the Fun of the Fair in Paris*. New York: Brentano's, 1927.

Reynolds, Bruce. *Paris with the Lid Lifted*. New York: A. L. Burt Company, 1927.

Richardson, Leslie. *Things Seen on the Riviera*. London: Seeley, Service, 1923.

Rolfe, William J. *A Satchel Guide to Europe*. Boston: Houghton Mifflin, 1924.

Ross, Cathy. *Twenties London: A City in the Jazz Age*. London: Philip Wilson Publishers, 2003.

Schauble, Peter Lambert. *First Battalion: The Story of the 406 Telegraph Battalion Signal Corps, U.S. Army*. Philadelphia: Bell Telephone Company, 1921.

Schoonmaker, Frank. *Come with Me Through Italy*. New York: R. M. McBride, 1929.

Shackleton, Robert. *The Book of New York*. Philadelphia: Penn Publishing, 1917.

Shanks, David C. *As They Passed Through the Port*. Washington, DC: Cary, 1927.

Shenk, Robert (ed.). *Playships of the World: The Naval Diaries of Admiral Daniel V. Gallery, 1920–1924*. Columbia: University of South Carolina Press, 2008.

Shneer, David, and Caryn Aviv. *American Queer, Now and Then.* Boulder, CO: Paradigm, 2006.

Snell, King W. *With the Army at Hoboken.* New York: McConnell, 1919.

Theoharis, Athan G., with Tony G. Poveda, Susan Rosenfeld, and Richard Gid Powers, eds. *The FBI: A Comprehensive Reference Guide.* Phoenix, AZ: Oryx, 1999.

Thompson, Mrs. Lucy. *To the American Indian.* Privately printed, 1916.

The Traveller's Handbook for Belgium, and the Ardennes. London: Thomas Cook, 1921.

The Traveller's Handbook for Normandy and Brittany. London: Thomas Cook, 1923.

The Traveller's Handbook for Switzerland, Including French Savoy and Italian Lakes. London: Thomas Cook, 1922.

Vygotsky, L. S., *The Collected Works of L. S. Vygotsky: Child Psychology, Volume 5.* New York: Plenum Press, 1998.

Wanderwell, Aloha. *Call to Adventure: True Tales of the Wanderwell Expedition, First Woman to Circle the World in an Automobile.* Toluca Lake, CA: Nile Baker Estate and the Boyd Production Group, 2013.

Whalen, Mark. *American Culture in the 1910s.* Edinburgh: Edinburgh University Press, 2010.

Wilgus, William J. *Transporting the A.E.F. in Western Europe, 1917–1919.* New York: Columbia University Press, 1931.

Wilmut, Roger. *Kindly Leave the Stage! The Story of Variety, 1919–1960.* London: Methuen, 1985.

Wilson, Robert Forrest. *Paris on Parade.* Indianapolis: Bobbs-Merrill, 1924.

Woodward, Christopher. *The London Palladium: The Story of the Theatre and Its Stars.* Huddersfield: Jeremy Mills Publishing, 2009.

Ziegler-McPherson, Christina A. *Immigrants in Hoboken: One-Way Ticket, 1845–1985.* Charleston, SC: History Press, 2011.

JOURNAL AND MAGAZINE ARTICLES

Cobb, Russell. "Why Do So Many People Pretend to Be Native American?" *This Land Press,* August 2014.

Green, Rayna. "The Tribe Called Wannabee: Playing Indian in America and Europe." *Folklore* 99, no. 1 (January 1988): pp. 30–55.

McFeely, William S. "The Black Cats of Amherst." *Amherst Magazine,* Spring 2010.

Meyer Zu Erpen, Walter J., and Joy Lowe. "The Canadian Spiritualist Movement and Sources for Its Study." *Archivaria,* Summer 1991, p. 4.

Willson, Perry. "The Nation in Uniform? Fascist Italy, 1919–1943," *Past and Present* 221, no. 1 (November 2013): pp. 239–72.

THESES

Britten, Thomas A. "American Indians in World War I: Military Service as a Catalyst for Reform." PhD diss., Texas Tech University, 1994.

Camurat, Diane. "The American Indian and the Great War: Real and Imagined." Master's thesis, University of Paris, 1993.

SELECTED DIGITAL ARCHIVES

Archives Départementales des Alpes-Maritimes, Archives Historiques L'Express et L'Impartial, Archives Historiques Le Temps, British Columbia Historical Newspapers, British Newspaper Archive, California Digital Newspaper Collection, *Corriere della Sera* Digital Archive, Fold3.com (Bureau of Investigation Old German Files), Old Fulton NY Postcards, Gallica, Genealogy Bank, Google News Archive, Hoboken Historical Museum, *La Stampa* Digital Archive, Library of Congress Digital Collections, Montana Digital Archive, Newspapers.com, Panama-California Exposition Digital Archive, Peel's Prairie Provinces, Royal Library of Belgium, Trove, Utah Digital Newspapers.

ARCHIVES/LIBRARIES

Archives and Museum of Literature, Brussels; London Metropolitan Archives; Ministry of Justice, Central Law Library, Rome; National Archives, UK; National Library of France, Paris; Rhode Island Historical Society; Royal Library of Belgium, Brussels; Washington State University.

ACKNOWLEDGMENTS

I'd like to thank my agents—Matthew Hamilton at Aitken Alexander Associates in London, and Anna Stein at I.C.M. Partners in New York City—for setting in motion the long process of turning my initial idea into this book. Without their help and encouragement, my book proposal wouldn't have caught the attention of Domenica Alioto and Claire Potter at Crown Publishing. I'm indebted to them not only for their decision to commission *King Con,* but also for the unremitting vigor and enthusiasm with which they've supported it. On almost every level, each draft of my book was significantly improved by Claire's editorial skills, wielded with supreme patience, tact, and sensitivity. Those last few epithets apply to her copyediting colleague, Michelle Daniel, too. At risk of sounding grovelingly sycophantic, I count myself fortunate to have ended up being published by a company that devotes such care to every aspect of the publishing process.

My book also benefited from masses of invaluable suggestions, comments, and corrections supplied by my friend the film historian Peter Krämer, who also provided me with various English translations of German newspaper articles. When dealing with the much greater volume of material in Italian, I was fortunate enough to be able to enlist the expertise of an Italian-speaking friend, Doralba Picerno. As well as translating large quantities of Italian text, she undertook research for me in several Italian archives, her fascination with Edgar Laplante and her amusement at his antics sustaining me through periods when I was feeling overwhelmed by the project.

So geographically far-reaching was the Edgar Laplante saga that, in order to keep to my research and writing schedule, I needed to hire other researchers, whose contribution I greatly appreciate. This other research was carried out by my friend Marc Fireman, who investigated some of Edgar's Californian adventures; by Christine Lamar, who delved round in the Rhode Island Historical Society's collection; and by Zach Conn, who trawled through Yale University Library's newspaper collection.

I remember once interviewing the novelist Will Self and commenting upon how surprised I was to find that nonfiction writing expanded my social circle. With deadpan humor, he remarked that fiction writing has a tendency to *shrink* your social circle. I'm extremely fortunate in having made so many cherished friends through my writing, friends who provided boundless support and practical assistance throughout the composition of this book. Those friends include Marc-Henri Glendening, Cathi Unsworth, Mike Meekin, Virginia Ironside, Keiron Pim, Will Buckley, and Jon Glover. In the case of Max Décharné and Katja Klier, that support extended to lending me their flat while I carried out London-based research.

Thanks are also owed to Keith and Dorothy Holmes, two of the blood relatives of Edgar Laplante's luckless second wife. I was touched by their generosity in sharing details of their family history. I'm grateful as well to the following archivists and librarians who contributed to my research, many of them going well beyond the call of duty: Cheryl Gunselman, manuscripts librarian at Washington State University Libraries; Alla Roylance, senior librarian at Brooklyn Public Library's Brooklyn Collection; Brian Merlis at the excellent BrooklynPix.com, one of the finest sources of material about that borough; Duncan Ball, information specialist at the Met Office, UK; Lisa Lipshires, reference librarian at Springfield City Library; Julienne Boudreau at the Cinémathèque Québécoise; Gail Loper at Fremont County Pioneer Museum; Christian Bach at the Bibliothèque Nationale de France; Cindy Brown at the Wyoming State Archives; Ian Pittock, assistant librarian, Map Department, Cambridge University Library, UK; Jack Mueller and Mary Hartman at the Laramie branch of the Wyoming Historical Society; Mike Thomason, research librarian at Pueblo Library; Edmund Dunne at the Archives and History Department of Manchester Central Library, UK; Catherine Mills, curator of library and archives at History San José; Michael Maloney, librarian/archivist at Grems-Doolittle Library; Gail and Liz at Libraries Unlimited South West, UK; Laura Hobbs, archivist (digital) at the Royal Archives, Windsor Castle, UK; Lisa Schoblasky, special collections services librarian at the Newberry Library; Adam M. Silva, the assistant curator/photography at the Library of Congress; and Luc Wanlin at the Archives et Musée de la Littérature, Brussels.

Lastly, I'd like to thank my partner, Jo Willingham, and my father, David Willetts, for taking my literary ambitions seriously even when there was more reason for skepticism than belief.

INDEX